MW01623679

THE STYLISH LIFE

COCKTAIL PARTIES

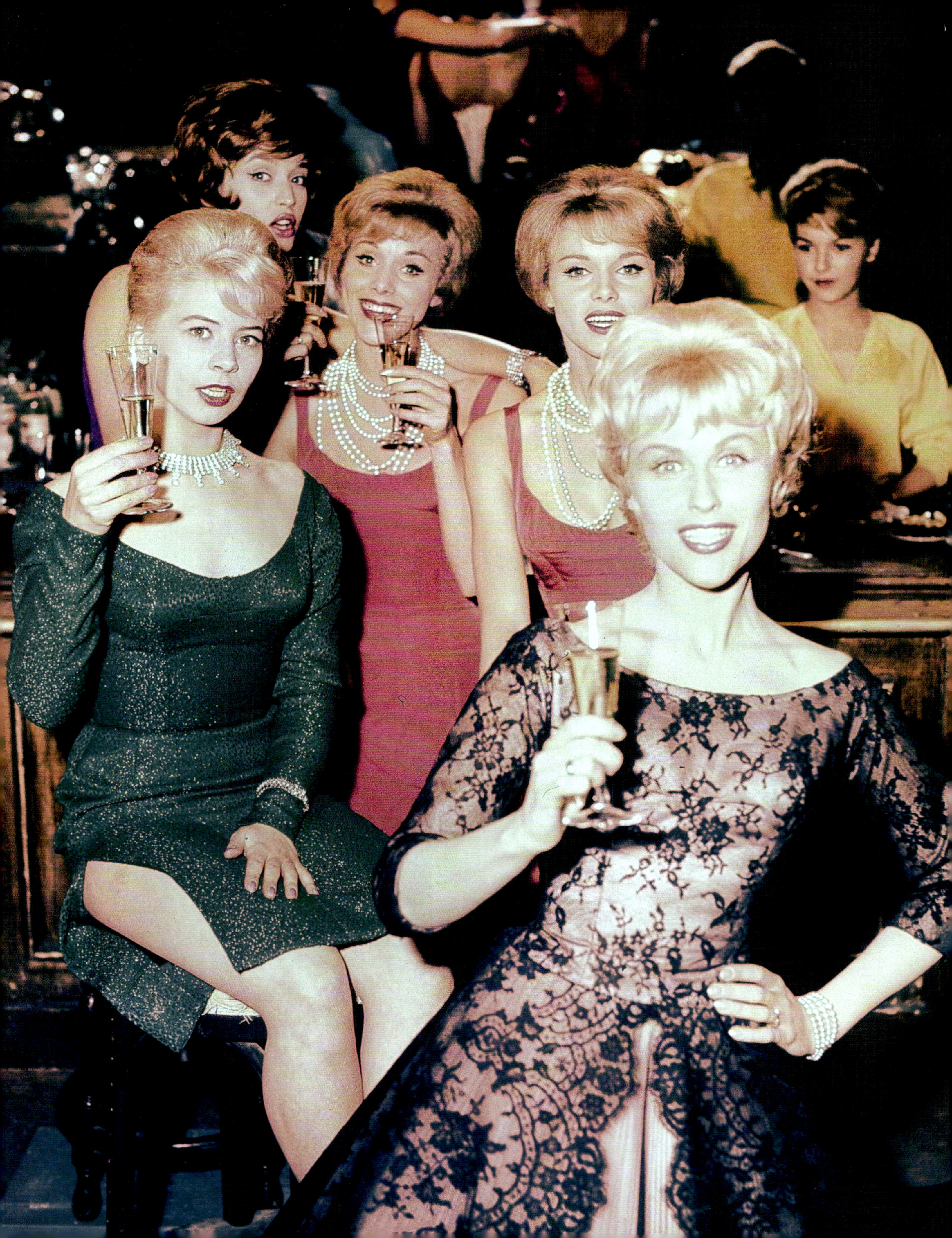

THE STYLISH LIFE

COCKTAIL PARTIES

Texts by Elizabeth Smith

teNeues

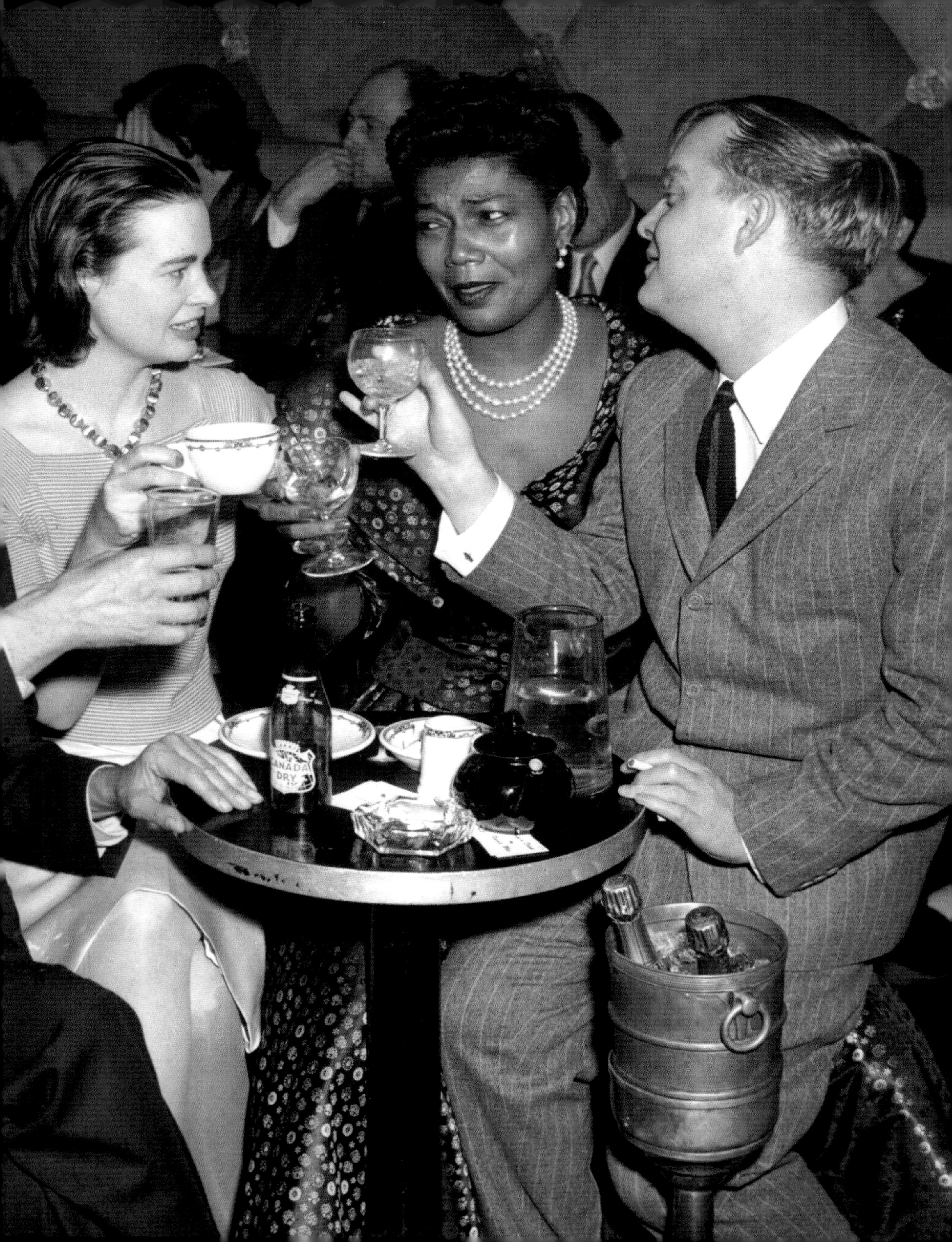
ANADA
DRY

CONTENTS

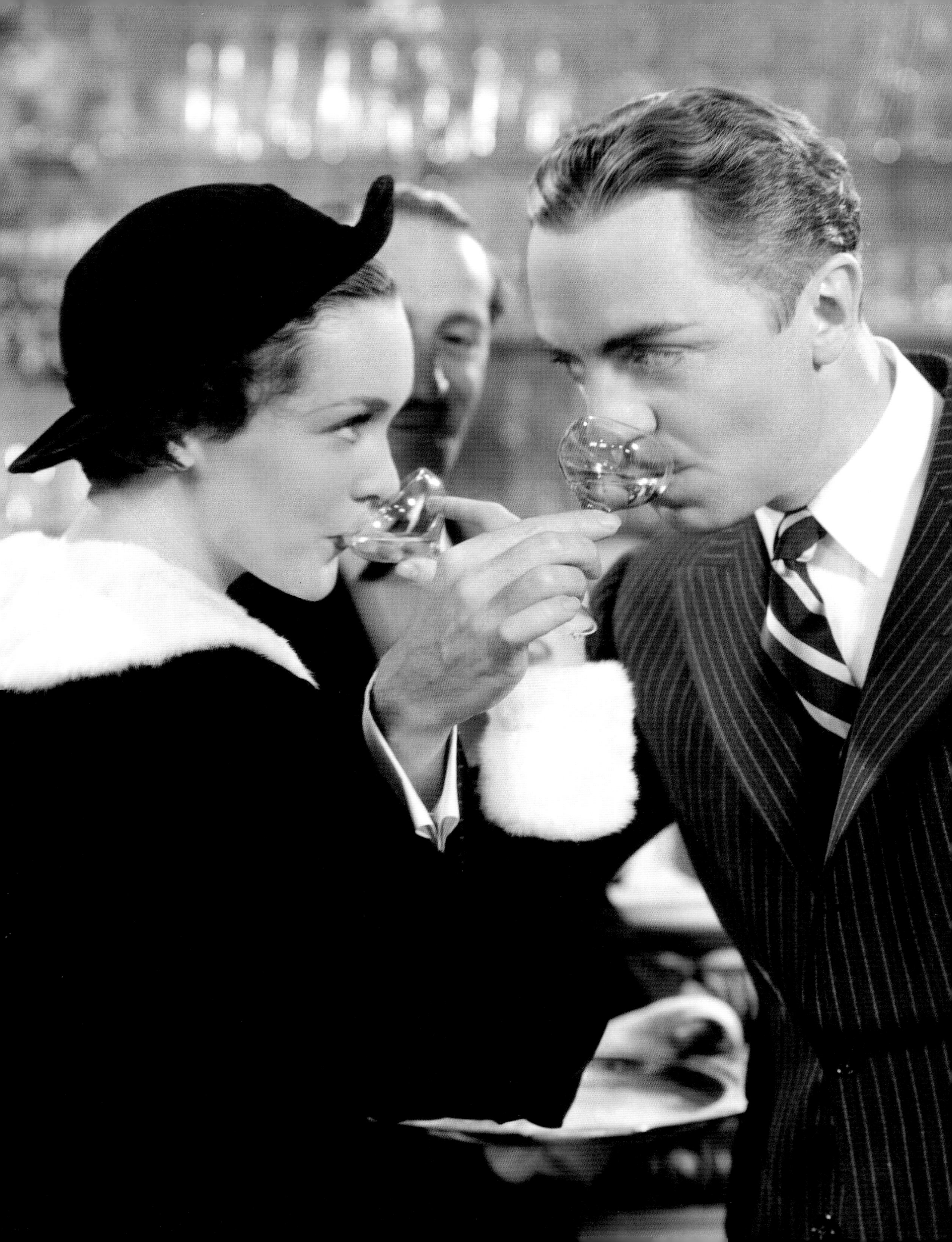

INTRODUCTION

ELIZABETH SMITH

"It's five o'clock somewhere!" Let's toast to cocktail hour, that magical, bubbly time between the workaday world and the evening, when special drinks, carefree indulgence, exceptional attire, and witty conversation raise spirits.

Today, we each sip our unique blend of cocktail alchemy—a Clover Leaf for traditionalists, a seventy-one-ingredient Commonwealth for adventurers, an Espresso No-Tini for Dry January. Yesteryear's tippling was simpler: ales and wines, shots of rum, whiskey, and brandy. British punches—concoctions of spirits, fruit juices, and spices—were set out in large bowls, inviting everyone to ladle out their share.

The word "cocktail" popped up in print in 1803, lauded as "excellent for the head." But where did the word come from? The French word for eggcup, *coquetier*? Revolutionary War troops toasting the "cock tail" on General Washington's hat? No one knows for sure, but by 1806, cocktails were the talk of the saloons. Enter professional bartenders, like Jerry "The Professor" Thomas, who stepped behind the bar with a bang. The godfather of flair bartending, his specialty was the Blue Blazer—a stream of flaming whiskey poured between two tumblers, a feat not even Tom Cruise in *Cocktail* could replicate. After Thomas's seminal 1862 book, *How to Mix Drinks: The Bon Vivant's Companion*, others followed, like Louisville's Tom Bullock, who served up a Mint Julep that could make a Kentucky Derby winner

Page 2: Prost! Salud! Sánte! Gānbēi! *Stylish ladies cheer the cocktail hour, 1961.* Page 4: *Gloria Vanderbilt, Pearl Bailey, and a puckish Truman Capote (perched on Bailey's lap) share a toast at New York's Blue Angel, 1955.* Opposite: *The urbane Nick Charles (William Powell) and Dorothy (Maureen O'Sullivan) drink to solving her father's disappearance in* The Thin Man *(1934).*

swoon. His cocktail book, *The Ideal Bartender*, was the first published by an African American—just as Prohibition turned off the lights and kicked everyone out.

In 1920, the Eighteenth Amendment made the production, transport, and sale of alcohol illegal, deflating the Golden Age of the Cocktail. Before Prohibition, the "what" and "how" to drink were straightforward: gentlemen (and never, *ever* ladies) partook in socially acceptable places. After Prohibition, the party kept going—underground, abroad, and at home—shaking up a seismic revolution. Men and women drinking together? High society rubbing shoulders with the average Joe? *Quelle horreur!*

Speakeasies, hidden behind secret doors in cafés or shops, offered enticingly illicit refreshments, drawing men and women to dance and drink the night away. Professional bartenders—and well-heeled tipplers—migrated to international watering holes on a Grand Tour of cocktails. Those stuck at home followed Clara Bell Walsh's lead. Back in 1917, Kentucky-born socialite Mrs. Walsh decided to give everyone an escape from wartime worries. One Sunday, she threw a party for fifty close friends, between noon and one o'clock. The first cocktail hour was born—and oh, pearls were clutched! "Cocktail Parties Are New Society Stunt" proclaimed one newspaper columnist haughtily. Fast-forward to 1933, the end of Prohibition, and cocktail parties were all the rage. (As we know, once the Champagne cork is popped, there is no way to get it back into the bottle!)

Today's cocktail culture is all about finding the style that suits your sip. Exclusive, hidden speakeasy enclaves beckon adventurous patrons. Craft trends look to the past. Mixologists create art out of chemistry. Cocktails are big business, with brands offering high-, low-, and no-alcohol options. Bartenders create sensory experiences, using CBD-infused bitters or artisanal hot sauces; garnishing with Darth Vader–shaped fruit or gummy brains à la *The Walking Dead*. Add your own twist to the eight classic recipes in the back of this book!

The possibilities are limited only by your fancy and daring—the essence of cocktail style. As T. S. Eliot wrote in his play *The Cocktail Party*, you do "no harm to find yourself ridiculous. Resign yourself to be the fool you are.... We must always take risks." So, raise a glass to the past, the adventures yet to come, and the magic that lies in the moment.

To living—with style—in the now!

Opposite: *Fashion muse Bianca Jagger savors a quiet moment with a cocktail at designer Halston's New York townhouse, 1978.*

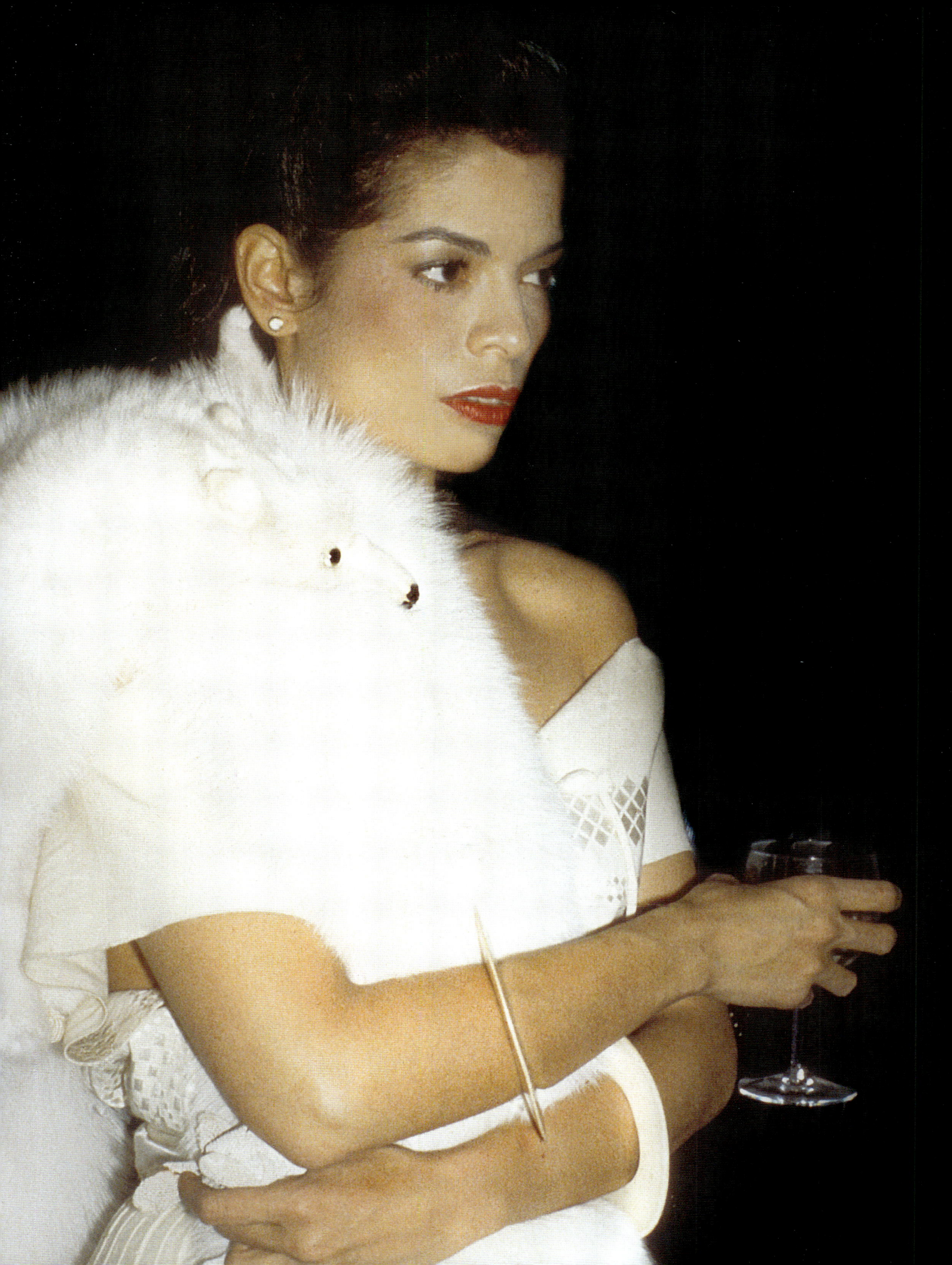

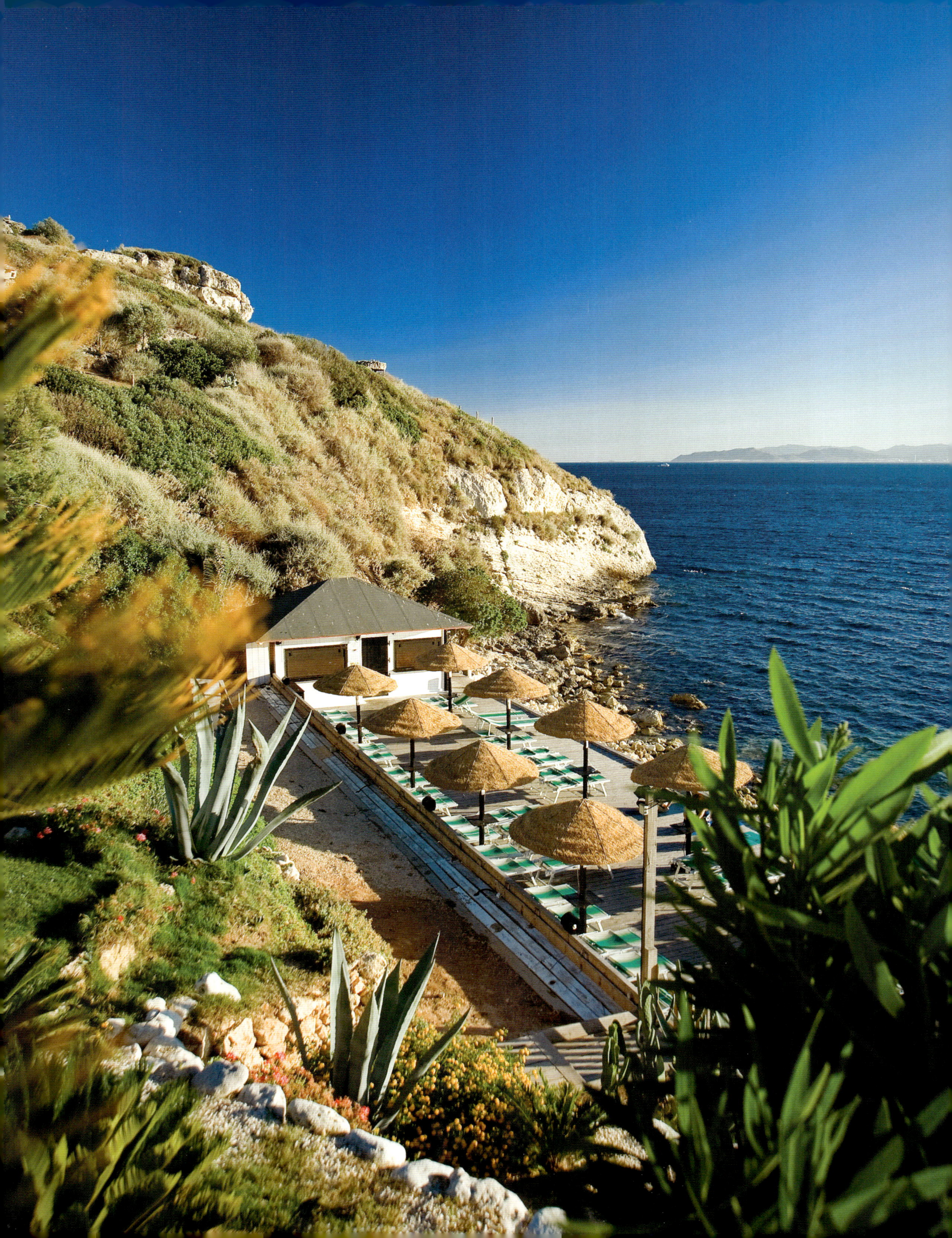

DESTINATIONS & EVENTS

WHERE TO BE AND BE SEEN

It's not just about what's *in* your glass, but *where* you're raising it. Picture-perfect settings across the globe make delicious cocktail destinations—think legendary hotel bars and celebrity watering holes, hopping hotspots, rooftop terraces, and serene gardens. Want an infusion of culture with your cocktail? Jazz clubs, poetry readings, and celebrity-studded galas offer their own kinds of twists. Fancy an ice bar in Tokyo or a swim-up bar at a hot spring in Iceland? Coming right up.

The high seas offer a chance to indulge on a luxurious cruise, or a well-stocked home bar might be your preferred mixer. With so many options, there's no wrong answer to the question, "What's the best way to enjoy a cocktail?" Although perhaps legendary bartender Harry Craddock of London's Savoy Hotel answered it best: "Quickly!"

The Grand Tour

When wealthy Americans fled Prohibition, they headed to Cuba, London, Paris, and beyond. They came, they saw, they sipped—and showed how to do it with style. London's American Bar at the Savoy Hotel was where world leaders like Winston Churchill (and his cabinet) and writers like Ernest Hemingway bellied up to the bar—in fact, even the Queen Mother often popped in for her gin and Dubonnet. Hemingway spent the Roaring 20s in cups with F. Scott Fitzgerald at the Ritz in Paris, and famously "liberated" it from Nazi occupation twenty years later (running up a tab for over fifty Martinis). Beside a Venetian canal, Harry's Bar has welcomed royalty and movie stars since 1931. There Katherine Hepburn, Gary Cooper, and

Opposite: *A Mediterranean cocktail paradise beckons at a Sardinian beachside café below Sella del Diavolo.*

Truman Capote savored its signature Bellinis, and it's still in the tender care of the Cipriani family, standing tall as one of Italy's National Landmarks.

For other classic cocktail ports of call, Raffles Hotel's Long Bar in Singapore birthed the Singapore Sling—cleverly created by bartender Ngiam Tong Boon to disguise a potent cocktail with fruit juices so that women could legally drink in public. In Cuba, La Bodeguita del Medio in Havana crowned the Mojito, while El Floridita's own Constantino Ribalaigua Vert elevated the frozen Daiquiri, which drew (you guessed it) Hemingway as a regular. In fact, visitors to El Floridita today dutifully raise their glasses to a bronze statue of Hemingway, the bar's "patron saint."

Every Pour Tells a Tale

From coast to coast, the cocktail bars at American hotels and restaurants have plenty of stories to tell—if only walls could talk! Steeped in Tinseltown glamour, the Polo Lounge is as classic Hollywood as Marilyn Monroe, who often enjoyed its signature Negronis. New Hollywood stars still rendezvous at Musso and Frank, to where Charlie Chaplin and Douglas Fairbanks would race on horseback, the loser paying the tab. On the East Coast, the Biltmore Hotel once welcomed guests via a tunnel from Grand Central Station, offering a direct path to ballrooms, gardens, and palm courts—oh, and cocktails, of course. Meanwhile, the Carlyle Hotel welcomes younger generations to clink glasses with Upper East Side society beneath Ludwig Bemelmans's whimsical murals, where Madeline and a cigar-smoking rabbit make their appearances.

In D.C., the Round Robin Bar keeps debate flowing with its famed Mint Juleps, uniting presidents, writers, and lobbyists of all political stripes. But perhaps the true mecca of the cocktail is the Big Easy. New Orleans's cocktail havens include where America's first cocktail, the Sazerac, was born—The Roosevelt Hotel's Sazerac Bar. And the literary ghosts of Eudora Welty and Tennessee Williams may still spin tales and savor sophisticated Vieux Carrés at Hotel Monteleone's revolving bar.

La Dolce Vita

Like pairing cocktails and hors d'oeuvres, there is an art to finding the perfect spot to indulge. The best limoncello aperitivo might be in a piazza on Sardinia or on the island of Capri, where beneath lemon trees an afternoon *passeggiata* (catching up with friends) lingers till the stars come out. Bubbly is obligatory at the French Riviera, where cocktail hour includes toasting the sunset from yachts in the turquoise waters of Nice and Saint-Tropez, or partaking of a Splash at Antibe's Hotel du Cap-Eden-Roc, topped with Champagne.

Rum-infused cocktails sing a siren call on the sun-kissed beaches of the Caribbean, or poolside after one snorkels with sea turtles by colorful coral reefs on Barbados, with that island's signature blend of rum, lime juice, sugar, nutmeg, and a dash of bitters. When snowy slopes beckon, après-ski ("after ski") soirées in alpine resort chalets from St. Moritz to Courchevel promise cozy fireside retreats and whiskey-imbued hot toddies after skiing the powder all day.

Al Fresco and at Home

Entertaining al fresco traces its roots to Tudor-era hunting parties, blending tradition and formality. But add a pool, and things get lively! Rumors hinted of all-night pool parties at the Garden of Allah Hotel on Sunset Boulevard, where Tallulah Bankhead swam in the buff, and at the Sunset Marquis in the 1970s, where the Ramones lived the rock-and-roll dream poolside after LA gigs. Today, Palm Springs, Miami Beach, Ibiza, or anywhere a shimmering pool invites can host DJ-fueled extravaganzas or sophisticated gatherings for the most discerning. The pinnacle of outdoor entertaining? Buckingham Palace, where the king and royal family greet thousands of guests. These formal gatherings, rooted in debutante presentation parties, are meticulously planned. However, modern al fresco can also be a laid-back, impromptu affair wherever one's garden grows or pool beckons. After all, convivial conversation just needs a little liquid refreshment.

In the 1950s and 1960s, cocktail parties found their home sweet home. In suburbia, as soon as cocktail hour struck, the scene was set: recipe guides, shakers, and swizzle sticks emerged alongside festive glassware and ingenious gadgets that crushed ice and puréed juices, all while hostesses in cocktail dresses served finger foods and Jell-O salads. Hi-fis playing Sinatra have evolved to home stereo systems pumping out disco beats and hip-hop jams and to playlists streaming hits from all decades. But the essence of a home cocktail party remains unchanged. With a cocktail in hand, truly home is where the heart is. Or as Noël Coward said: "A perfect Martini should be made by filling a glass with gin then waving it in the general direction of Italy."

Following pages: *Five o'clock aboard a Chinese junk in Fort Lauderdale features cocktails and good friends (plus a stirring game of chess), 1970.*

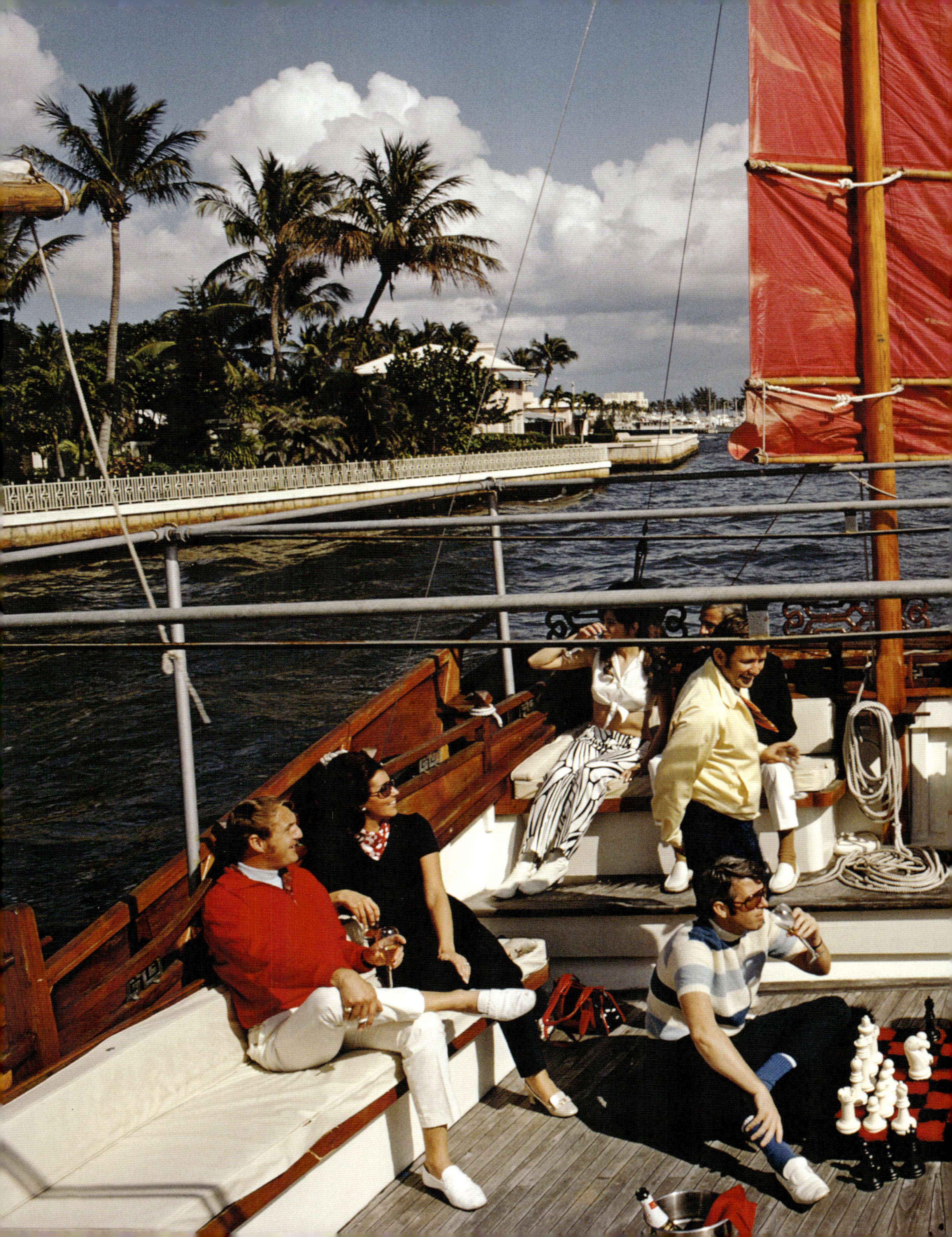

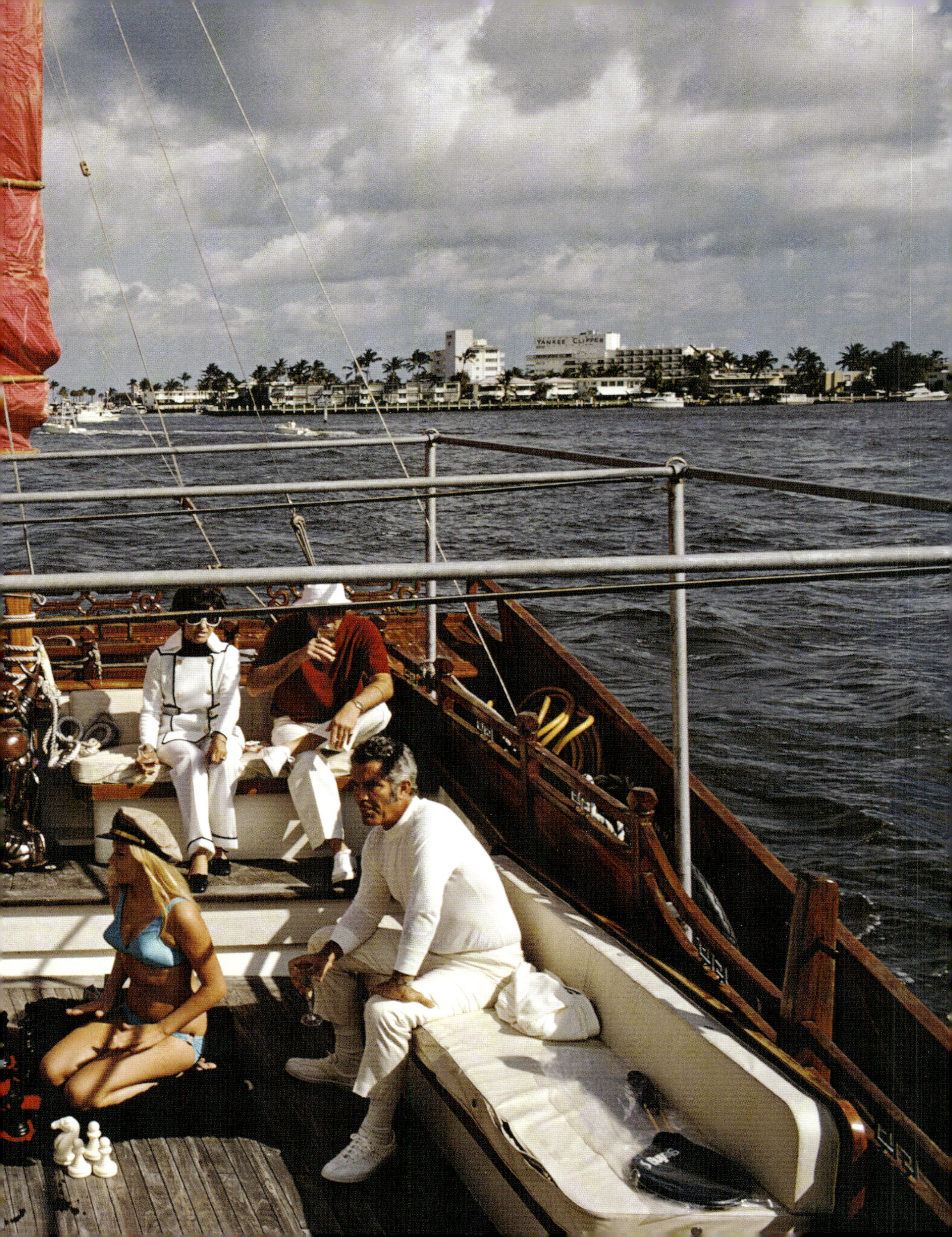
YANKEE CLIPPER

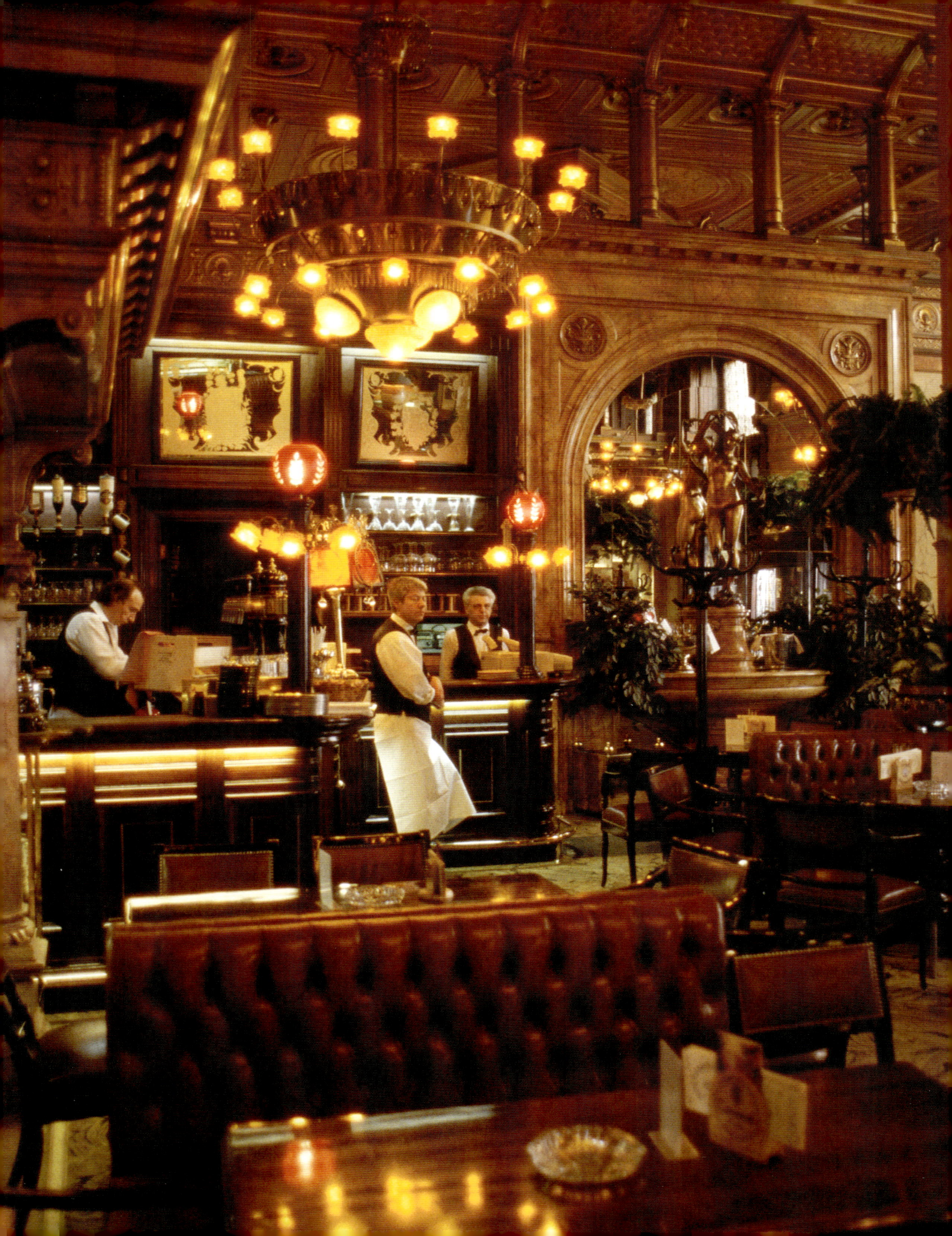

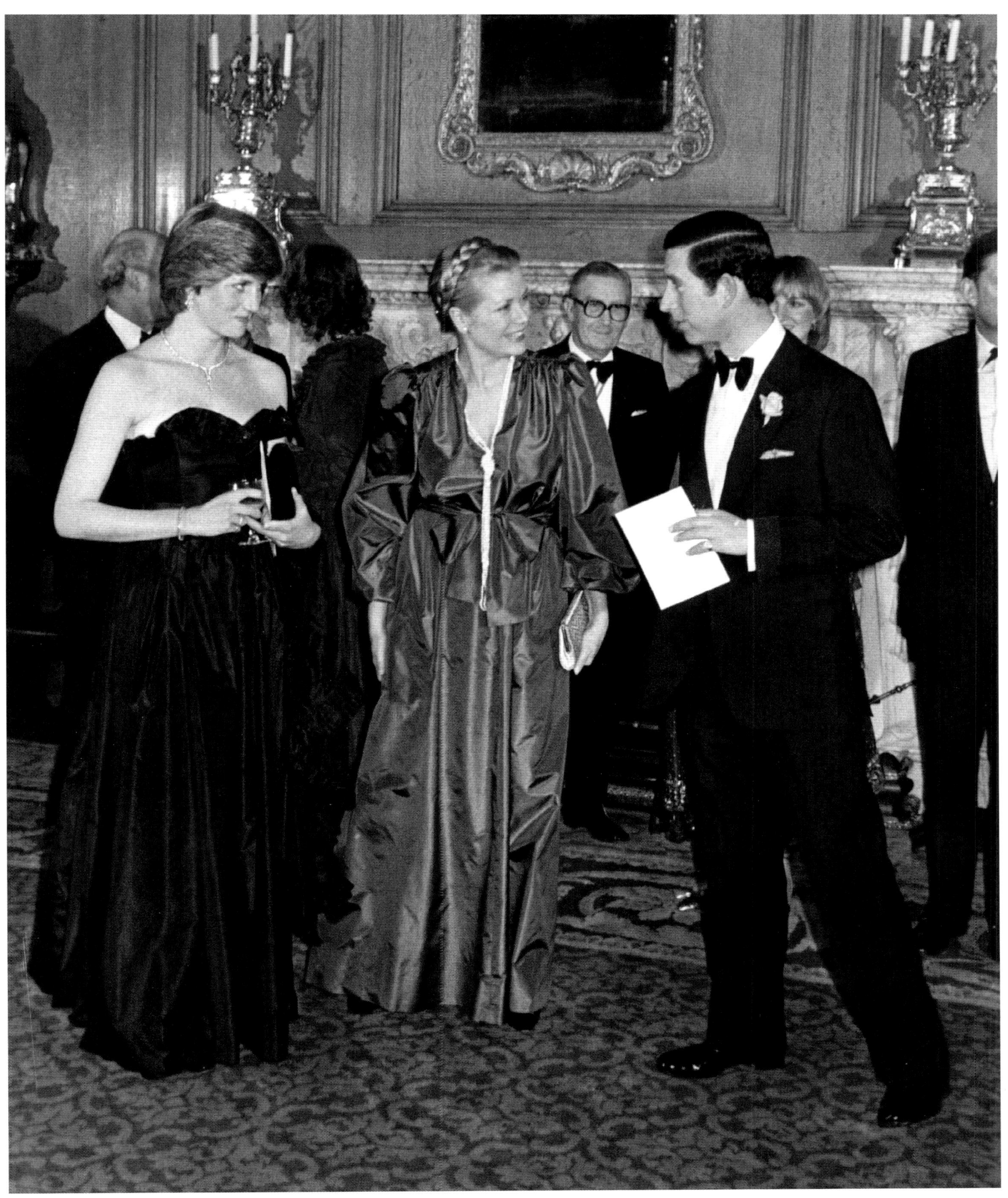

Opposite: *The grand art nouveau bar at Brussel's Hotel Métropole is home to the Black Russian (vodka and Kahlua).* This page: *Princess Grace of Monaco, Charles, Prince of Wales, and his then fiancée, Lady Diana Spencer, enchant at Goldsmiths Hall, London, 1981.*

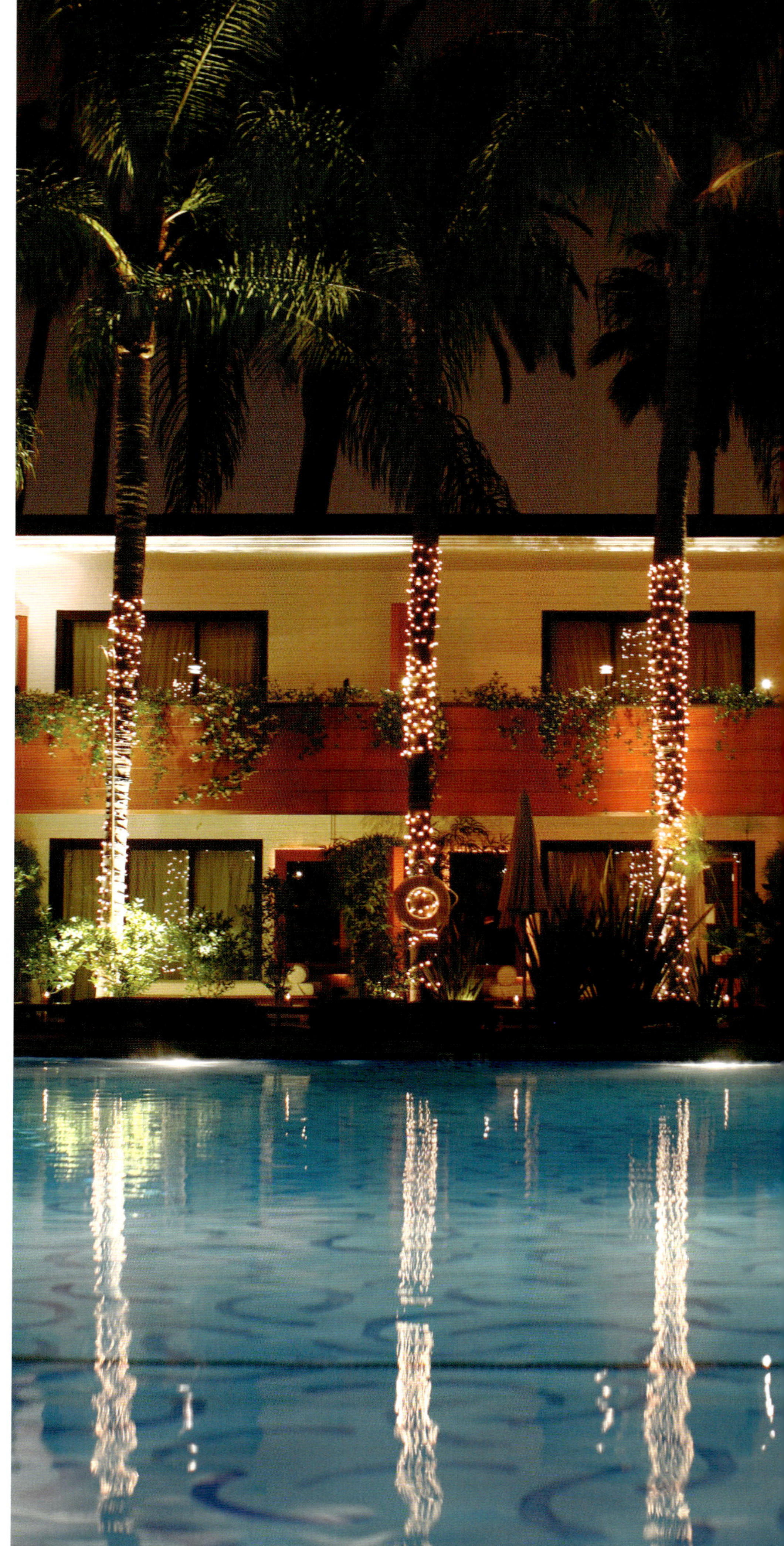

Opposite, clockwise from left: *Artist David Hockney's underwater mural at the Roosevelt's Tropicana Bar shimmers with Hollywood allure; A summer resort bar offers a place to sip in good company, 1960; An aloof llama is guest of honor at an author's book-signing cocktail party, 1953.*

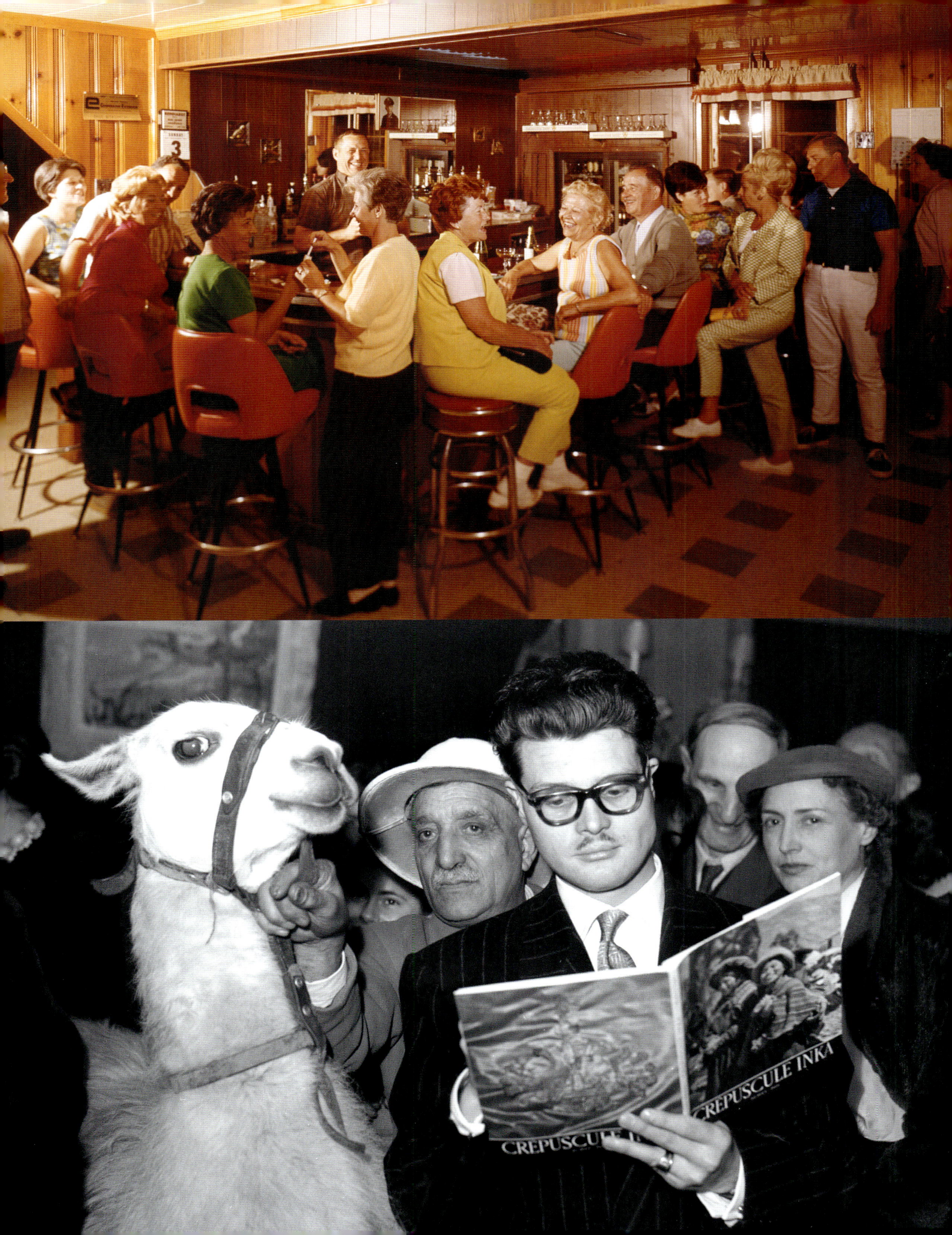
CREPUSCULE INKA

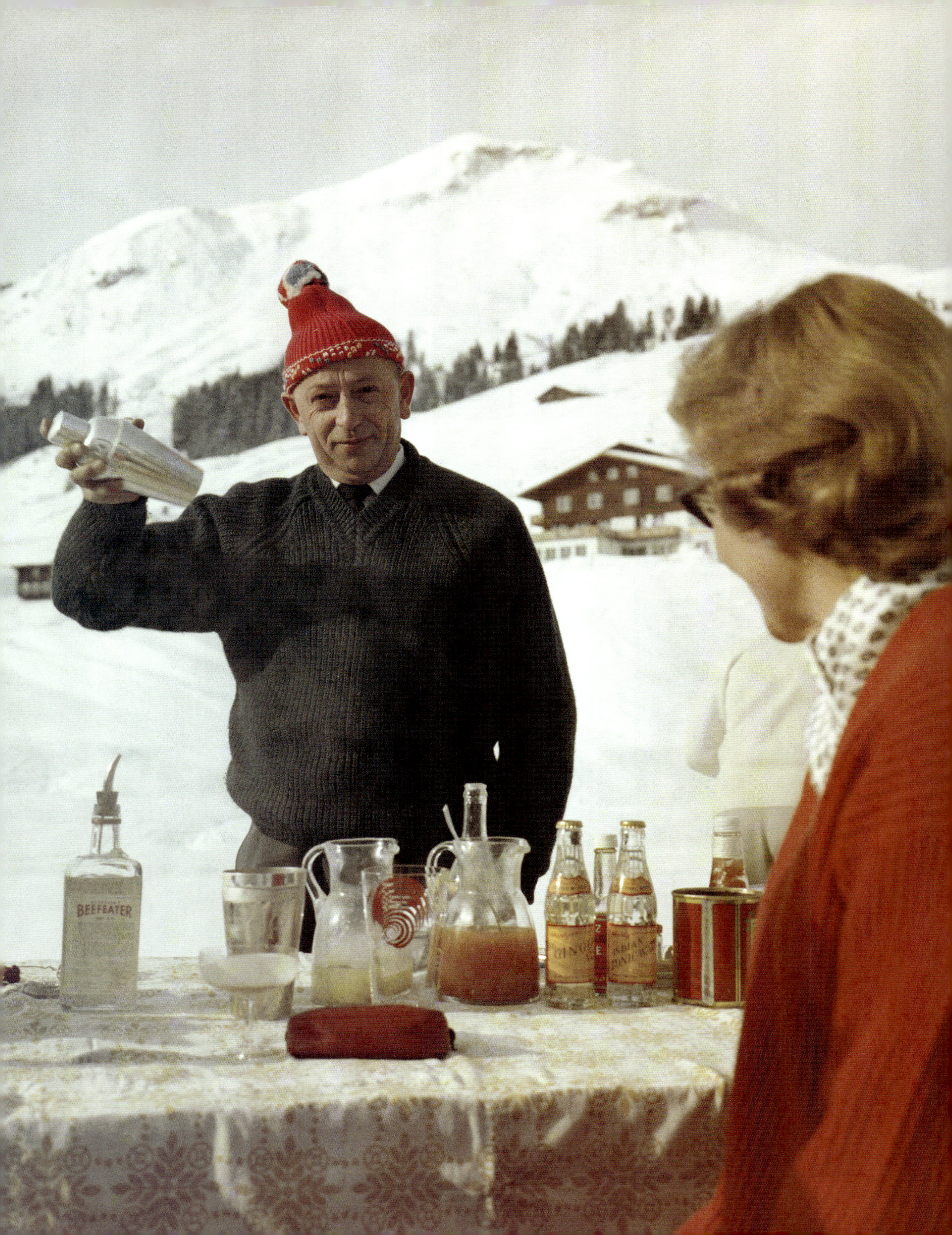
BEEFEATER
INDIAN

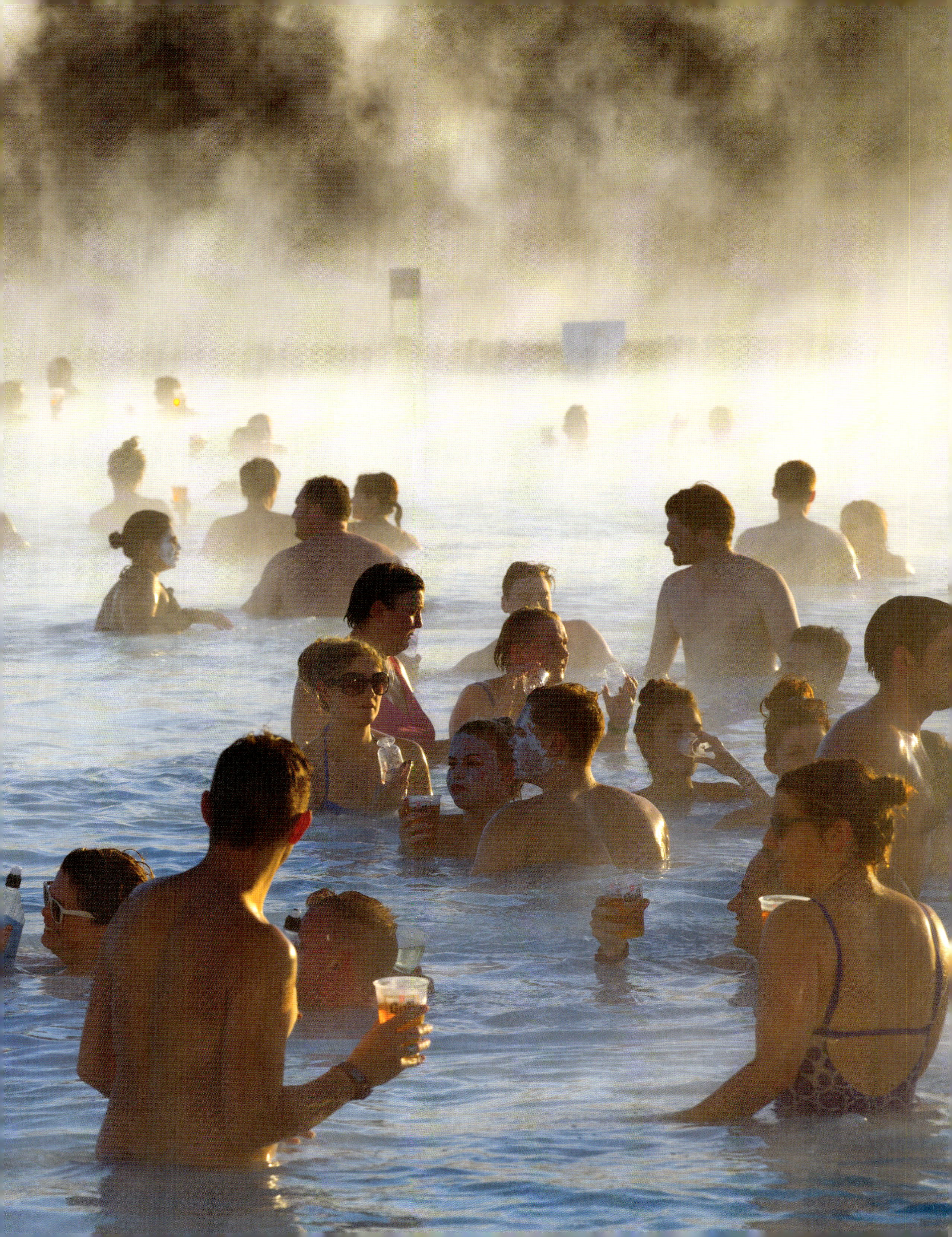

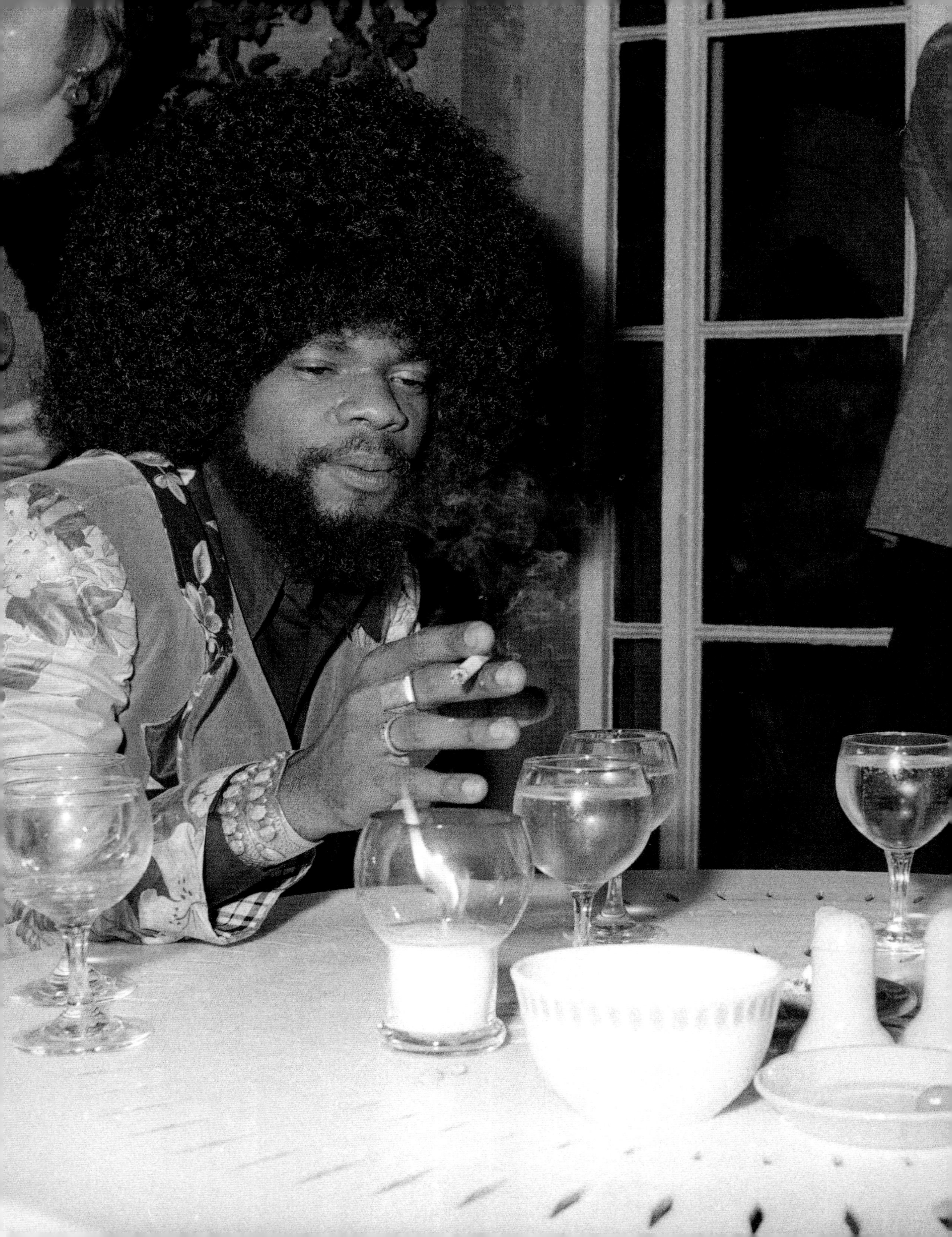

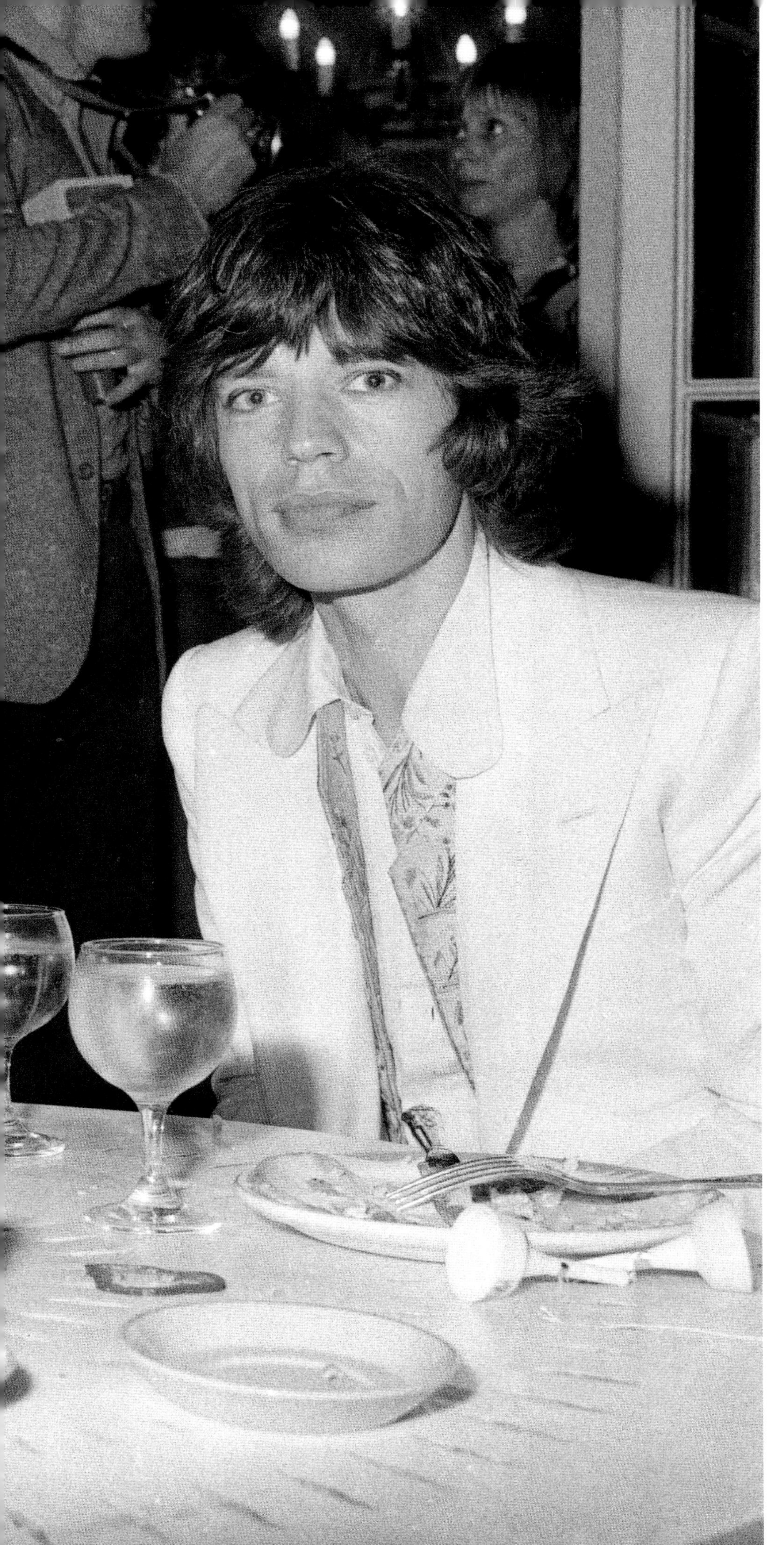

Previous pages, left: *A cheerful bartender mixes drinks for après-ski revelers at the Ice Bar, Hotel Krone, in Lech, Austria, 1960*; right: *Surrounded by lava fields, bathers chill out and drink up in Iceland's geothermal Blue Lagoon, 2014*. Opposite: *Rockstars Billy Preston and Mick Jagger have a few rounds at a bash for the Rolling Stones, Blenheim Palace, 1983.*

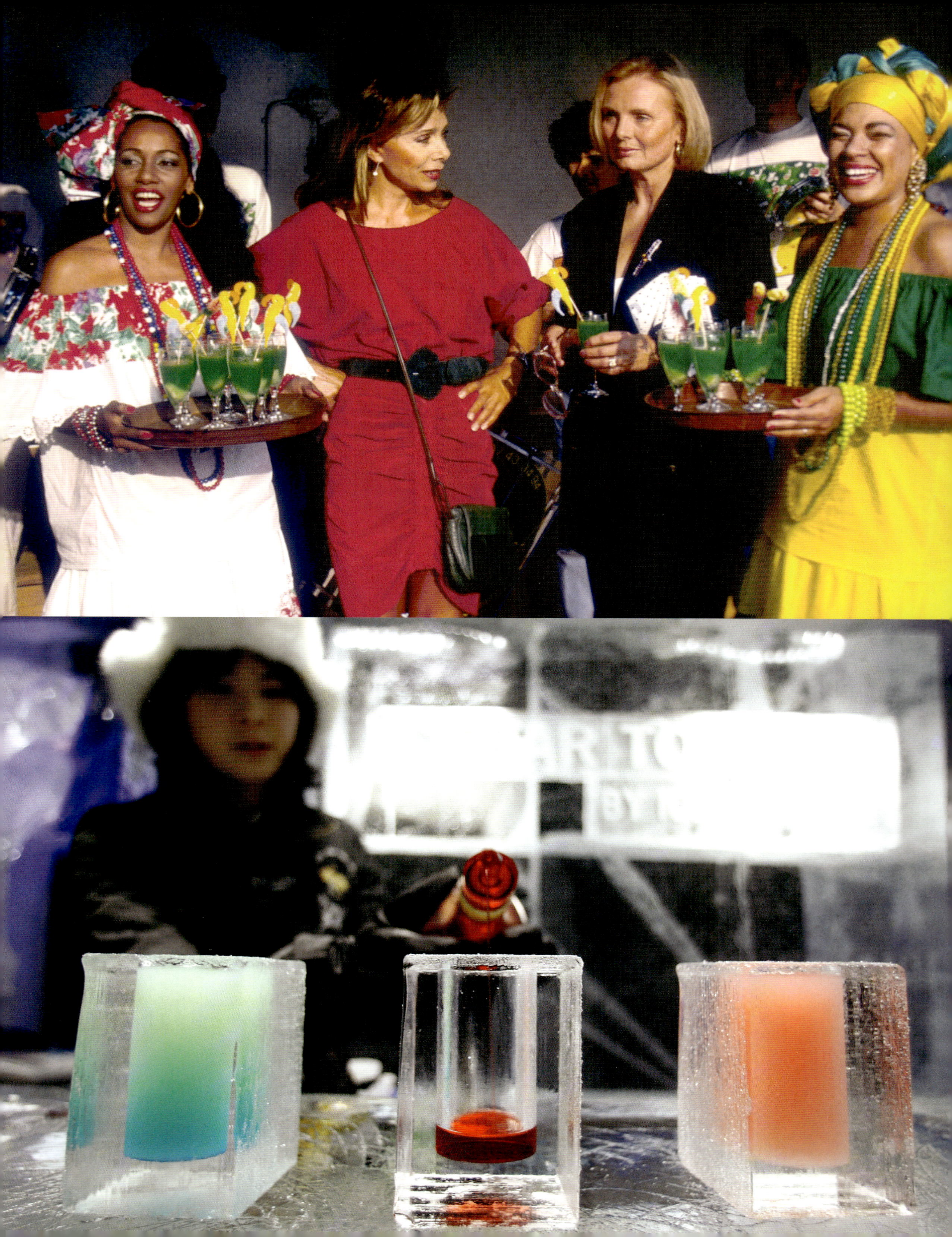

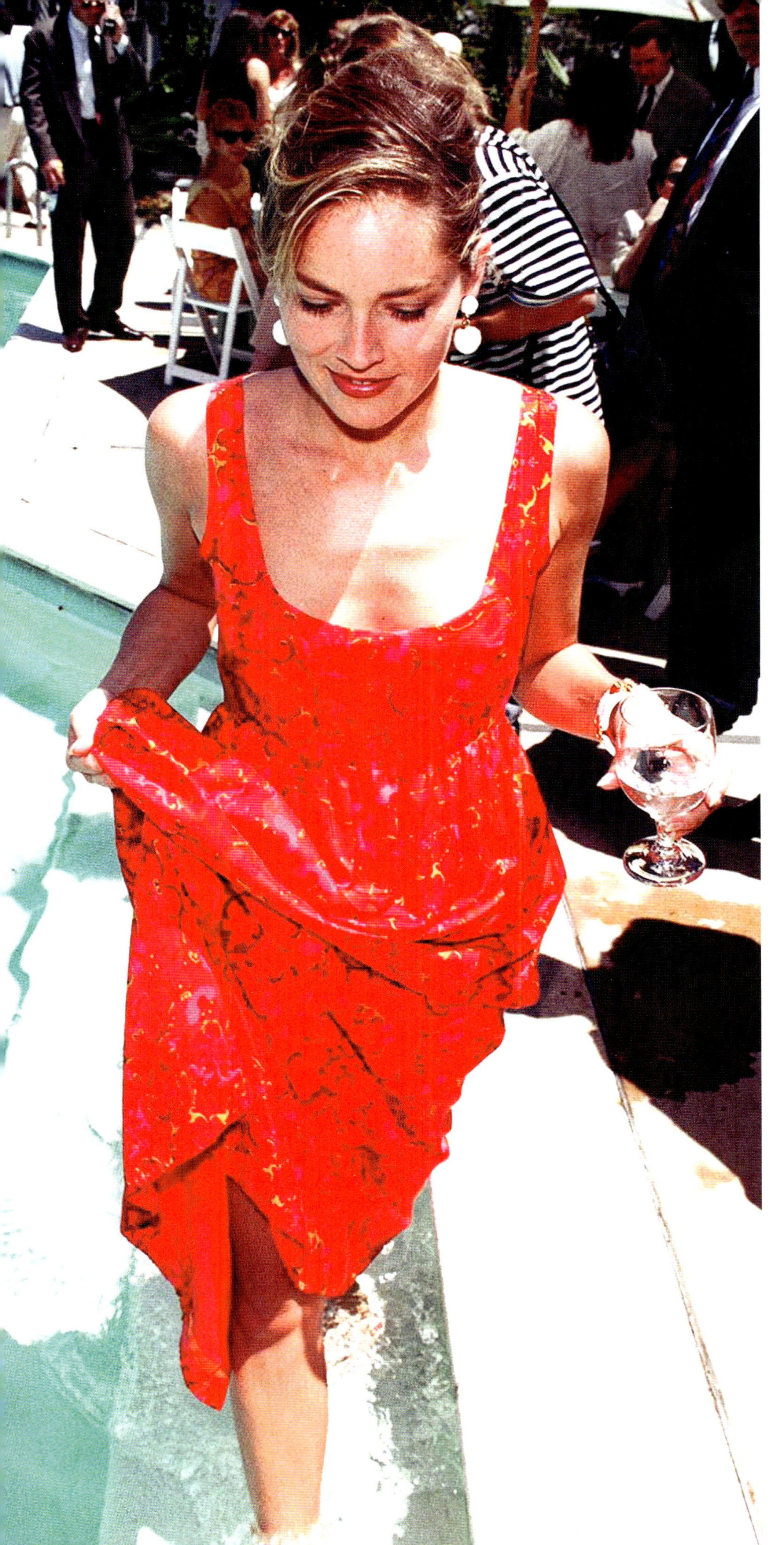

Clockwise from top left: *Brazil's spirit sambas through the Caipirinha (cachaça, lime juice, sugar, and tropical fruit garnish); Drink in hand, actress Sharon Stone cools off during a Bel Air party, 1994; Drinks chill at Tokyo's Icebar made from ice cut from Sweden's Torne River*. Following pages: *Sugar, coffee, Irish whiskey, and cream—bartender Paul Nolan stirs Irish Coffees to life at the Buena Vista café on Fisherman's Wharf, San Francisco, 2011.*

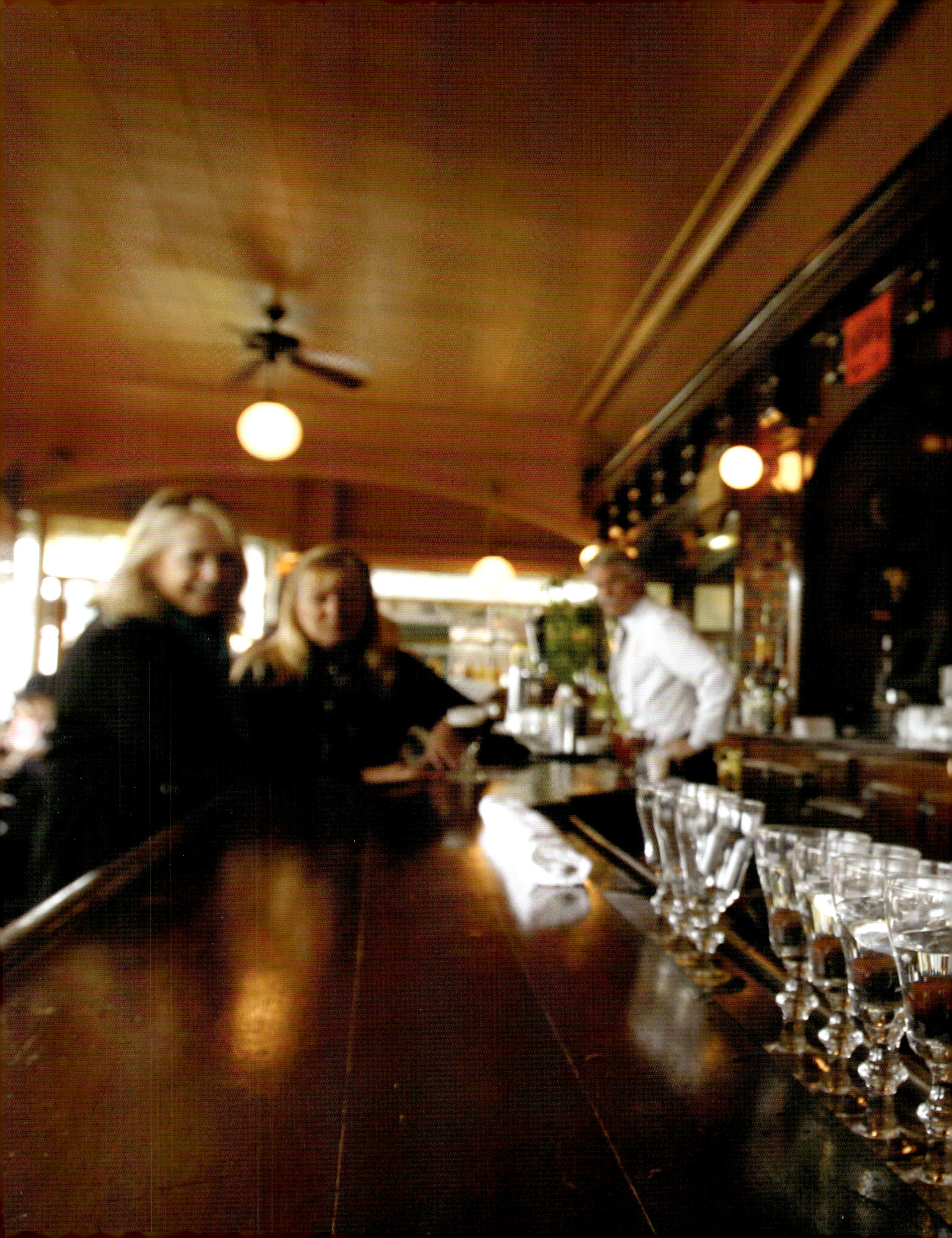

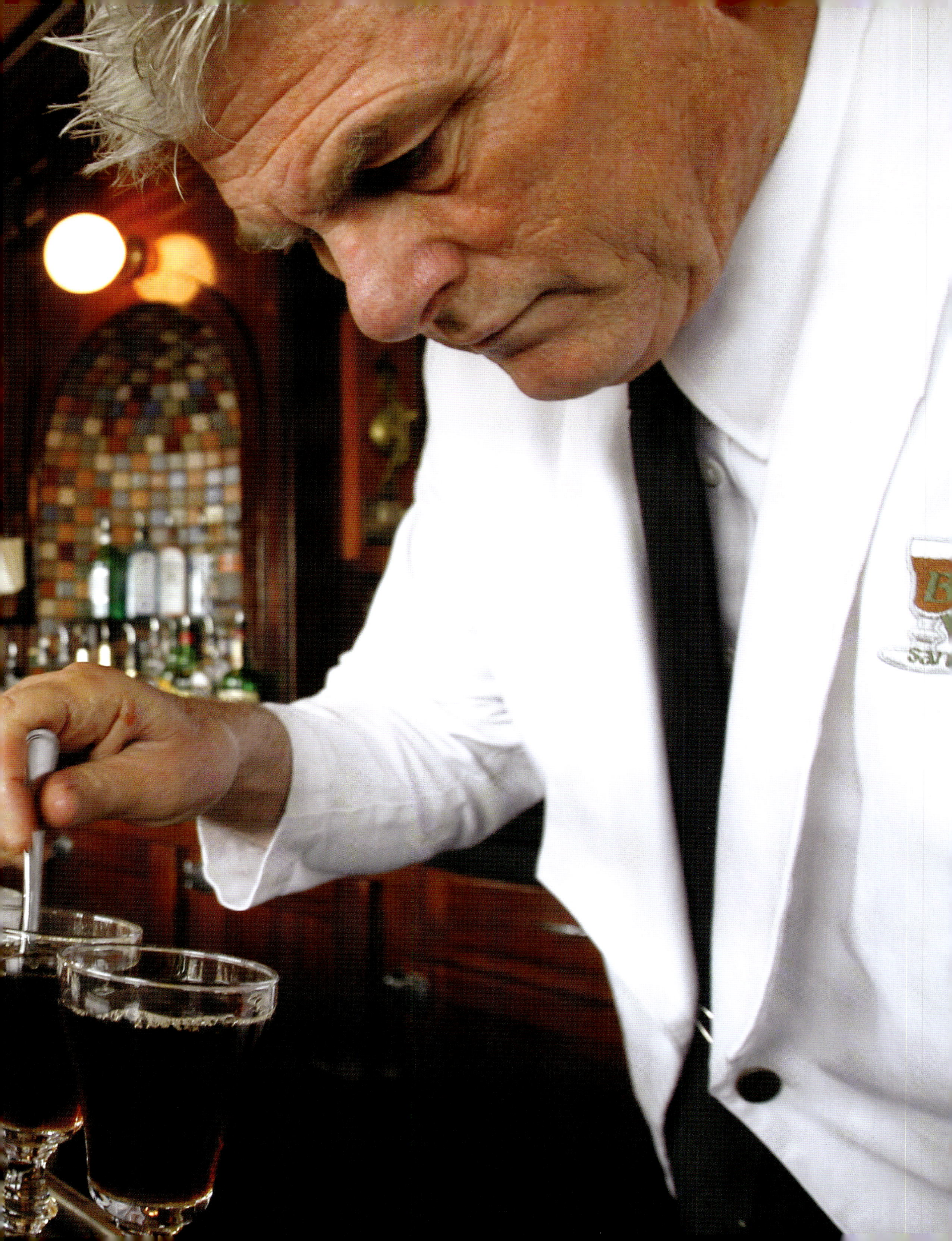

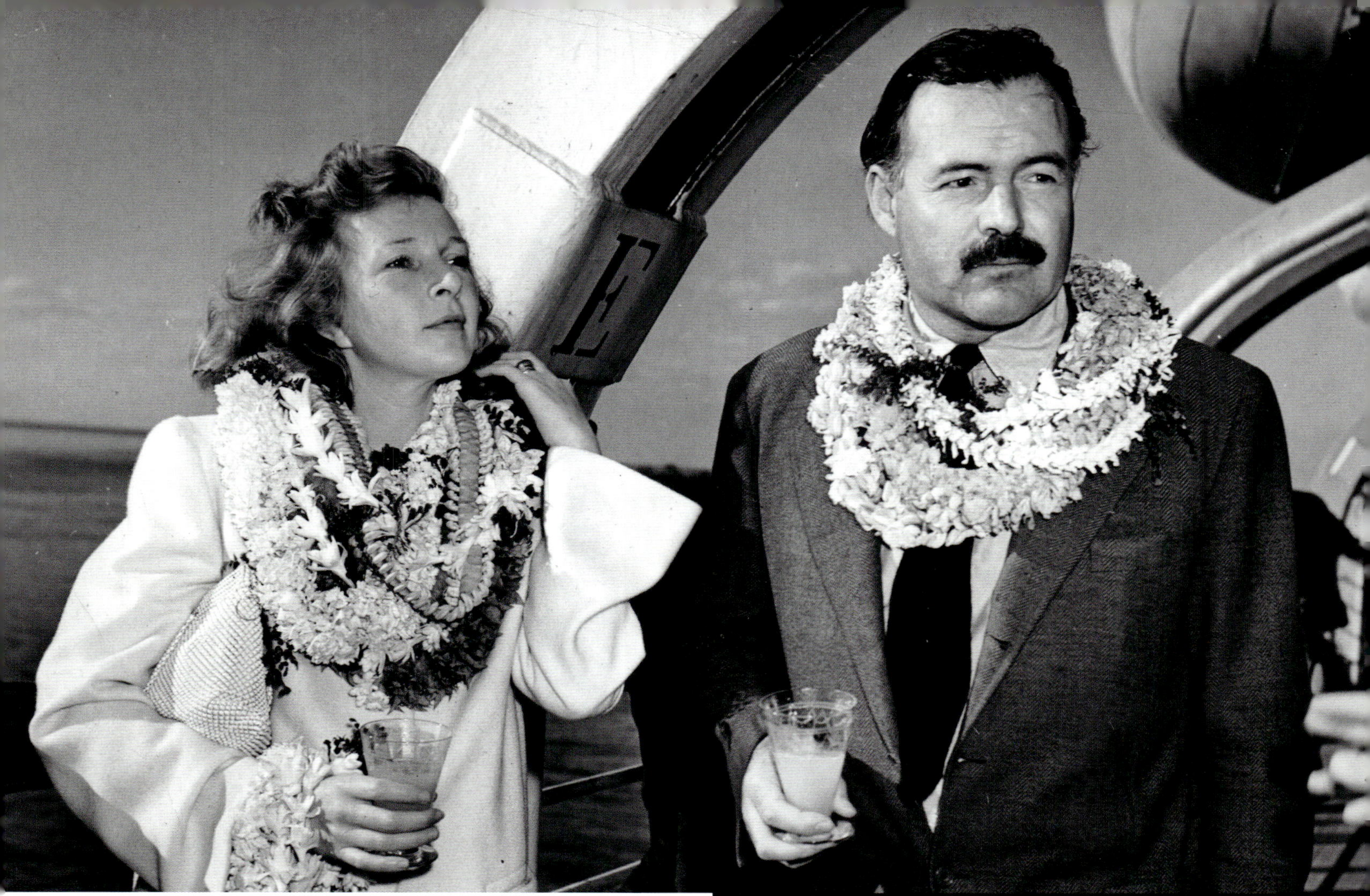

Clockwise from top left: *Despite a turbulent marriage, journalist Martha Gellhorn and author Ernest Hemingway make peace on the high seas with leis and cocktails, 1941; A zesty lemon aperitif at a sidewalk bar on Capri is as refreshing as Mediterranean breezes, 1959; At a 1987 cocktail fundraiser, stars Matt Dillon, Debbie Harry of Blondie, and Richard Gere unite for Art Against AIDS.*

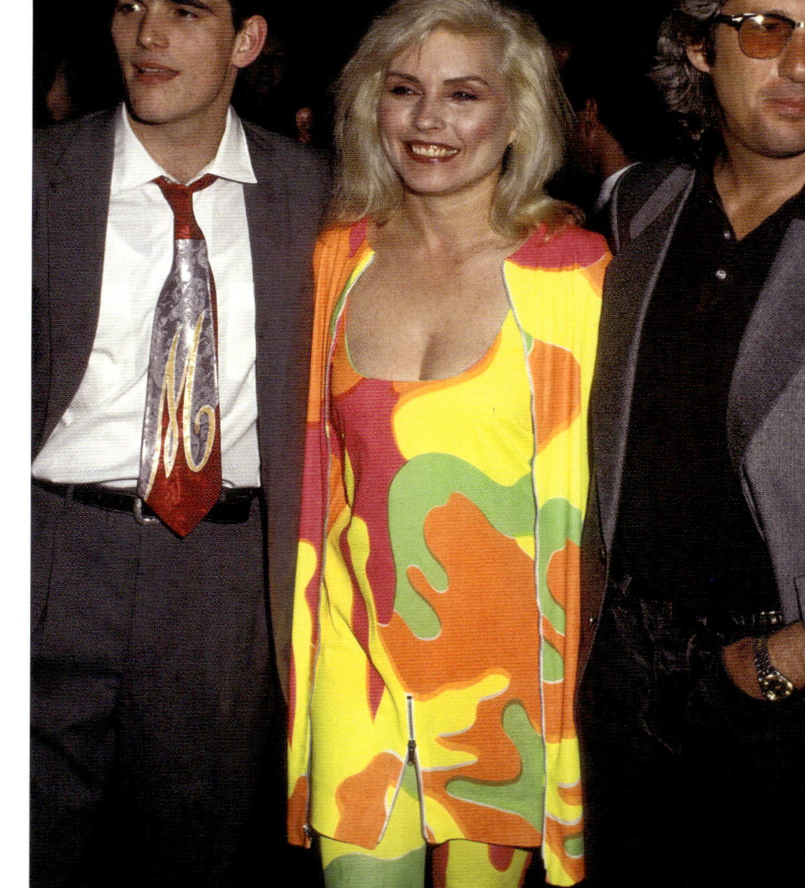

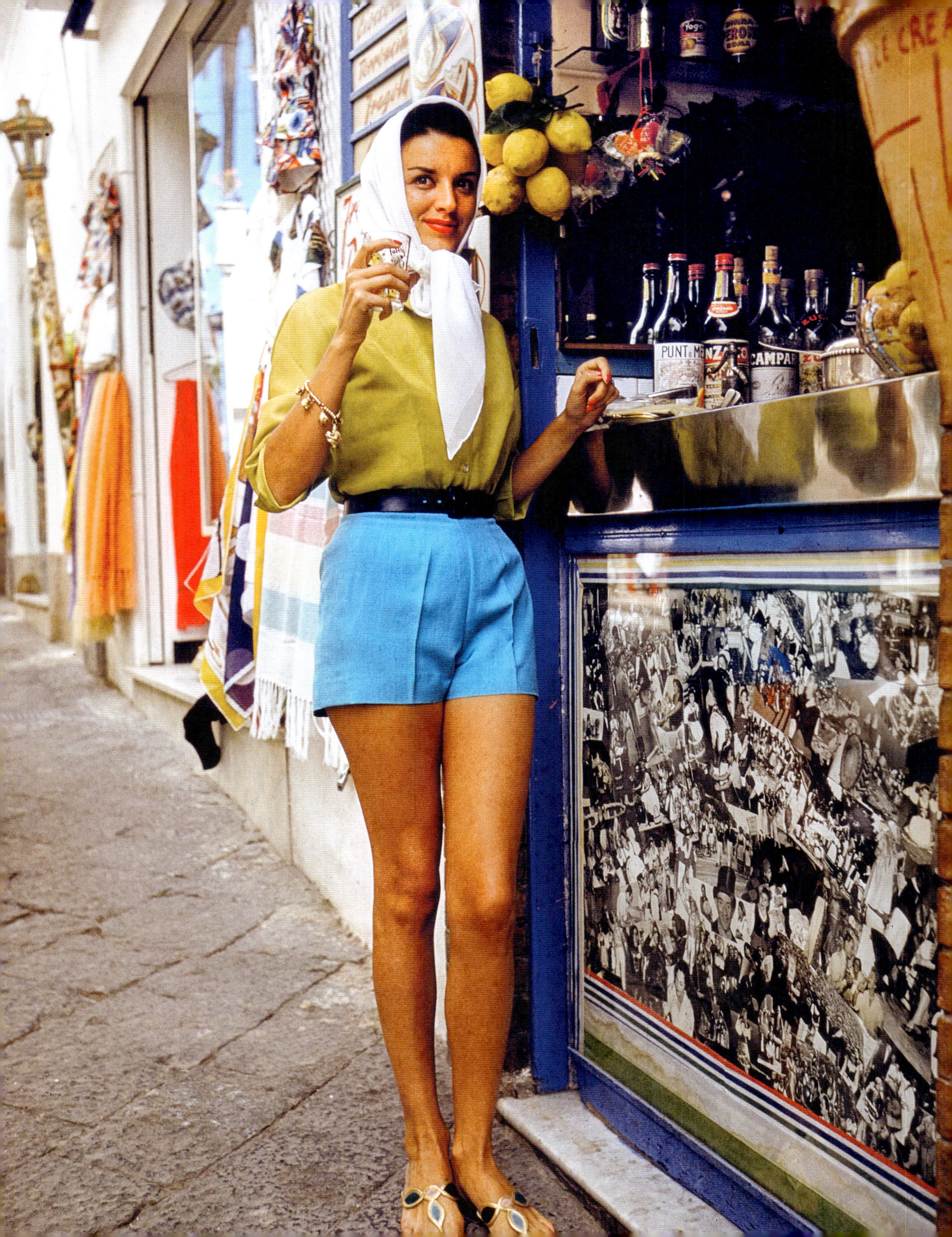
PUNT e ME
CAMPAR

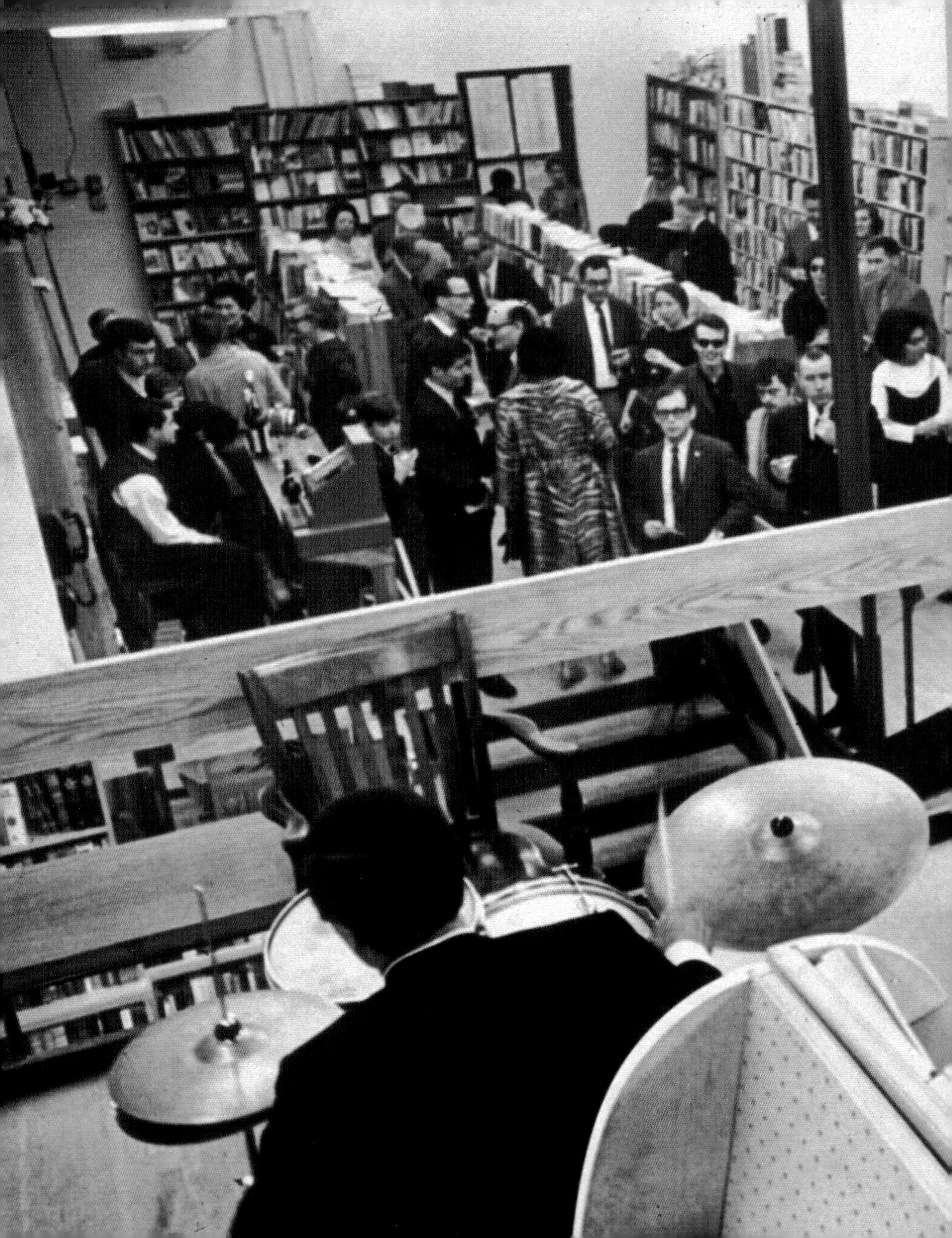

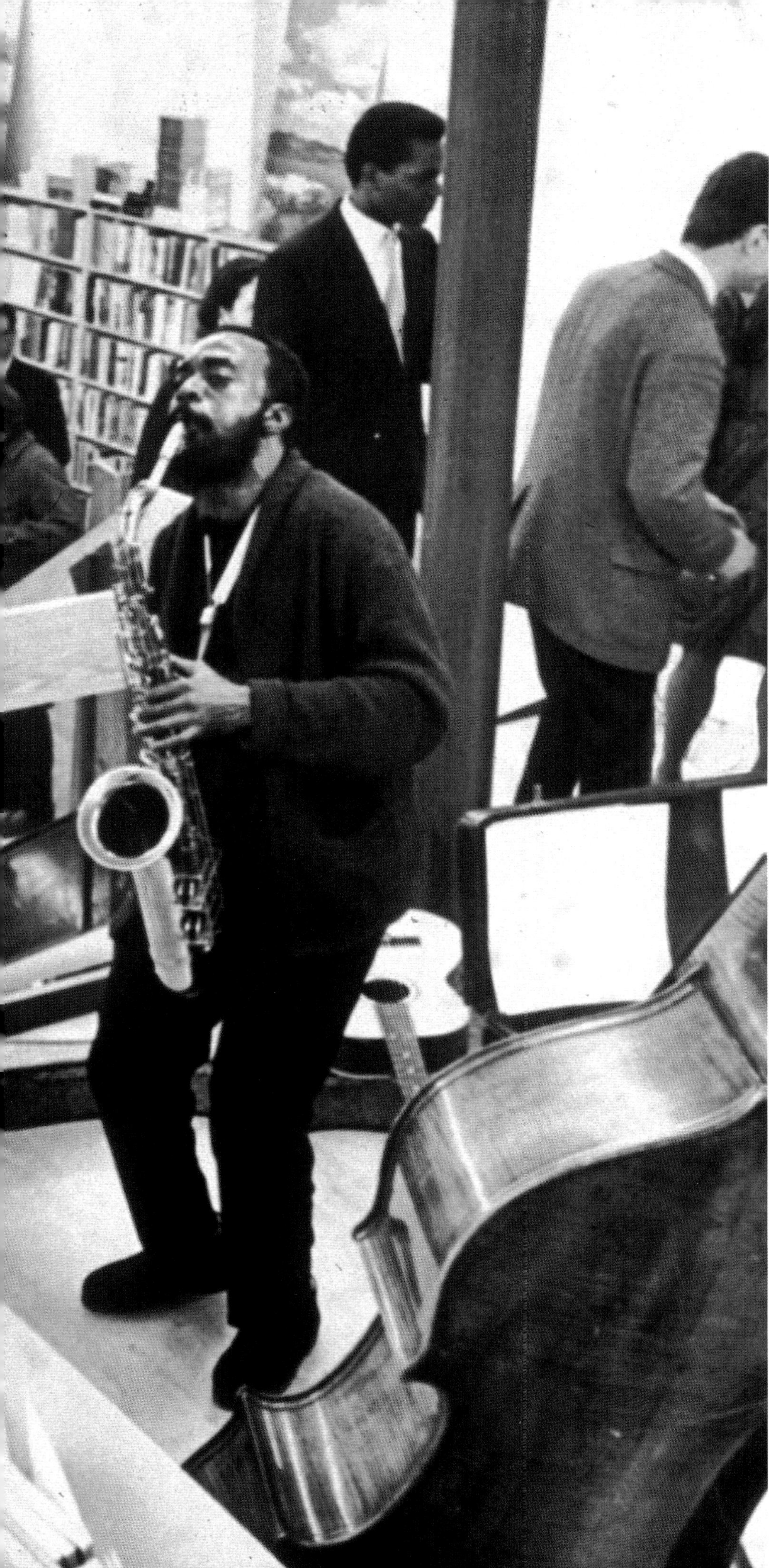

Opposite: *Partygoers dig a jazz trio's riffs at a party celebrating the famed Eighth Street Bookshop in New York's Greenwich Village, 1965.* Following pages: *Impeccable aprés-ski style reigns at Gstaad's Palace Hotel, Switzerland, 1984.*

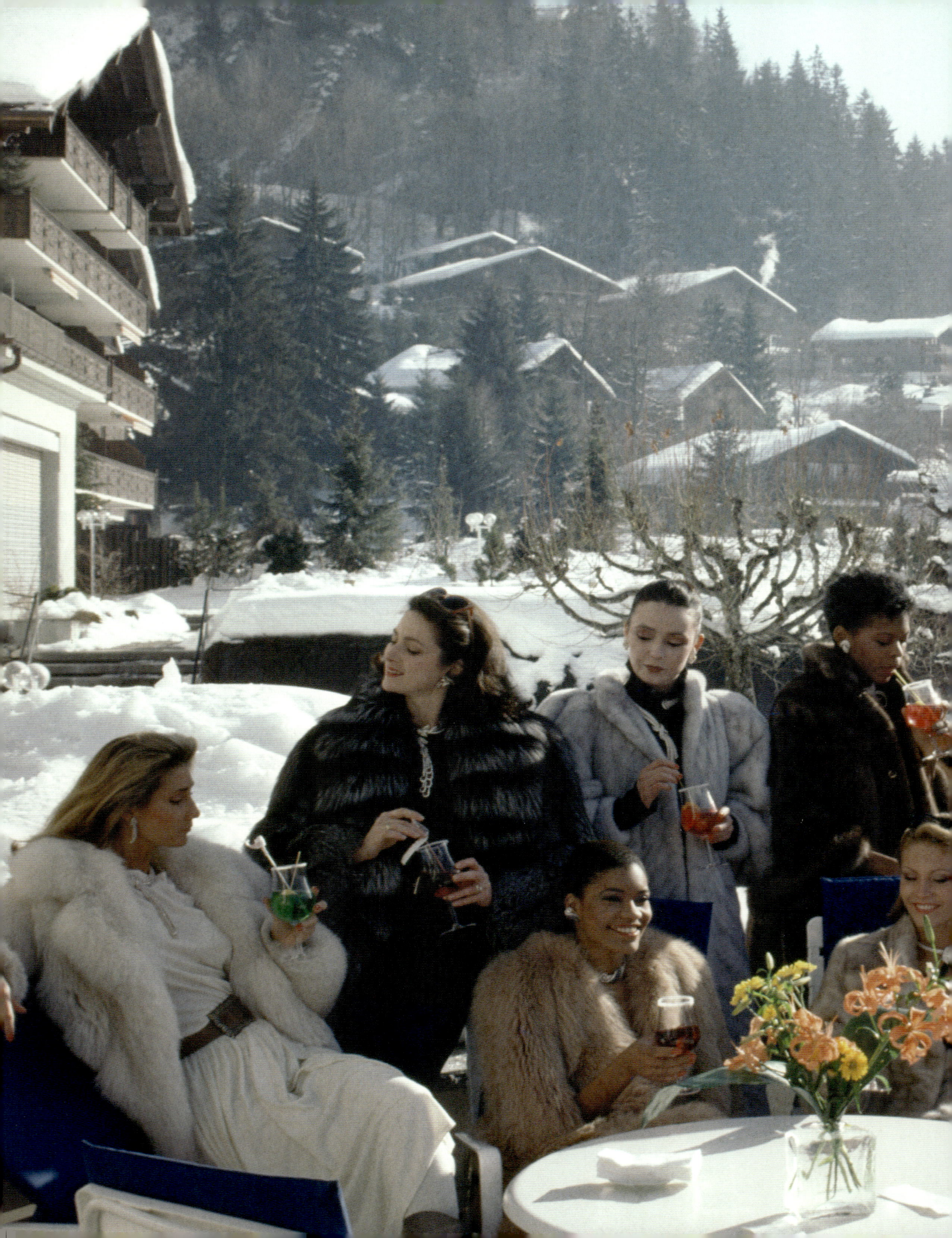

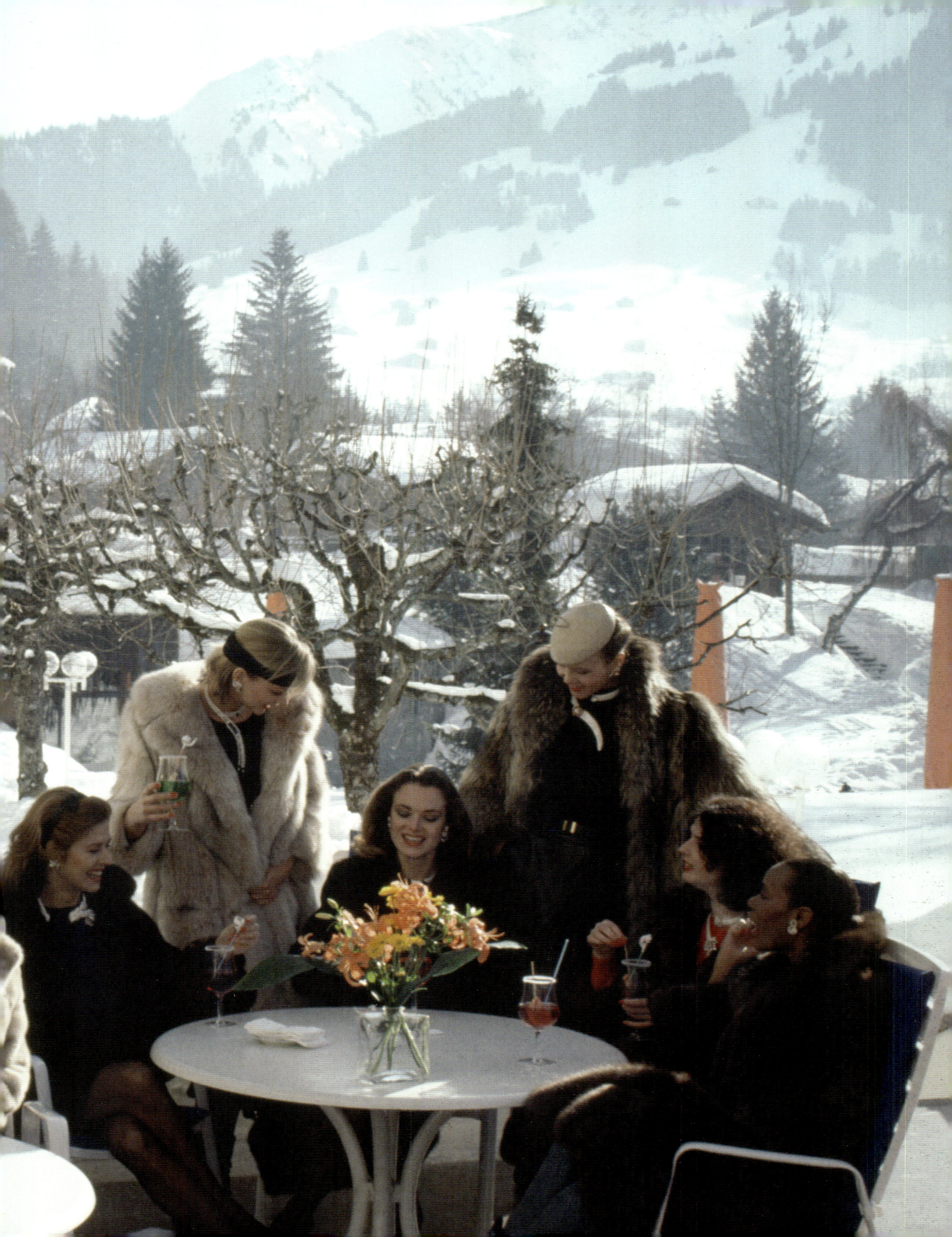

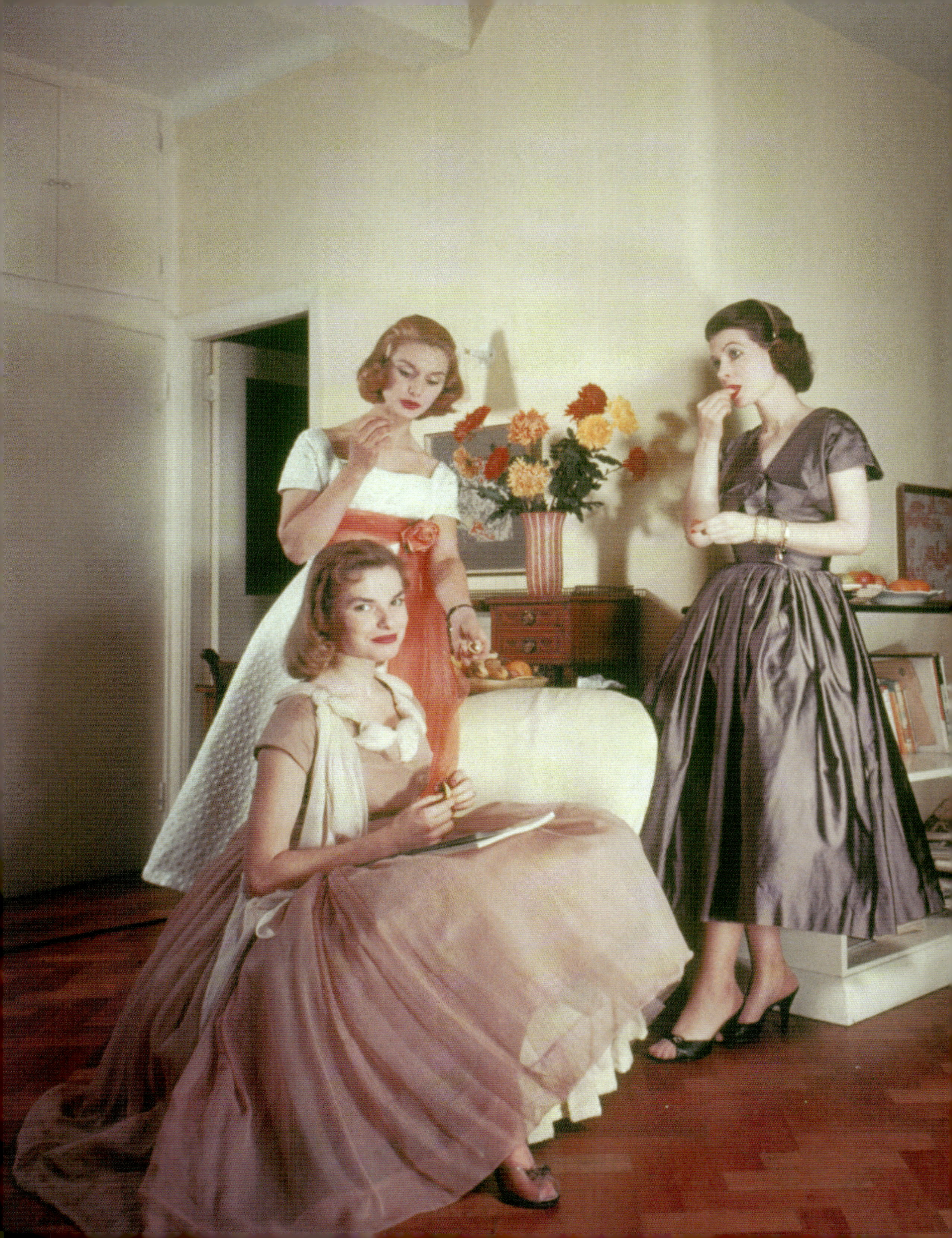

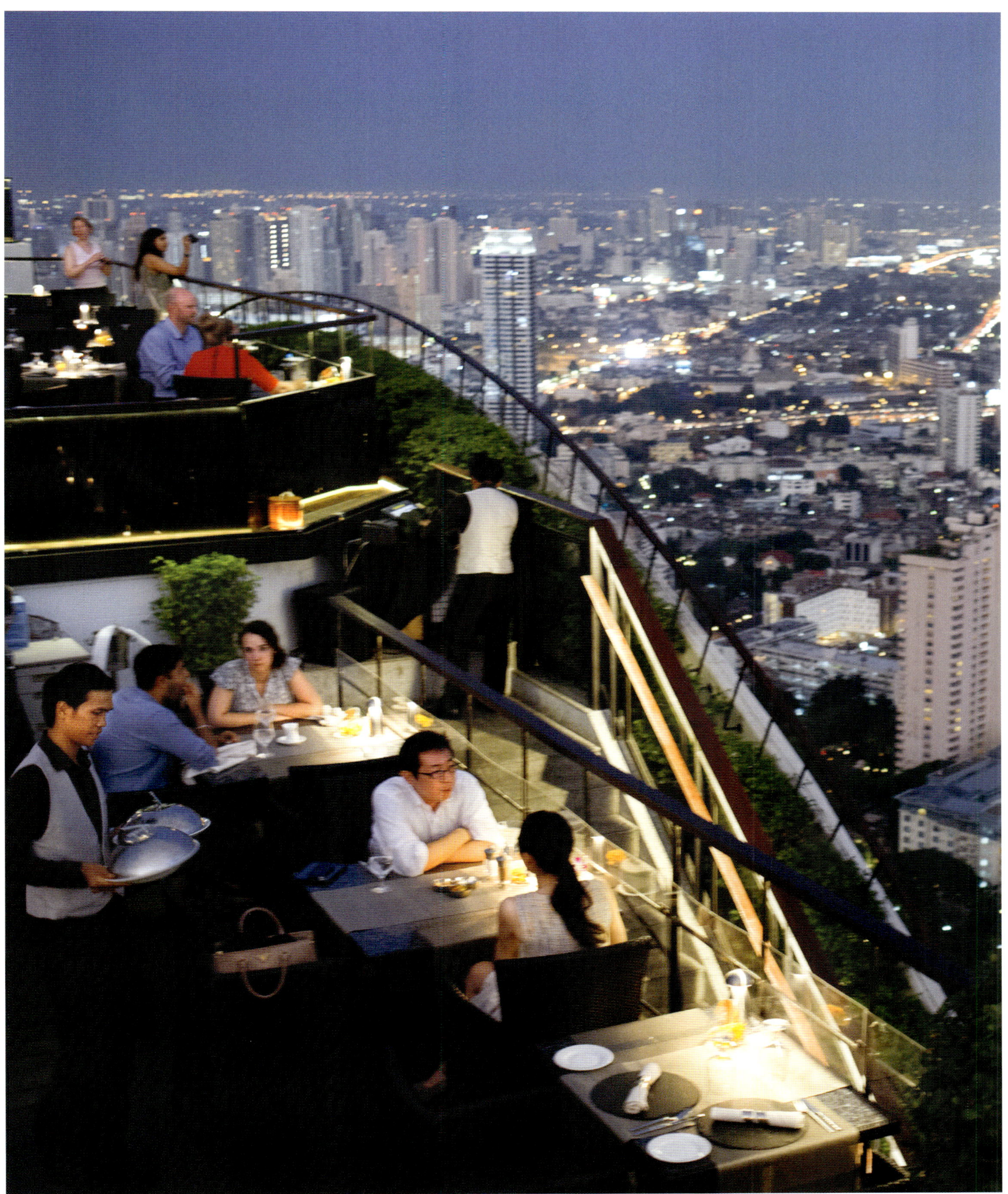

Opposite: *Elegant young ladies daintily nibble on hors d'oeuvres at a cocktail party, circa 1955.* This page: *Sky-high 360-degree views of Bangkok enthrall at the Vertigo Bar and Restaurant, on the roof of the Banyan Tree Hotel.* Following pages: *Guests sip and mingle at a serene poolside soirée in Santa Barbara, California, 1975.*

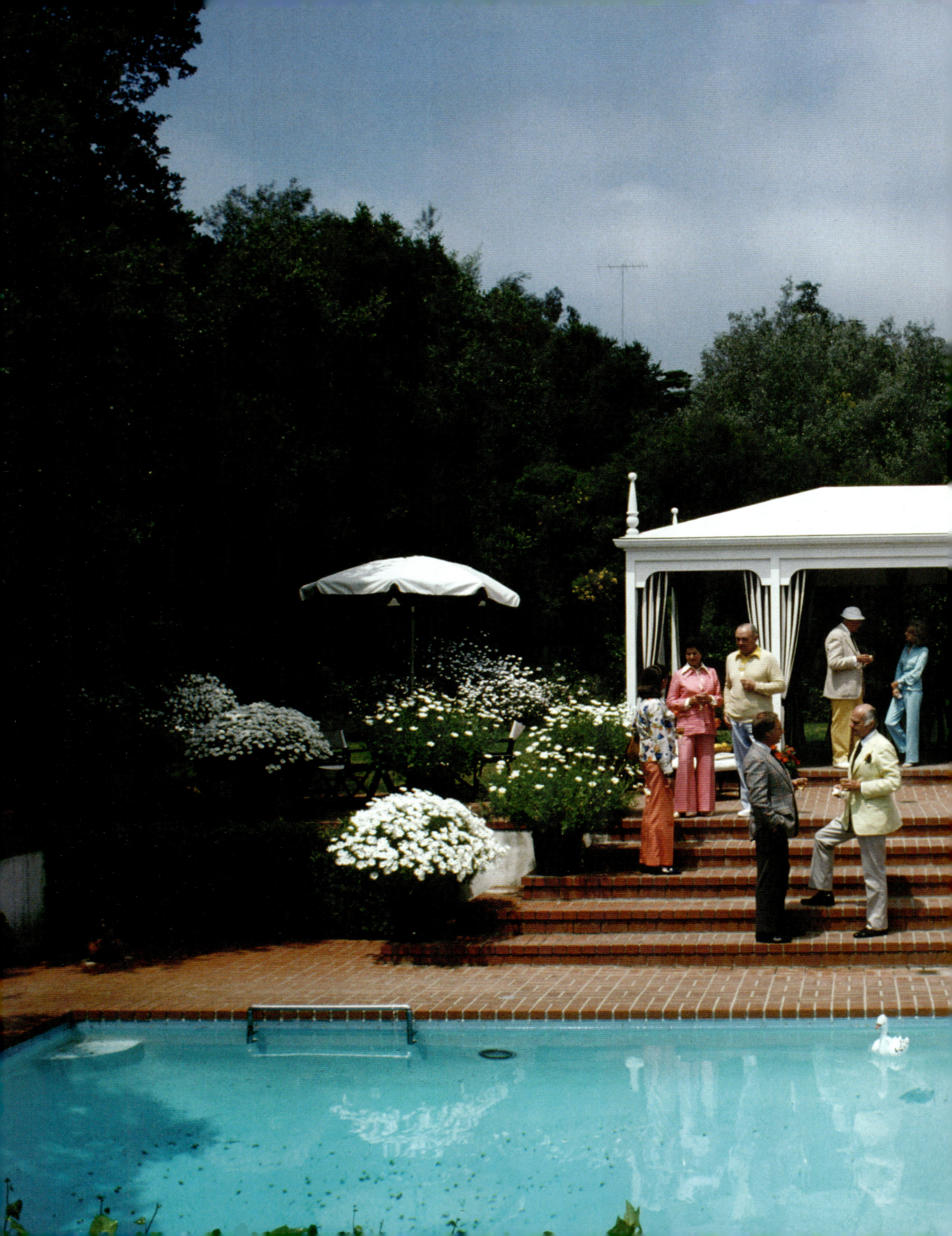

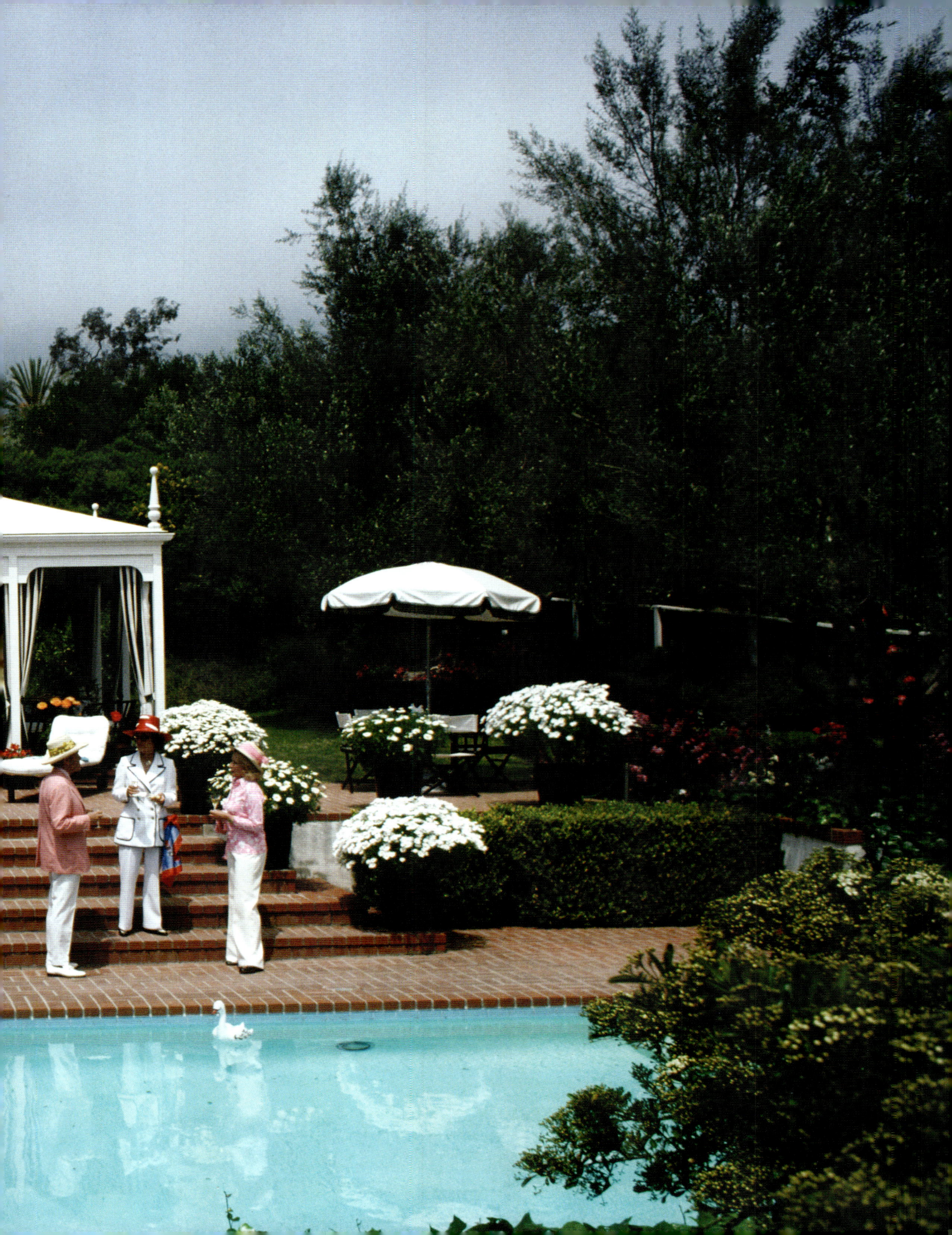

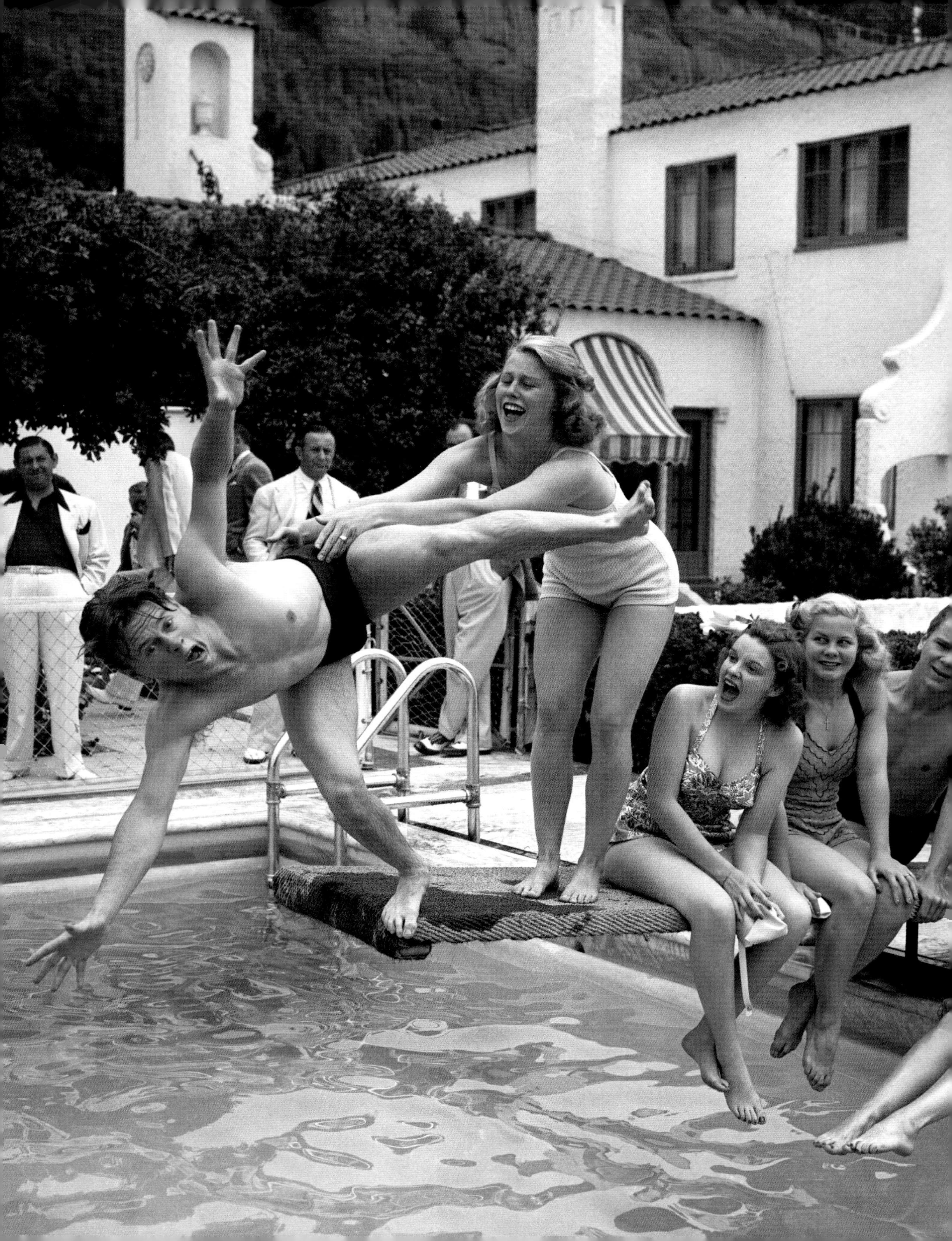

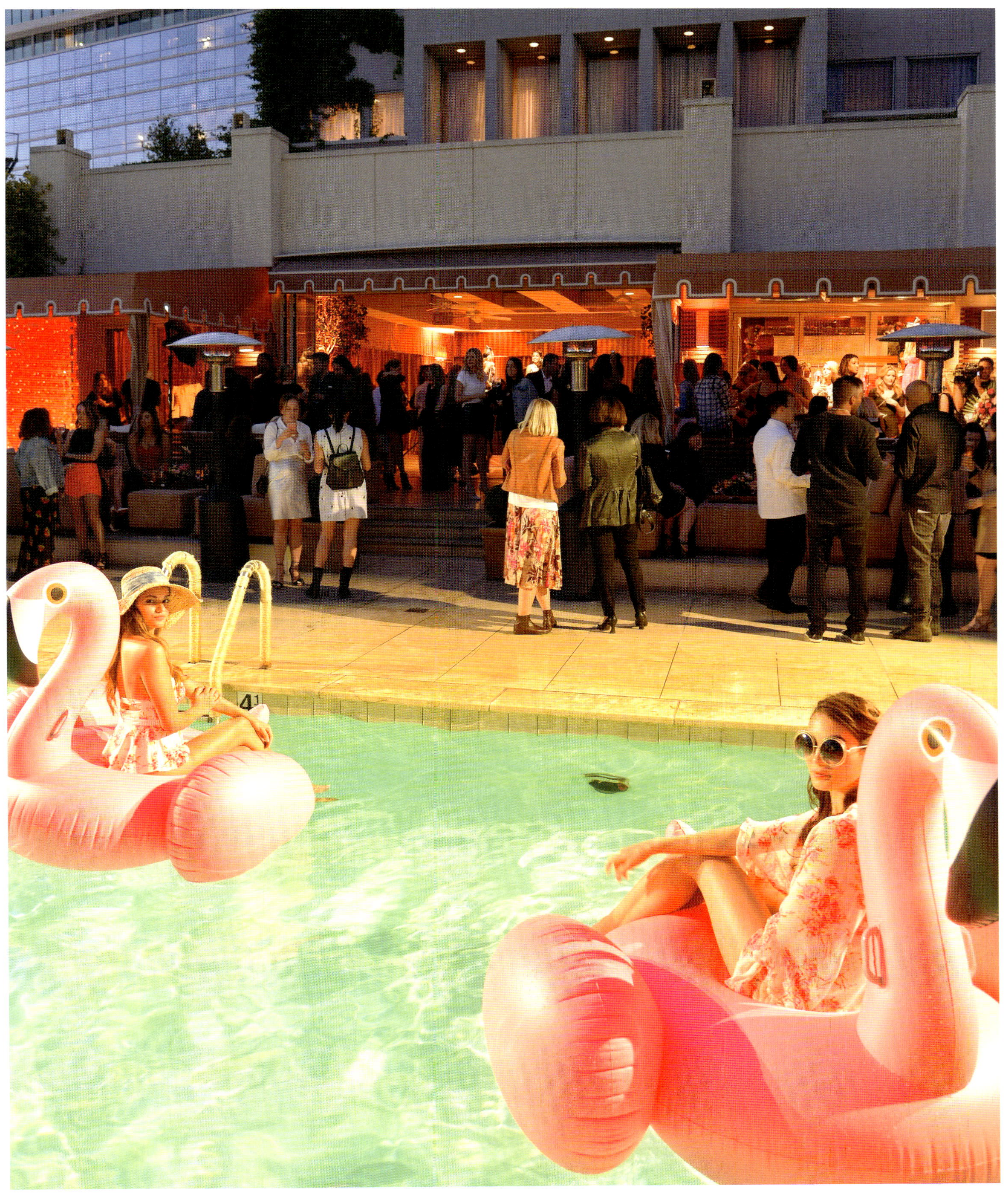

Opposite: *Mickey Rooney makes a splash during Judy Garland's birthday pool party at Louis B. Mayer's Santa Monica beach home, 1939.* This page: *Pink flamingo floats add a dash of whimsy at designer Betsey Johnson's extravaganza, West Hollywood, 2016.*

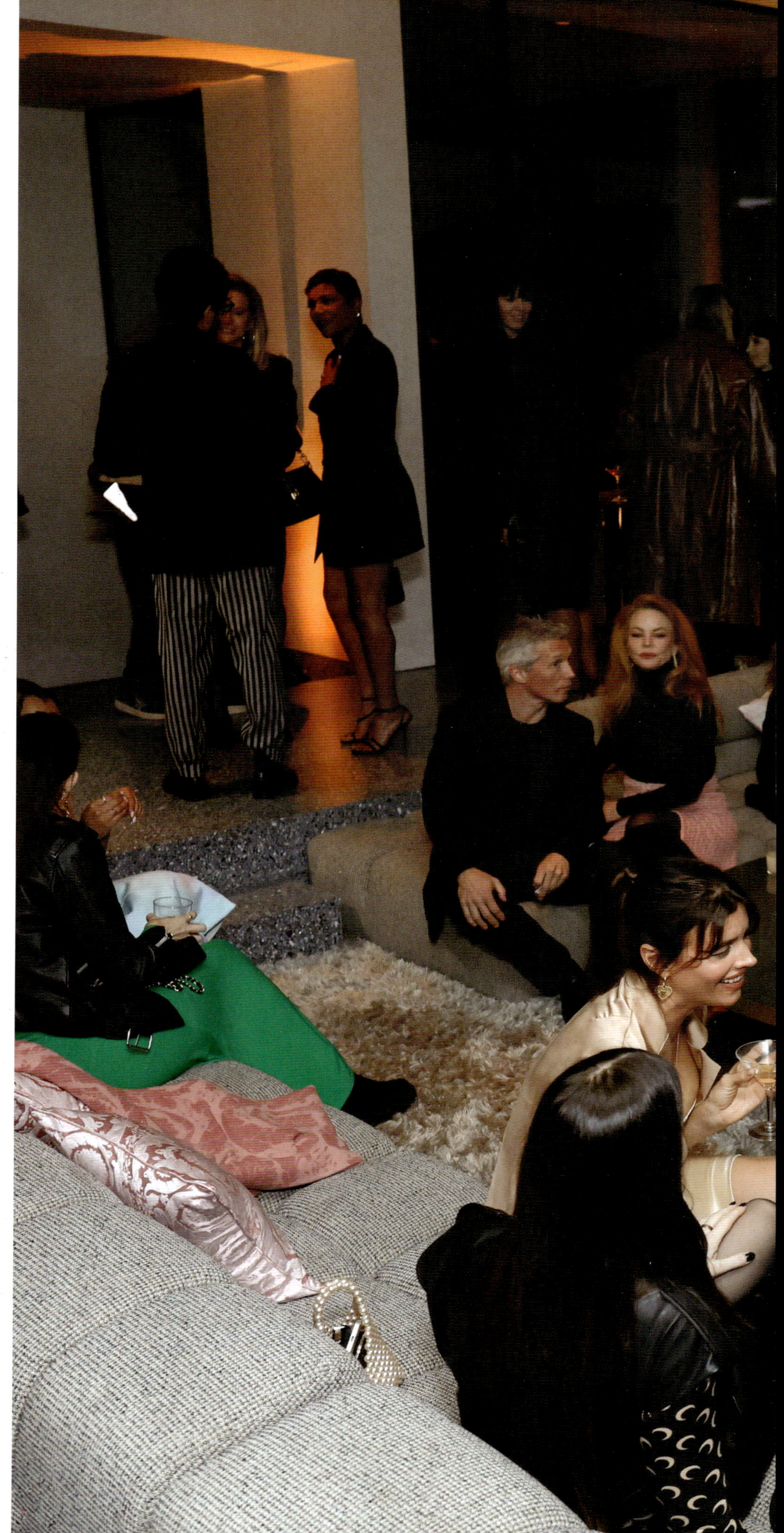

Opposite: *Cocktails and conversation mix at Donatella Versace's cocktail party in Los Angeles, 2024.* Following pages, left: *Two stylish women harmonize with a member of a barbershop quartet during cocktails al fresco, 1970*; right: *Genteel conversation and cocktails fill a languid Parisian afternoon, 1948.*

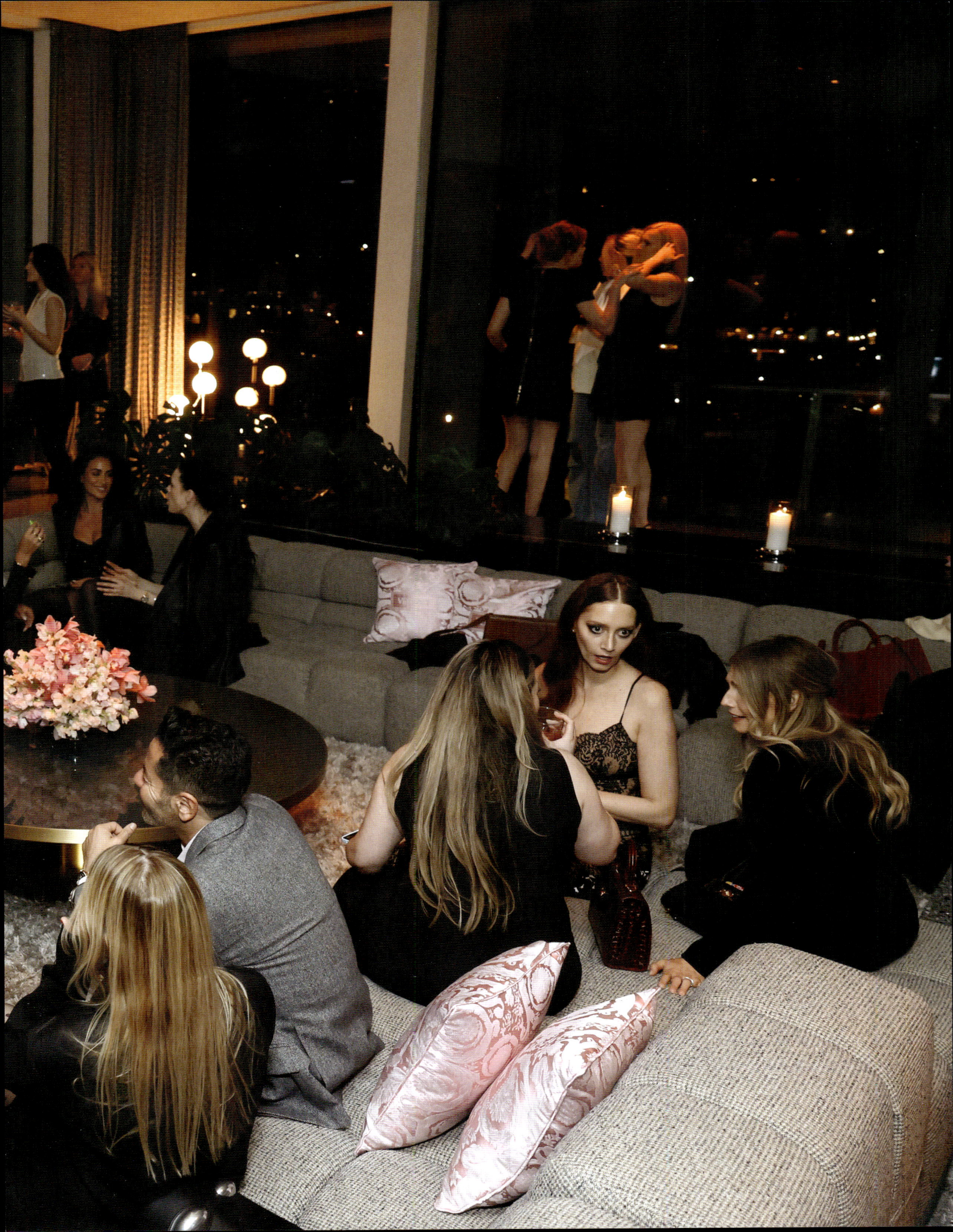

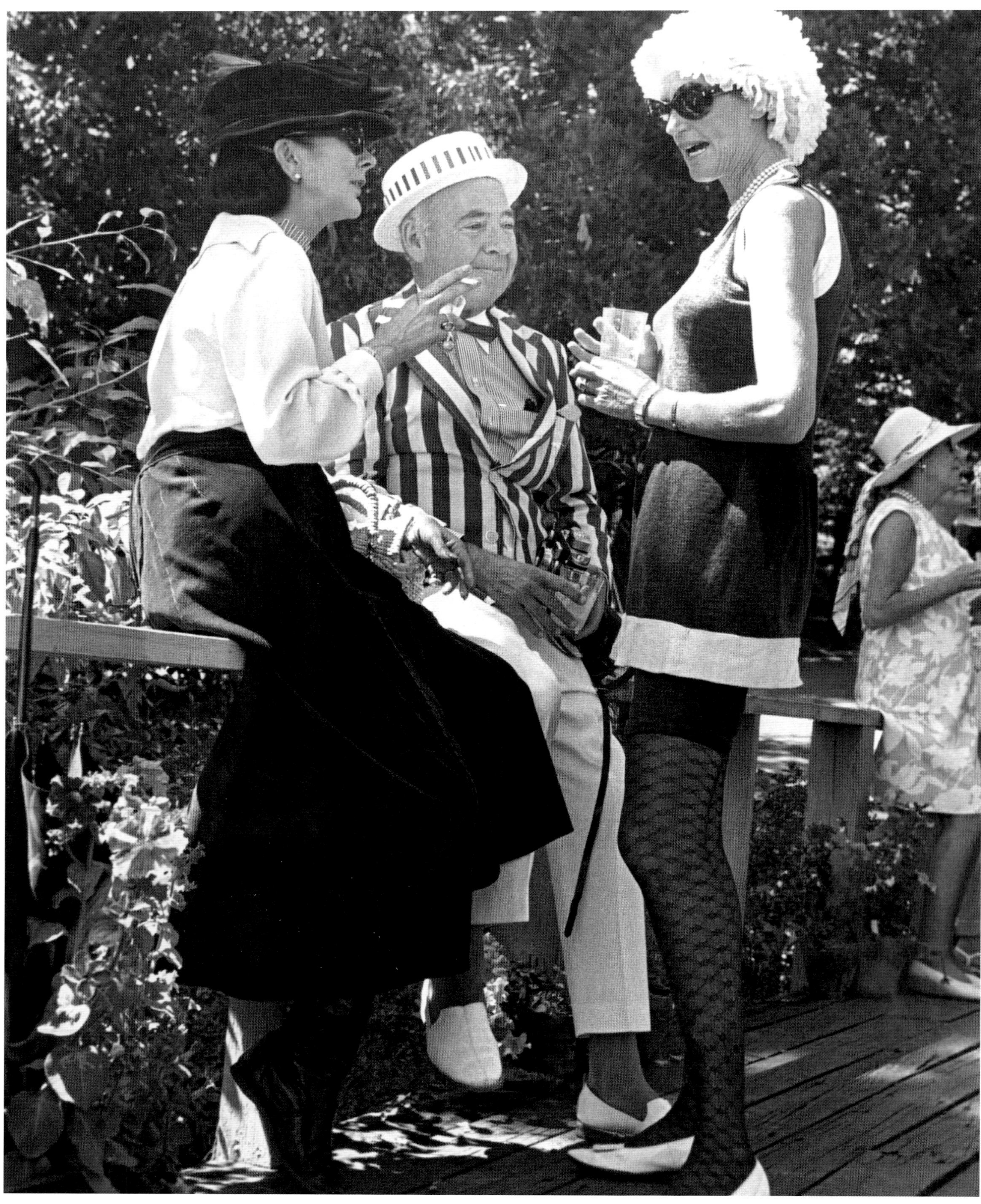

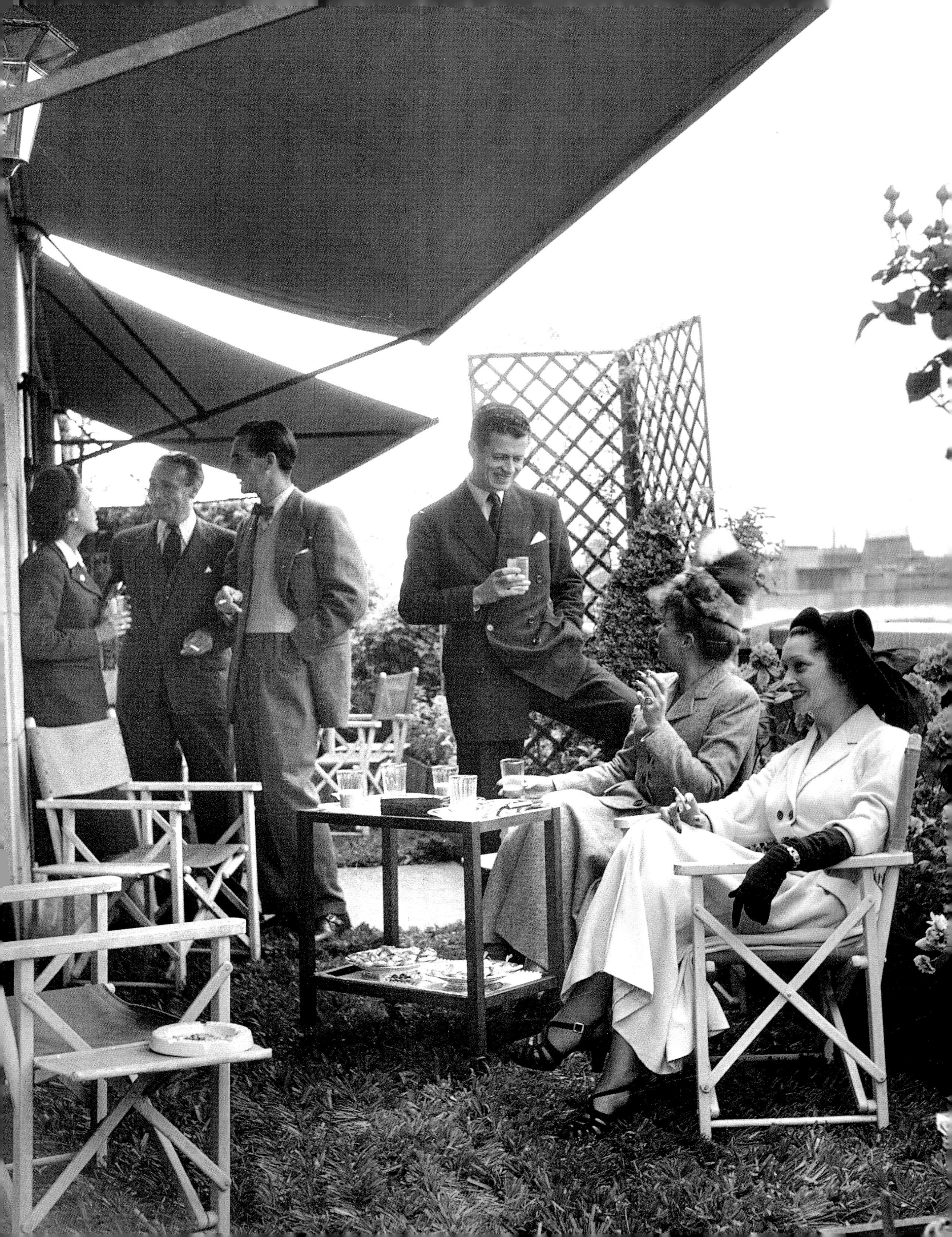

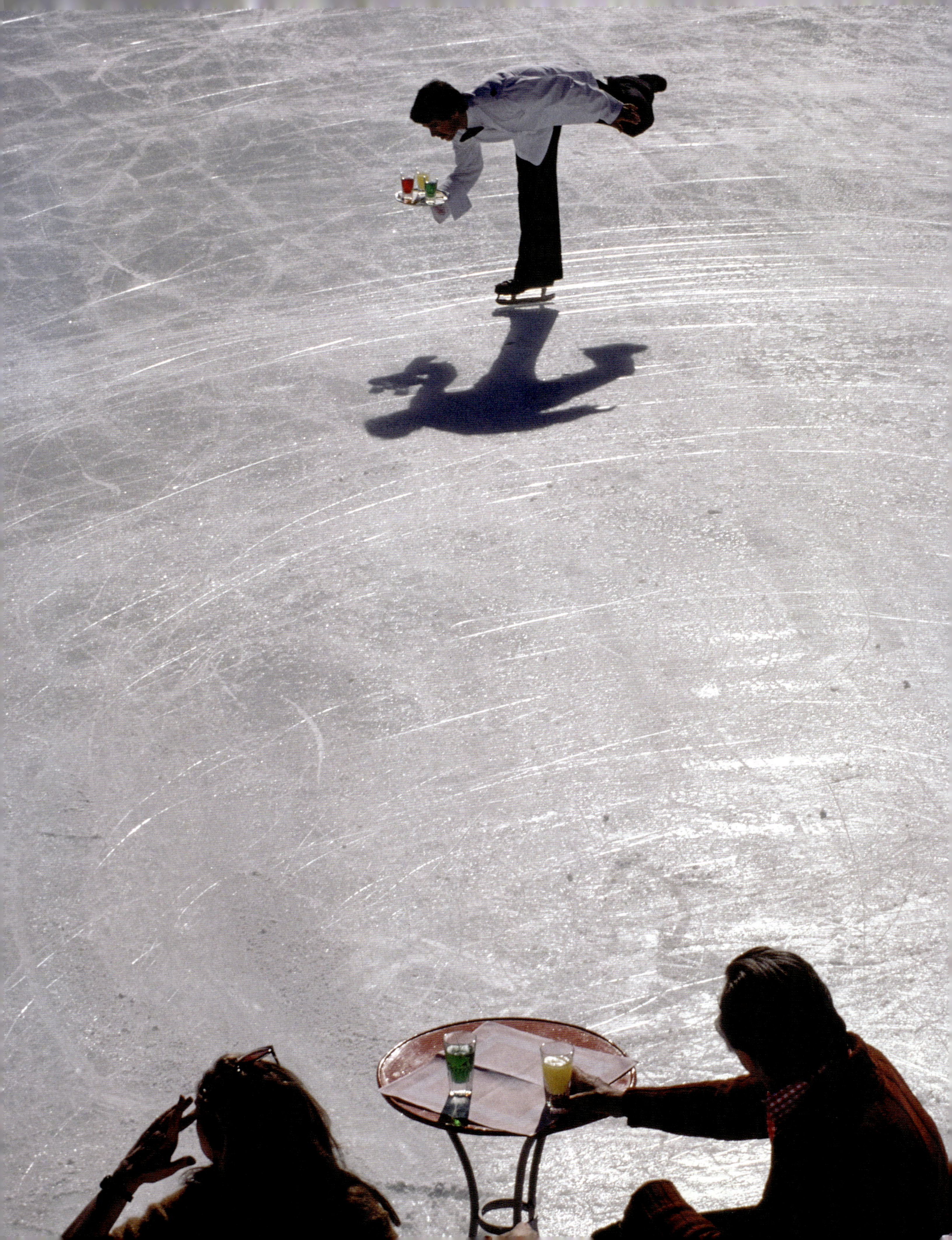

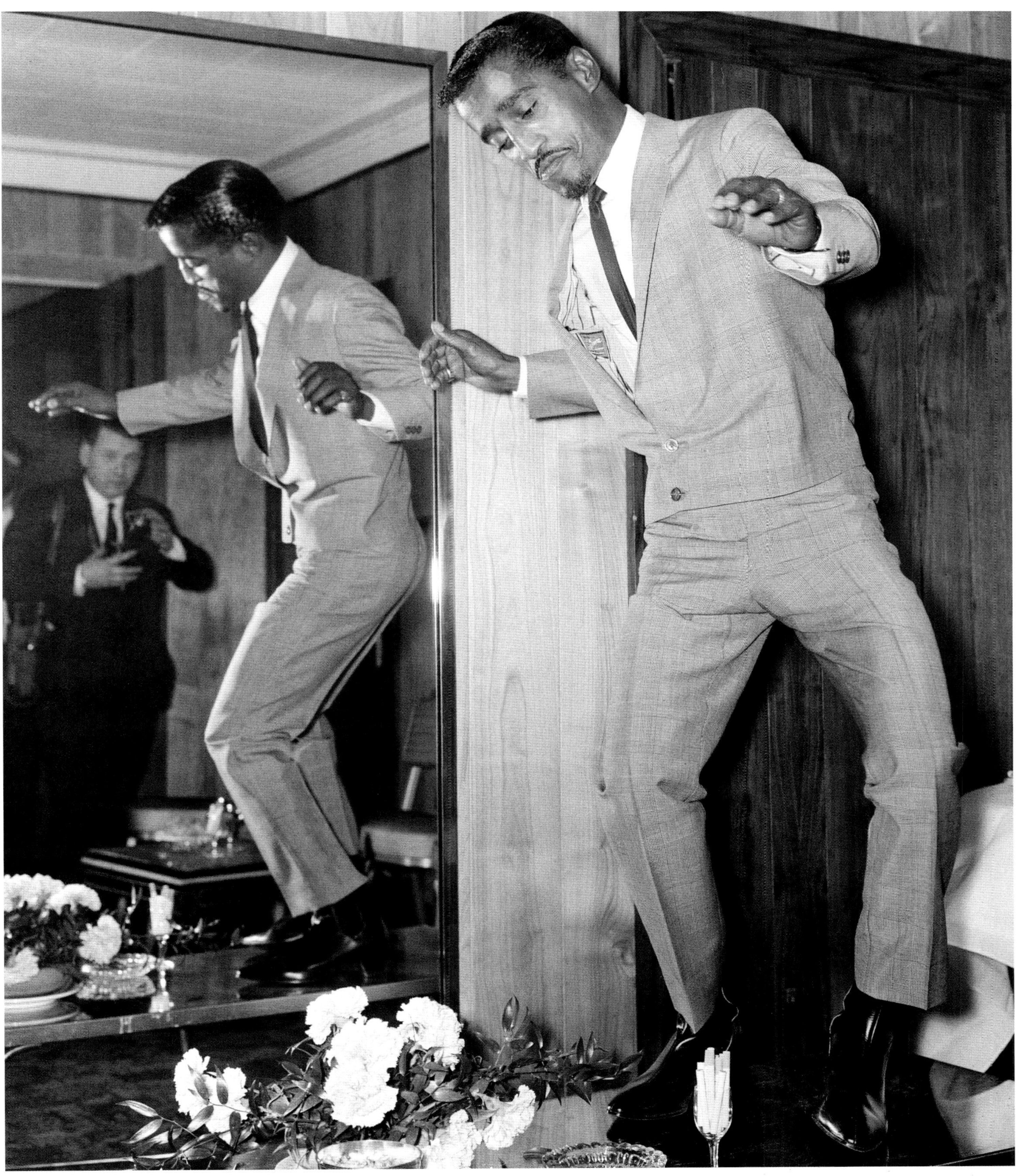

Opposite: *A skating waiter serves guests at the Palace Hotel, St. Moritz, Switzerland, 1978.* This page: *Sammy Davis Jr. shakes up the cocktail scene at the May Fair Hotel, London, 1966.* Following pages, left: (top) *A neon sign celebrates Las Vegas's 24/7 cocktail culture*; (bottom) *The Havana's El Floridita is home to the Daiquiri*; right: *The Biltmore Hotel advertises a reprieve for travelers passing through Grand Central Station, New York, 1935.*

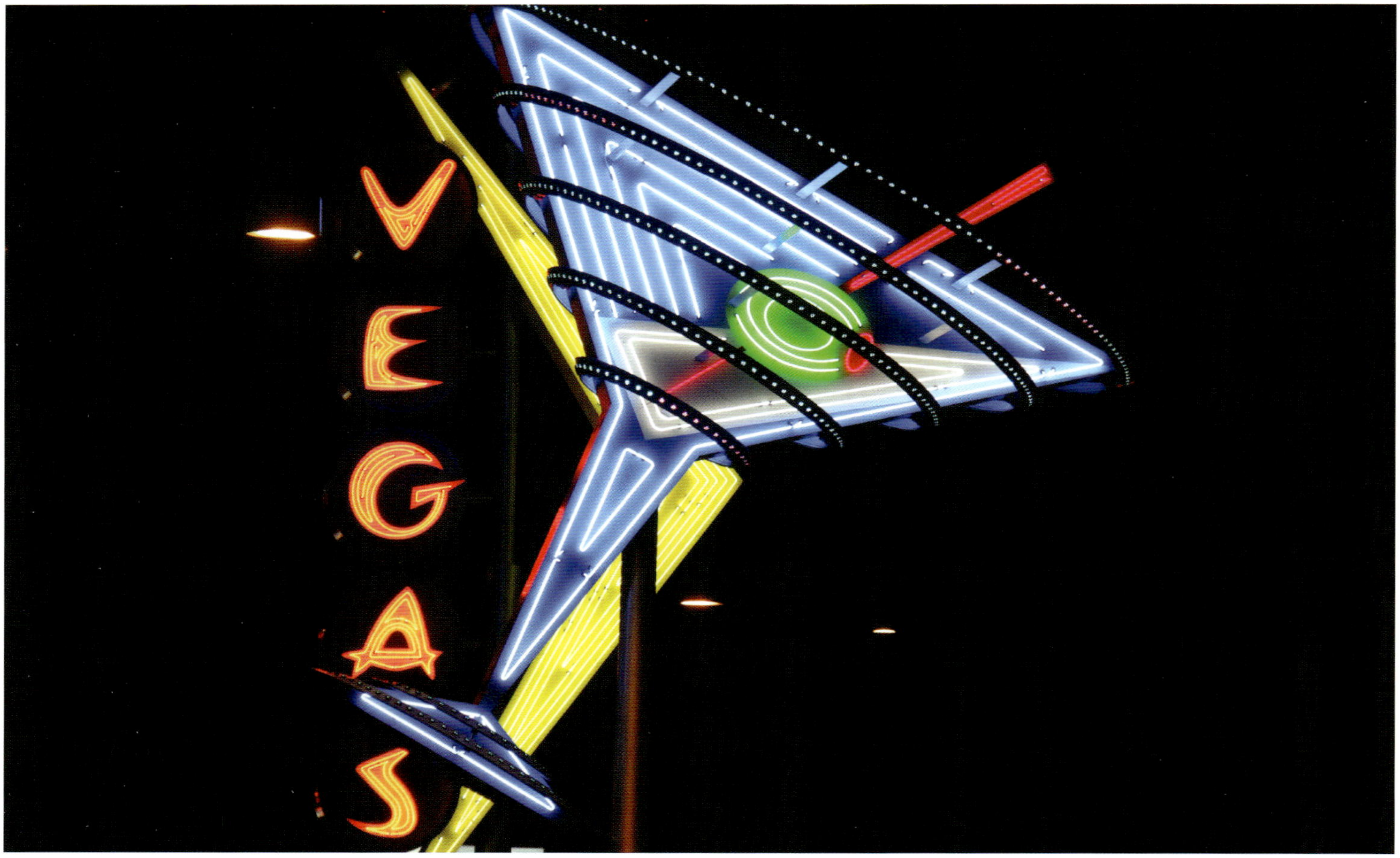
VEGAS

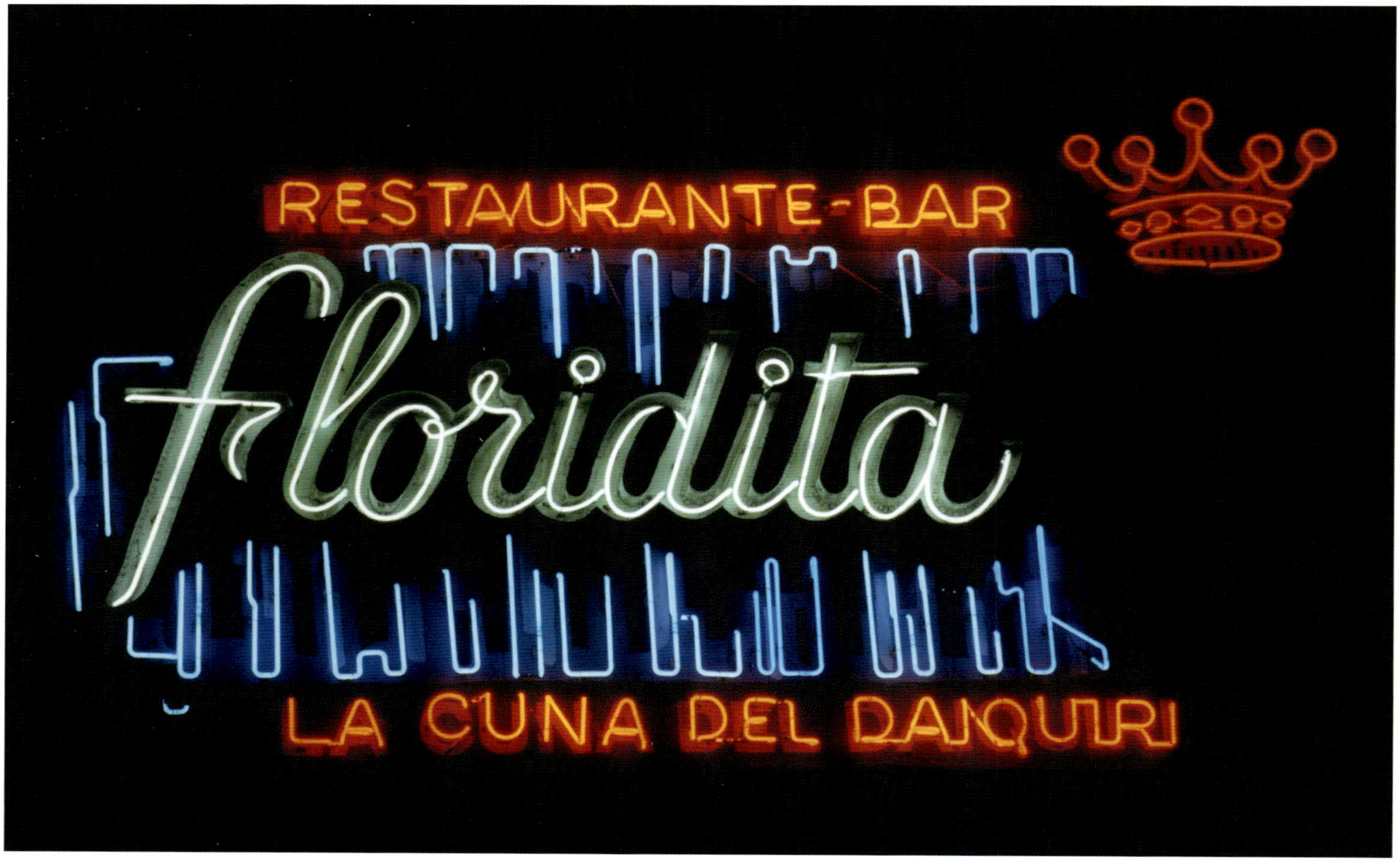
RESTAURANTE-BAR
floridita
LA CUNA DEL DAIQUIRI

COCKTAIL HOUR IN THE MADISON ROOM OF

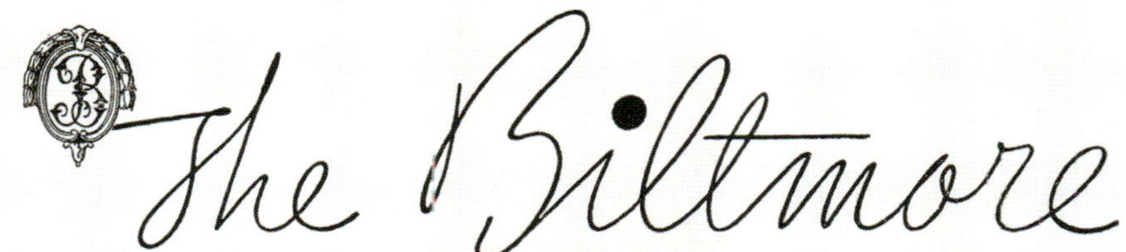

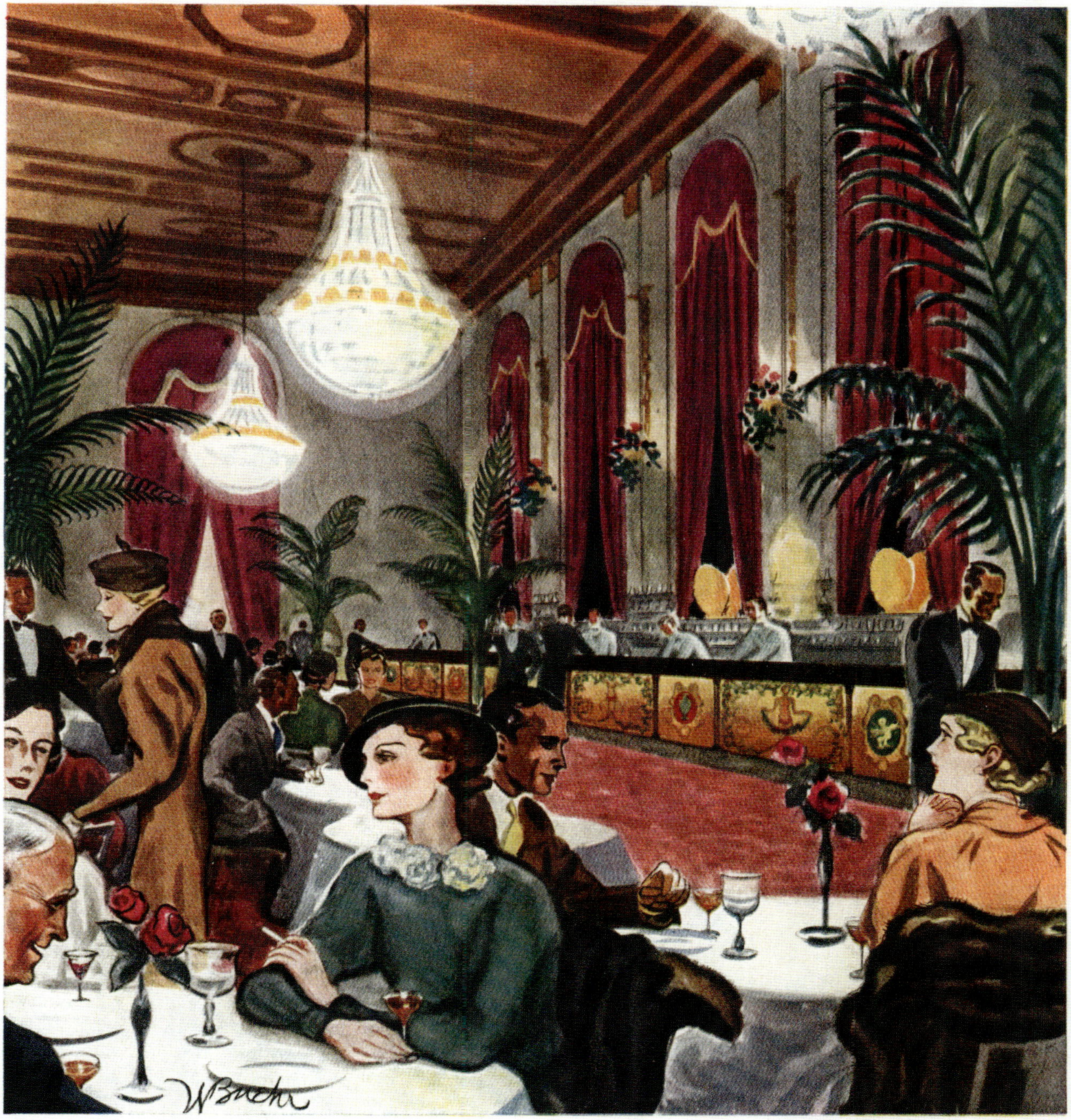

PAUL WHITEMAN *plays again! You may catch his smart rhythms drifting across the* **PALM COURT** *from Le Casino Bleu and into this famed room, as you enjoy the cocktails born at its magnificent bar. In this* **MADISON ROOM** *of gay continental mood, discriminating New Yorkers dine and wine, as of old. In the Palm Court they enjoy an apéritif. In* **LE CASINO BLEU** *they come for tea, dinner and supper dancing.*

BOWMAN-BILTMORE HOTELS CORPORATION • OPERATORS OF THE BILTMORE AND THE COMMODORE

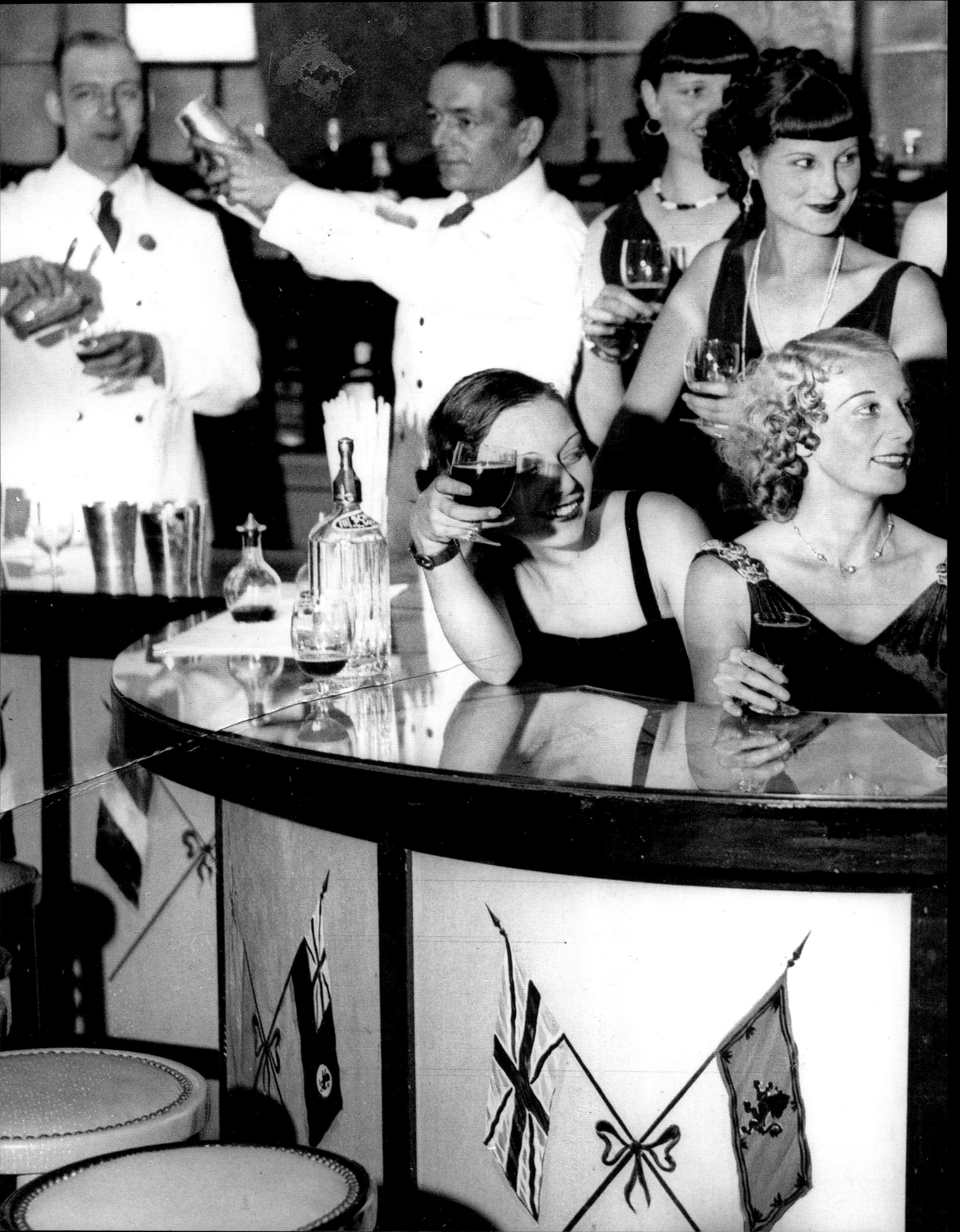

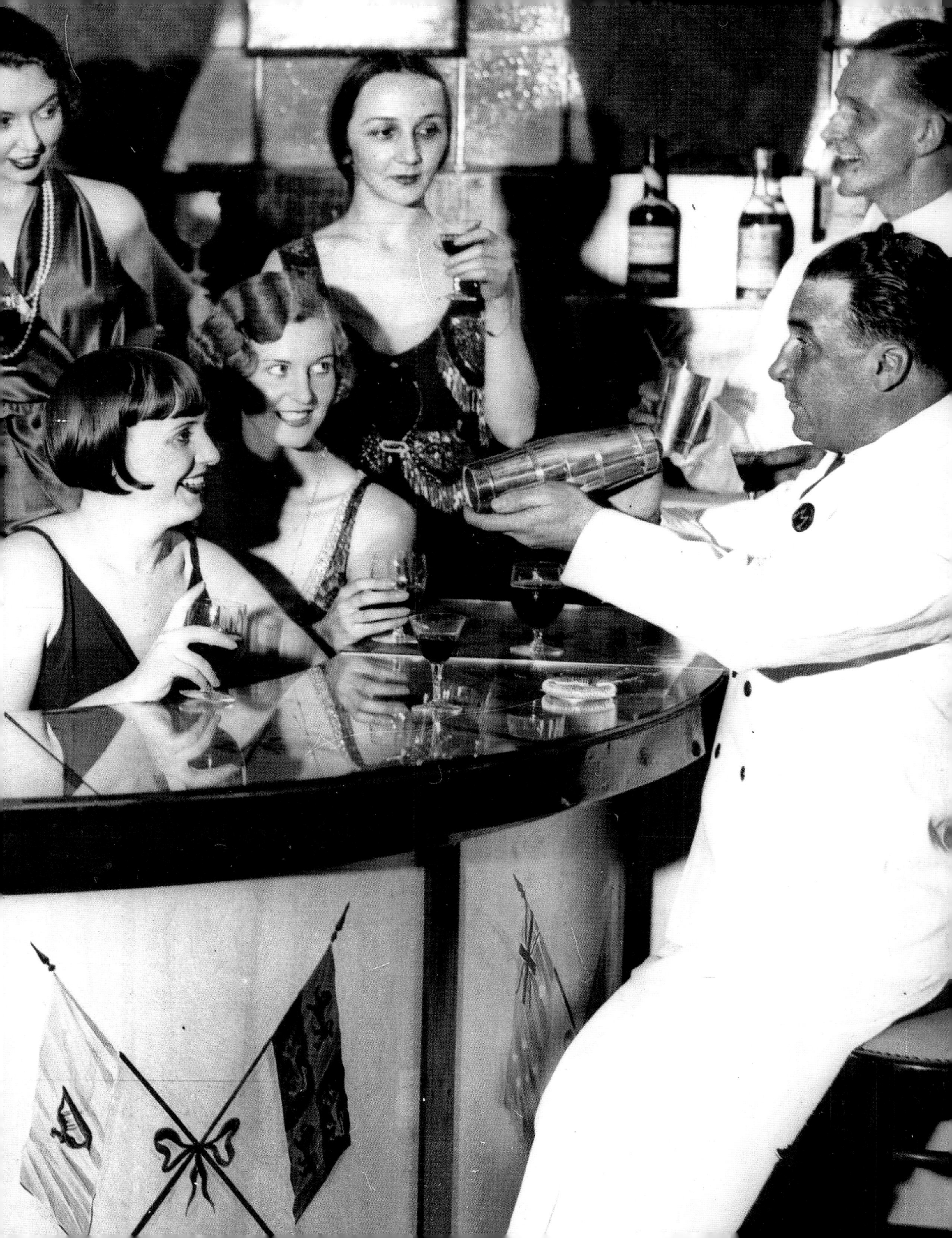

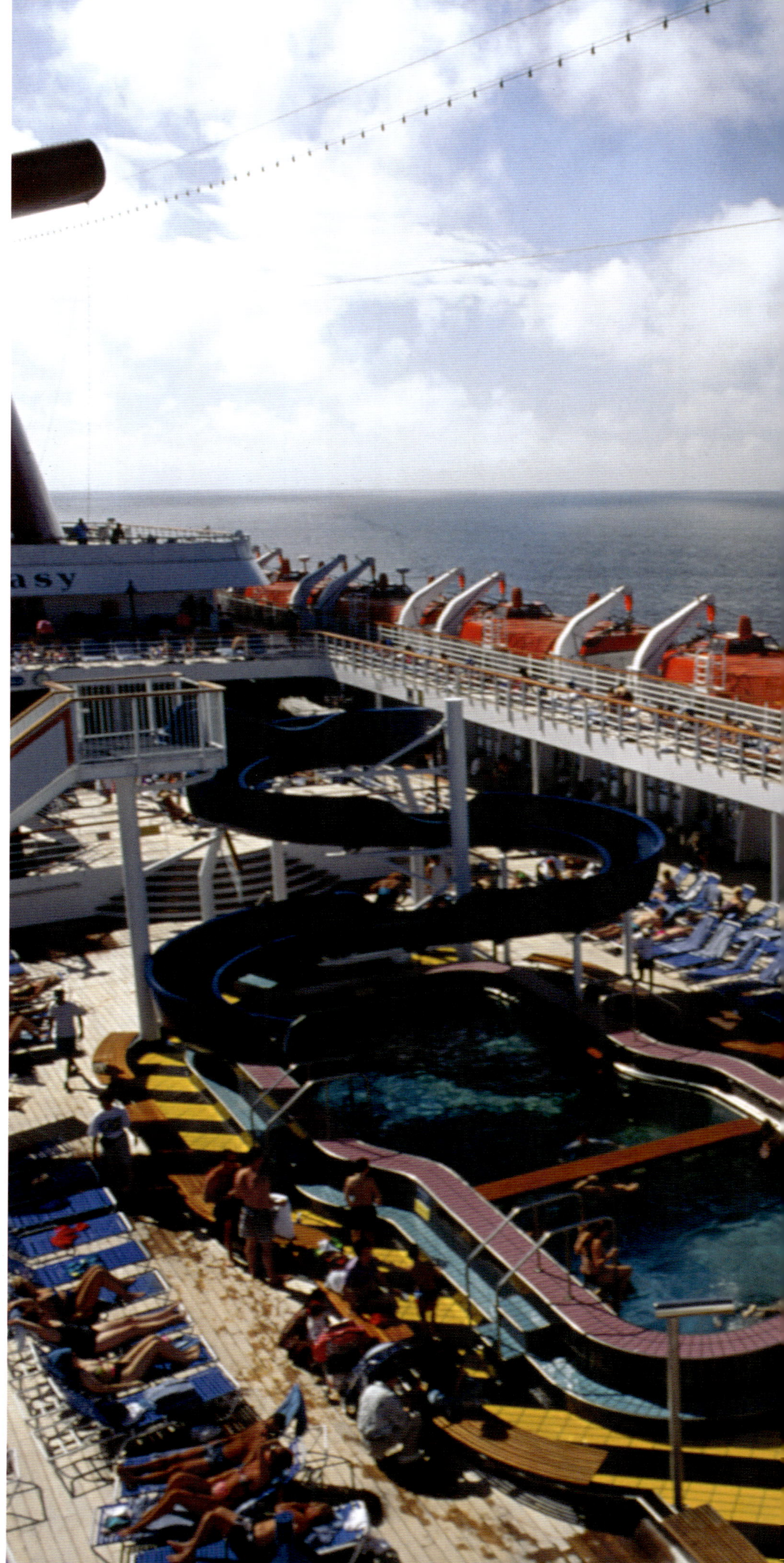

Previous pages: *Barmaids and bartenders strike a pose at Murray's, a risqué club in London's Soho, 1932.* Opposite: *A bartender offers a mid-voyage refreshment on the lido deck of the the cruise ship* Carnival Ecstasy, *2014.*

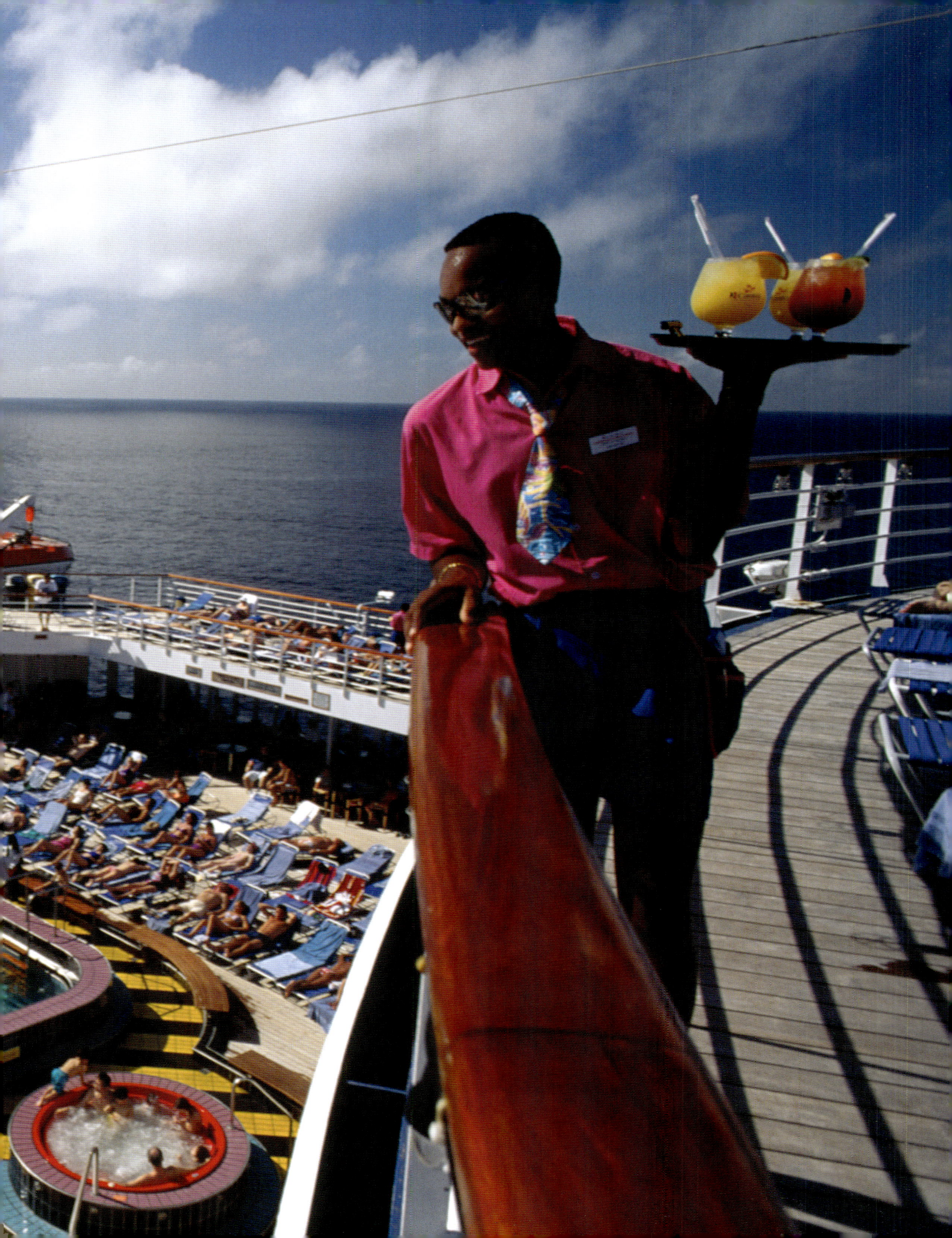

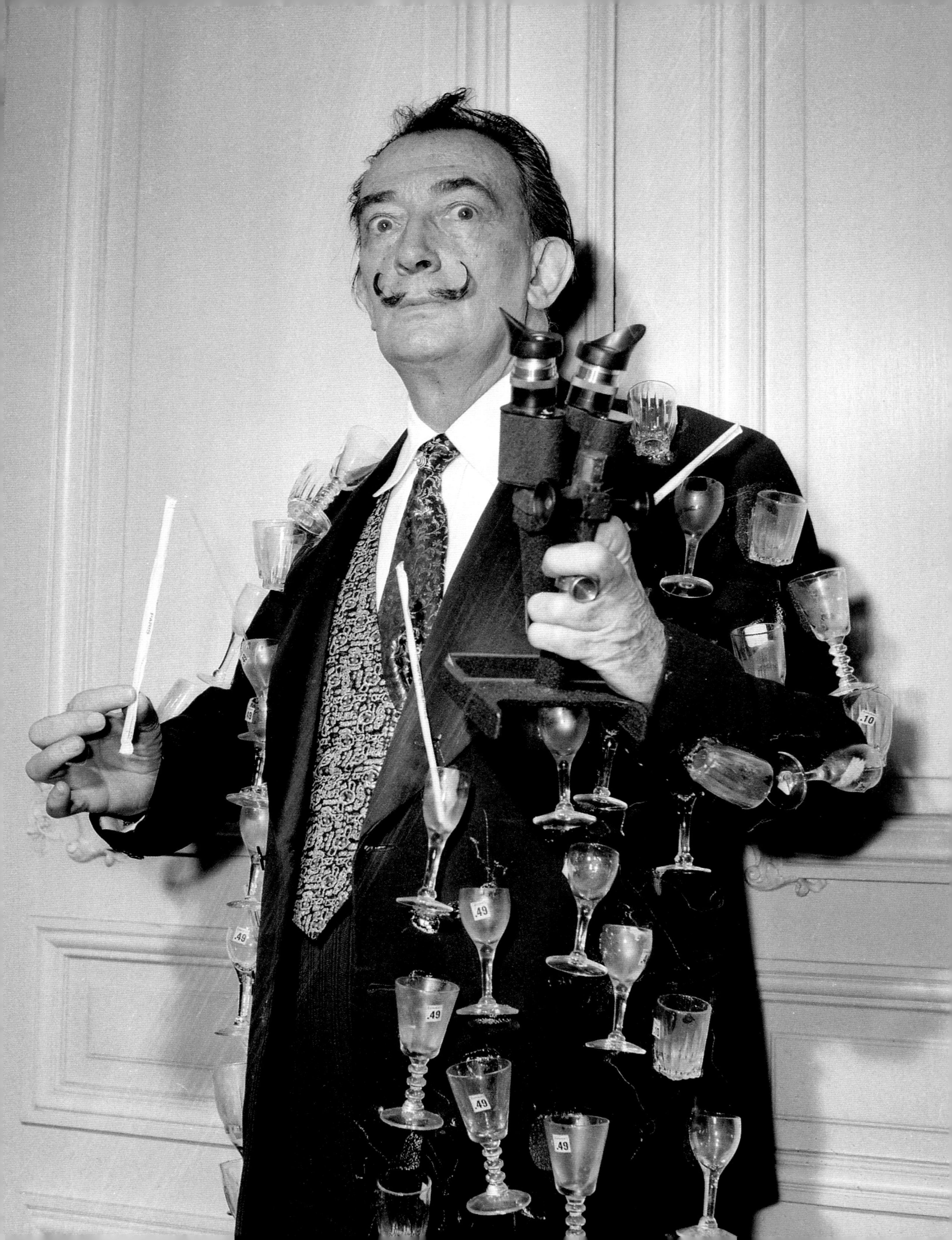
.10
.49
.49
.49
.49
.49

PEOPLE

LEGENDS AND CHARACTERS

What truly makes a party? The people! A good party is composed of a unique blend of people profiles, as artfully orchestrated as a good cocktail with unique proportions of bitter, sweet, sour, spicy, and salty flavors. In the best host's hands, a giddy, powerful concoction emerges, garnished with a delicious buzz of talk and laughter.

Etiquette maven Mrs. Emily Post had harsh words for those who don't have a "sense" for people. Those who do, she stated, are great hosts and hostesses. Those who don't, well, they are mediocre (shudder!) or failures. Making sure that your shindig doesn't wither on the social vine is like learning to make a proper Old Fashioned: you might need to pore through guidebooks for step-by-step instructions, learn by trial and error—or just drink deep from lessons of the greats.

The Hosts

Being a brilliant host is an art—think of it as knowing how to add a perfect splash of aromatic bitters to a cocktail. Born in Iowa, Elsa Maxwell became party planner to the stars, an inspired impresario who counted Jacqueline Kennedy and other high-society figures among her friends. The original hostess with the mostest, Elsa pioneered the theme party, staging "murders" at upper-crust estates with actors playing detectives and popularizing the scavenger hunt as party game. Her legendary "come as you are" parties meant guests arrived at odd hours, even with shaving cream smears and hair in curlers. Elsa's secret? A fresh idea and a sense of humor make a party; bores break it.

Opposite: *Surrealist artist Salvador Dalí wears* Aphrodisiac Dinner Jacket *(1964), whose drinks are sipped through straws, blurring the line between viewer and masterpiece.*

A host learns the fine line separating just right and too much. Truman Capote orchestrated the party of the century on November 28, 1966. Fresh off his best-seller *In Cold Blood*, Capote spent months perfecting his guest list for a black-and-white masked ball at New York's Plaza Hotel. His 540 guests included European aristocracy, American politicians, New York socialites, artists, actors, and his beloved "Swans" like Babe Paley and C.Z. Guest. Capote kept the food simple and the Taittinger flowing. At midnight, masks came off, and Capote was the toast of the town—until he dished out his friends' secrets in *Esquire*. Shunned, he learned the hard way: a dash of intrigue is delightful, but a splash of betrayal is never forgotten.

The Life of the Party

Every bash needs that person whose zest for life is infectious. Their stories and jokes sparkle like Prosecco, keeping the party alive. The French call them "bon vivants"—those who live well and share it, because true bon vivants aren't just in it for themselves; they ensure everyone has a blast. Think Liza Minnelli lighting up Studio 54, or Leonardo DiCaprio, the party magnet. Then there are the quieter types—the diplomats, spouses, and BFFs—who can charm and entertain without the spotlight.

Quiet types at parties also play a crucial role. Their standoffishness might mask a keen eye and ear for the most entertaining stories to tell their friends at the exclusive afterparty. Also, still waters run deep—that wallflower might be an Albert Einstein-level genius just recharging their brain for the next bon mot. Or another Rod Stewart, whose shyness in groups hides a rock-and-roll presence on stage and a philanthropist off it. Like balancing honey's sweetness with citrus's sour pucker, these opposites, in the right proportion, enhance everyone's experience.

The Divas

Divas are divine, darling! They don't open doors—doors are opened for *them*. As fiercely confident as Grace Jones, a diva makes an entrance, adding the spice to any mix. Avant-garde style icon, disco queen, provocateur—Jones is the queen and she knows it. But spicy doesn't always have to burn. Fiery and driven, music icon Diana Ross knows her worth and demands it. When she jumped atop Studio 54's DJ booth on its closing night to sing her hits, she wasn't hogging the spotlight but sharing her love for friends and memories. A diva's joie de vivre gets everyone moving, mingling spice with sweet and sour, and kicking the party into high gear.

Like a more complex hit of spice, the center of every entourage holds a unique kind of diva, one who thrives in the company of extraordinary friends. In the 1970s, Halston's tight-knit bunch, dubbed "The Halstonettes" by André Leon Talley, followed him everywhere. Celebrities like Liza Minnelli, Marisa Berenson, and Loulou de la Falaise, along with Halston's favorite models like Pat Cleveland and Alva Chinn, were his constant companions. Not all entourages are large, but they're always close-knit, like Stella McCartney's circle of BFFs, including Cara Delevingne, Gwyneth Paltrow, and Liv Tyler. The most famous entourage, Andy Warhol's Factory, spun in perpetual orbit around the artist. In the midst of socialites, drag queens, musicians, and intellectuals, Warhol used to say, "One's company, two's a crowd, and three's a party."

The Movers and Shakers

A pinch of saltiness brings out the sweetness and balances the bitter. Steely and opinionated, yet open to new ideas and people, movers and shakers can read the room. They can be as charming and well-connected as a young JFK, cheerfully holding forth before any number of people on a wide spectrum of political, intergenerational, and cultural topics. Others, like fashion powerhouse Anna Wintour with her famous bob and dark sunglasses, command attention. She doesn't suffer fools but knows quality when she sees it. Movers and shakers find ways to add their bracing, salty intellect to the mix—and elevate the common to the uncommon.

The embodiment of soft power, the bartender masters connection and persuasion, whether crafting top-shelf cocktails or mocktails. The best bartenders juggle the crowd, making each feel like royalty. They're as versatile as one-time sailor and Forty-Niner Jerry Thomas, whose 1862 classic, *How to Mix Drinks: The Bon Vivant's Companion*, is still in print today. They're pioneers like Ada Coleman, who trained Harry Craddock at the Savoy Hotel, or Dale DeGroff, who ignited the cocktail renaissance at New York City's Rainbow Room. They're not just mixologists; they're sages who know just the right kind of salty, spicy, sour, sweet, or bitter story to tell.

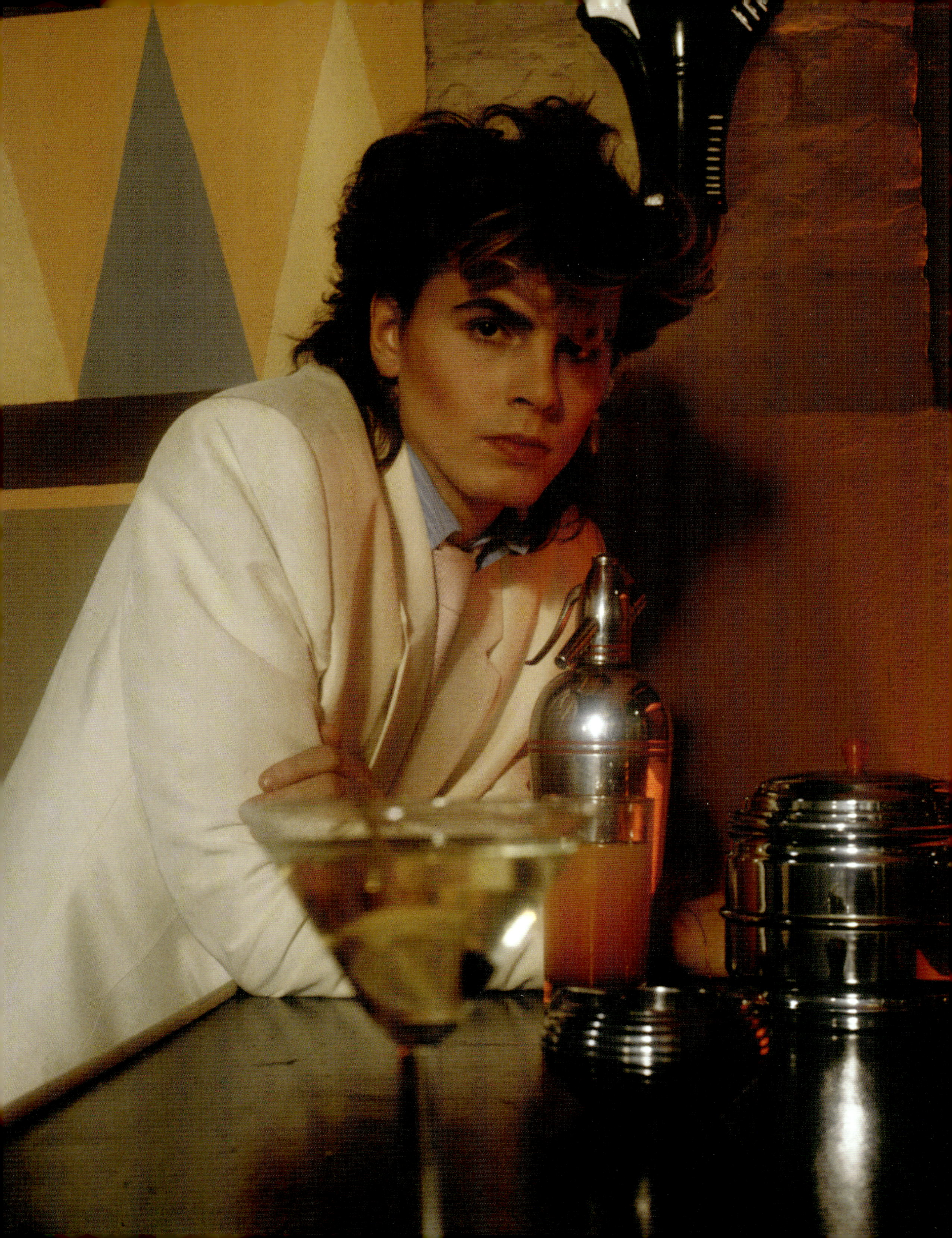

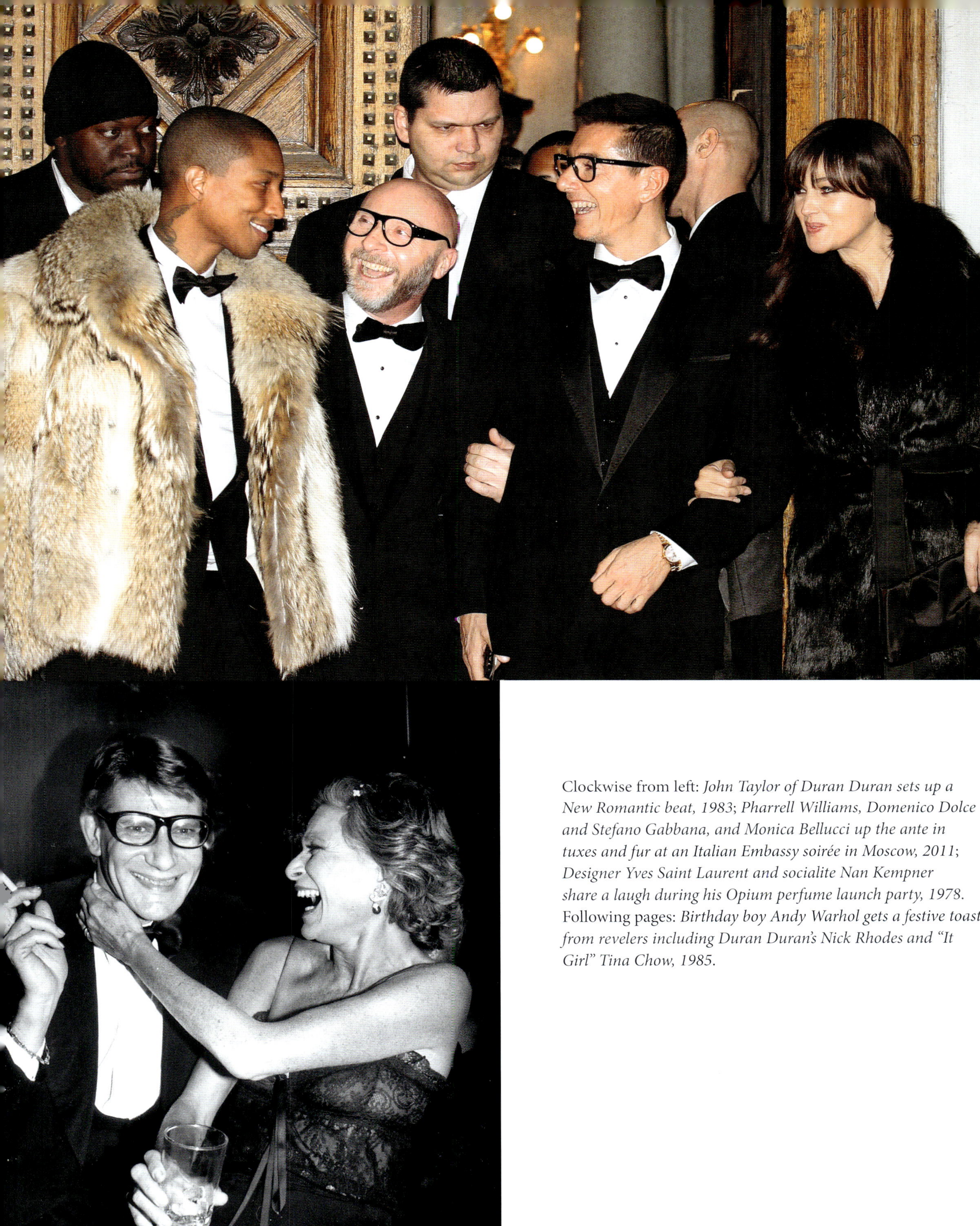

Clockwise from left: *John Taylor of Duran Duran sets up a New Romantic beat, 1983; Pharrell Williams, Domenico Dolce and Stefano Gabbana, and Monica Bellucci up the ante in tuxes and fur at an Italian Embassy soirée in Moscow, 2011; Designer Yves Saint Laurent and socialite Nan Kempner share a laugh during his Opium perfume launch party, 1978.* Following pages: *Birthday boy Andy Warhol gets a festive toast from revelers including Duran Duran's Nick Rhodes and "It Girl" Tina Chow, 1985.*

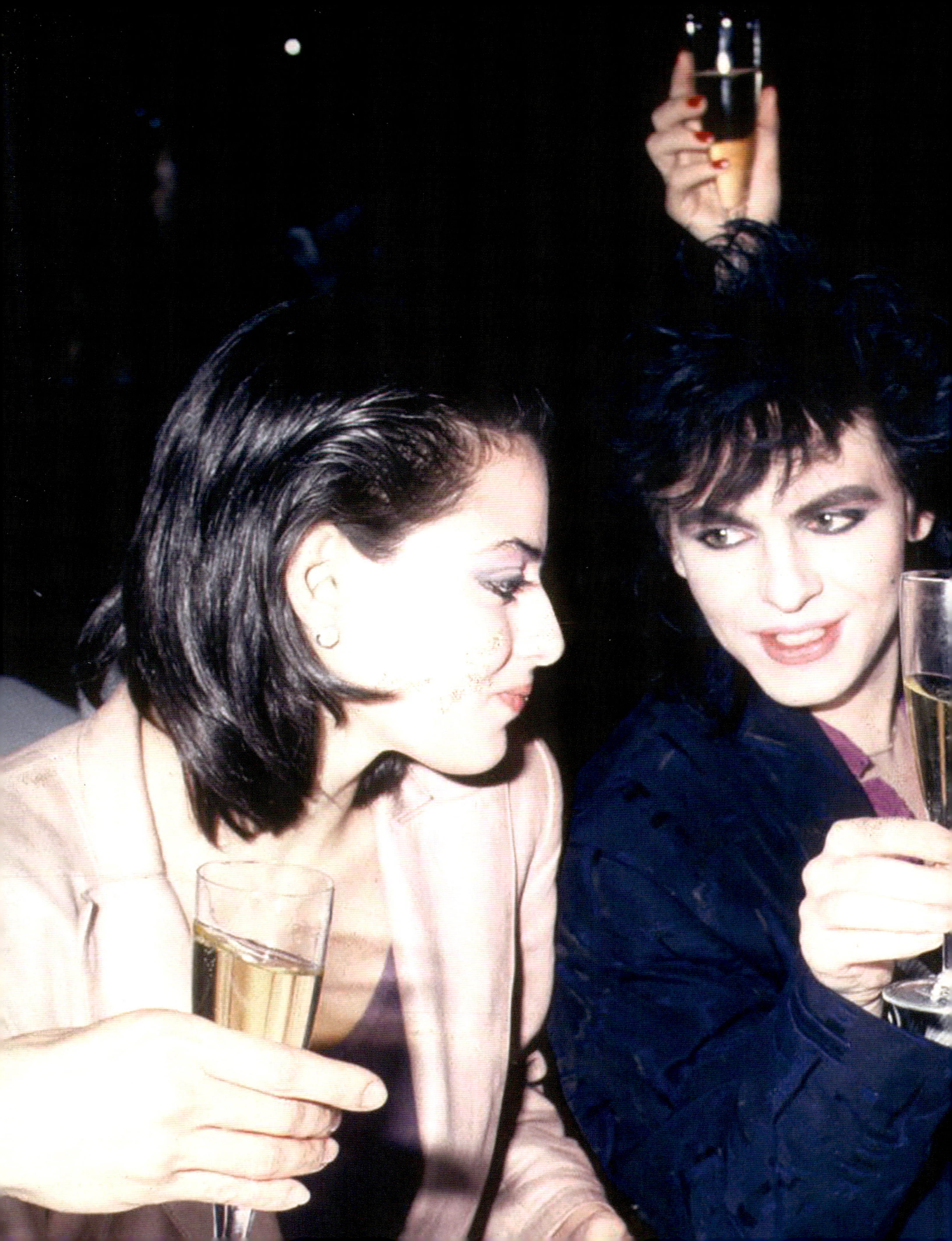

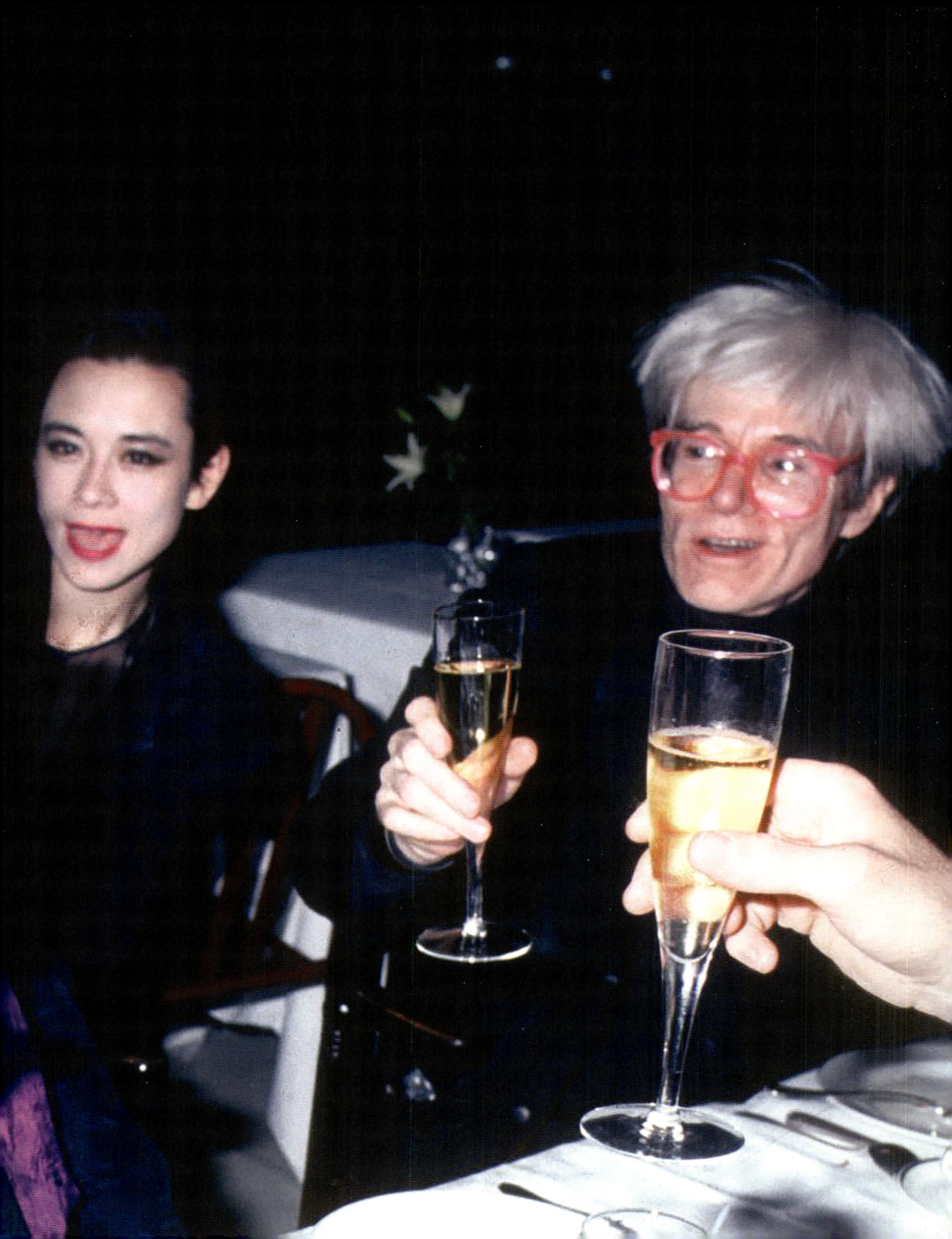

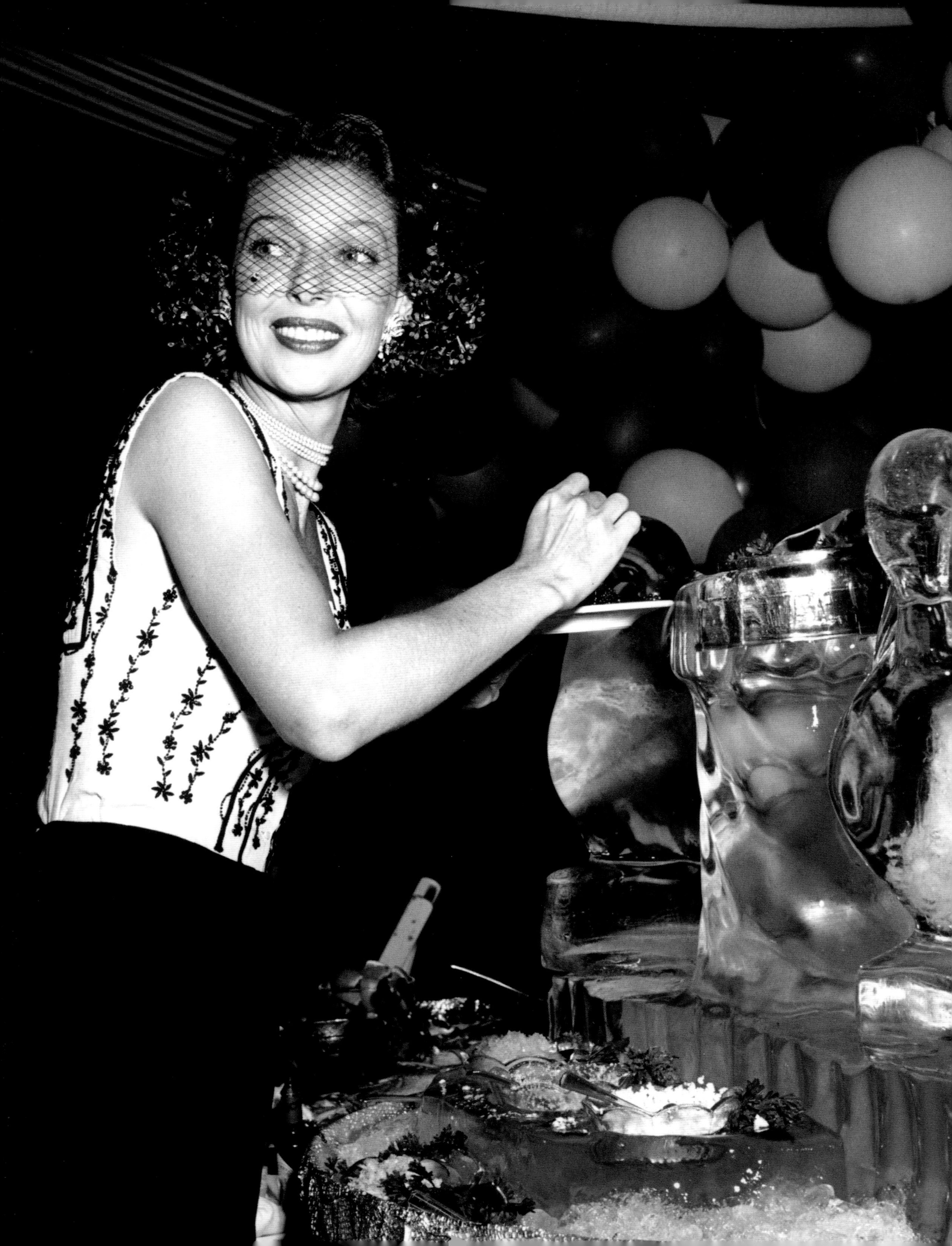

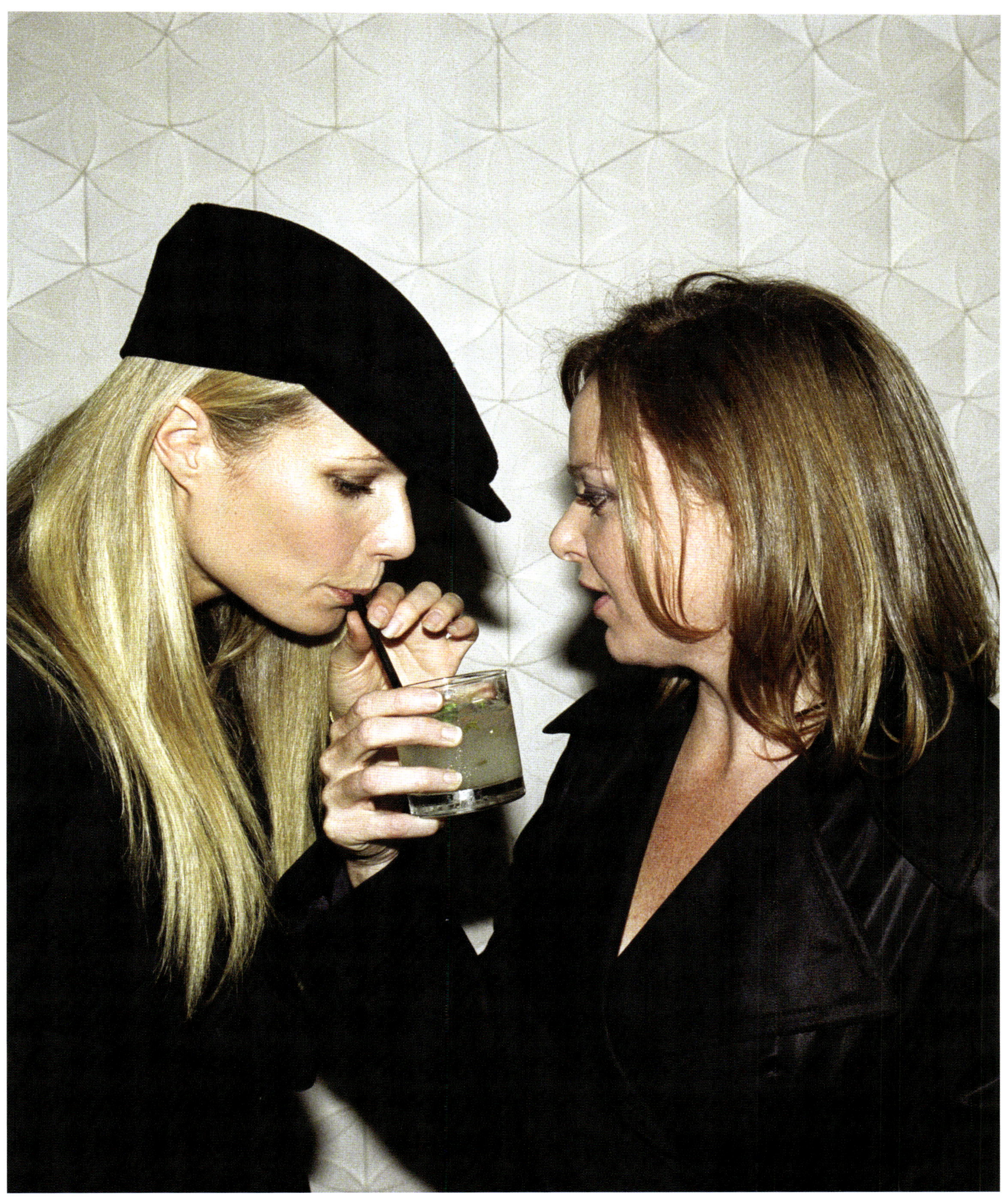

Opposite: *Actress Loretta Young's smile shines brighter than the ice sculptures at a Hollywood Ice Follies cocktail party, 1952.* This page: *Fashion designer Stella McCartney shares a Mojito with BFF Gwyneth Paltrow, at the opening of McCartney's new store, 2002.*

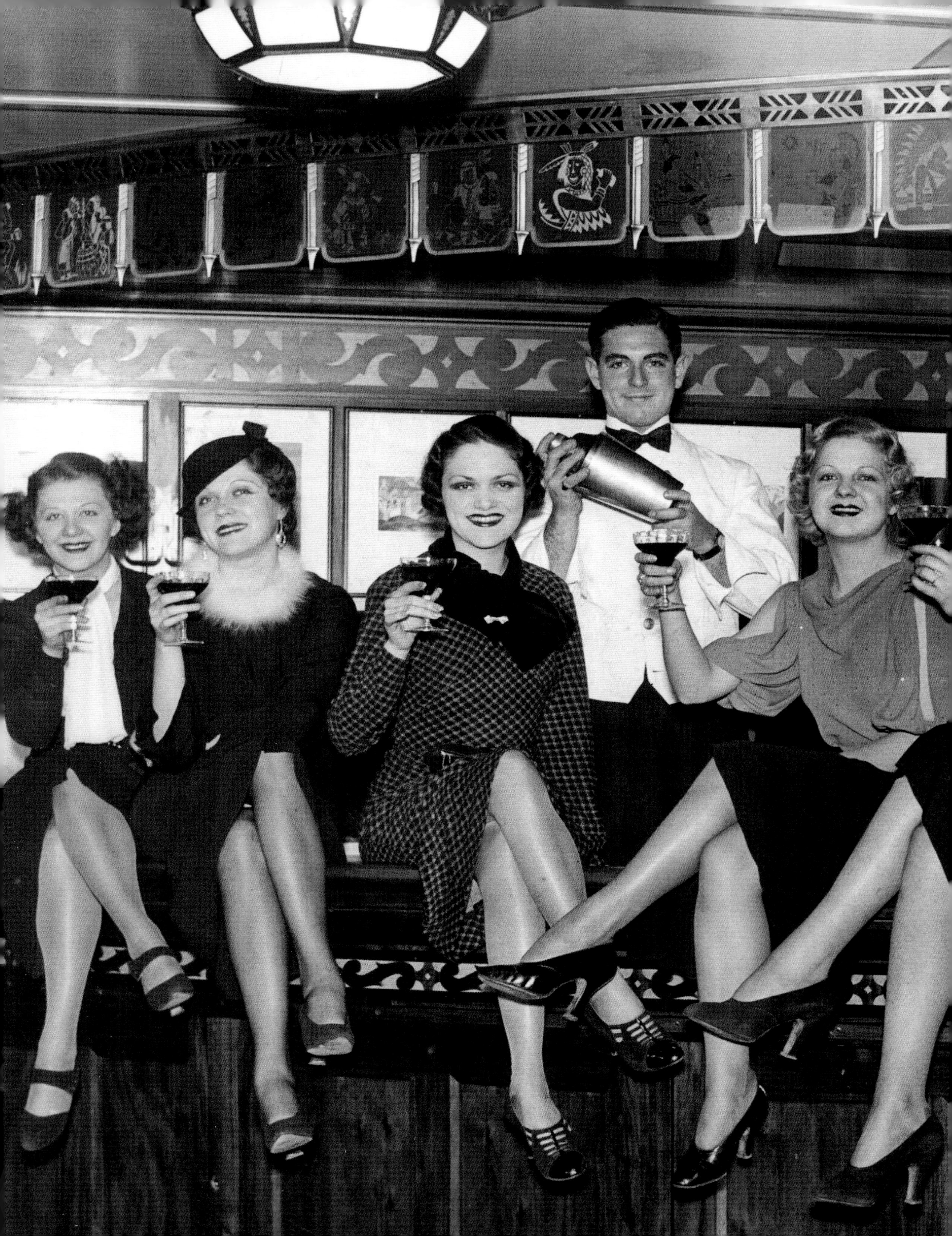

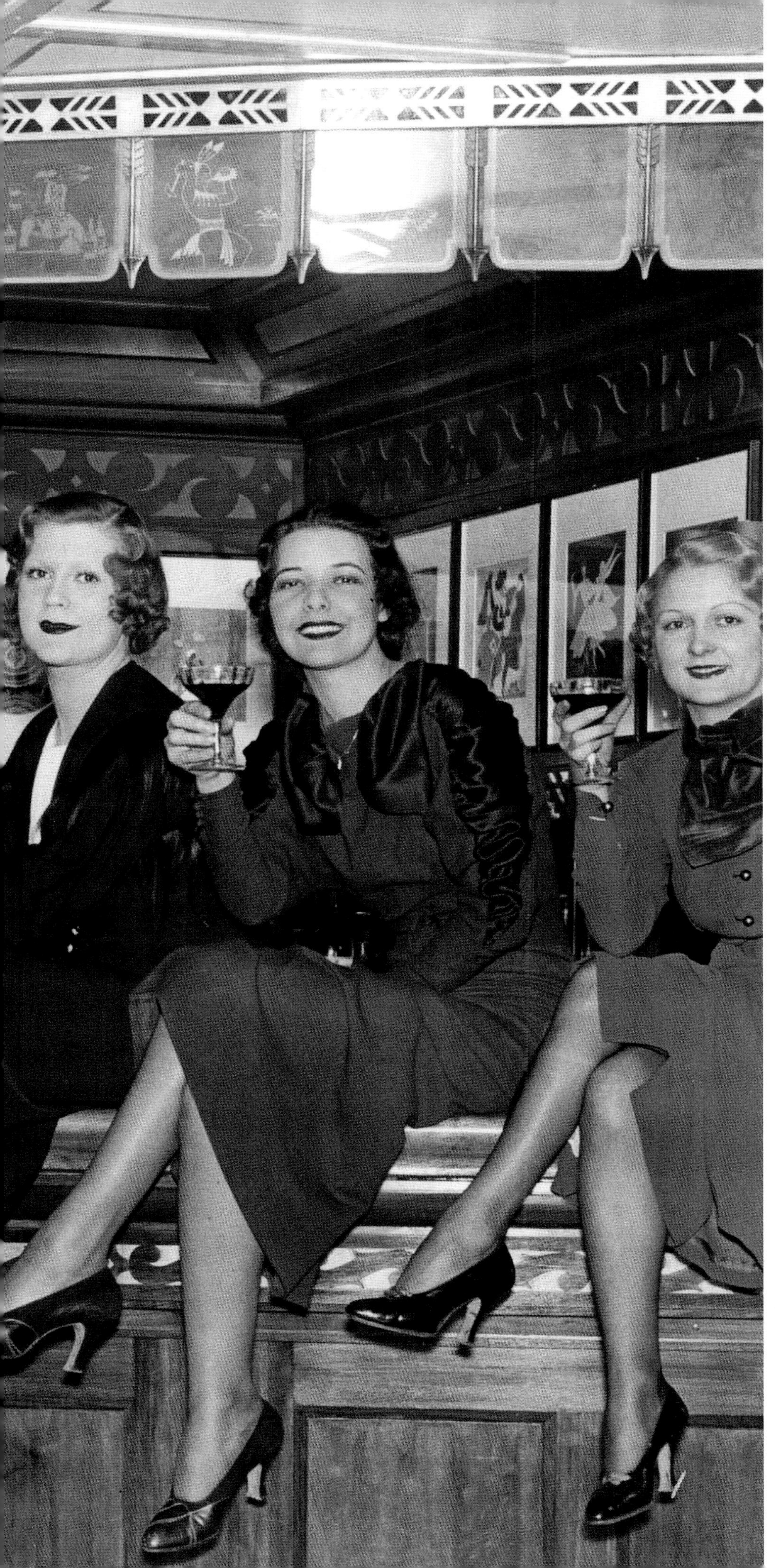

Opposite: *Onboard the luxury liner SS* Manhattan, *a group of women toast "goodbye and good riddance" to Prohibition, December 5, 1933.*

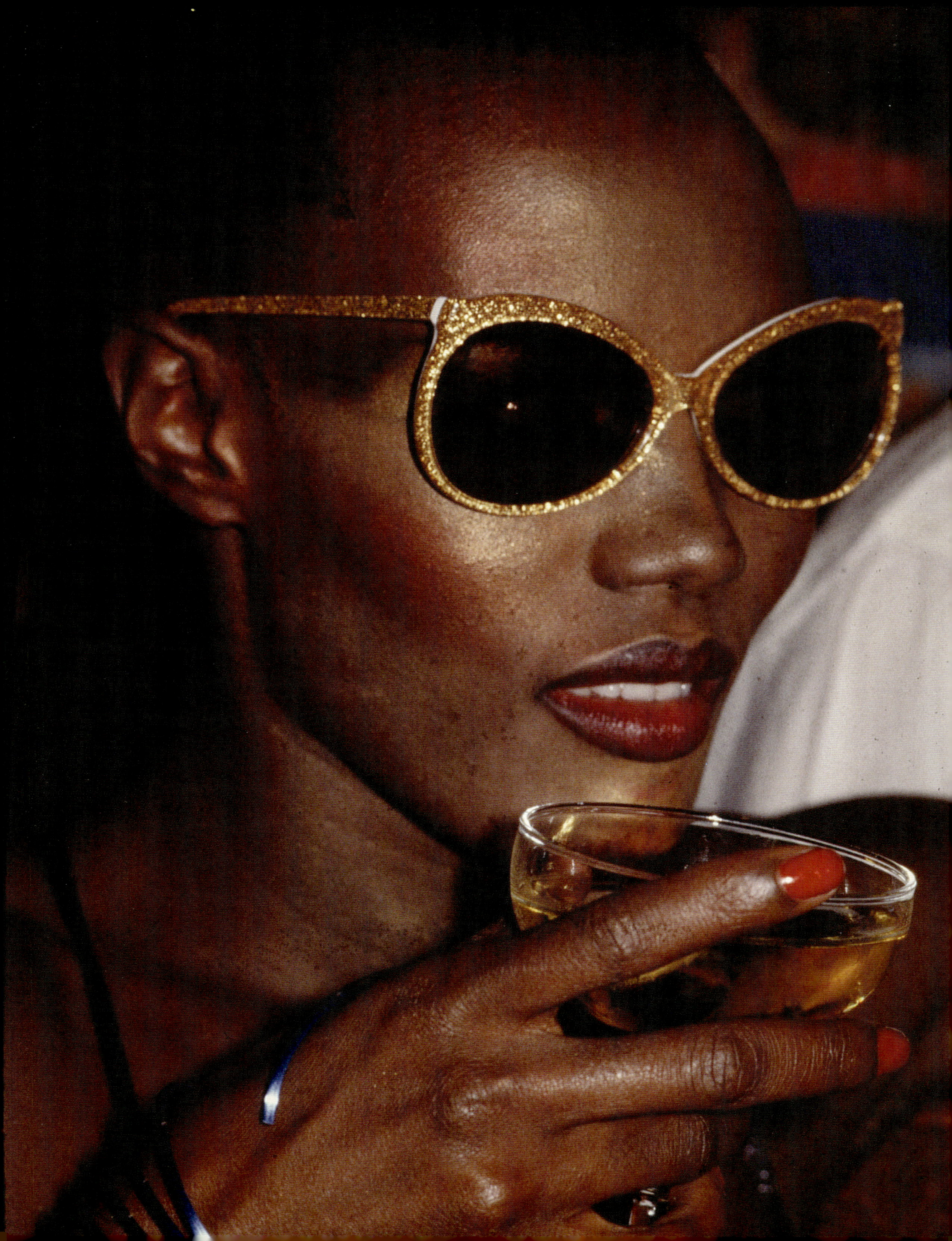

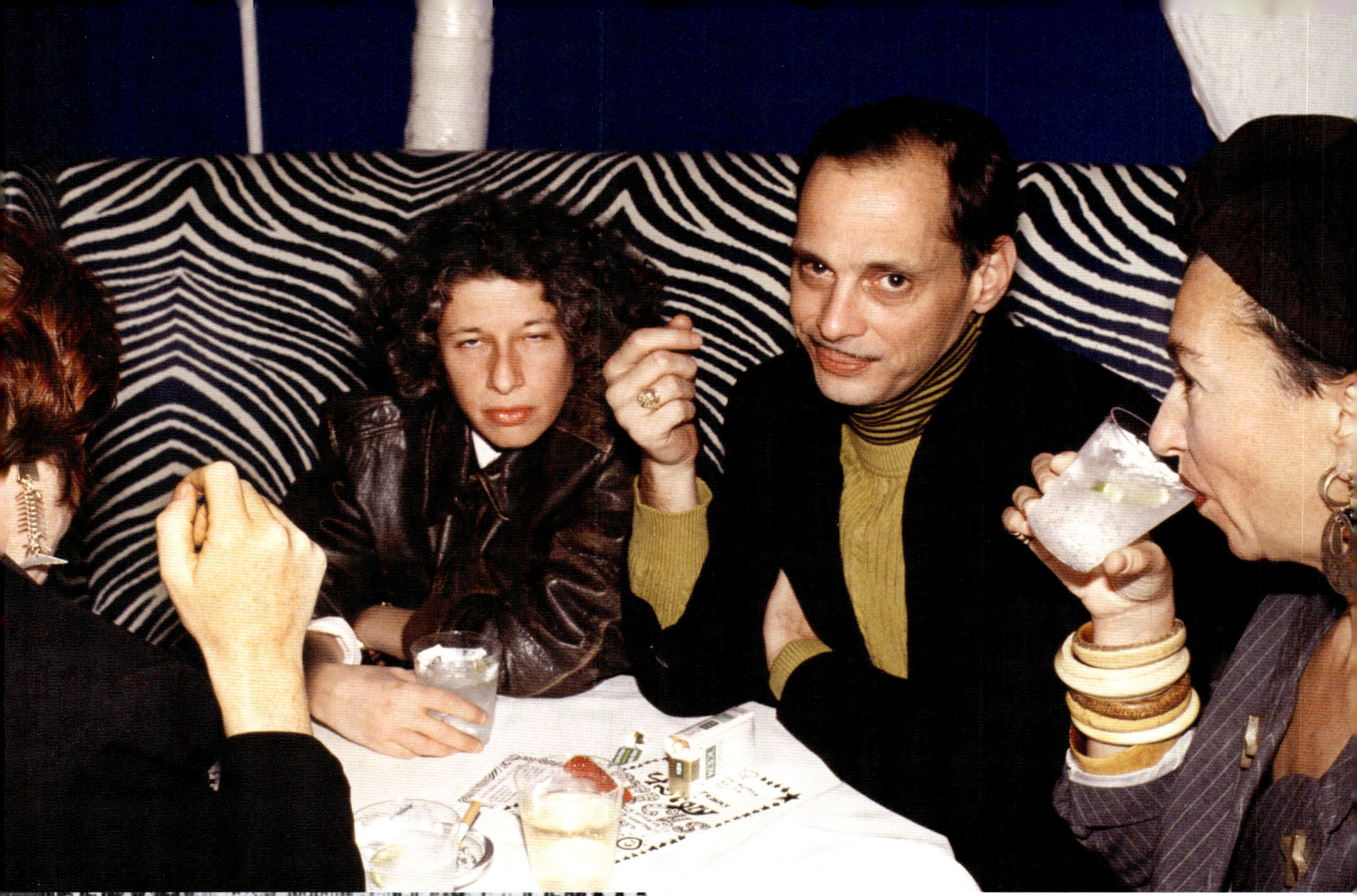

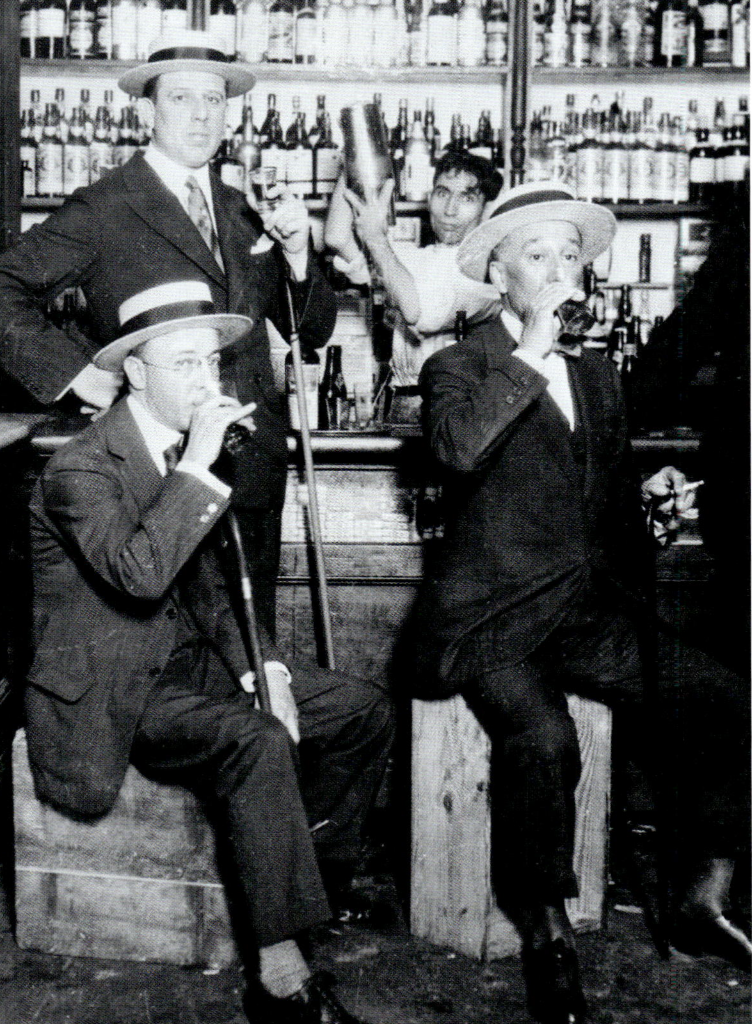

Clockwise from left: *Singer and fashion muse Grace Jones celebrates her birthday, drawing A-listers—and go-go boys—onto Le Farfalle's dance floor, 1978; A late night blurs into morning at New York's El Morocco club, with Fran Leibowitz, John Waters, and Henny Garfunkel, 1988; Tipplers in straw boater hats live it up at a Prohibition-era "underground" gin joint.*

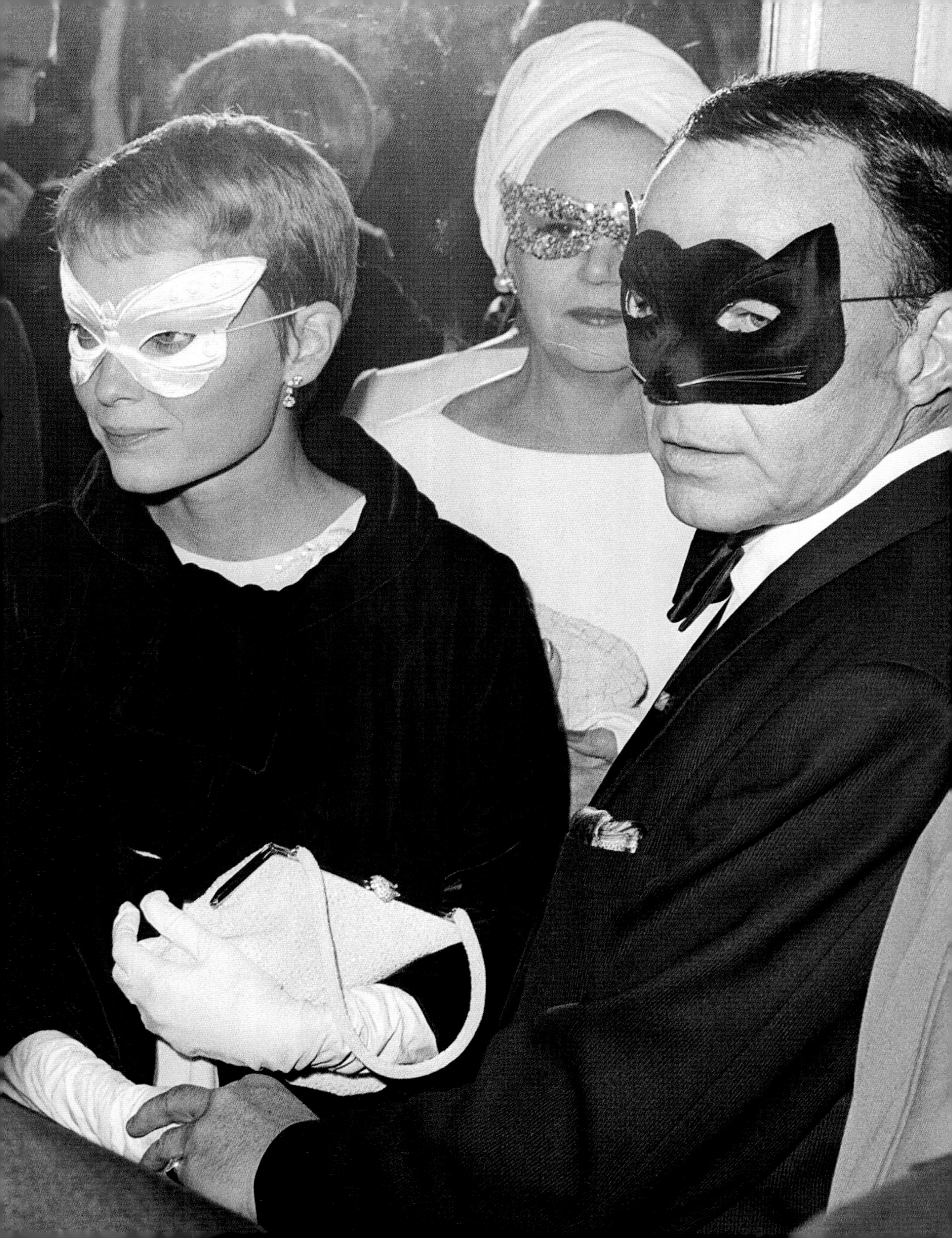

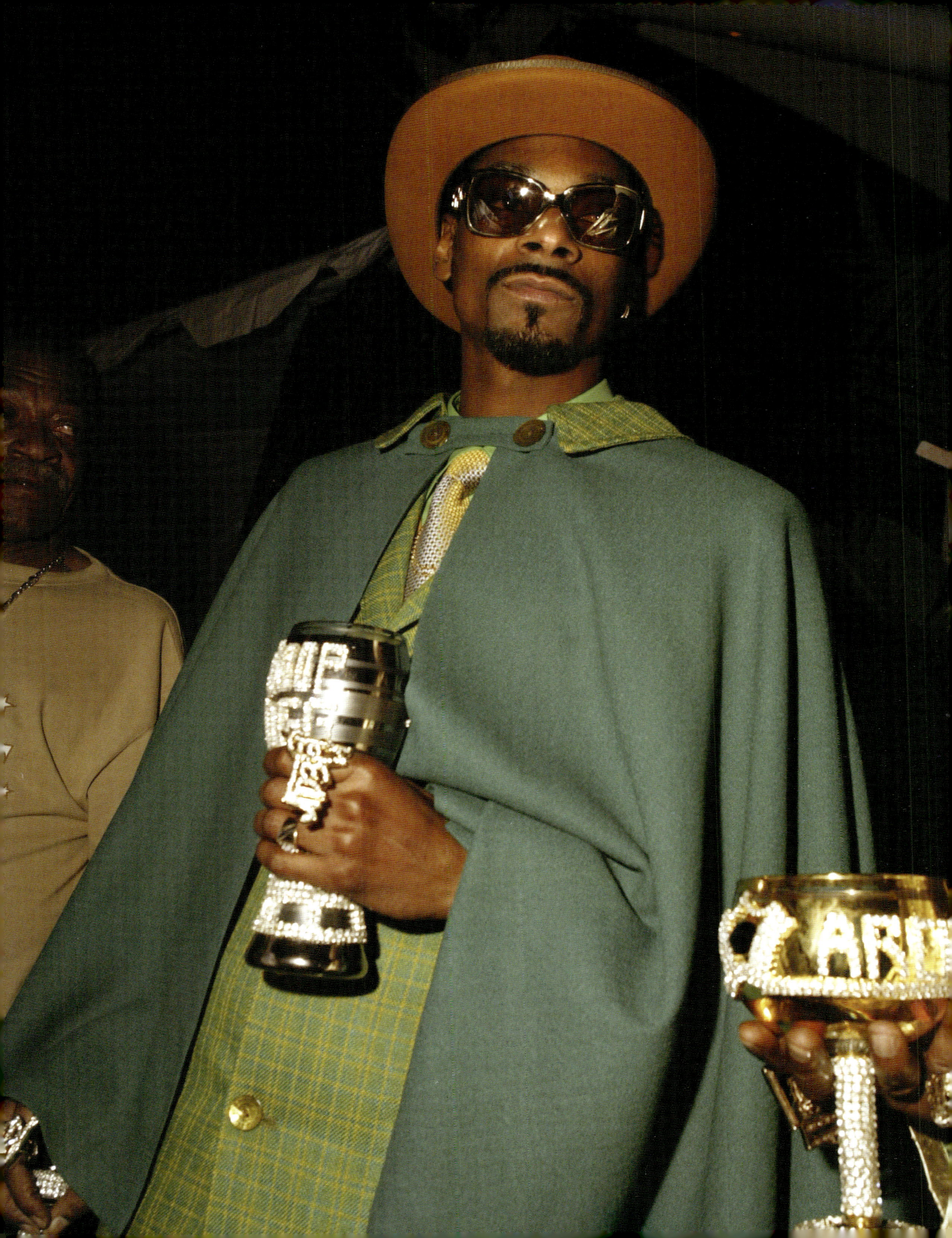

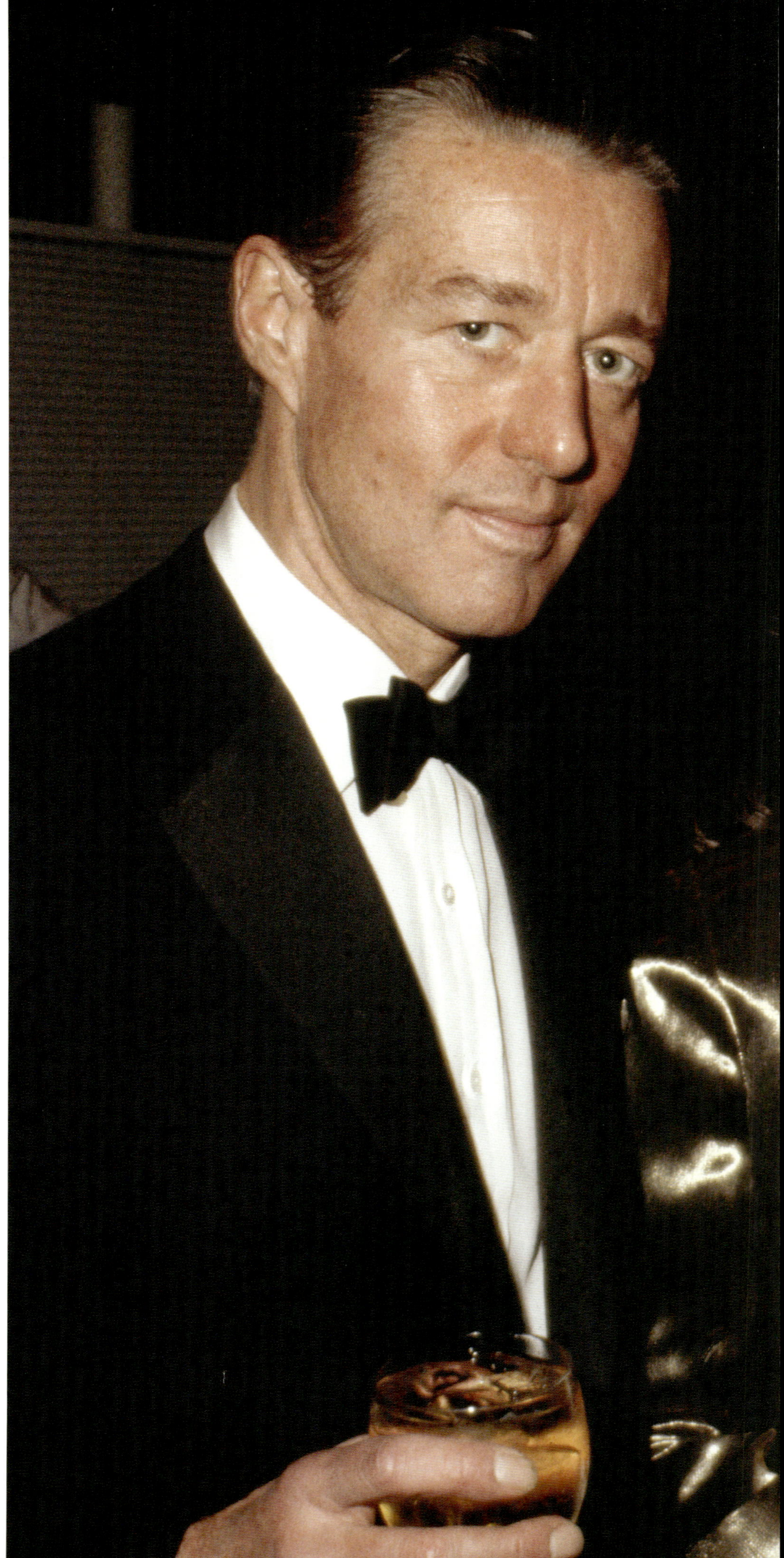

Previous pages, left: *Masked but unmistakable, Frank Sinatra and his wife, actress Mia Farrow, enter Truman Capote's Black and White Ball, 1966*; right: *Grammy nominee Snoop Dogg presides over the good vibes at a post-Grammy bash at White Lotus, Los Angeles, 2004.* Opposite: *Birds of a stylish feather flock together—designer Halston, Candice Bergen, and Liza Minnelli at a cocktail party, 1980.*

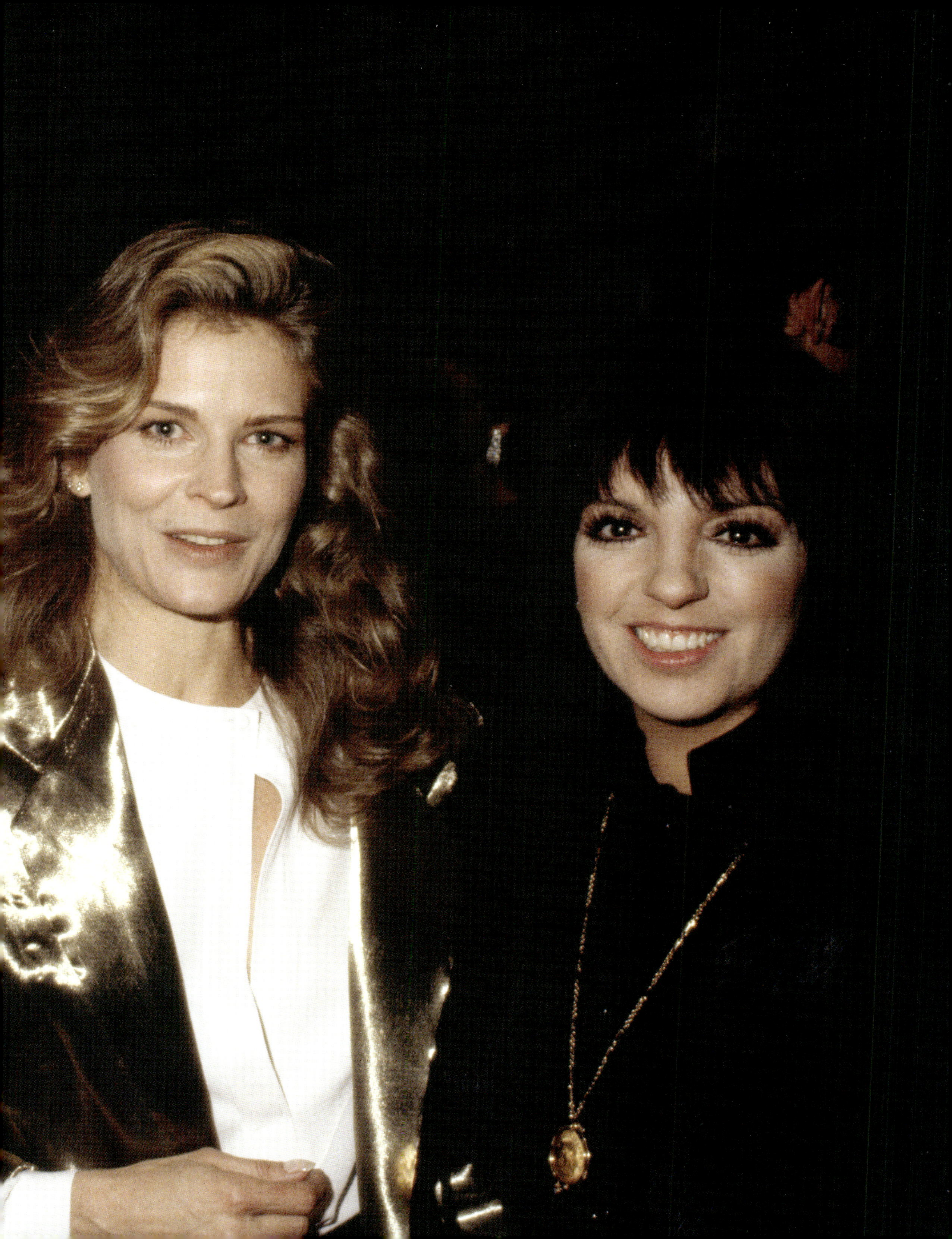

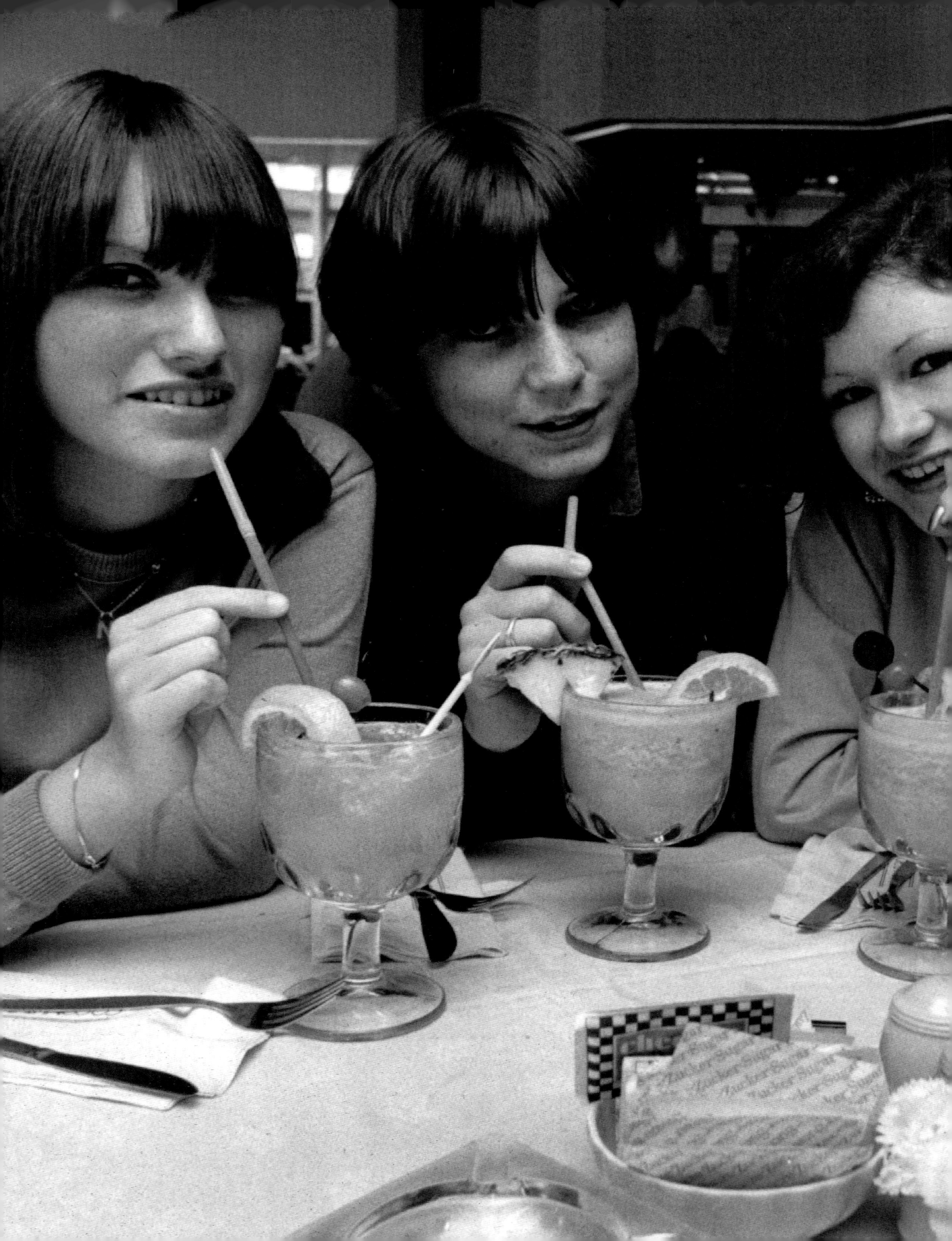

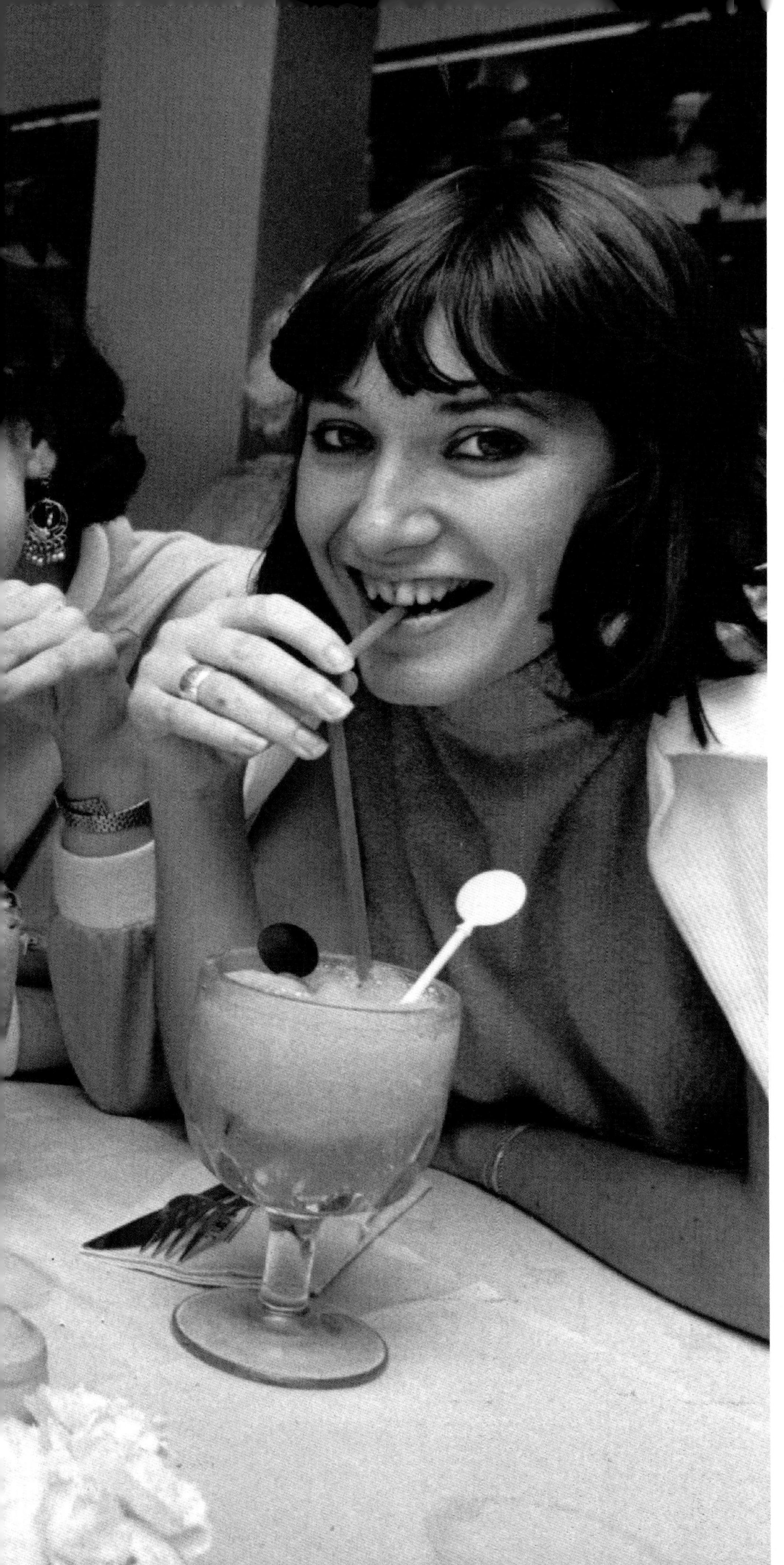

Opposite: *A giggling quartet of British gal pals sip fruity cocktails, 1980.*

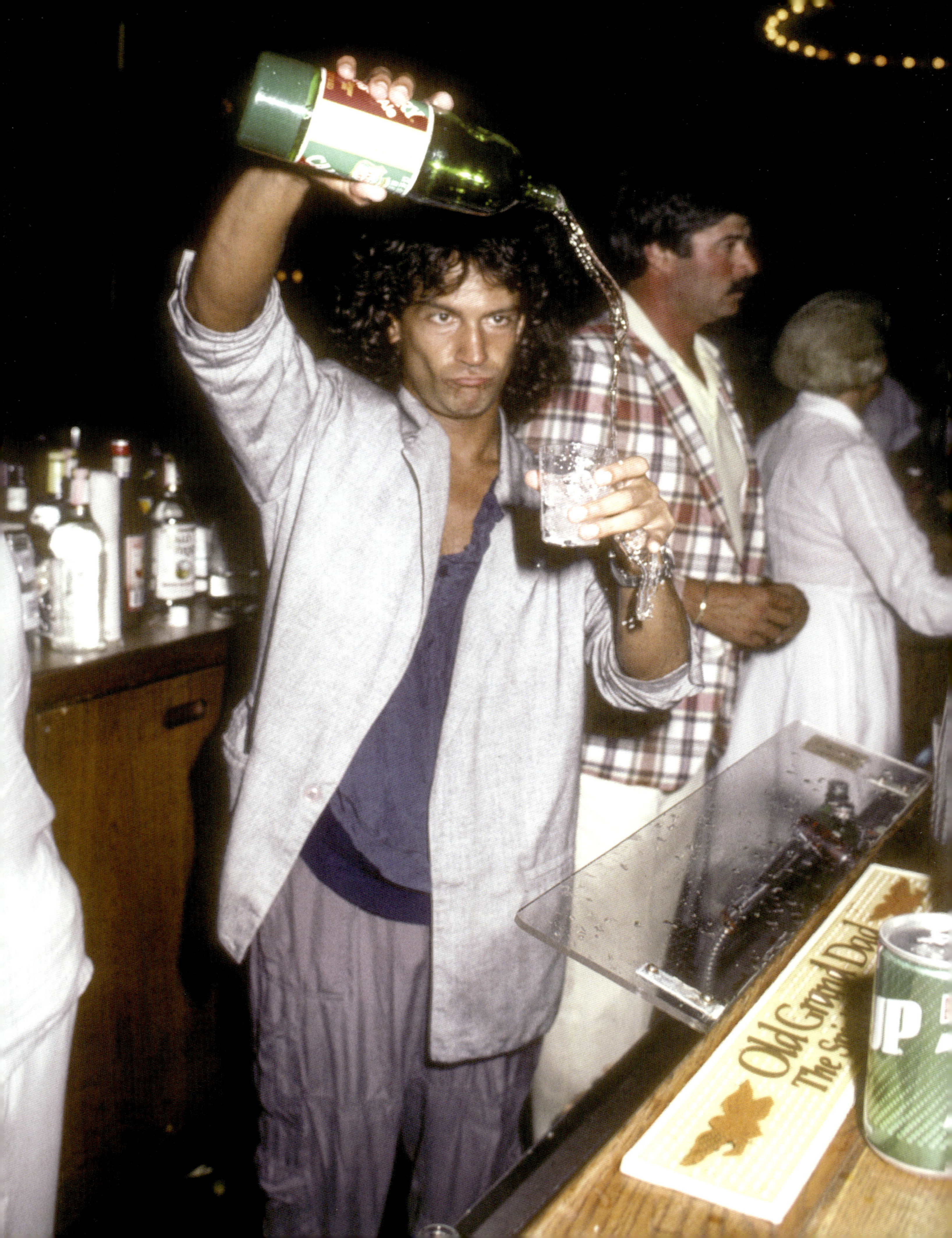
Old Grand Dad

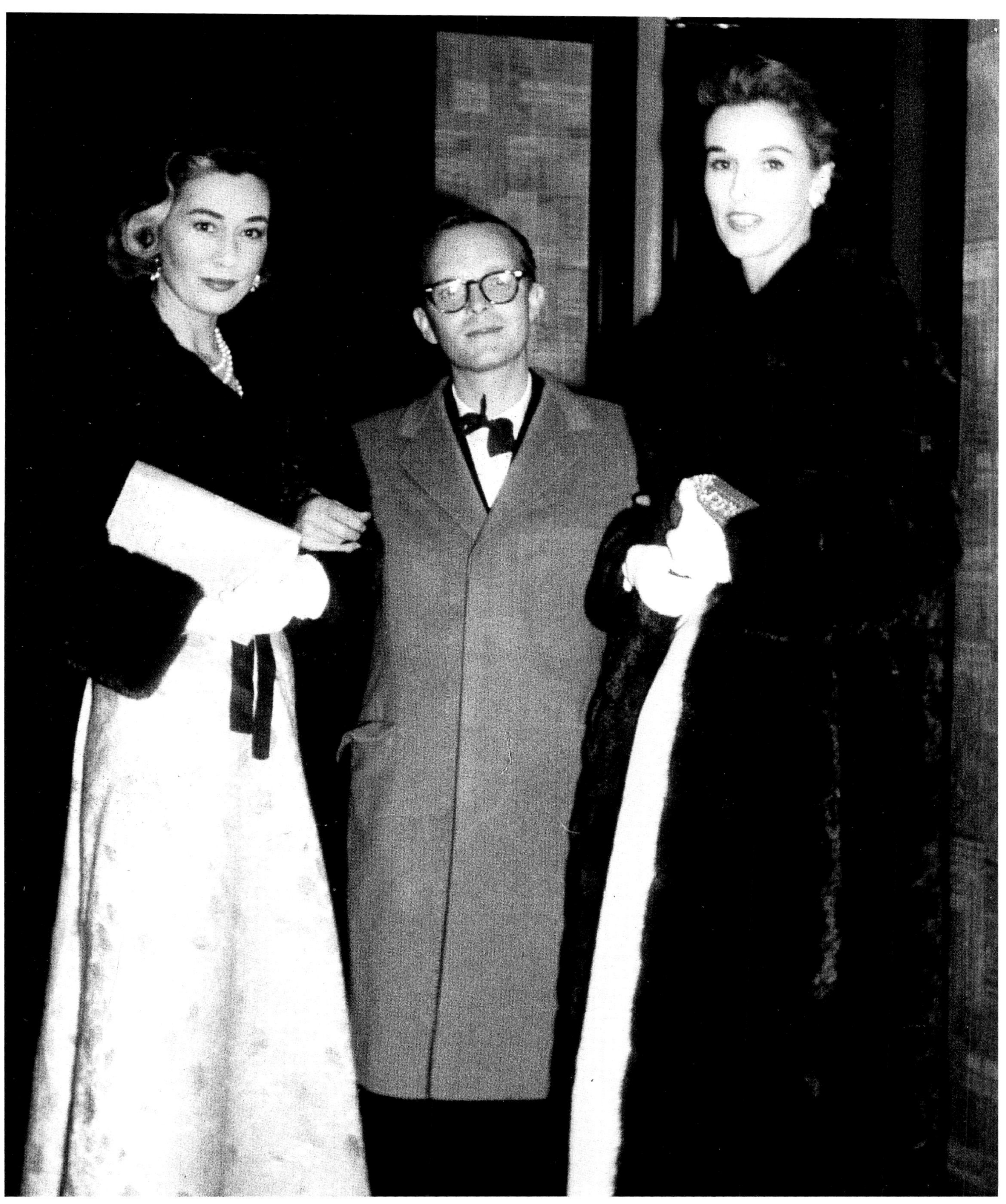

Opposite: *Musician Billy Squier mixes charity with a splash of rock 'n' roll at a Montauk fundraiser, 1985.* This page: *Writer Truman Capote sails in on the arms of two "Swans," Jeanne Murray Vanderbilt* (left) *and Barbara "Babe" Paley* (right), *circa 1957.*

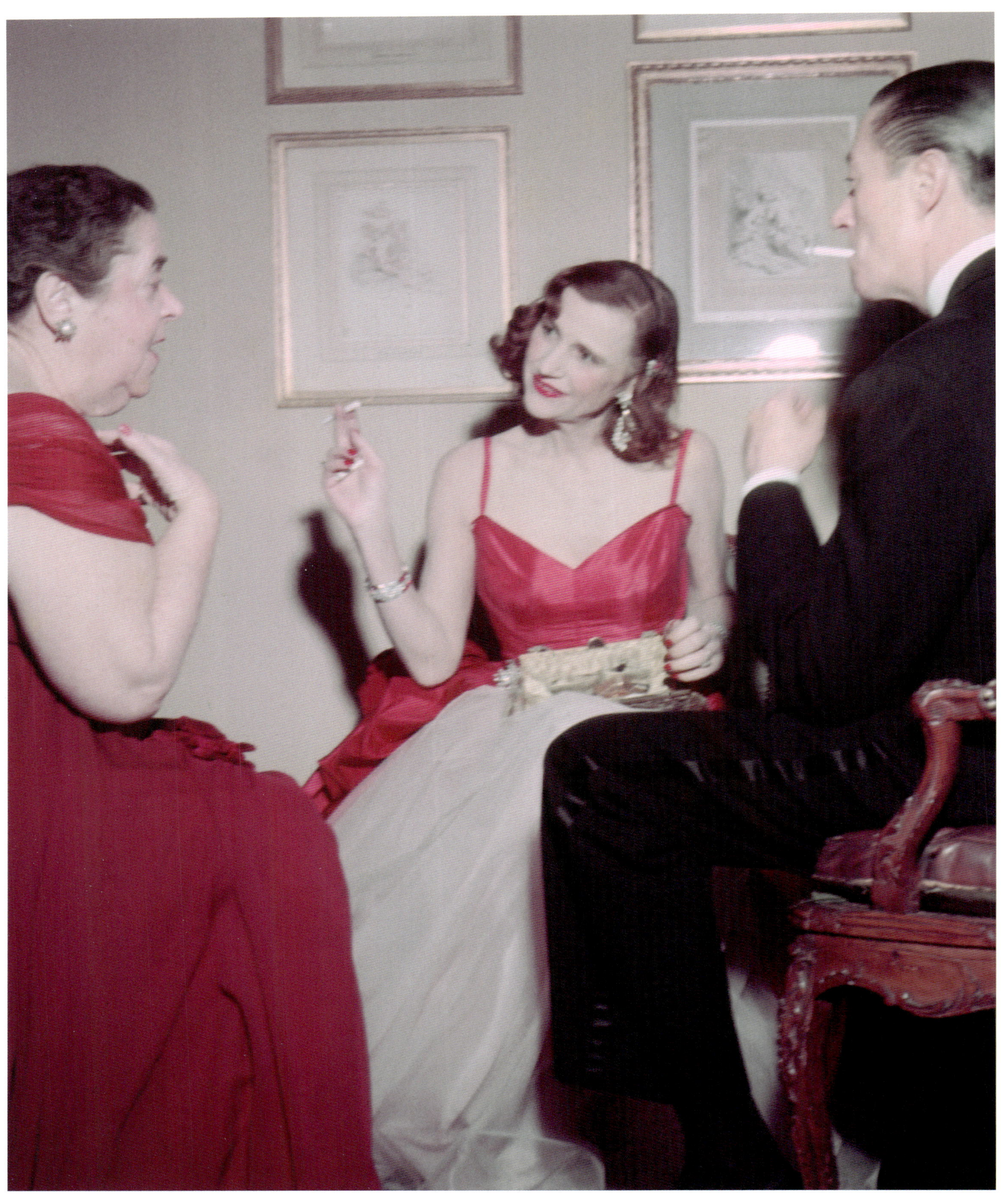

This page: *"Let's misbehave!" Society hostess Elsa Maxwell* (left) *and songwriter Cole Porter* (right) *gossip with a friend on New Year's Eve, 1952.* Opposite: *A giddy Ingrid Bergman reacts to Lucille Ball during a star-studded soirée in Bergman's honor, 1959.*

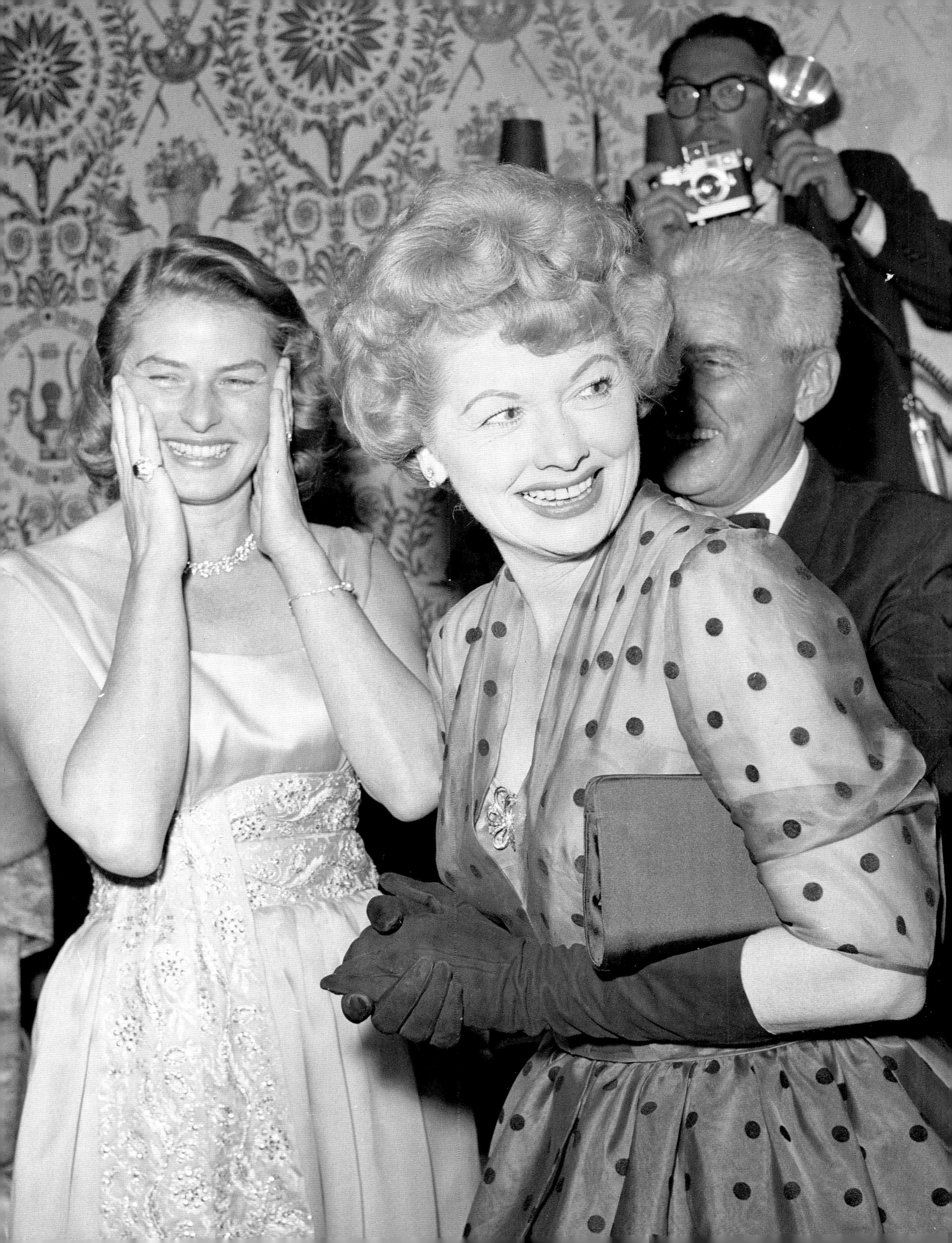

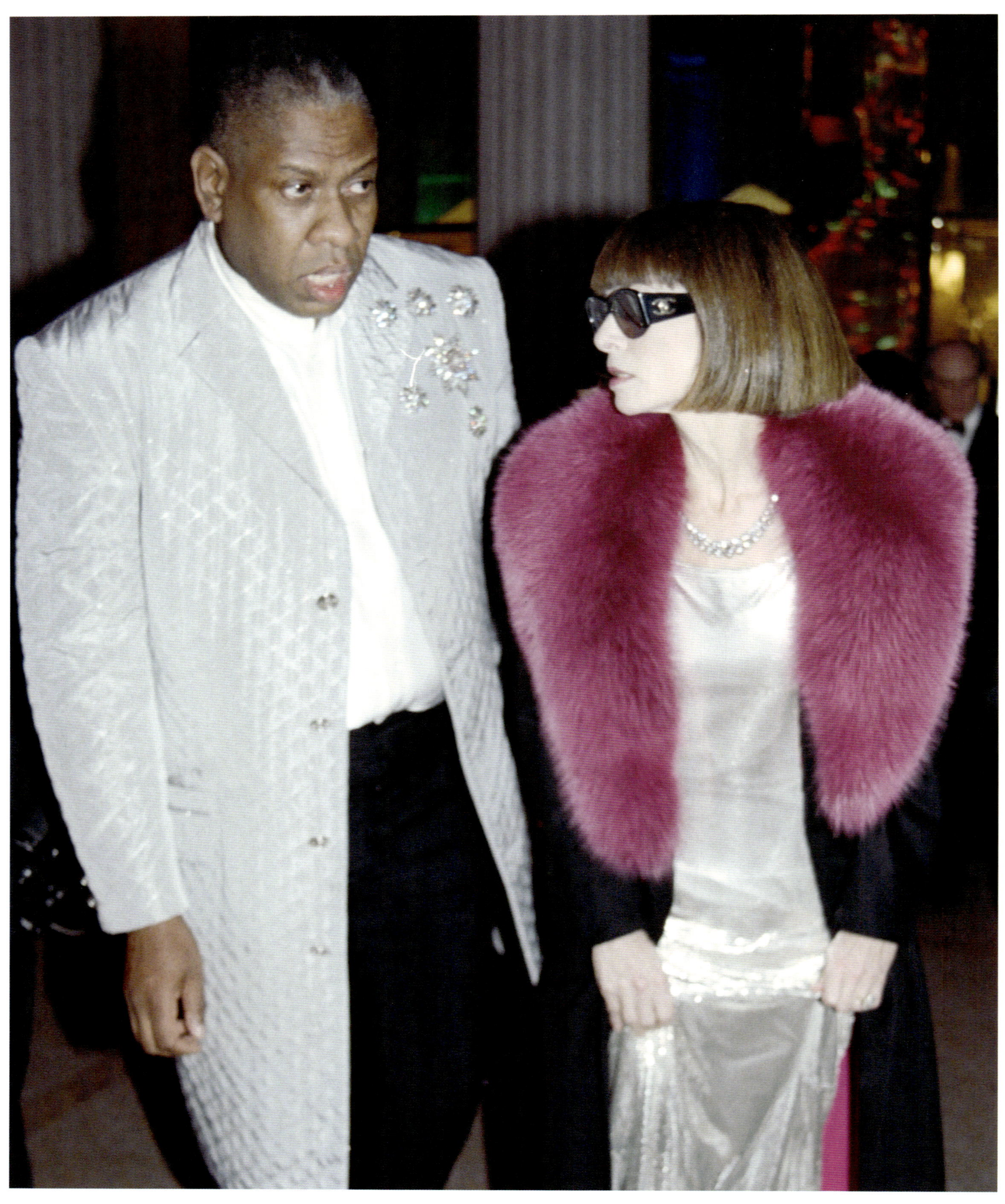

This page: *Anna Wintour and André Leon Talley stand supreme at the Costume Institute's Met Gala, 1997.* Opposite: *At designer Karl Lagerfeld's late-1970s bash, guests and staff don eighteenth-century court costumes.*

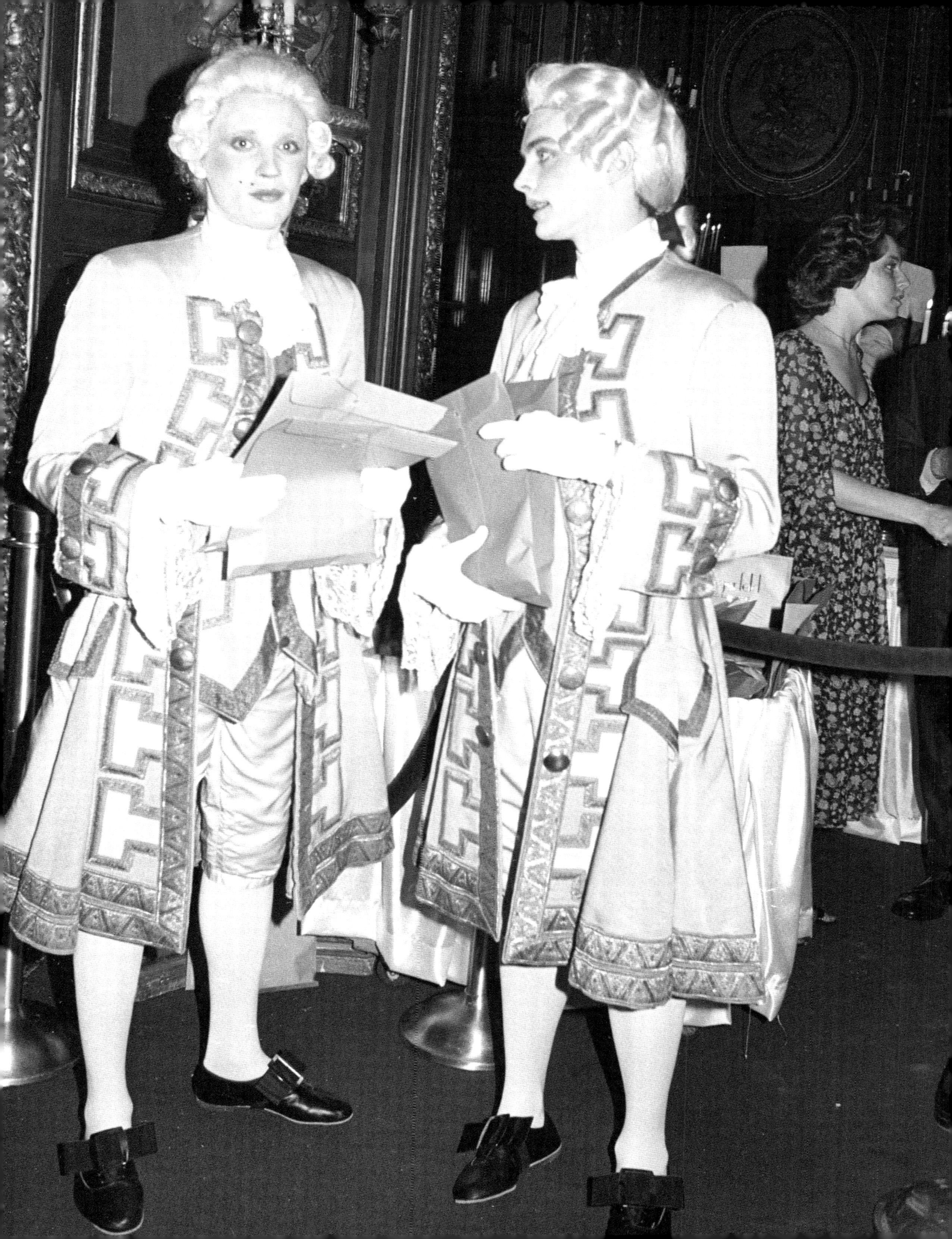

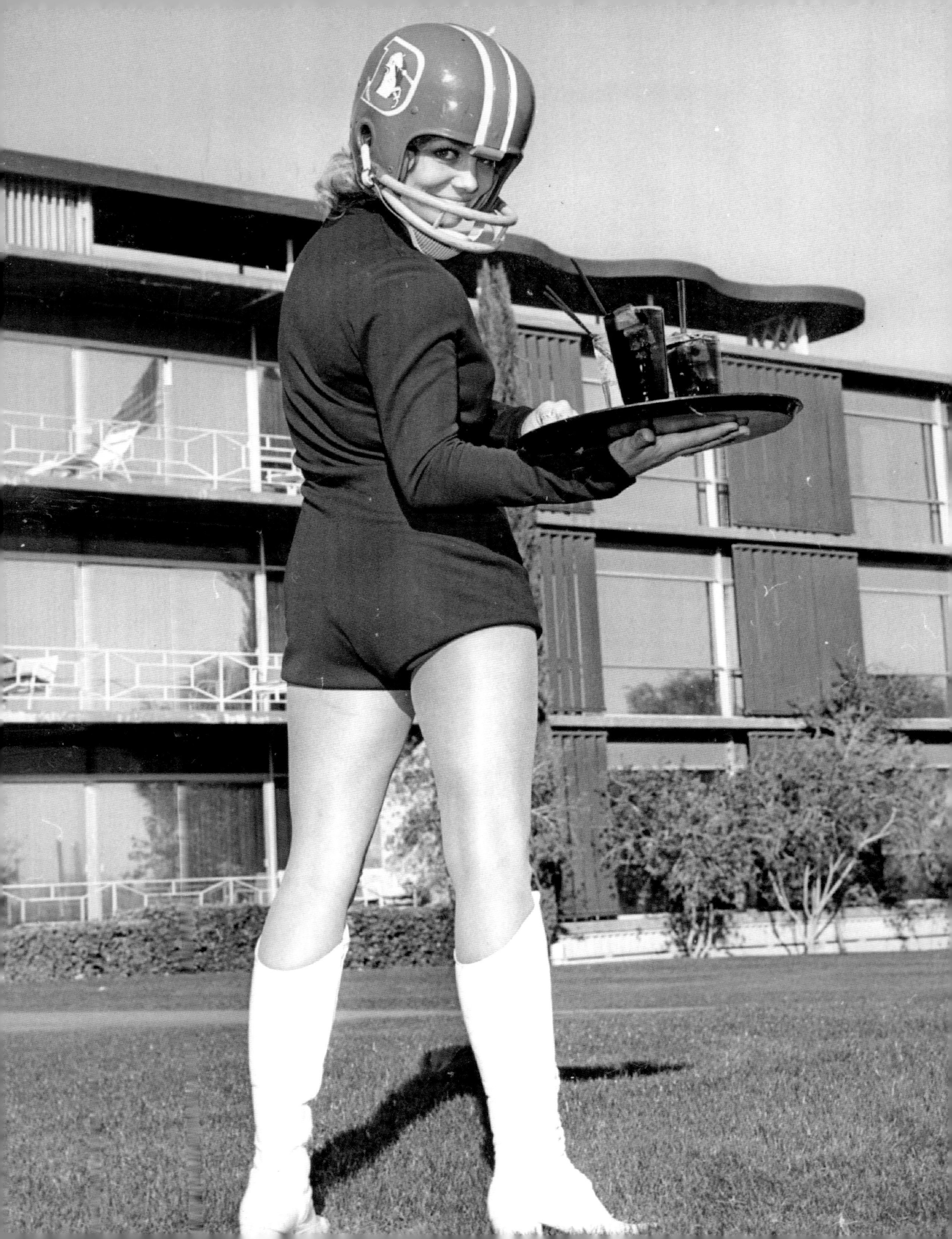

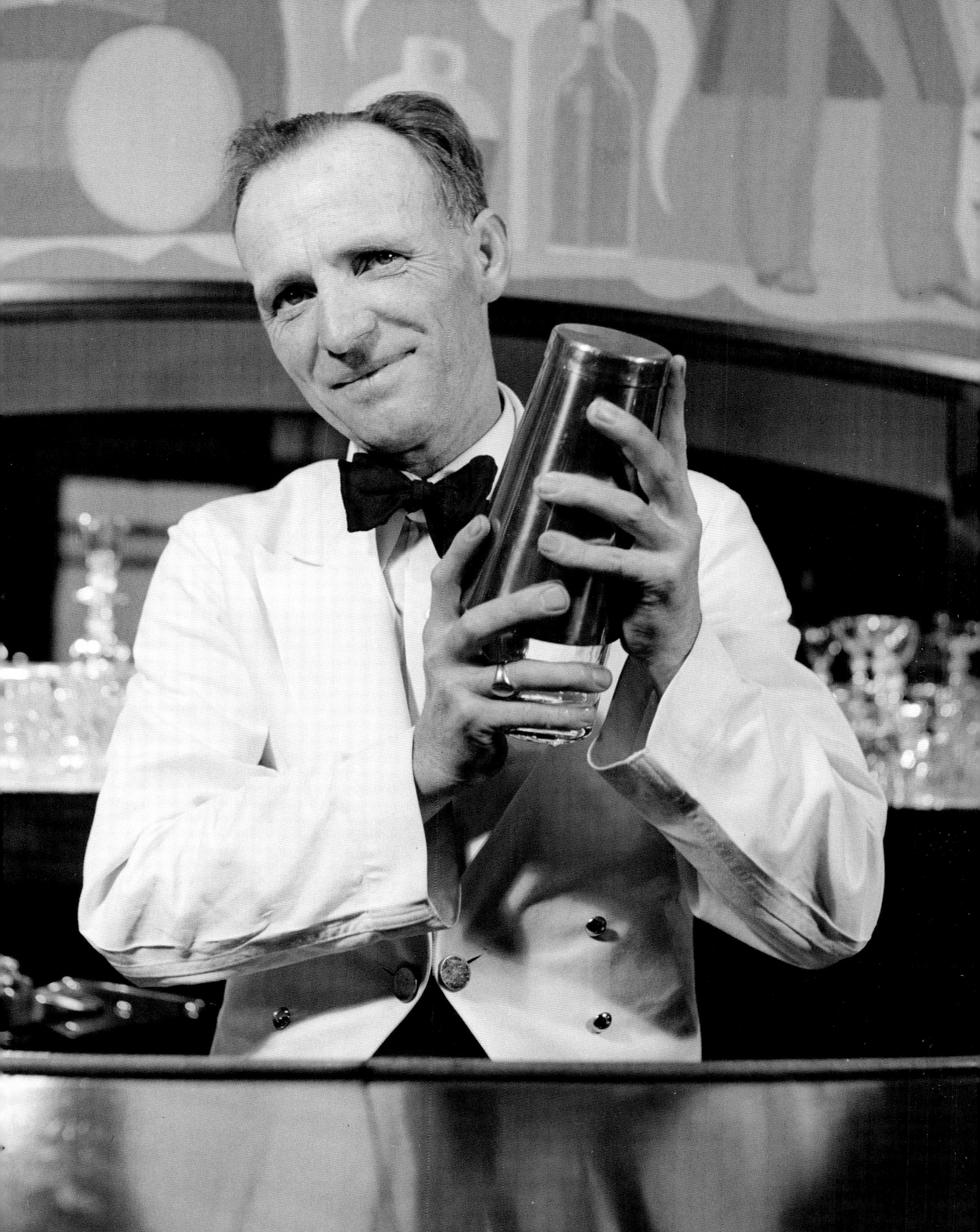

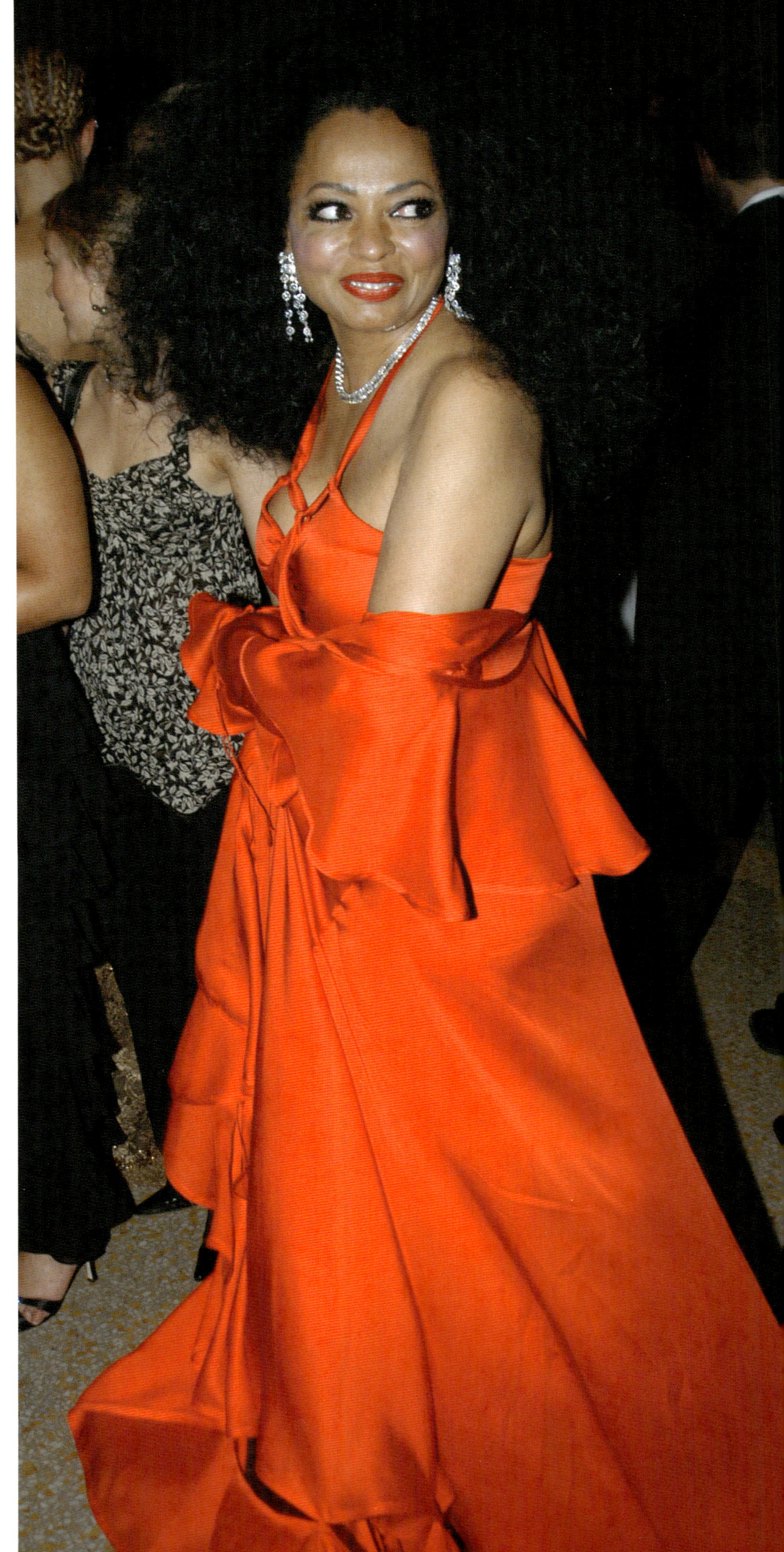

Previous pages, left: *A Denver Broncos fan serves touchdown-worthy drinks at the Desert Inn, Las Vegas, 1971*; right: *A cordial bartender readies a spirit-boosting cocktail at New York's Sky Lounge, 1942*. These pages, clockwise from left: *Diana Ross sweeps into the Costume Institute's Met Gala, 2003*; *Dashing undergrad and future US president John F. Kennedy discusses political theory at a White House garden party, circa 1939*; *1980s cocktail party style makes a statement as bold as the decade itself.*

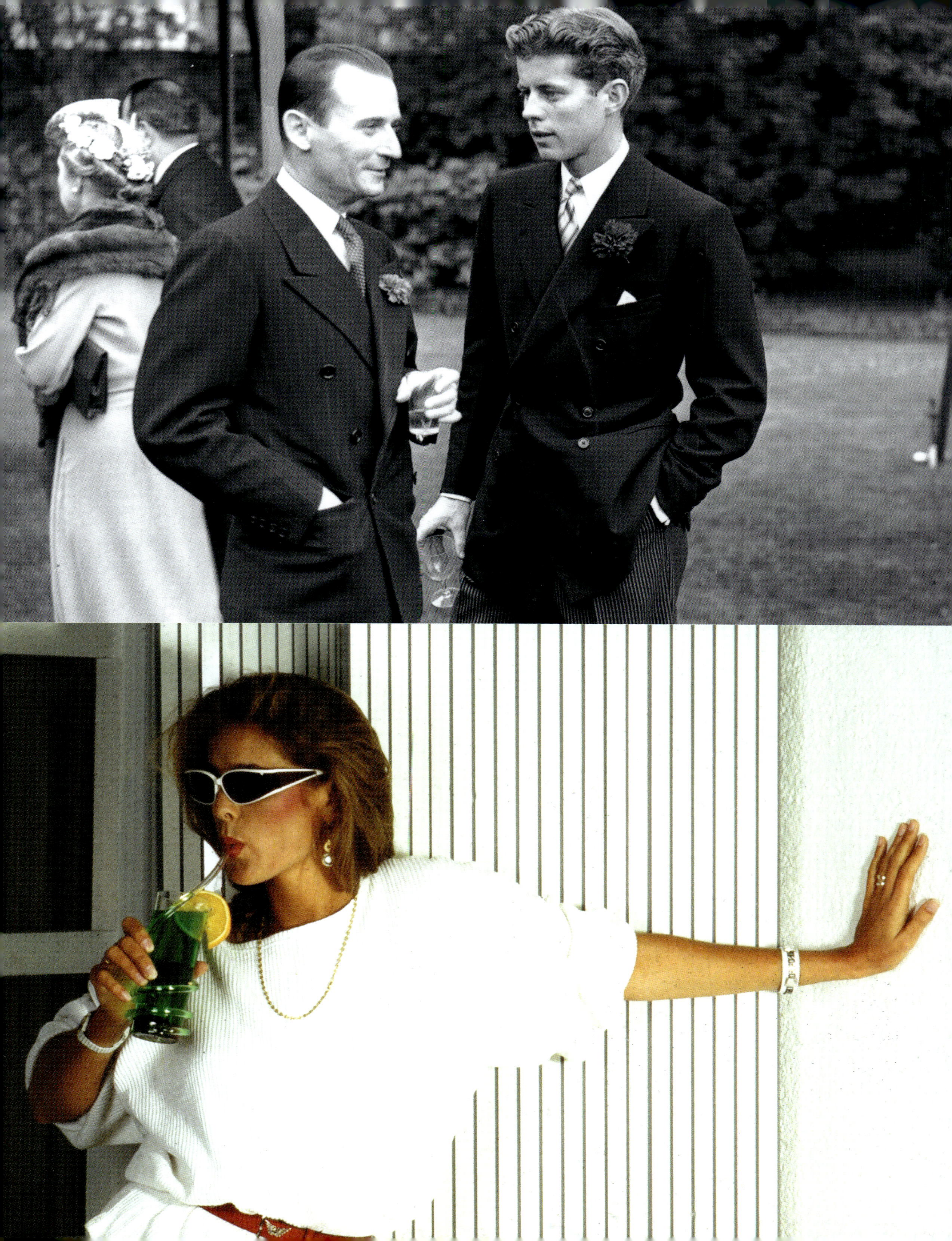

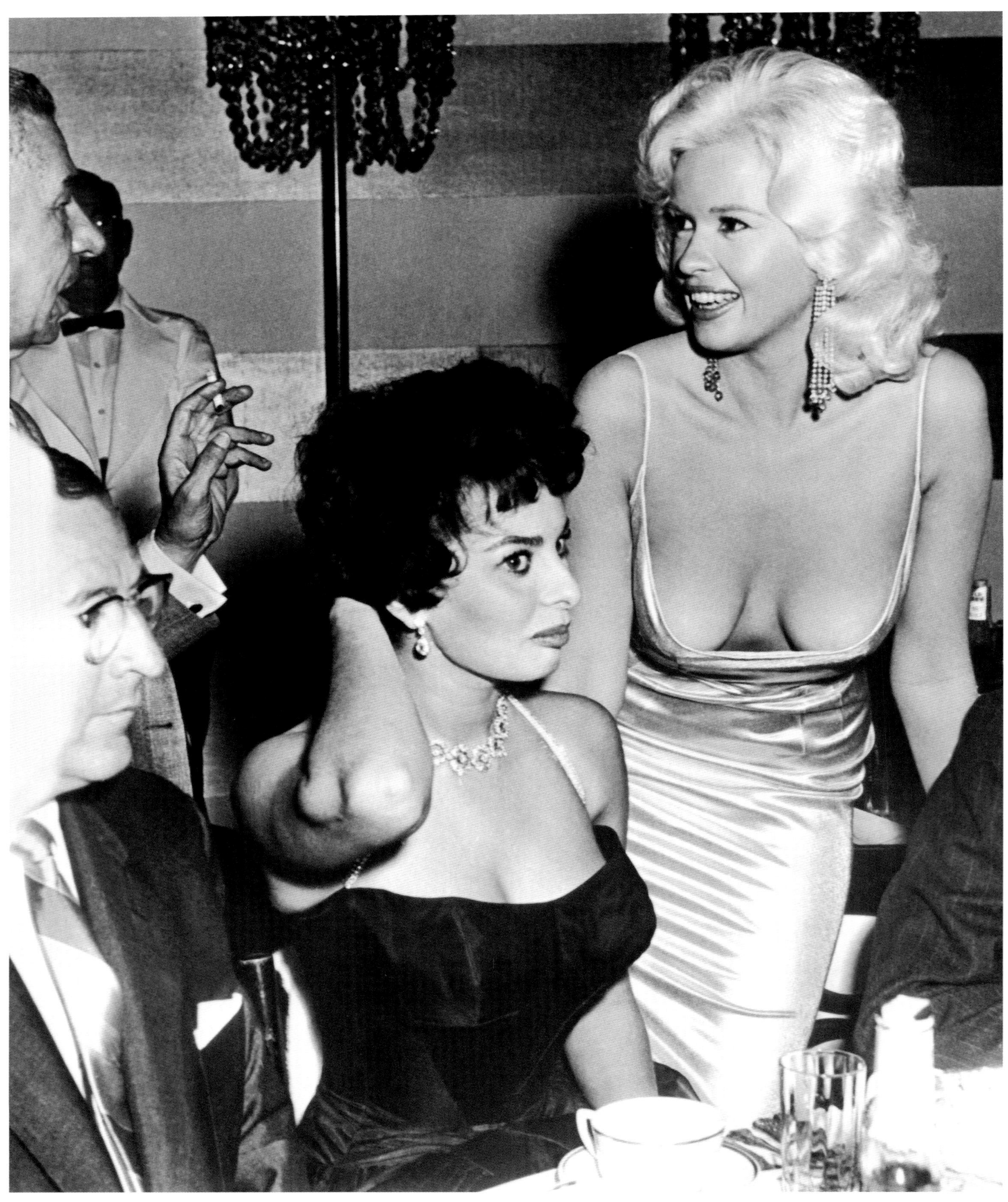

This page: *A fashionably late Jayne Mansfield makes an appearance at Sophia Loren's table, Los Angeles, 1957.* Opposite: *The best guests dress for the party—like casual wear for sunset cocktails on the beach.*

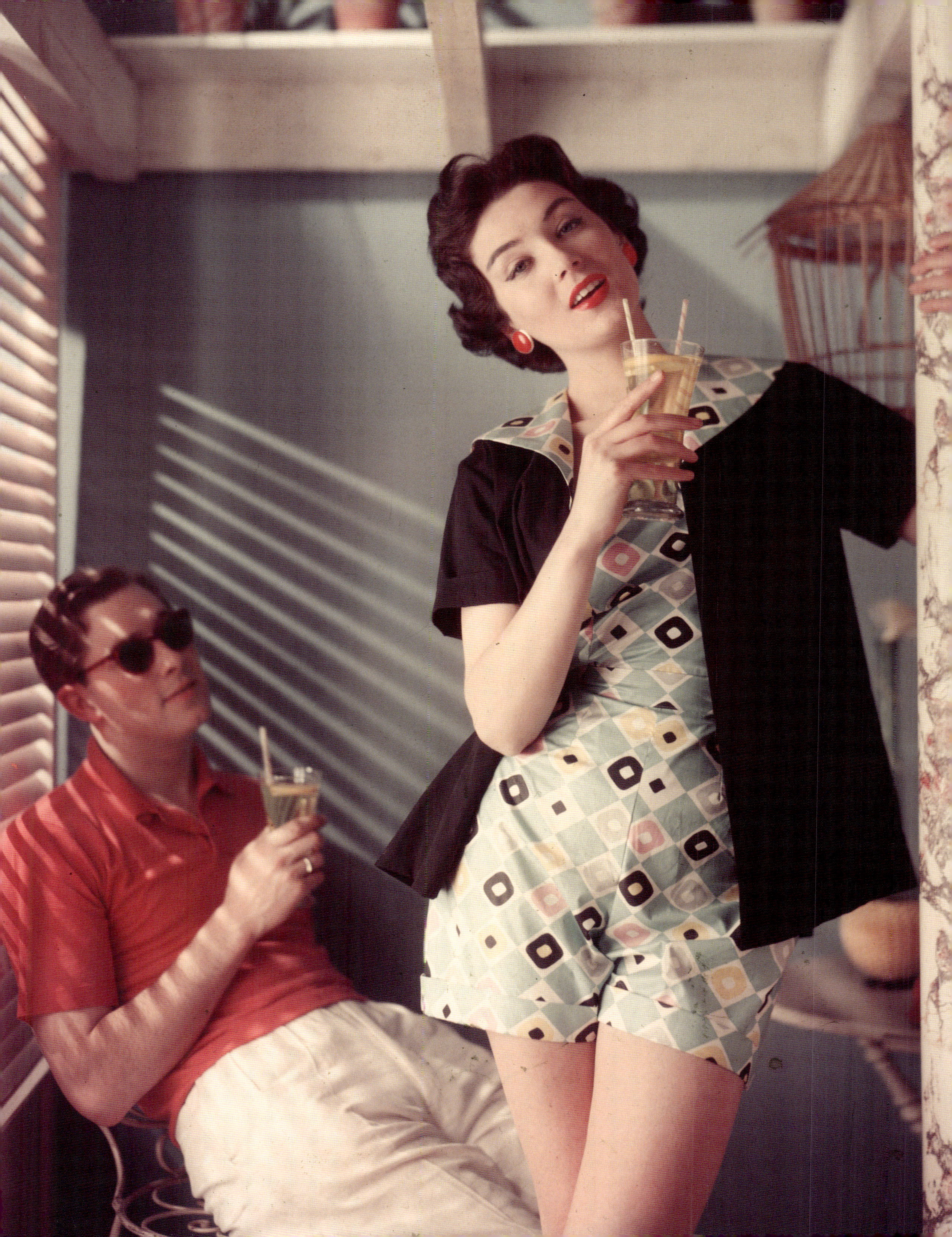

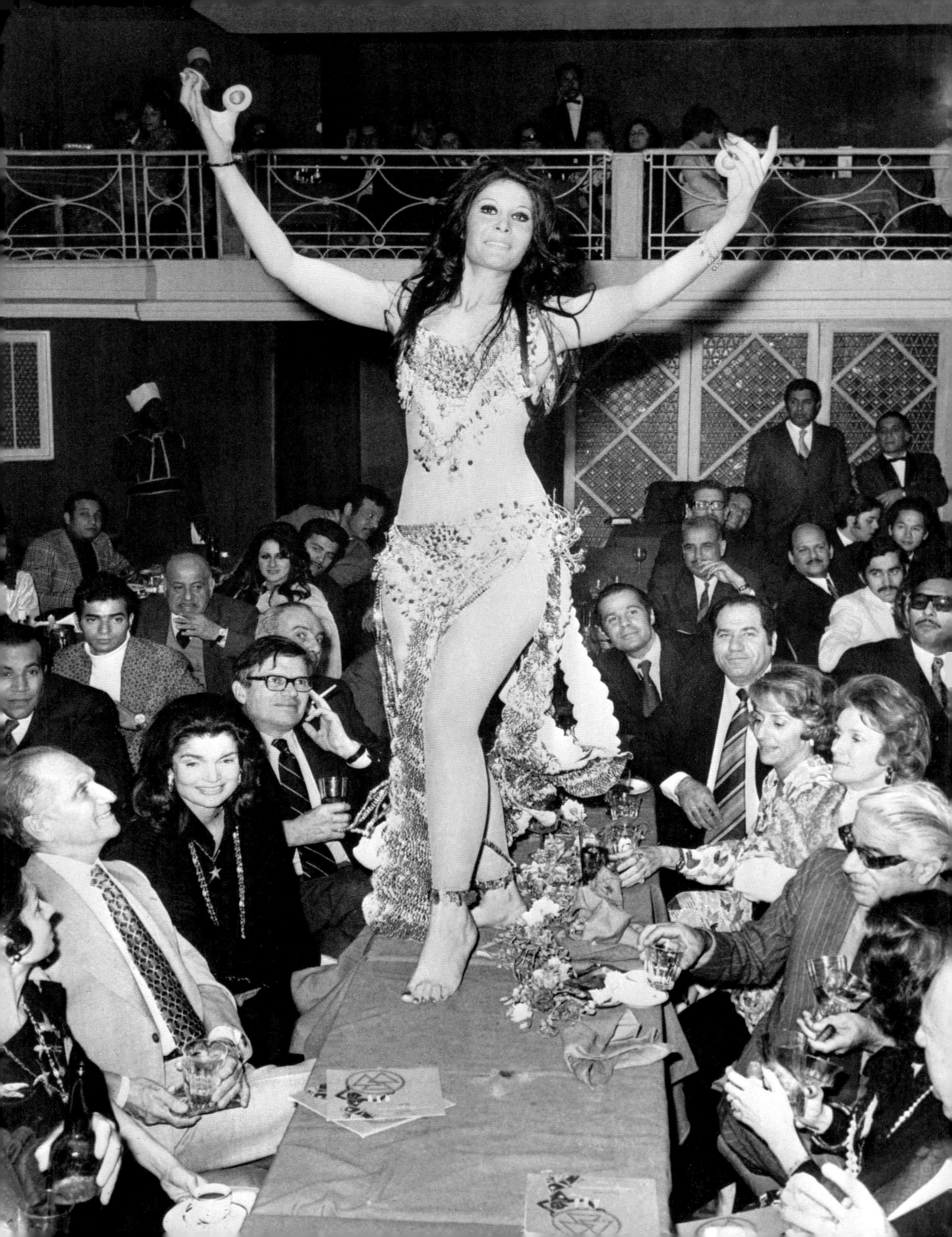

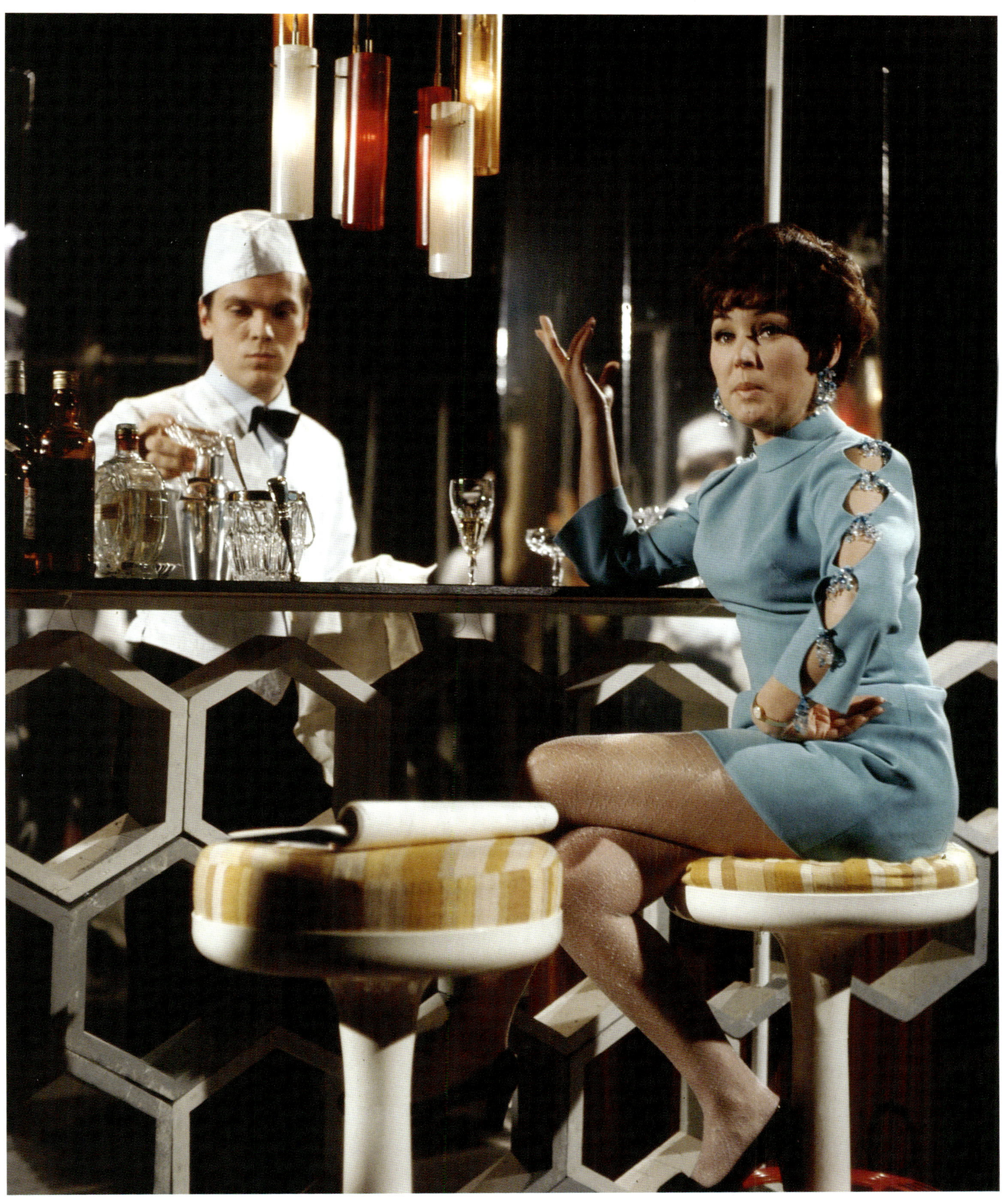

Opposite: *Appreciative guests Jacqueline Kennedy Onassis and Aristotle Onassis watch a bejeweled belly dancer at a private party for millionaires in Cairo, 1974.* This page: *A self-assured woman savors a solo cocktail in style.*

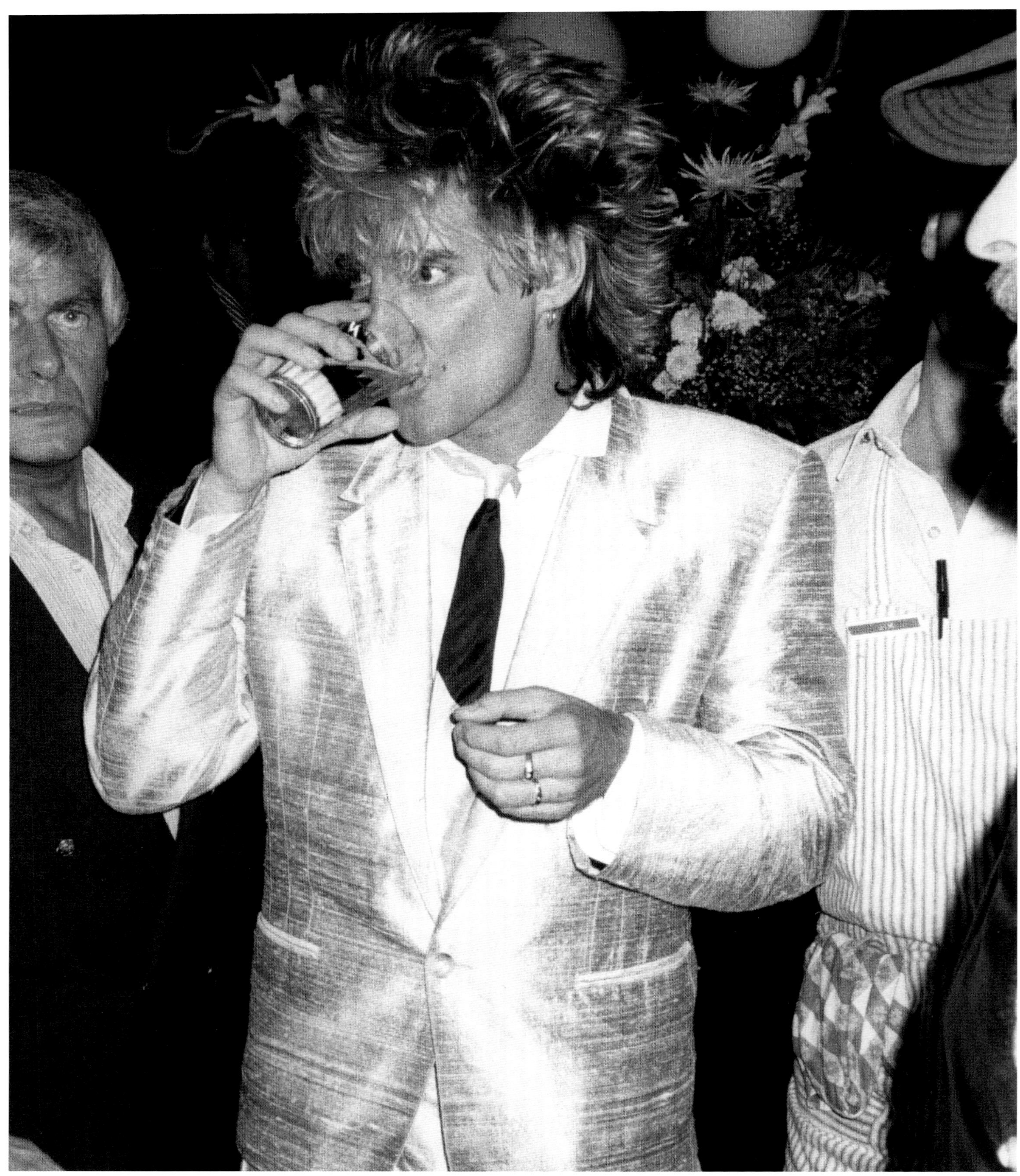

This page: *Rocker Rod Stewart steps out during cocktail hour, circa 1990.* Opposite: *Costumed antics turn an after-dark cocktail party into the talk of the town, 1952.* Following pages, left: *Press Secretary Bill Moyers dances the Watusi (and outrages members of Congress) at a Washington cocktail party, 1966*; right: *After partaking in fun at New York's Boom Boom Room, comedienne Ziwe and actress Emily Ratajkowski head home, 2022.*

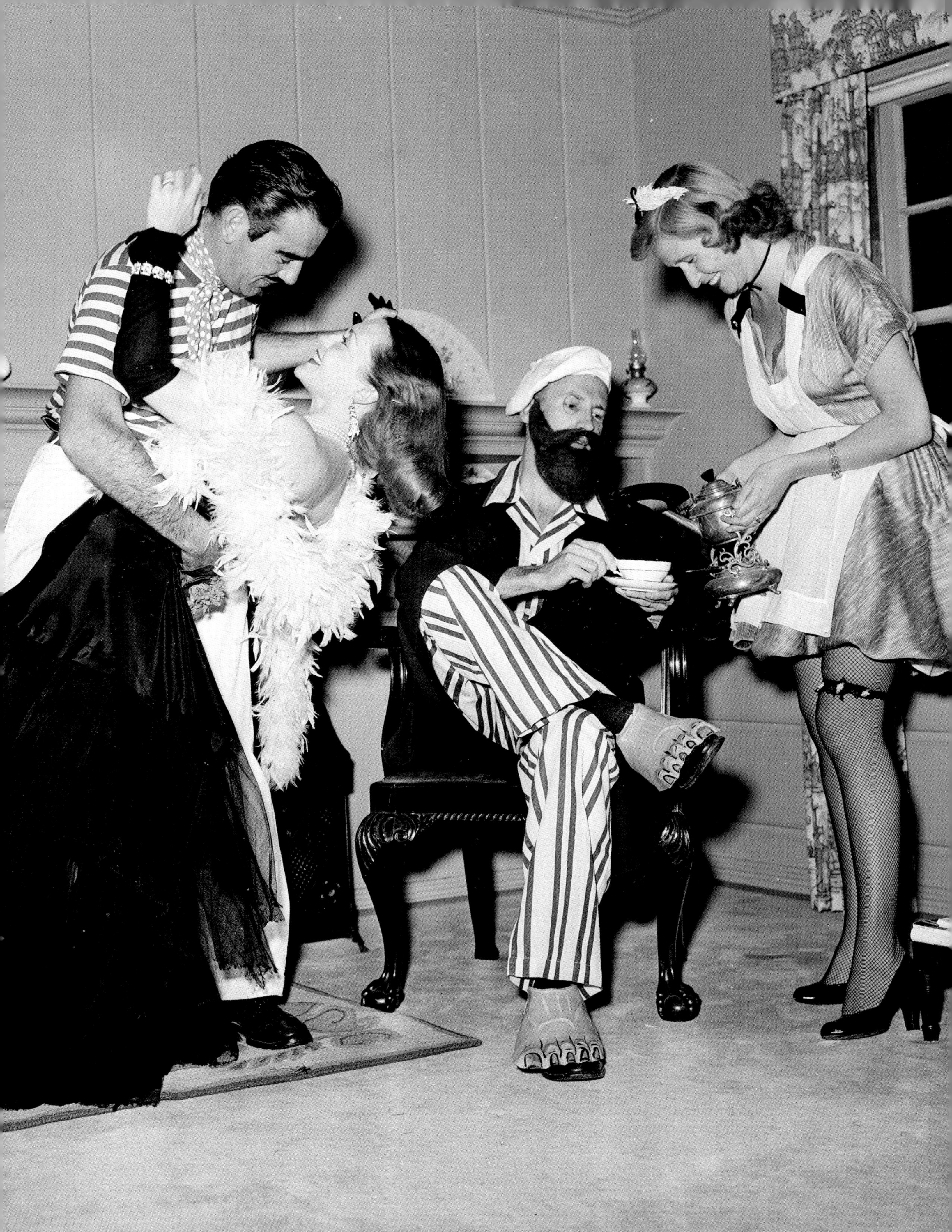

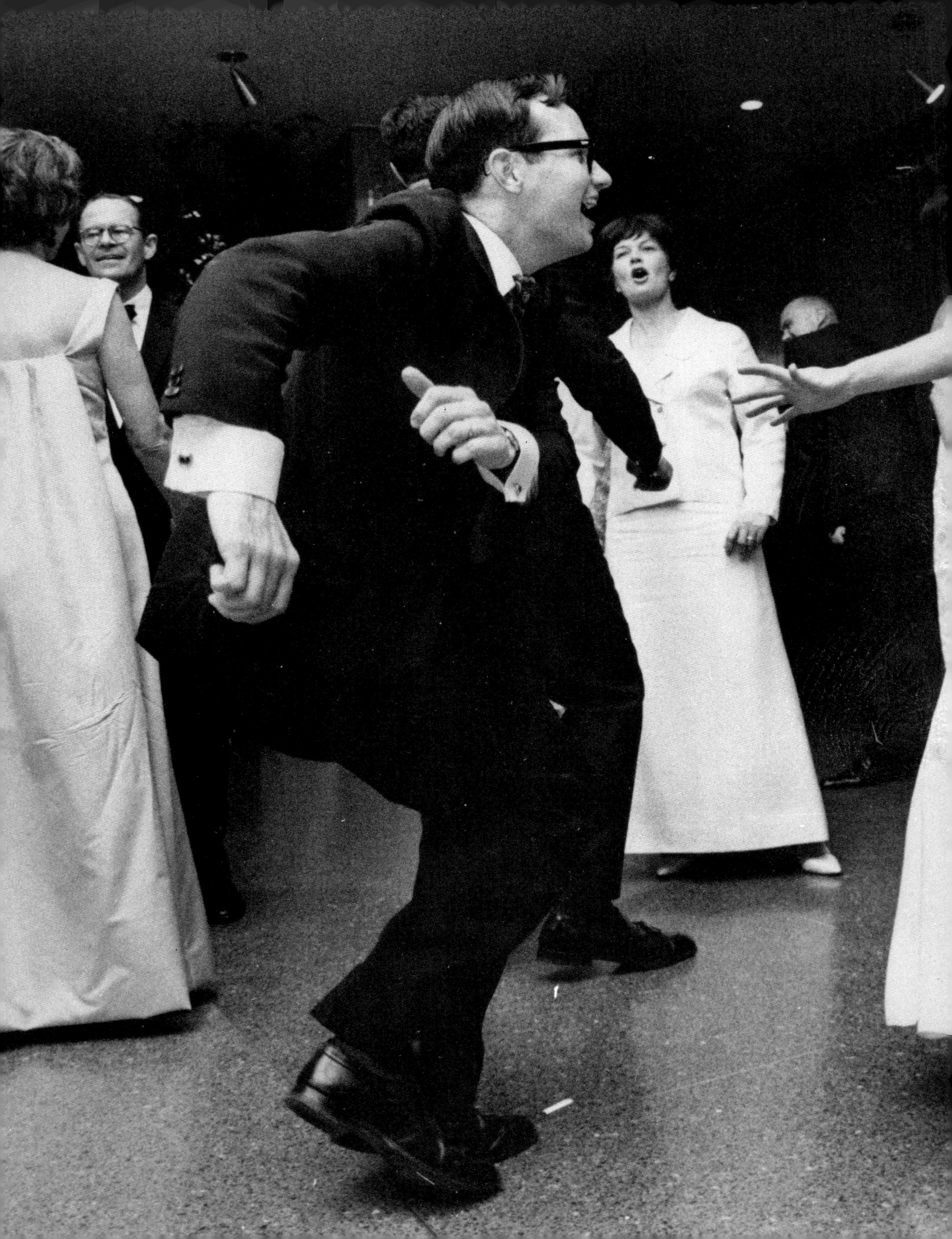

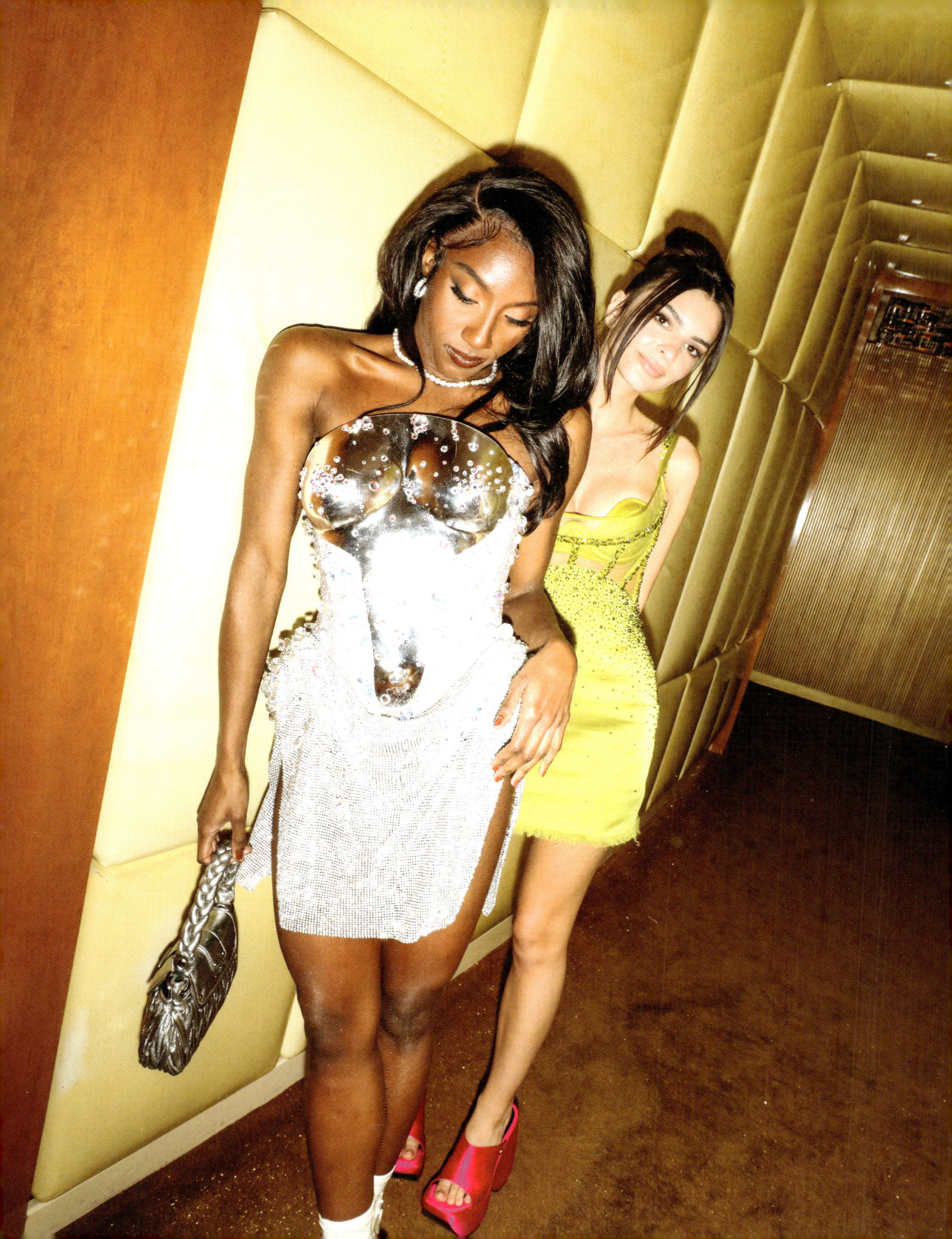

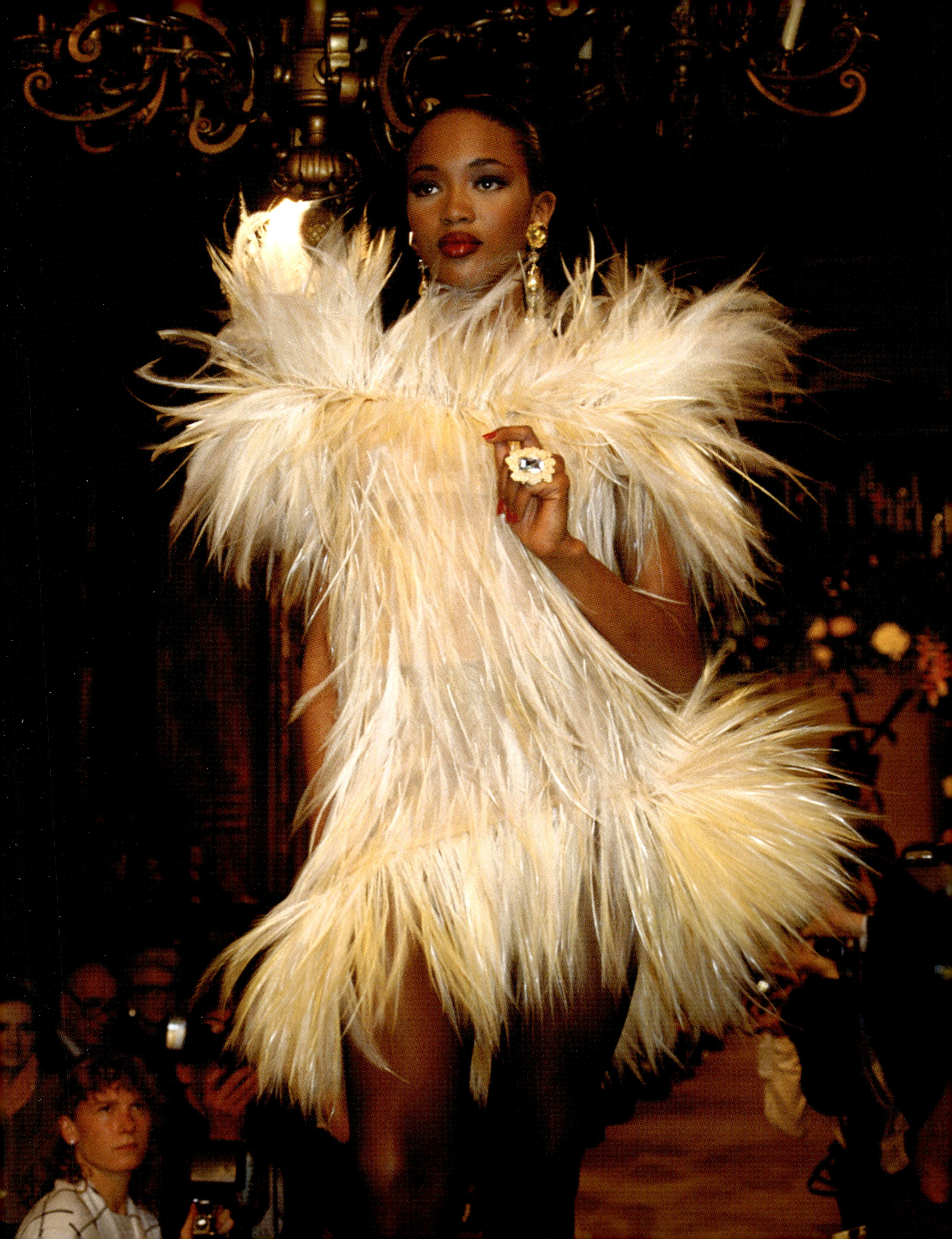

FASHION

THE DRESS CODE

So, what *is* a cocktail dress? Is it merely "something to spill cocktails on," as Jean Arthur quipped in the 1930s film comedy *The Ex-Mrs. Bradford*, playing opposite the dapper William Powell? Or does it and the *heure de l'apéritif* share a certain *je ne sais quoi*? Why *is* defining cocktail attire as elusive as trying to catch a Champagne bubble? "You know it when you see it," as the saying goes. And we know it's neither black-tie nor workaday—and *definitely* not ordinary.

The story of how we sip in style began at the turn of the twentieth century, when ladies broke free from their corsets and jazzed up their day frocks to knock back Old Fashioneds. Today, the cocktail hour wardrobe is as diverse as the menu at a mixologist's paradise. Their common sartorial thread? What else but a shared spirit of "Let's shake things up!"

Glad Rags and Wingdings

In the Roaring 20s, when Prohibition had everyone in the United States doing the Charleston around restrictive alcohol laws, giddy flappers and swells snuck drinks at speakeasies. French couturiers Coco Chanel and Jean Patou snipped away at evening gowns, turning them into short frocks decked out with beads and embroidery. Even the fellas tossed stuffy spats and canes for snazzy suits in eye-popping patterns. A drink called the Bee's Knees was the cat's pajamas, turbans were all the rage, and everyone walked like an Egyptian in designs inspired by Tutankhamun's tomb's sensational discovery.

Opposite: *Model Naomi Campbell stirs up haute couture in an Yves Saint Laurent fur cocktail dress and dazzling cocktail ring, Paris, 1987.*

The Great Depression sank everyone's spirits—and hemlines dipped. But instead of dwelling on harsh economic realities, cocktail revelers channeled their inner movie stars, downed Singapore Slings, and danced as if there were no tomorrow. Cary Grant and Clark Gable inspired men to dapper up in trim suits and dashing fedoras. Bette Davis and Jean Harlow, assisted by legendary costume designers Adrian and Edith Head, showed women how to glam up soirées in backless gowns, dripping with fur and feathers. "Let's think only of today, and not worry about tomorrow!" advised Zelda Fitzgerald. Cheers to that!

Cocktail Couture

"A woman doesn't need to be beautiful to wear one of my dresses," Cristóbal Balenciaga proclaimed. "The dress will do all that for her." This was fashion to a T in the 1950s, the golden age of cocktail parties. During World War II, people had little time for frivolity; cocktail attire was as drab as yesterday's Champagne, although designers like Norman Norell wove in much-needed sparkle. When wartime restrictions eased, fashion blossomed in French couturier Christian Dior's hands with his New Look's nipped-in waists and voluptuous skirts. Dior dubbed one of his creations a "cocktail dress"—and voila! Just as the perfect garnish transforms a Martini, the cocktail dress made every cocktail hour a party.

Living rooms in 1950s America became like runways, with impeccably turned-out homemakers serving up fashion as varied as the canapés they offered to their guests—from full and pencil skirts to sheaths and hostess gowns, from peek-a-boo sheer stunners to exuberantly polka-dotted frocks. Women's cocktail accoutrements rose to the occasion with long gloves, playful hats and fascinators, matching parure, and kitten heels and stilettos. Not to be outdone, men donned double-breasted suits with wide lapels and pleated pants that signaled a more prosperous era, while Ivy Leaguers ditched tradition with the more relaxed "sack" suit. Frank Sinatra, on the other hand, kept it classy in a timeless slim-fitting suit, narrow tie, and fedora. His tip? "Try not to sit down because it wrinkles the pants." Perfect advice for the standing-only cocktail hour.

Rule Breakers and Trend Setters

Before London's Youthquake and social revolutions began shaking up happy hour, the early 1960s were as smooth as John F. Kennedy's favorite Daiquiri, and as chic as Jacqueline Kennedy's coordinated sets. After Yves Saint Laurent dropped his sensational "Mondrian" dress in the mid-1960s, cocktails became a sartorial happening. Space-age style blasted off with vinyl looks and futuristic helmets straight out of an André Courrèges fever dream. Pop Art colors and wild Op Art geometry lit up the scene, while street fashion joined the party with hippie prints and boho vibes. Men embraced their inner peacock with hip-hugging velvet pants and platform shoes, grooving in bold patterned shirts and scarves. Speakeasy chic swung back into style, with flapper dresses, paisley, and pinstripes populating rock festivals as well as poetry readings.

Then, in the 1970s, the cocktail hour went all-night clubbing. The Polyester Decade's popular Harvey Wallbanger cocktail could be a bit much—a little like the heady disco soirées that were as risqué as any Jazz Age party. Heads turned at Studio 54 when Yves Saint Laurent revamped 1940s glam for the dance floor, until hot pants and halter tops shimmering with sequins stole the show. Leisure suits, wide lapels, and flared pants burnished men's playboy image while style flipped the gender script, with Bianca Jagger dancing the night away wearing Halston's tuxedo. Amid all the glitz, women dashed from board meetings to cocktails wearing Diane von Furstenberg's versatile wrap dress—a straight-up fashion tour de force with a twist of elegance.

Shaking Up the Scene

Power moves and power suits dominated the 1980s. Men and women rocked big hair, bigger shoulder pads, and accessories bolder than a Long Island Iced Tea. But not every cocktail outfit was a powerplay—take Giorgio Armani's loose, unstructured suit on Richard Gere's hustler in 1980's *American Gigolo*, or the pastel-soaked blazers and t-shirts of TV's *Miami Vice*. Throughout the decade, cocktail dresses tuned in to Princess Diana's fairy-tale-to-fierce evolution, from a layered "New Romantic" vibe to the cheeky-chic looks of Karl Lagerfeld's Chanel and Christian Lacroix.

Then the 1990s crashed the party with anti-fashion rebellion. Silhouettes and proportions went avant-garde with Rei Kawakubo and Yohji Yamamoto and minimal with Tom Ford. Silky slip dresses slid into formalwear territory while grunge ripped up the rulebook, paving the way for a cocktail fashion scene that welcomed influences from all corners. The renaissance of cocktail culture in the 2000s brought in creative mixologists and killer concoctions—and brought back mid-century glamour thanks to *Mad Men* and Prohibition looks à la *Boardwalk Empire*. Today, ditching stuffy etiquette and formal dress codes has become *de rigueur*, with cocktail parties as come-as-you-are affairs, and variations on the LBD making appearances from morning to night. From flirty frocks to sleek suits, cocktail styles are as varied as the fizz in your drink—with looks to savor, style to flaunt, and rules to break.

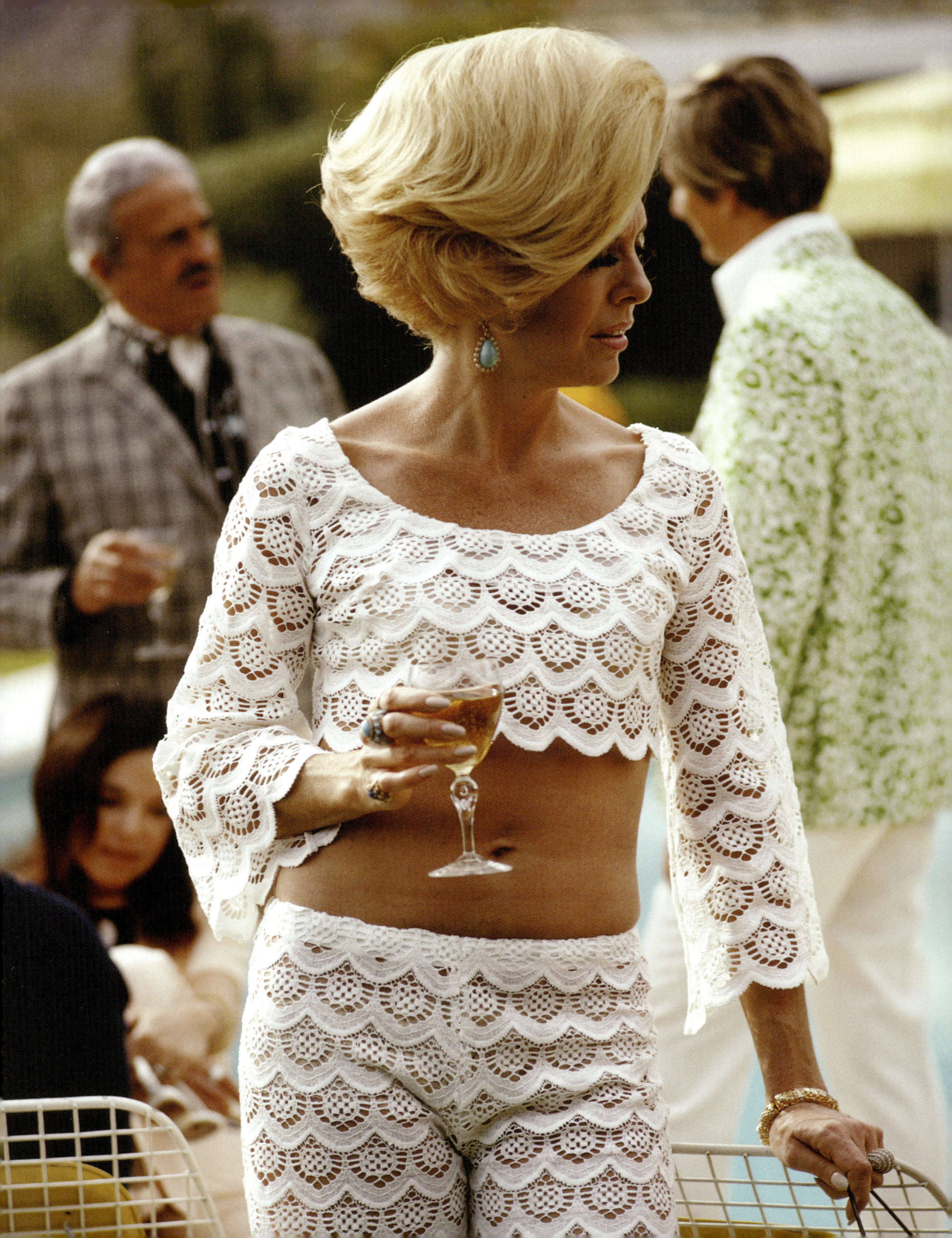

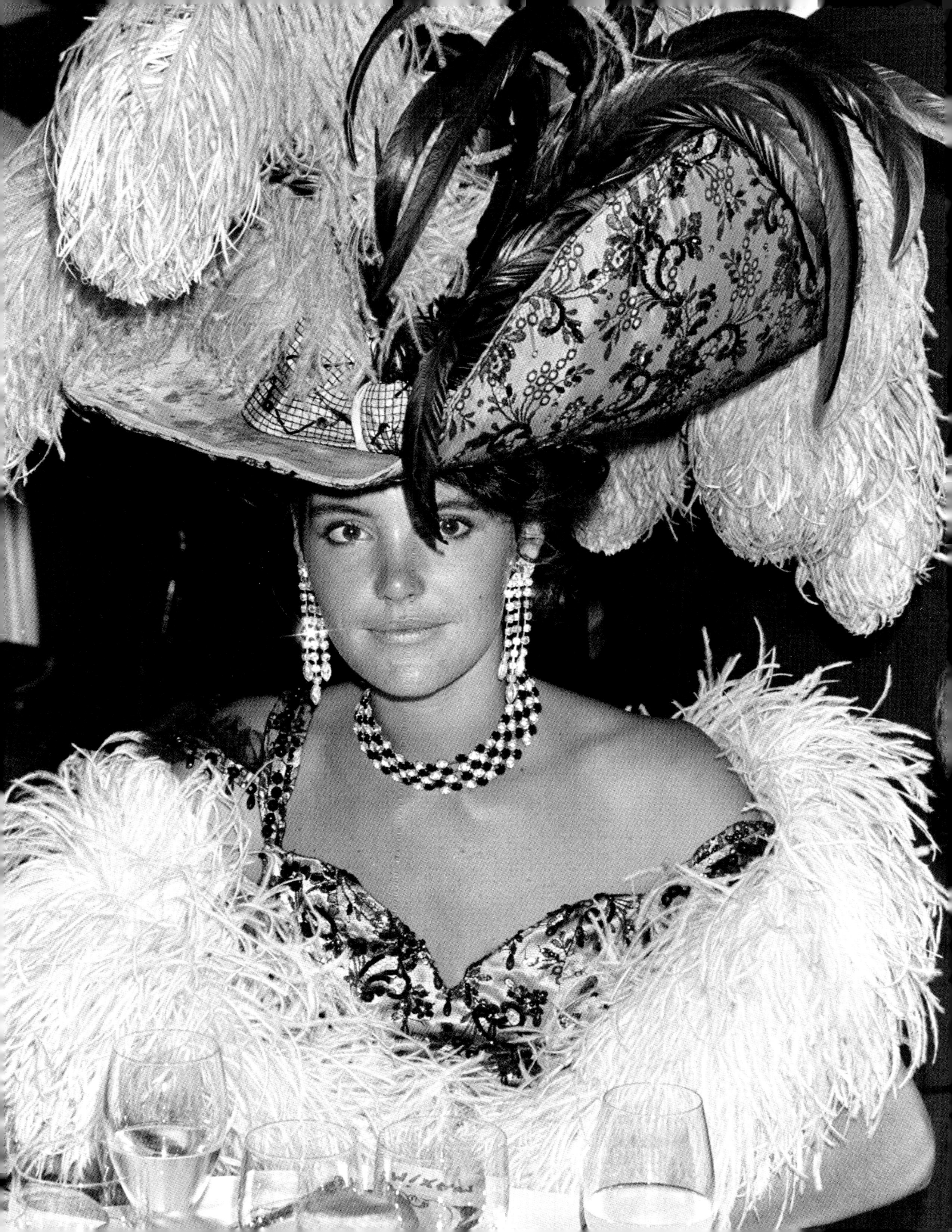

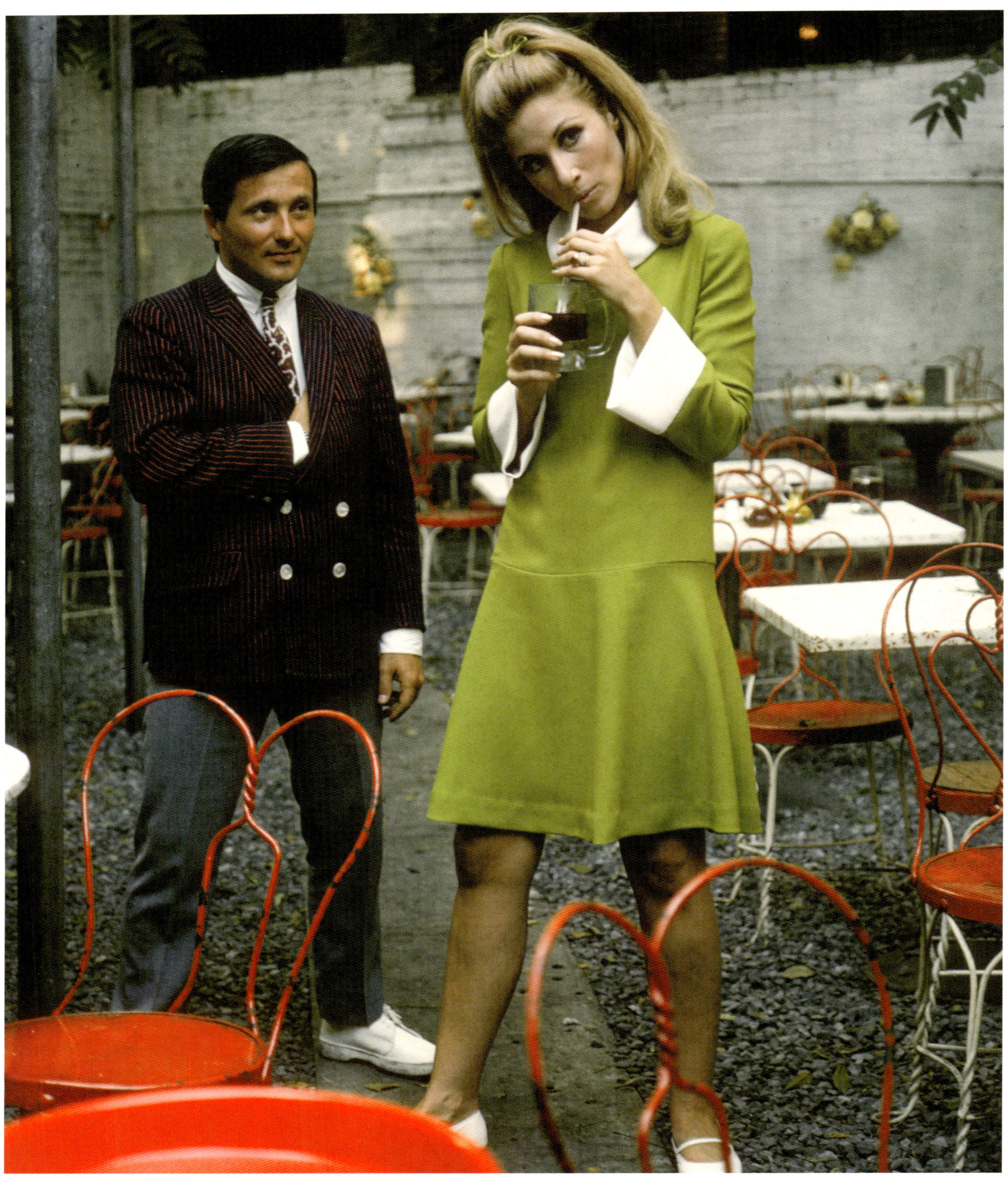

Previous pages, left: *In a white lace ensemble, California socialite Helen Dzo Dzo Kaptur pauses poolside at a Palm Springs party, 1970*; right: *A plumed hat radiates vintage glamour at Maxim's nightclub in Paris, 1985.* This page: *1960s style swings with Warhol Superstar Baby Jane Holzer's mod green dress and her companion's purple pinstriped double-breasted blazer.* Opposite: *A dose of New Romanticism adds dreaminess to cocktail hour, circa 1982.*

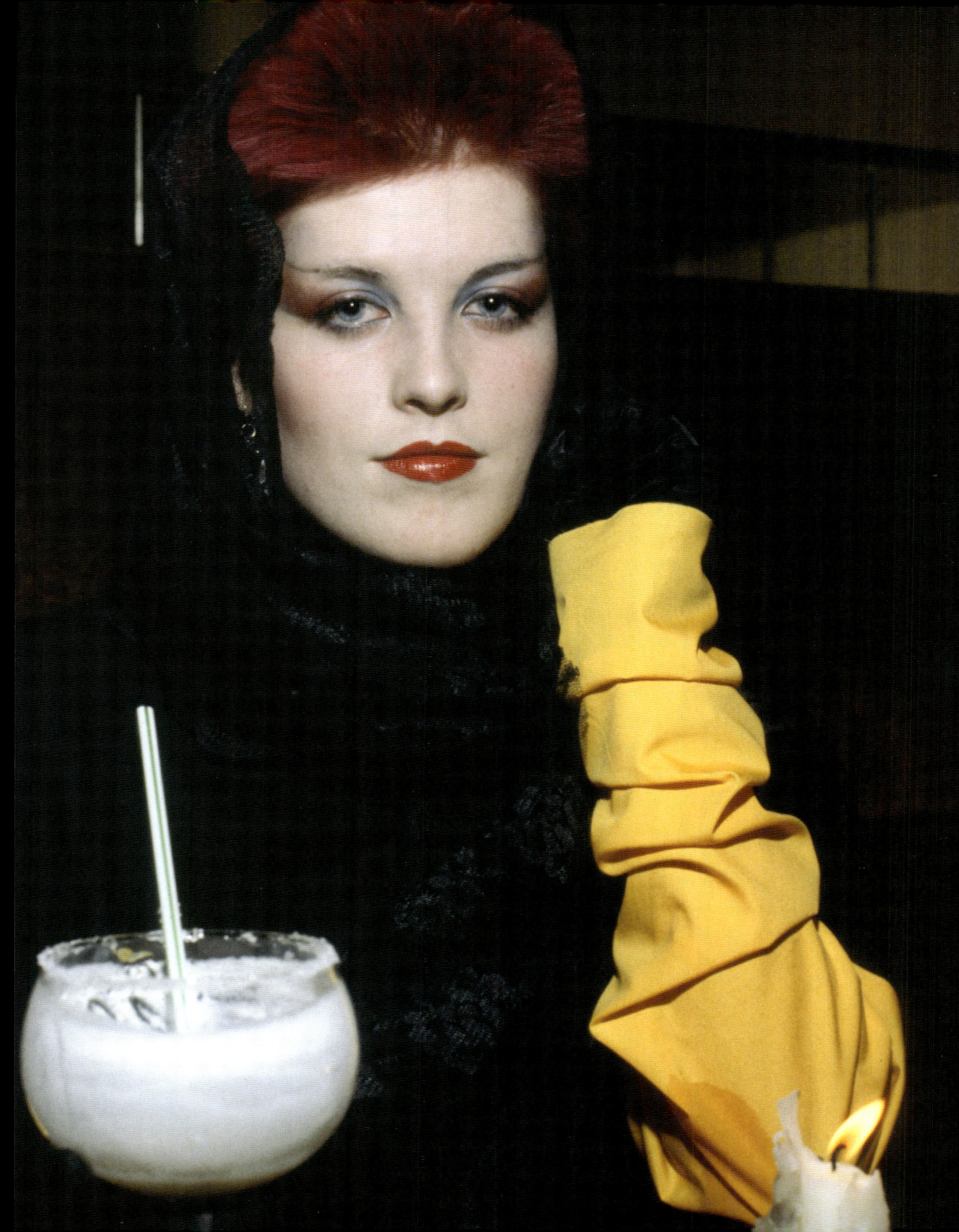

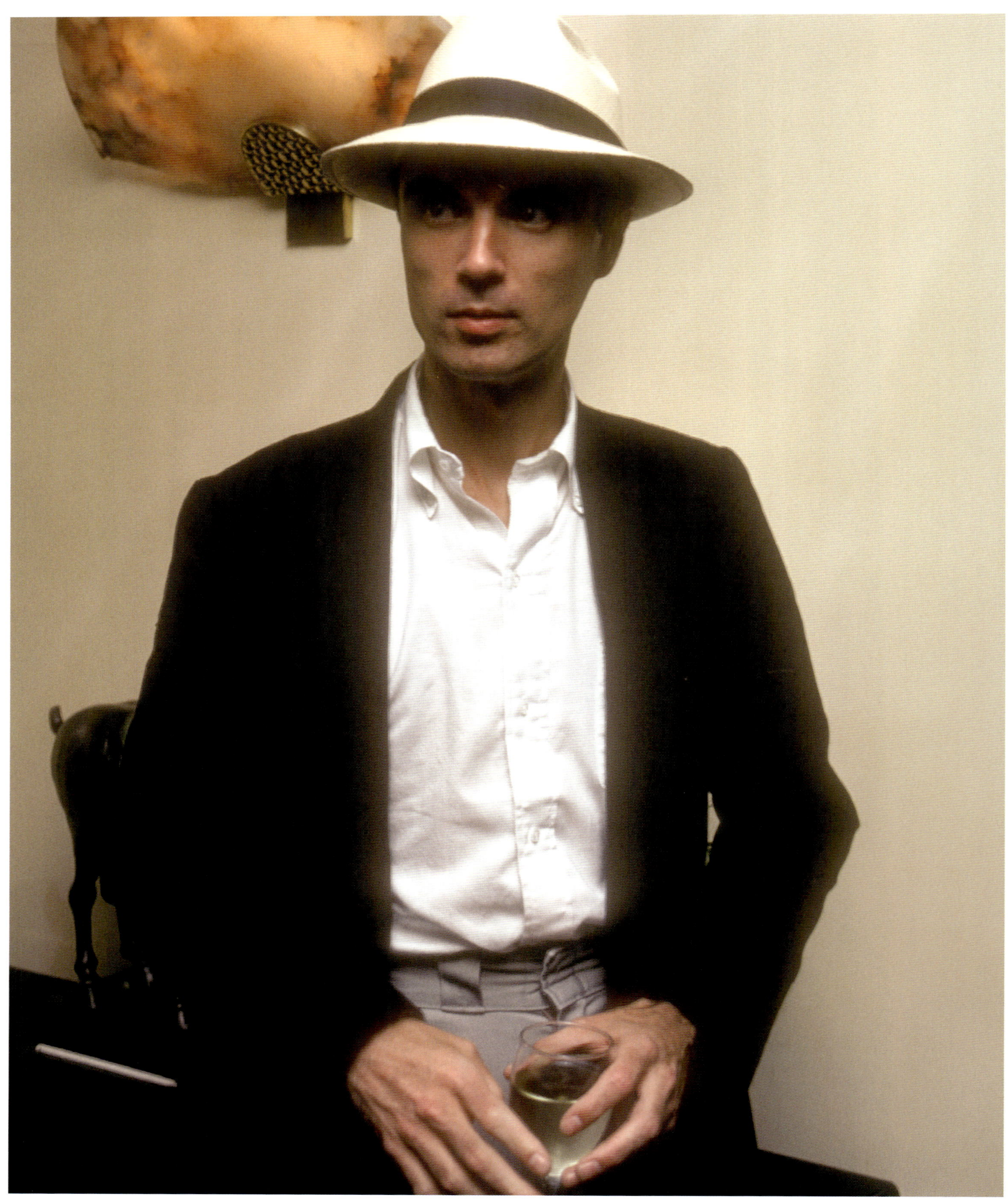

This page: *Talking Heads' frontman David Byrne shows how to top off a party with a Panama hat at Mr. Chow's, New York, 1981*. Opposite: *Sans masks, Lee Radziwill* (left) *has a tête-a-tête with a friend with ornately braided hair after Truman Capote's Black and White Ball, 1966.*

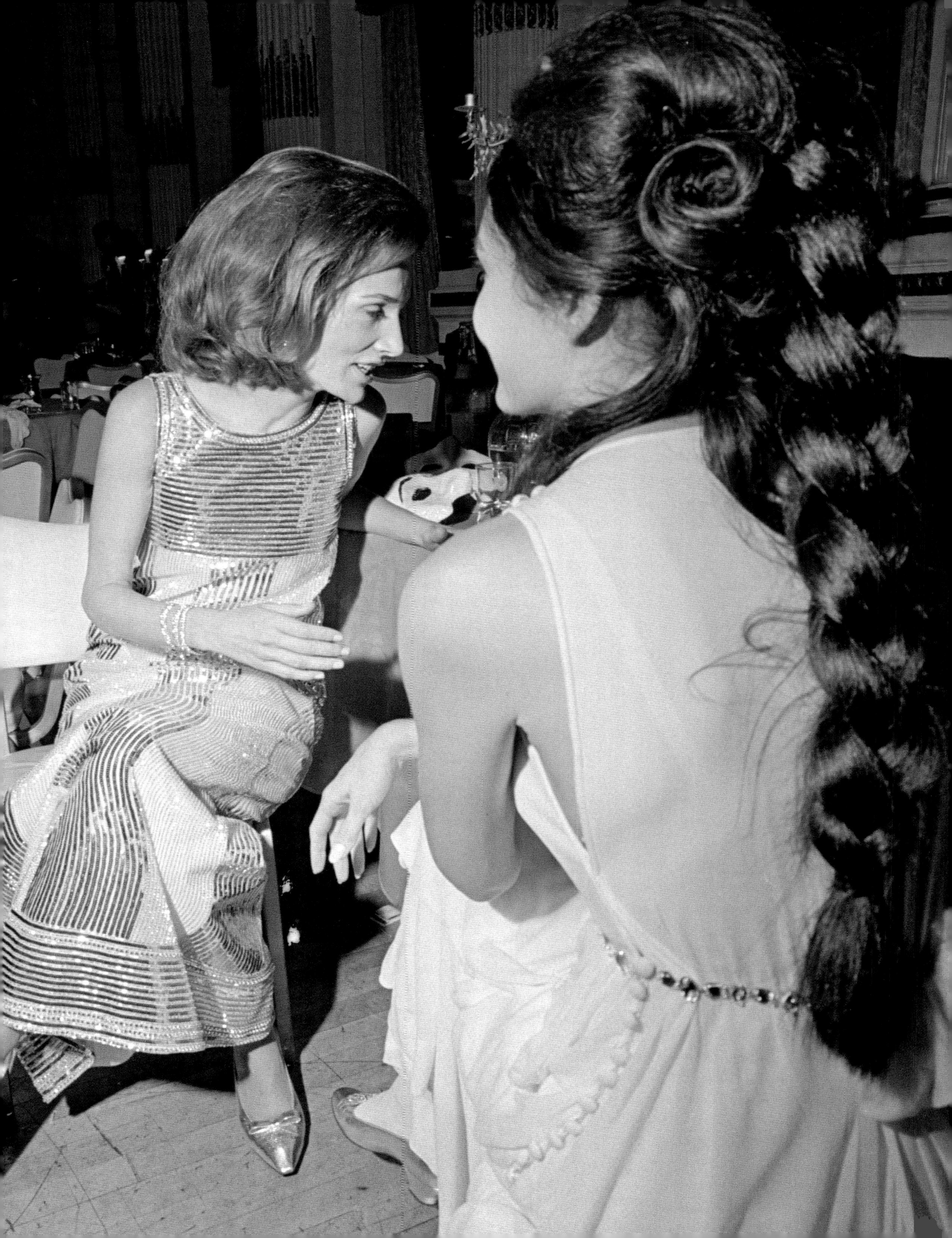

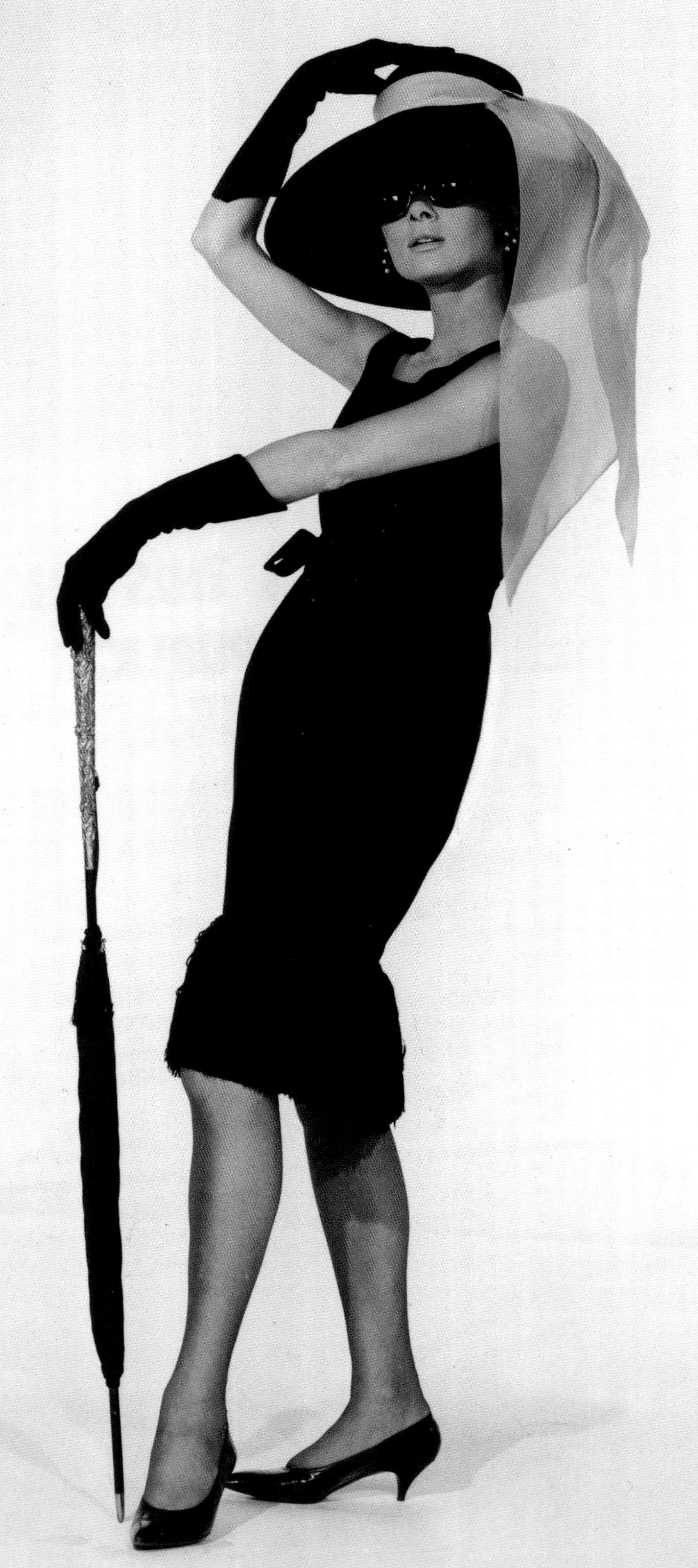

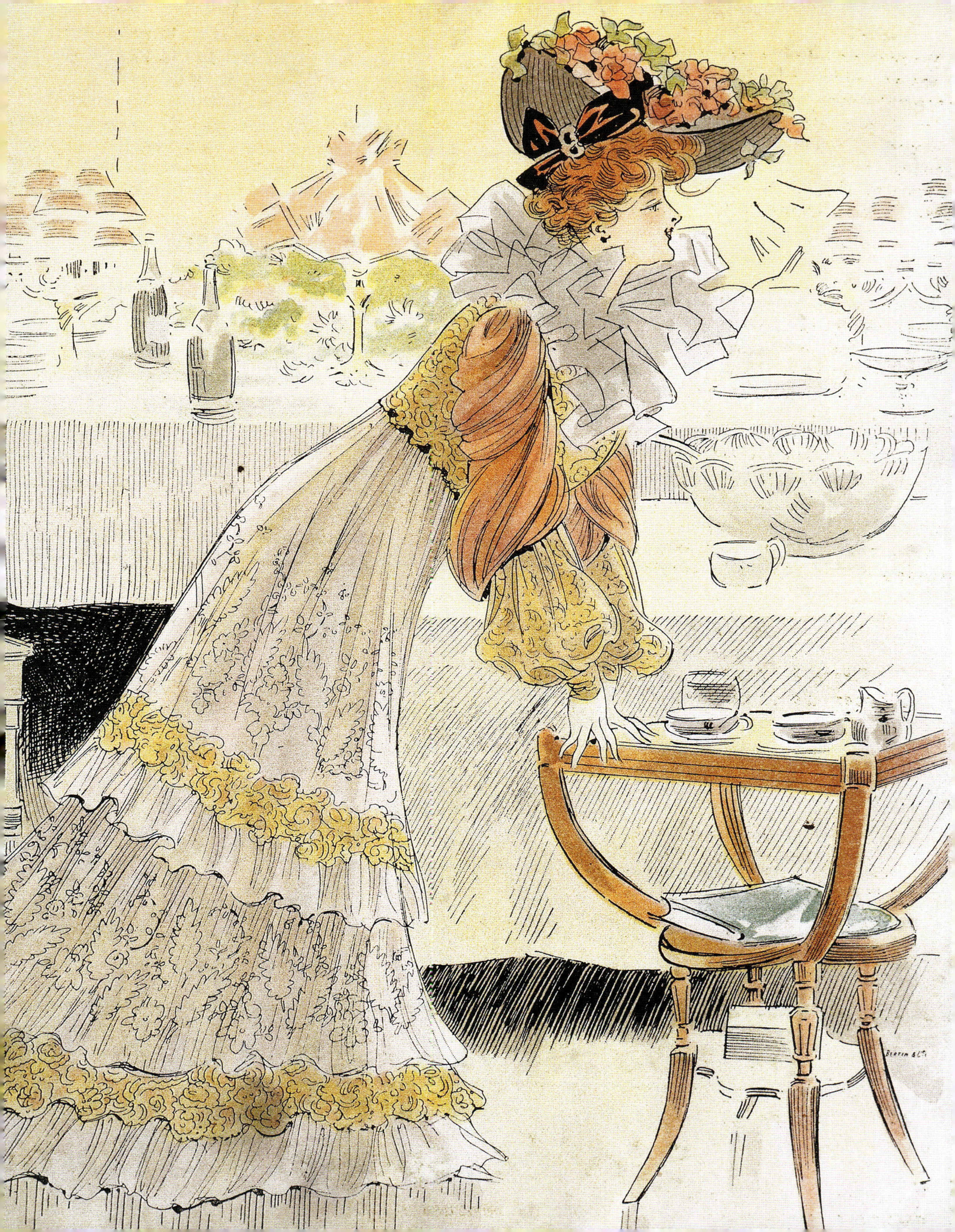

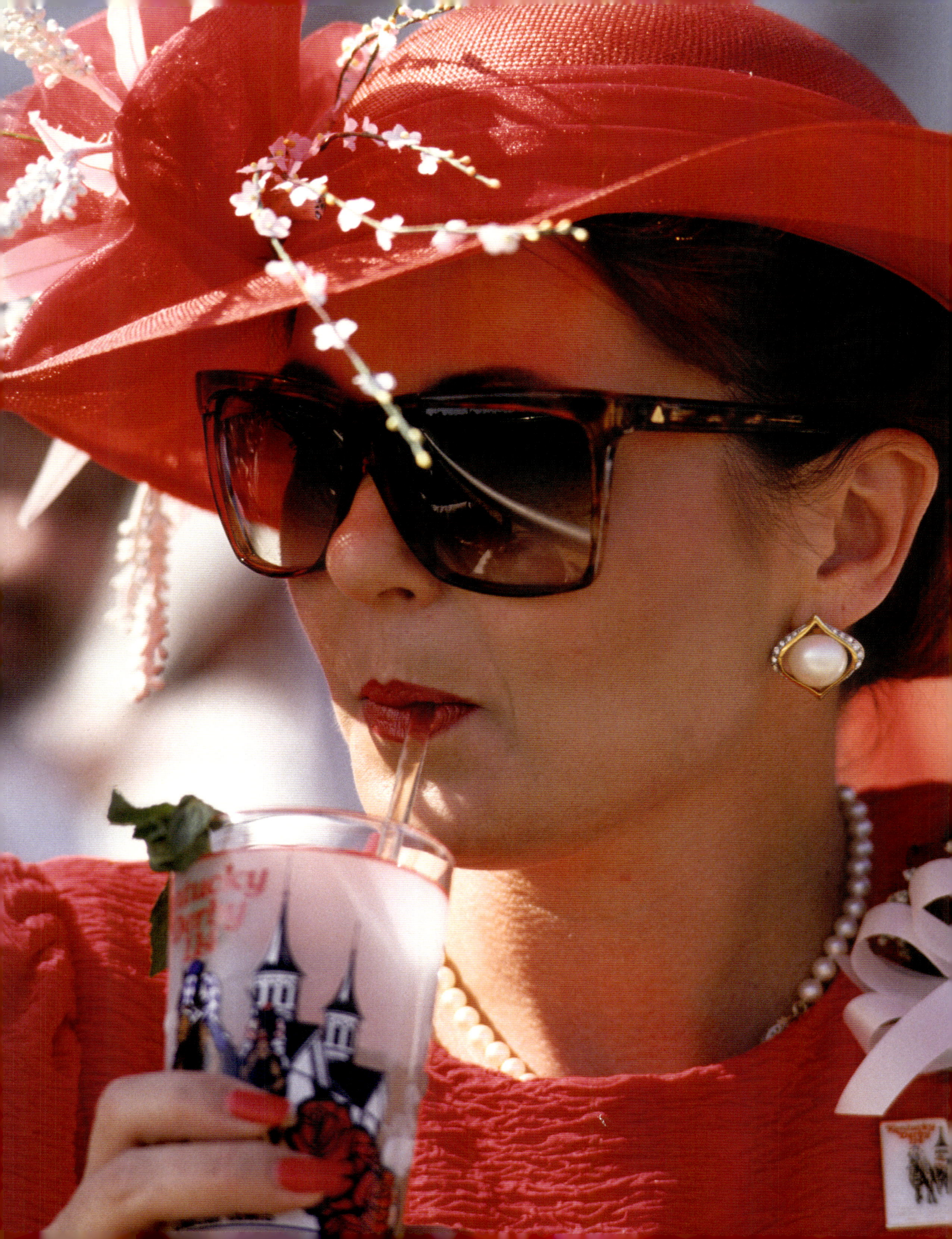

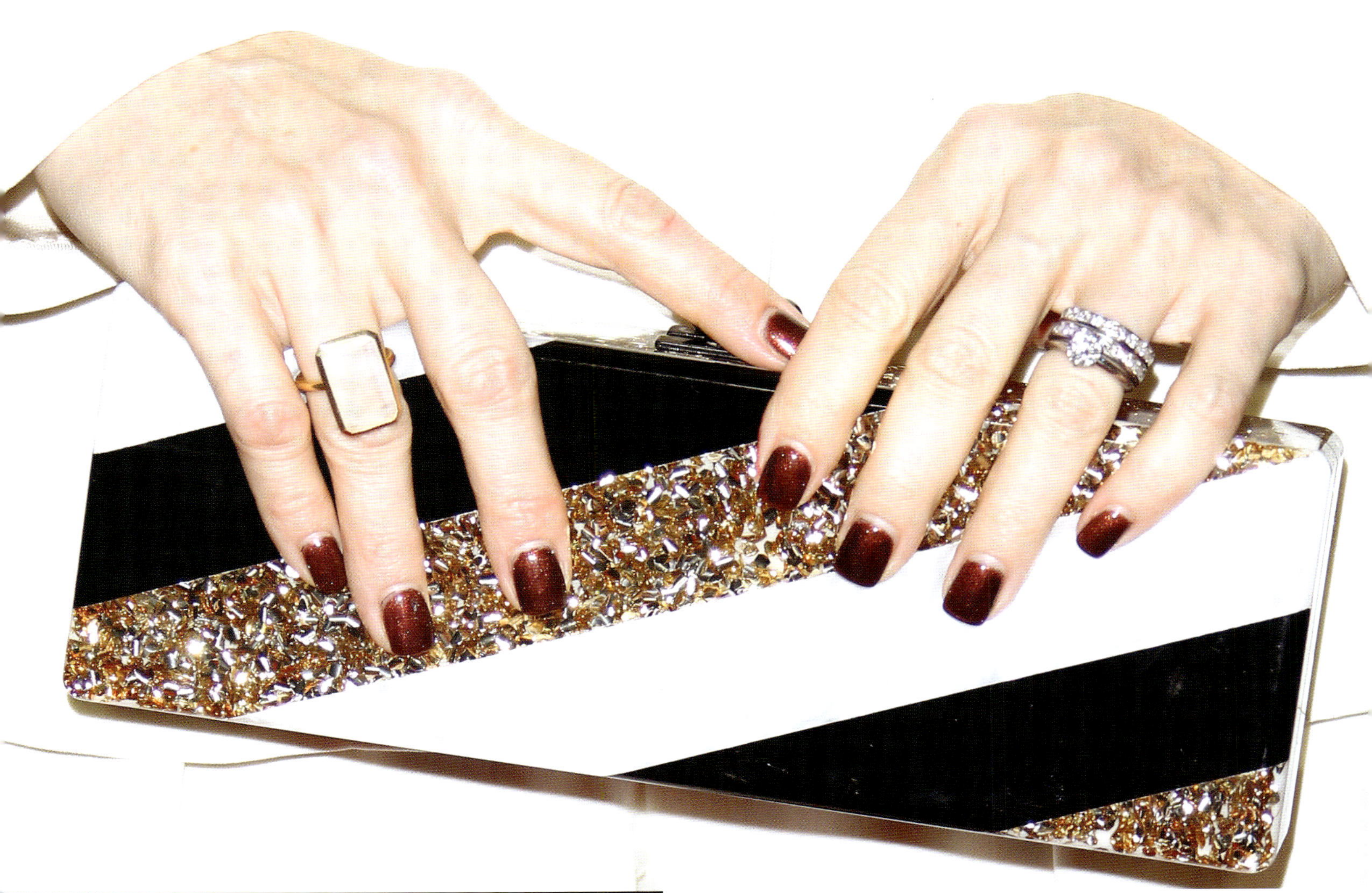

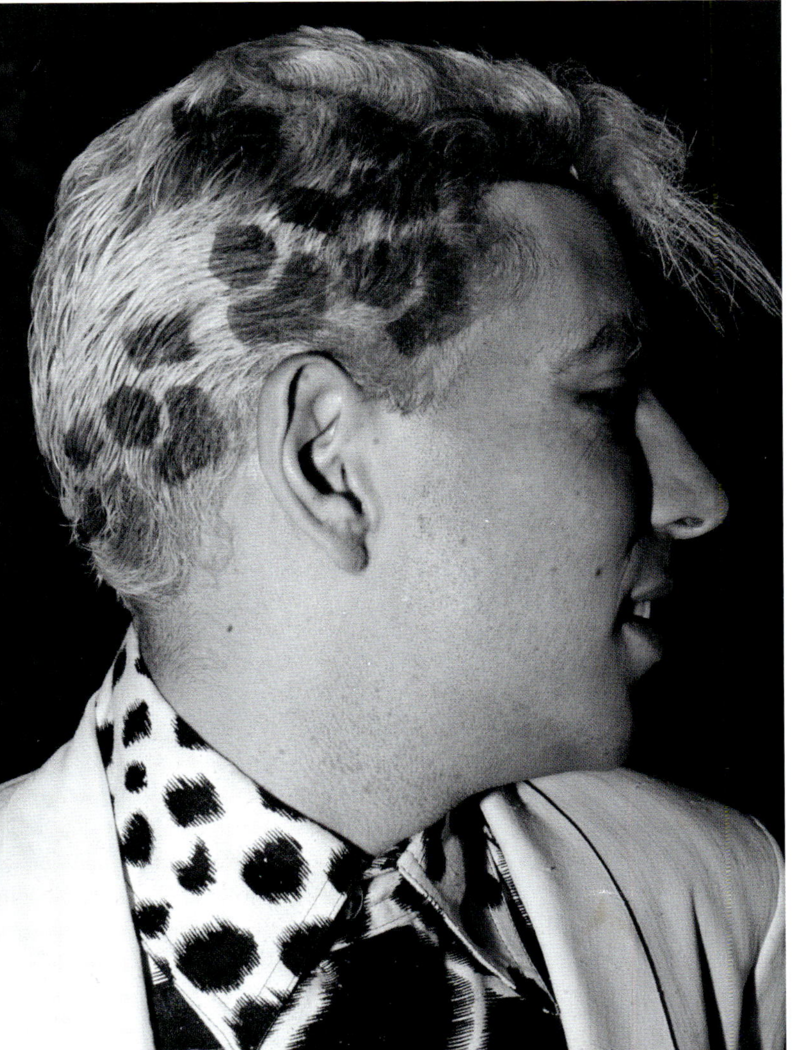

Previous pages, left: *The LBD that launched a thousand hostesses was Hubert de Givenchy's* au courant *take on Old World elegance, worn by Audrey Hepburn as Holly Golightly in* Breakfast at Tiffany's *(1961)*; right: *The picture of 1901 femininity, a society hostess readies a drinks tray in a flowing dress with puffed sleeves and extravagant collar, topped with a lavishly flowered hat.* These pages, clockwise from left: *A winning late-1980s Kentucky Derby look pairs red lipstick and nails with a dress and chic hat—plus a Mint Julep, of course; Golden Globe glitz finds center stage with this sleek clutch and cocktail ring, Los Angeles, 2014; A leopard-print shirt and dyed hair impact to the max at a 1984 networking event, San Francisco.*

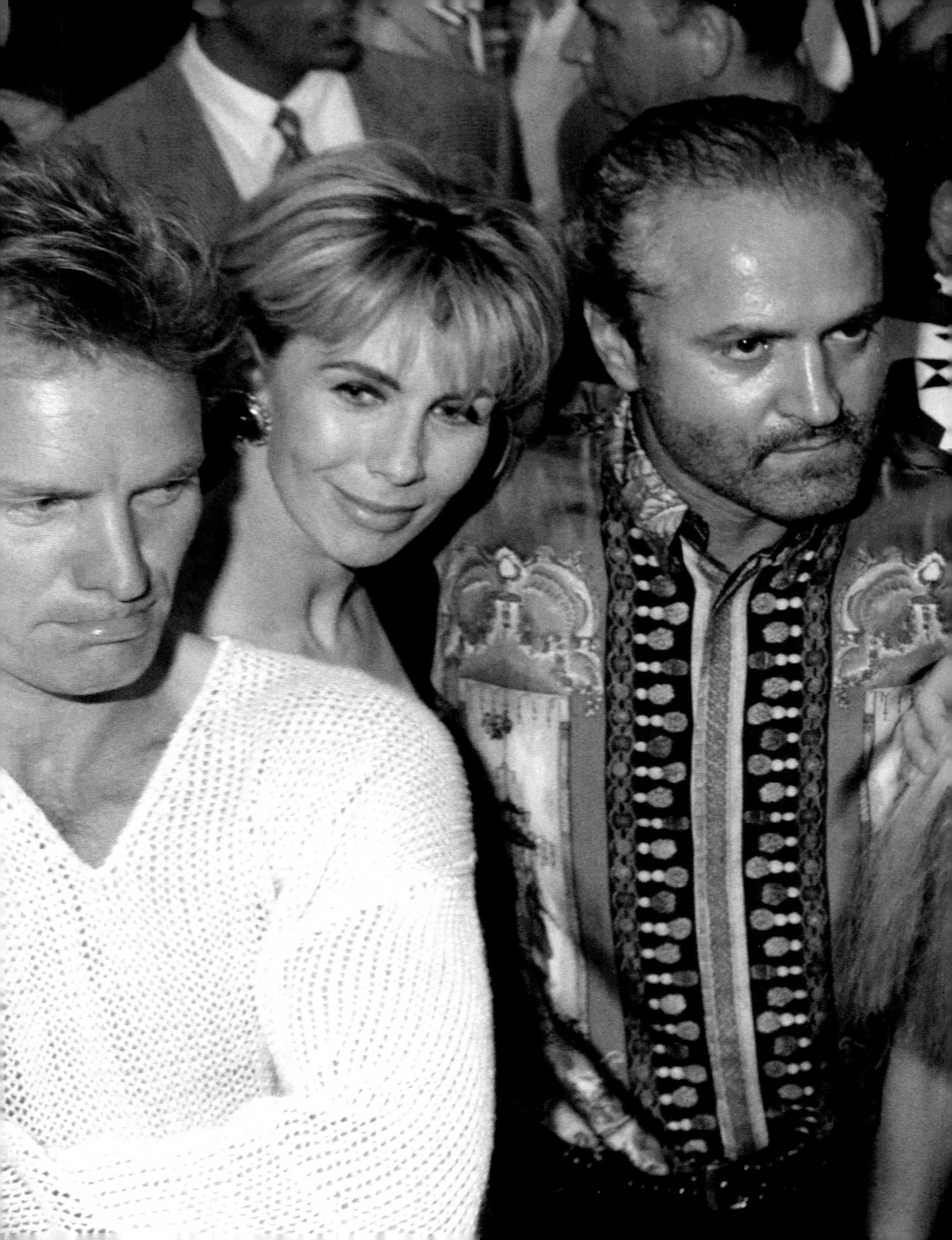

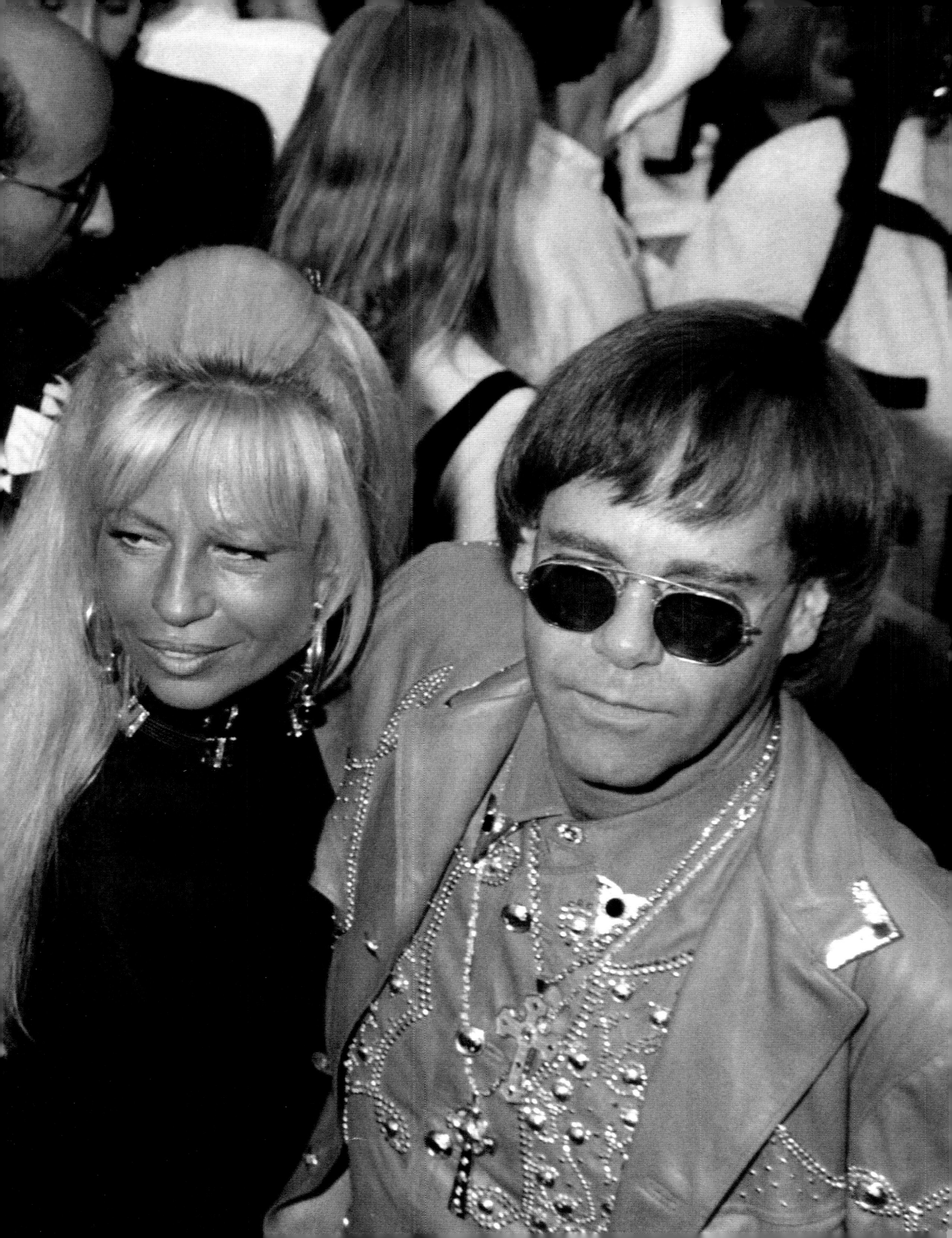

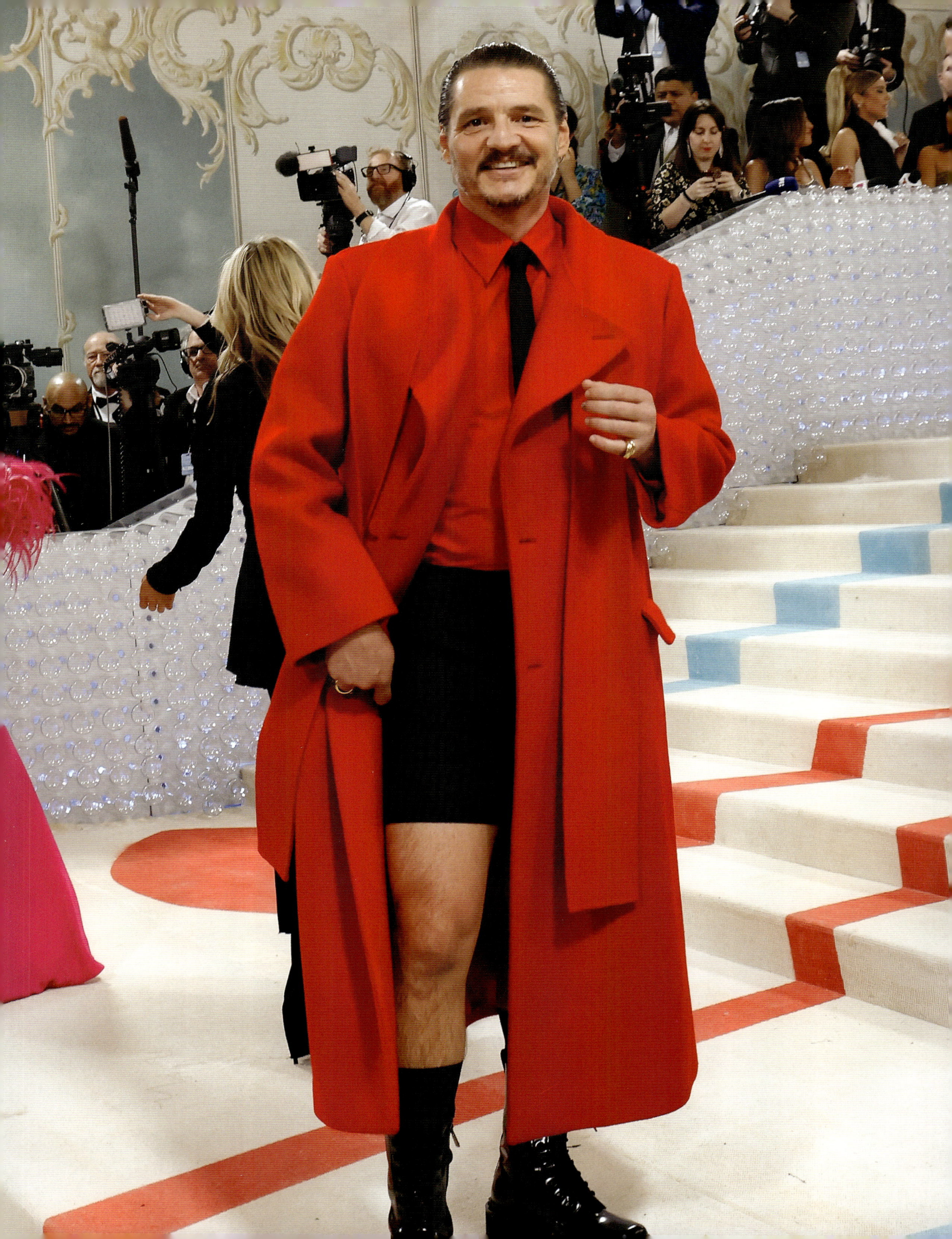

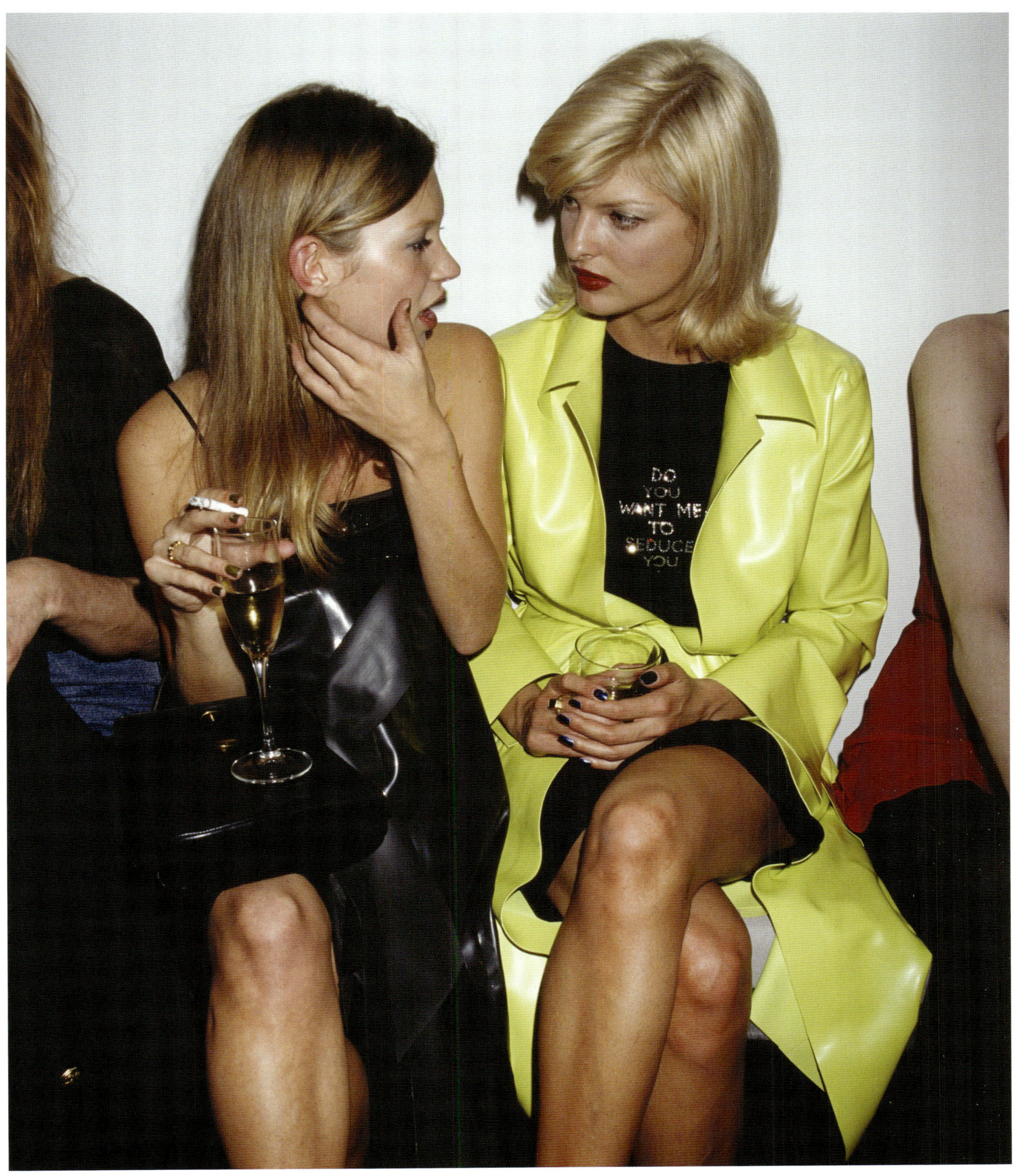

Previous pages: *Signature Versace baroque prints and a studded-leather suit outshine Sting and Elton John at Gianni Versace and Donatella Versace's London boutique party, 1992.* Opposite: *Pedro Pascal's structured red jacket, lace-up boots, and shorts shake up men's semiformal dress codes at the Costume Institute's Met Gala, 2023.* This page: *Kate Moss and Linda Evangelista channel 1990s glam at a Soho loft party, New York, circa 1996.*

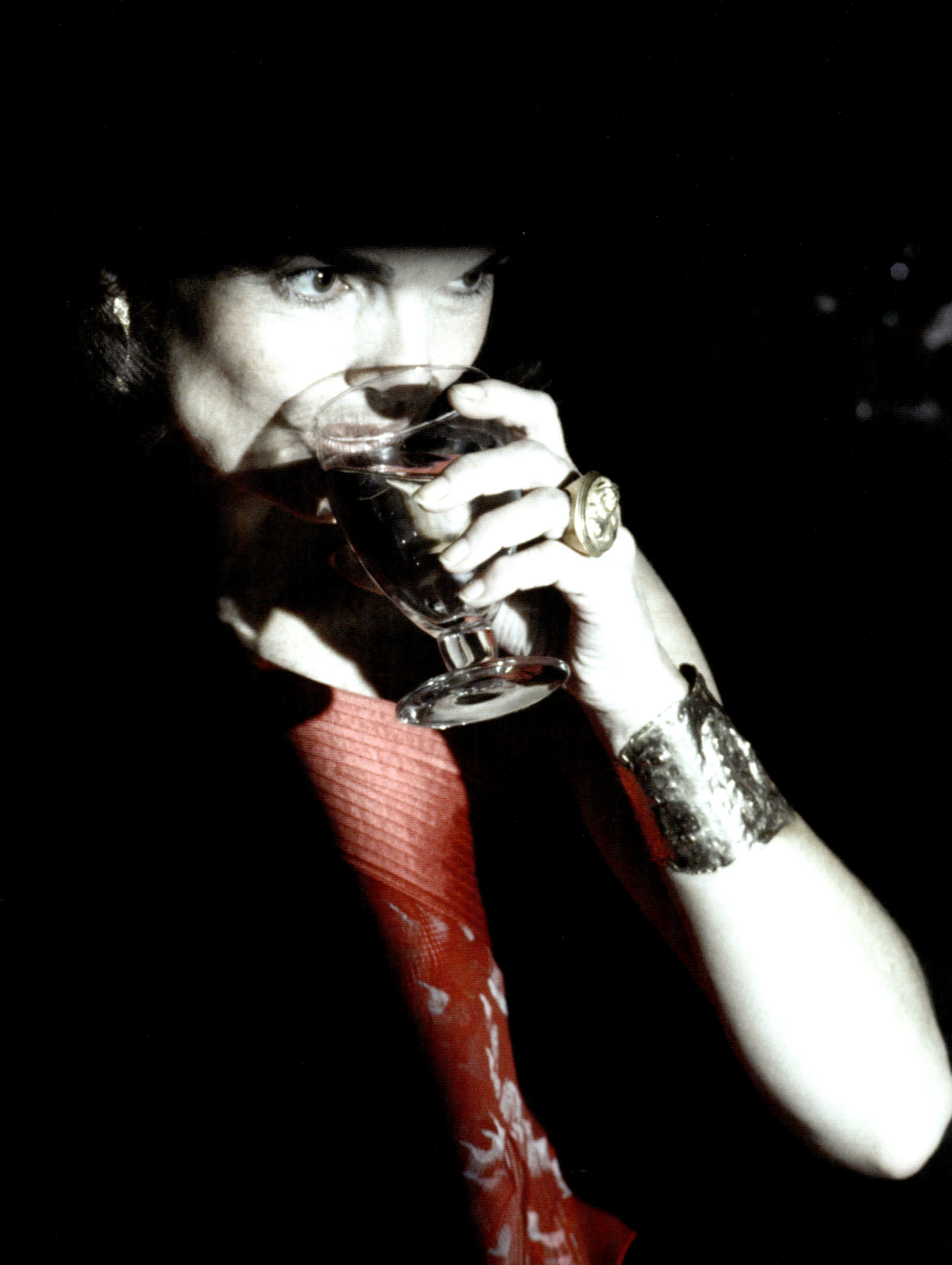

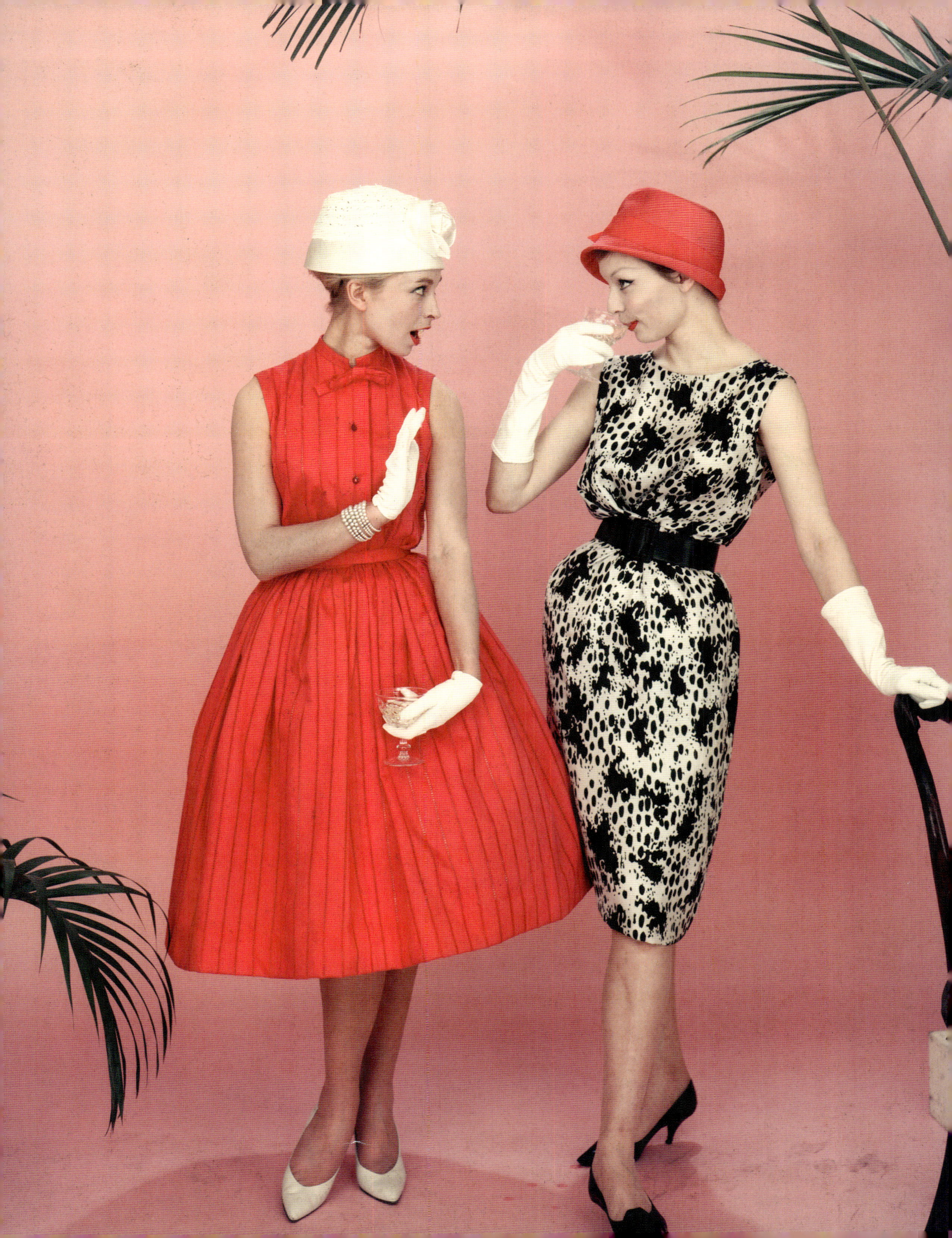

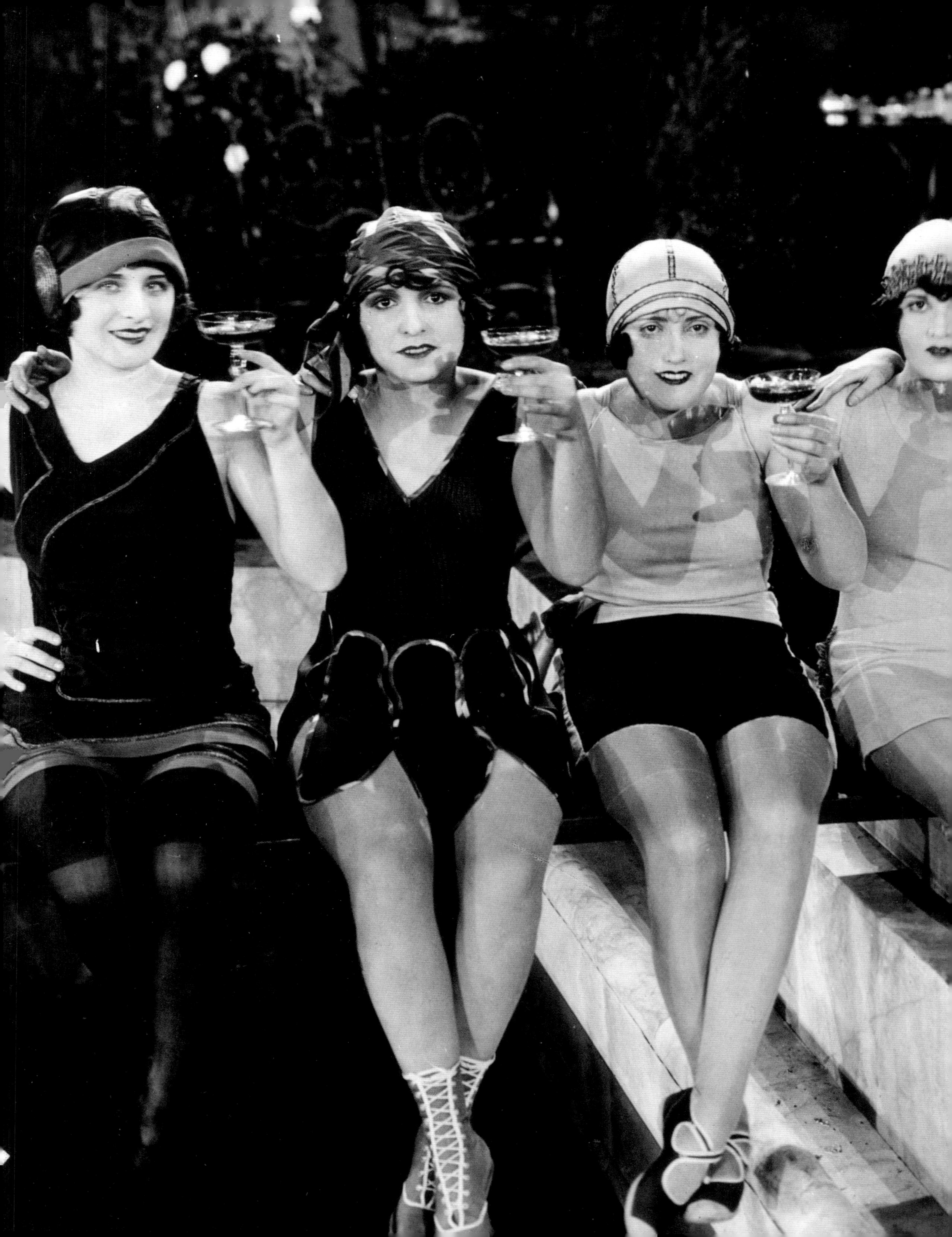

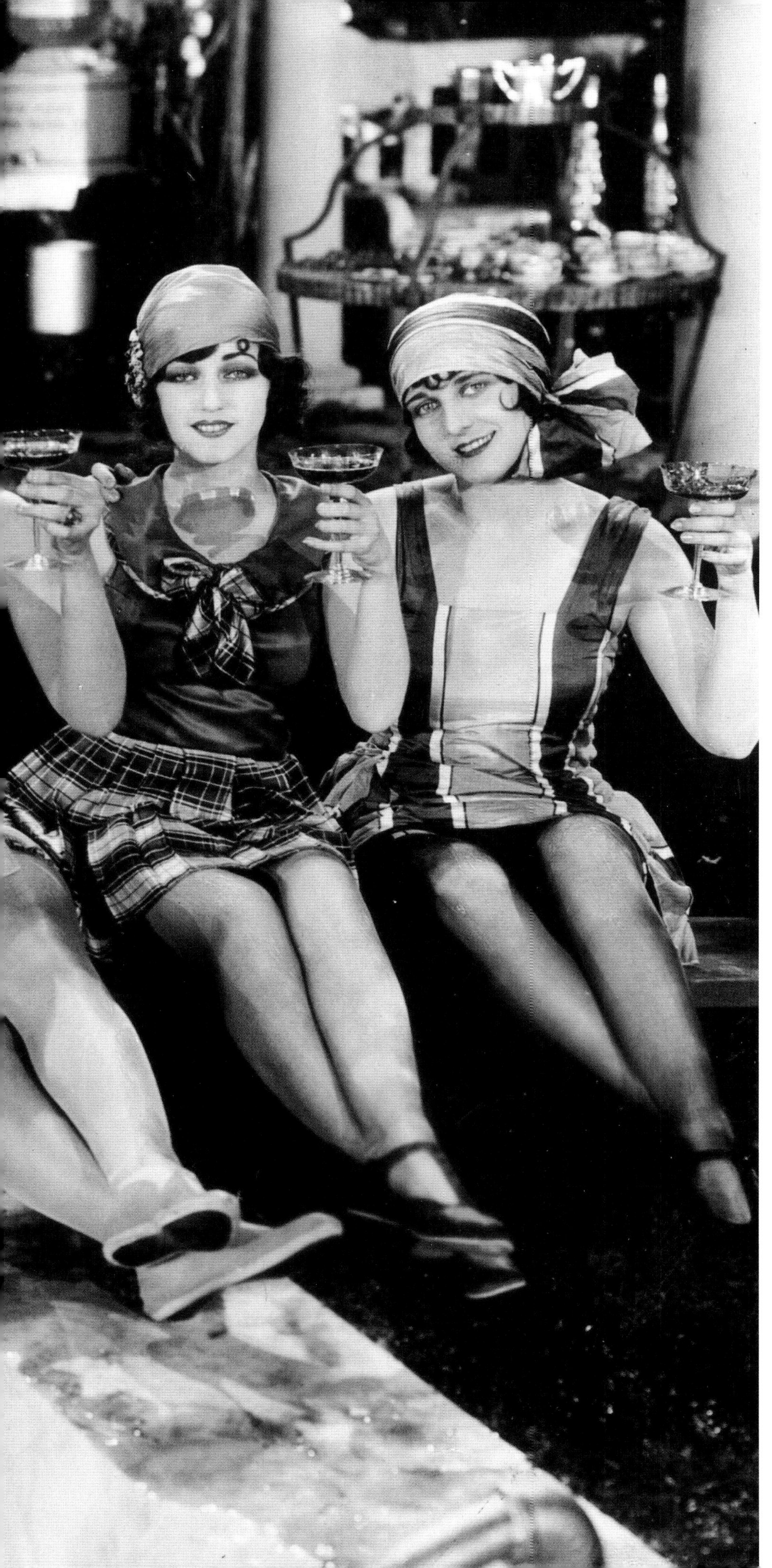

Previous pages, left: *Jacqueline Kennedy Onassis's silver cuff and cocktail ring steal the spotlight at the Met Opera, New York, 1976*; right: *Hats, kitten heels and stilettos, and gloves paired with festive frocks provide next-level cocktail hour flair, circa 1955.* Opposite: *Fashionable women of the Roaring 20s raise a glass to their liberating style: bobs, loose dresses, and a daring reveal of legs.*

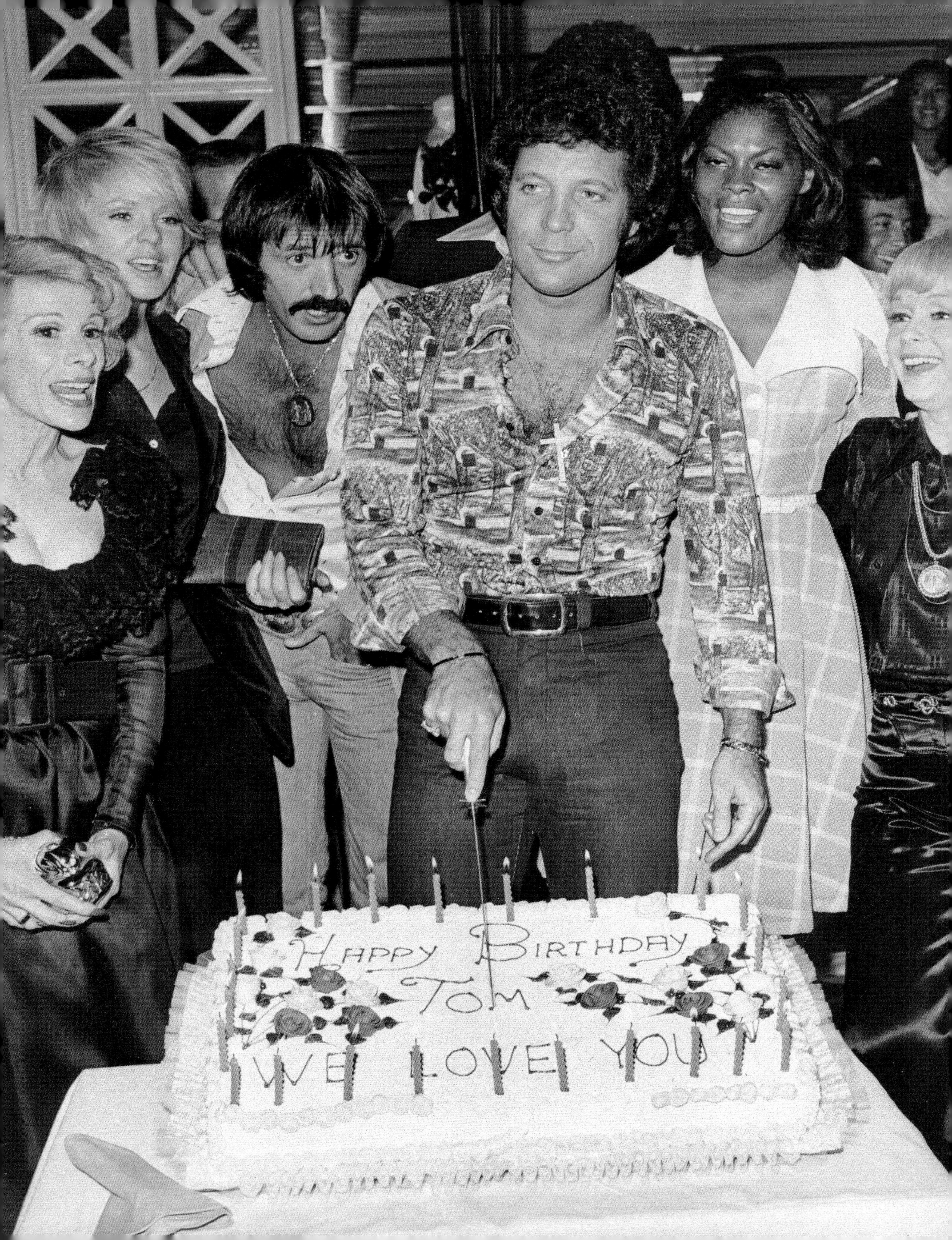
HAPPY BIRTHDAY
TOM
WE LOVE YOU

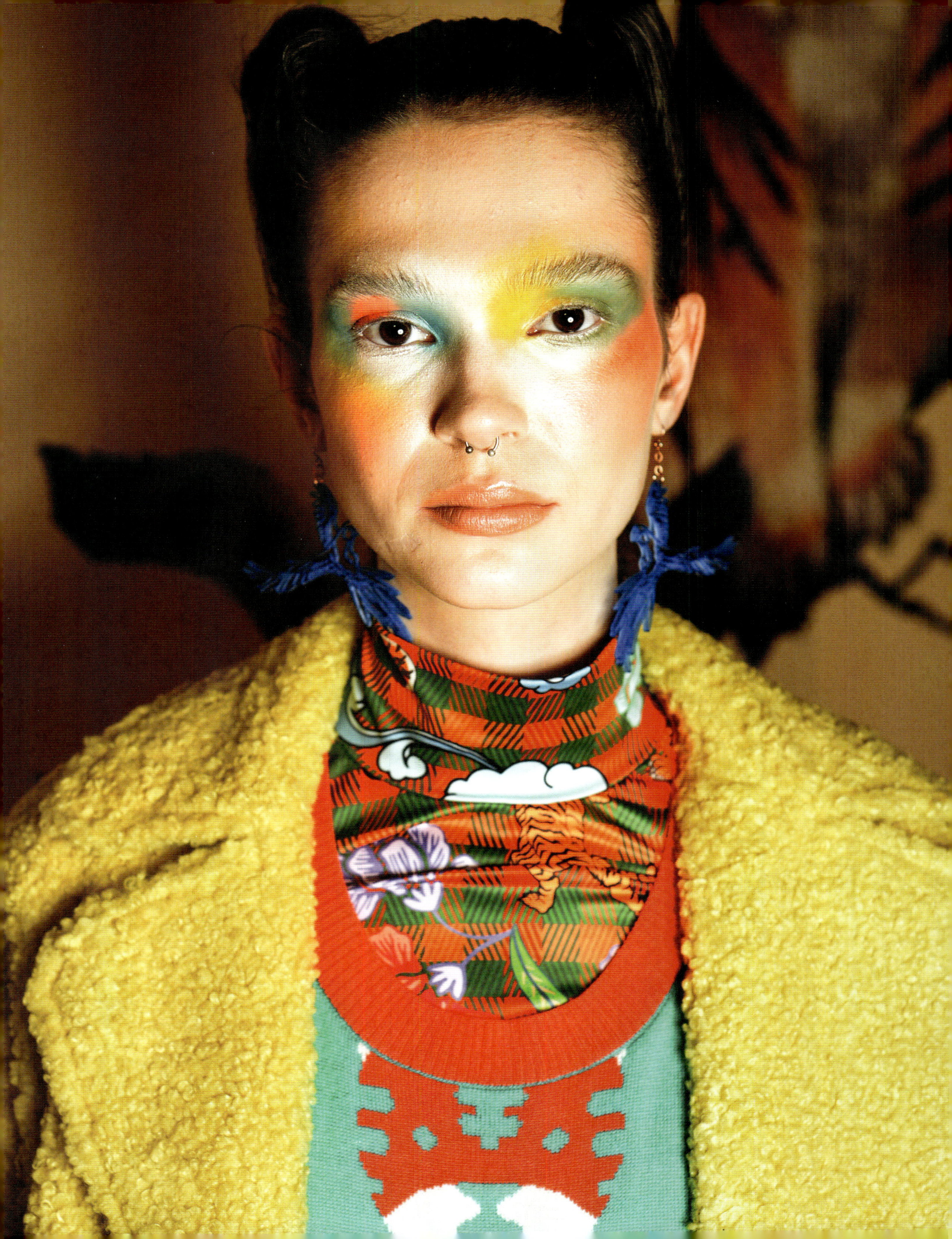

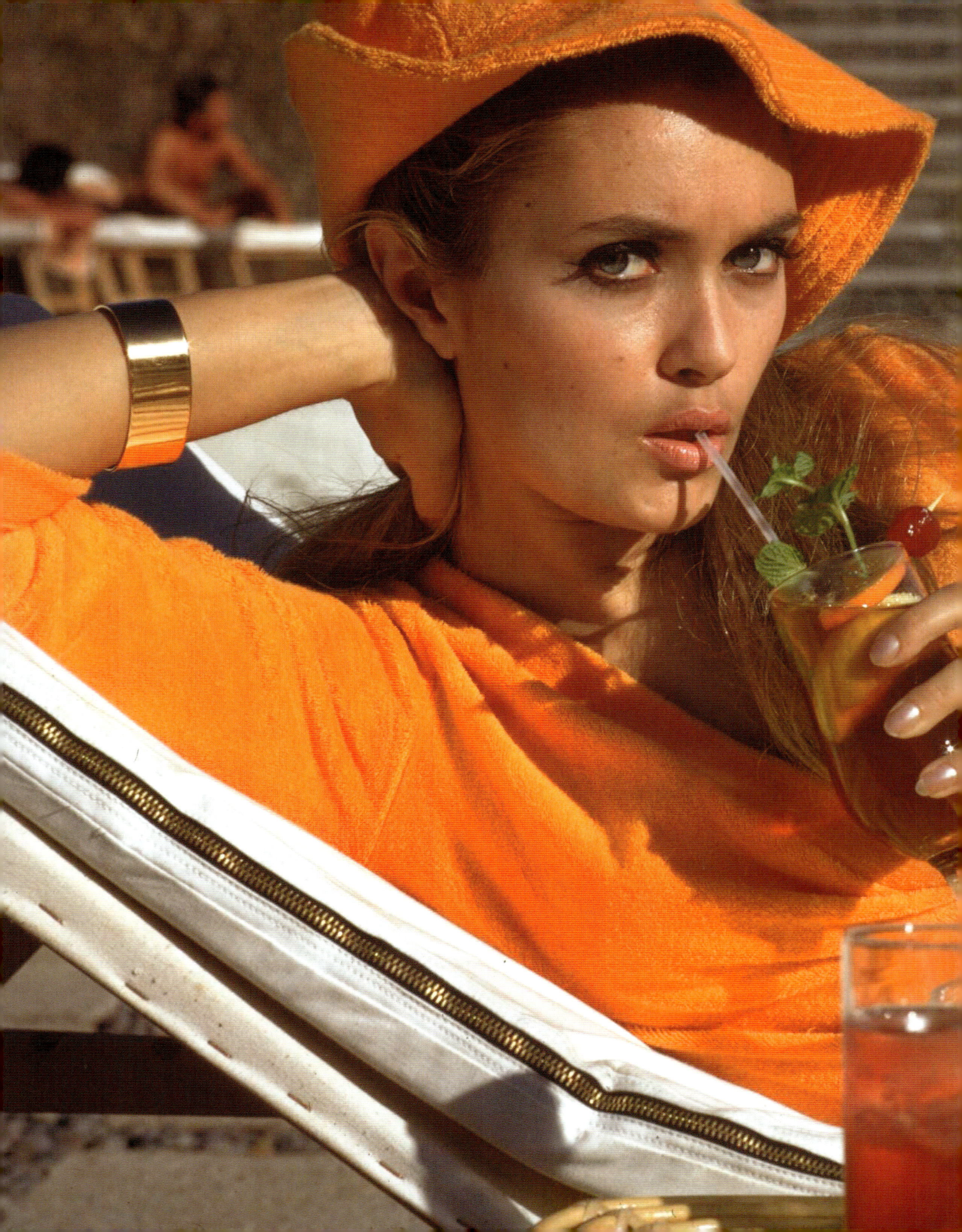

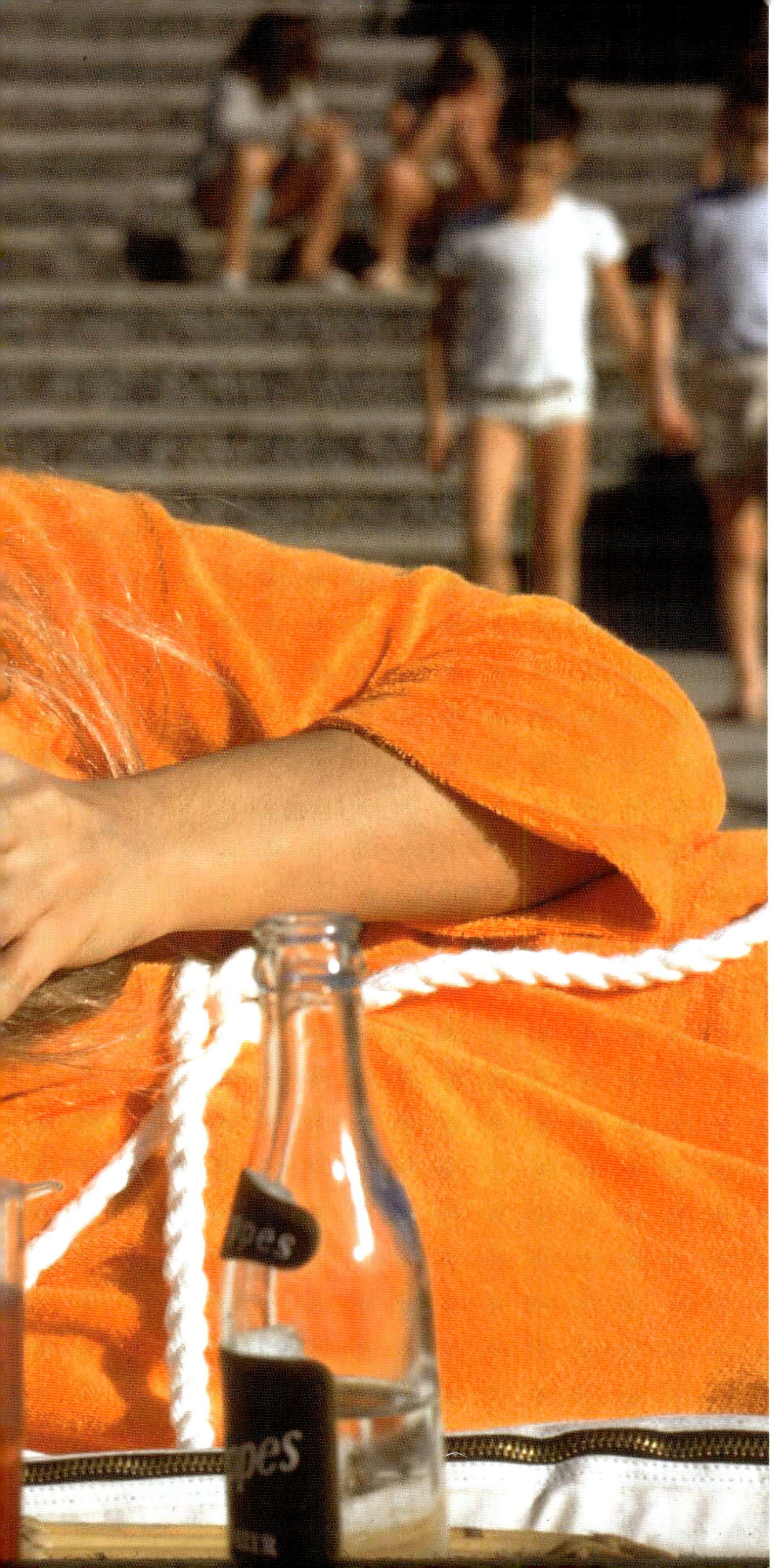

Previous pages, left: *A star-studded 2 a.m. party for singer Tom Jones is a showcase for men's peacock fashion, 1974*; right: *Bold color makes a sophisticated splash at a Hong Kong cocktail reception, 2019*. Opposite: *Lounging in Spain, actress and animal rights activist Alexandra Bastedo sips in relaxed style, 1969.*

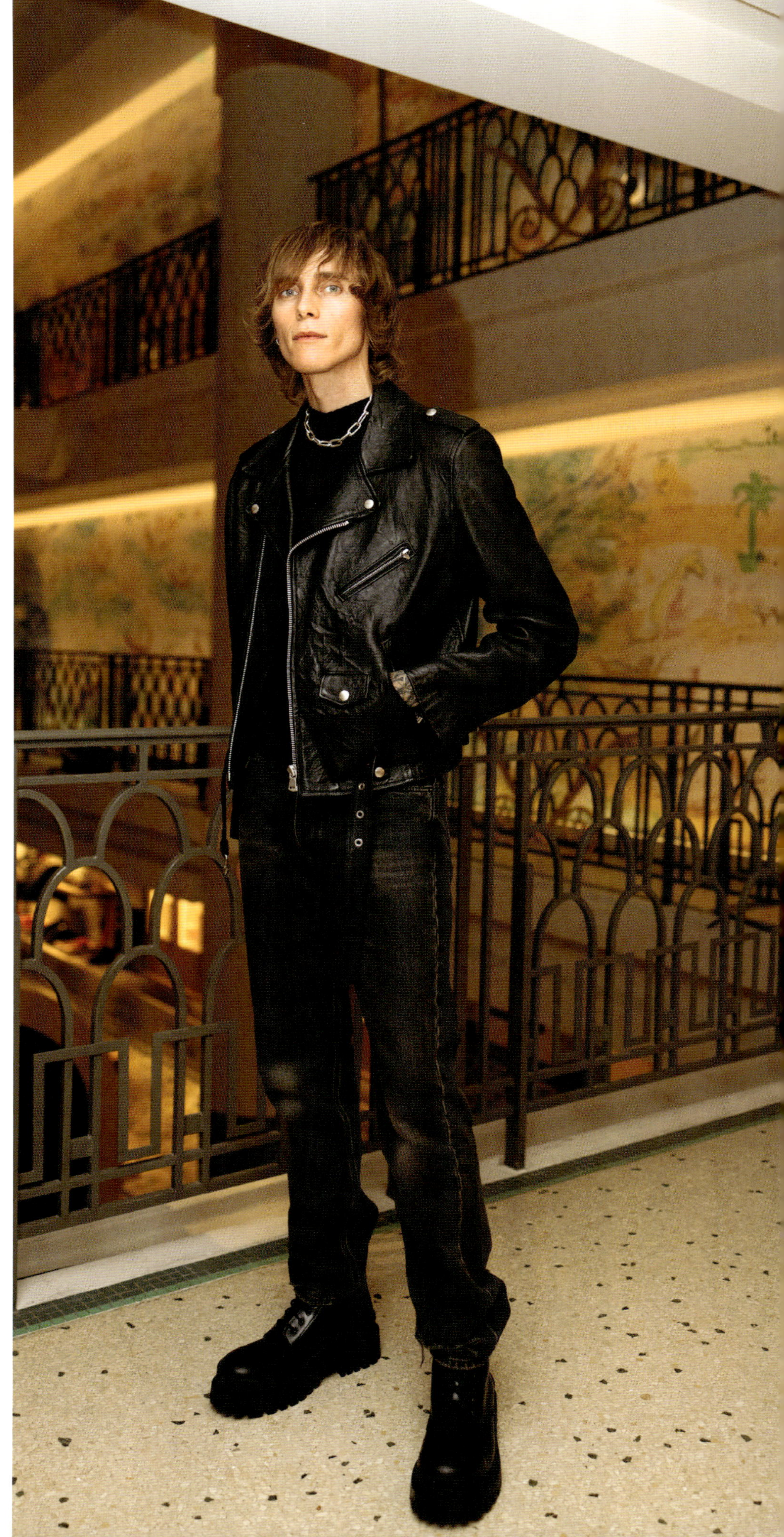

Clockwise from left: *Punk* á la *twenty-first-century minimalism rises to the occasion at a Paris Fashion Week party, 2021; Flowing satin dresses in vibrant floral hues on a veranda*—na última moda *during cocktail hour in tropical Brazil, 1985; Fur-trimmed coats add an aristocratic* je ne sais quoi *to women judging a cocktail contest in France, 1929.*

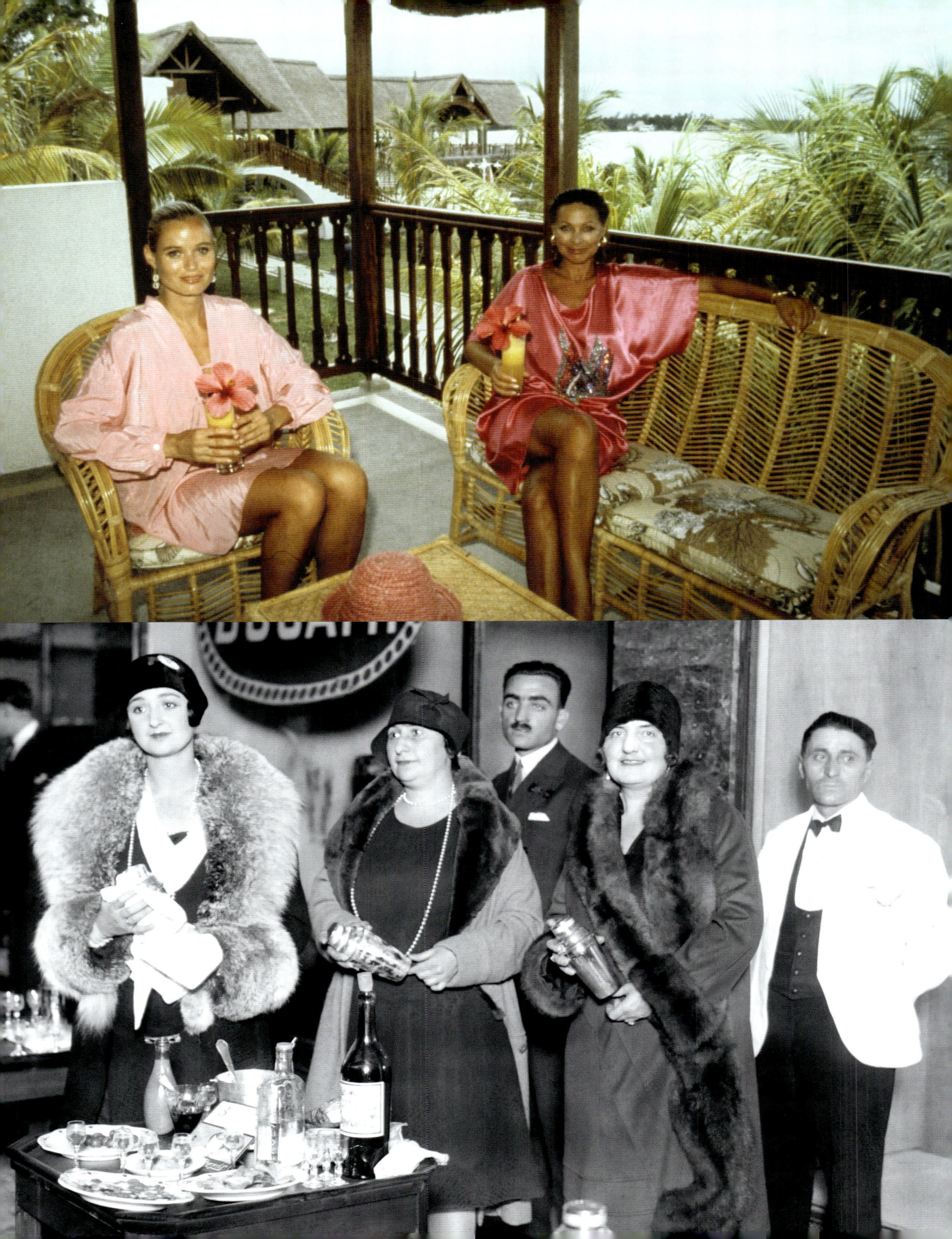

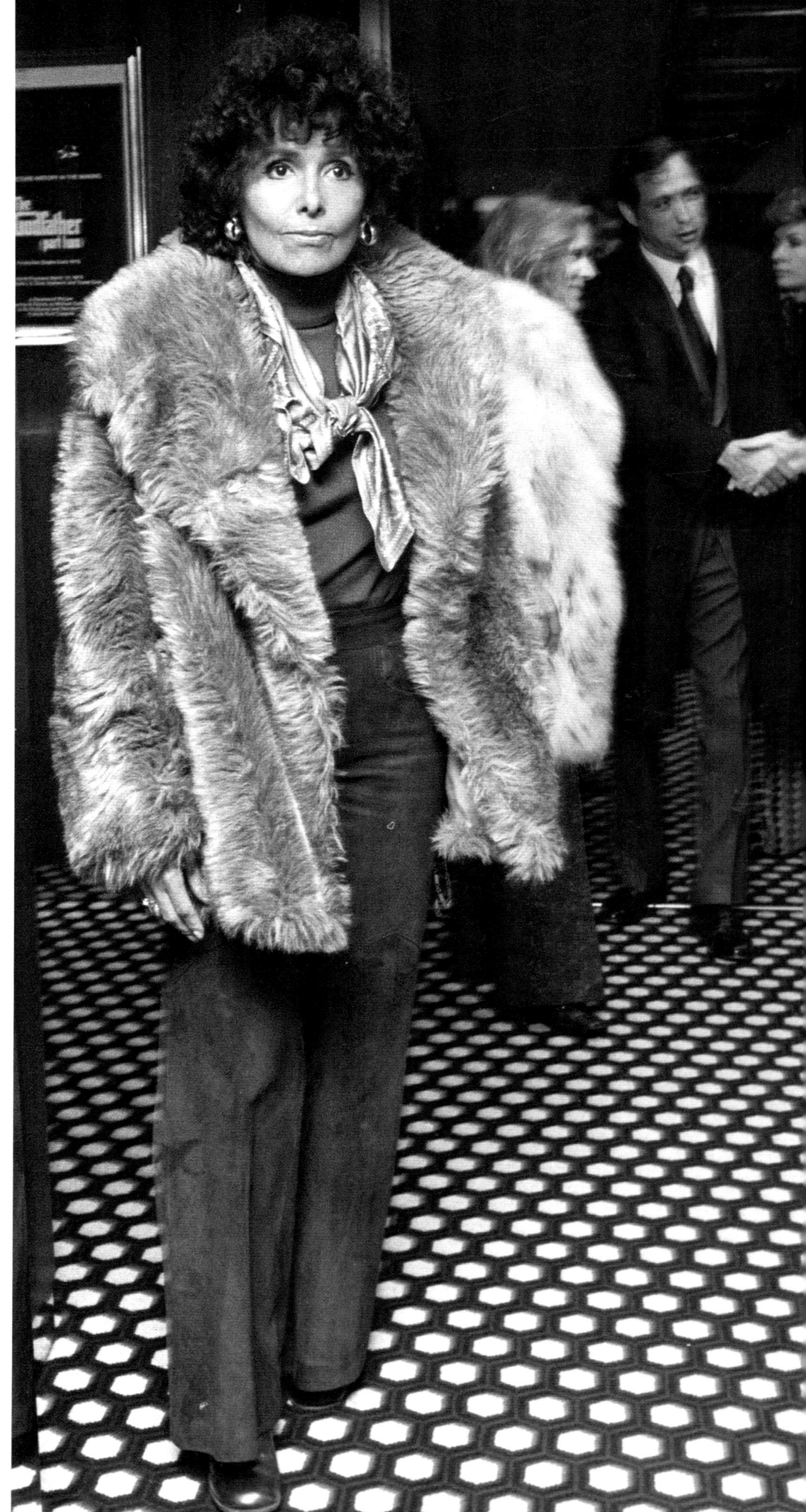

Clockwise from left: *The indomitable Lena Horne makes her entrance in a fur coat over purple suede pants and sweater, 1973; Ingrid Bergman adjusts an earring, a snowy-white fur stole draped over her shoulders, Cannes Film Festival, 1956; Hollywood royalty Clark Gable, Van Heflin, Gary Cooper, and James Stewart laugh it up in white tie at a New Year's party held at Romanoff's in Beverly Hills, 1957.* Following pages: *Slinky dresses, pantsuits that hug every curve, flared pants, and leisure suits fuel 1970s disco fever.*

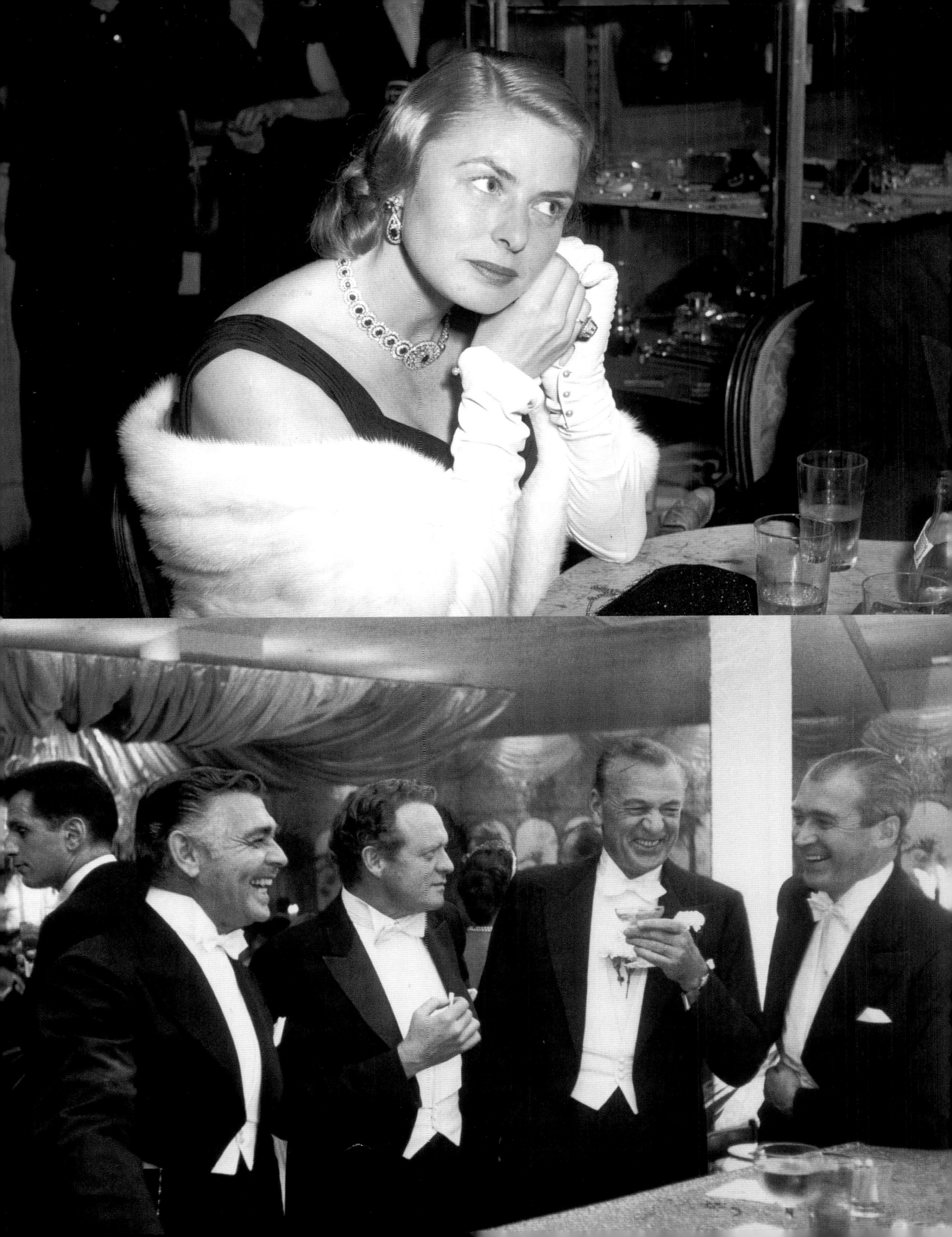

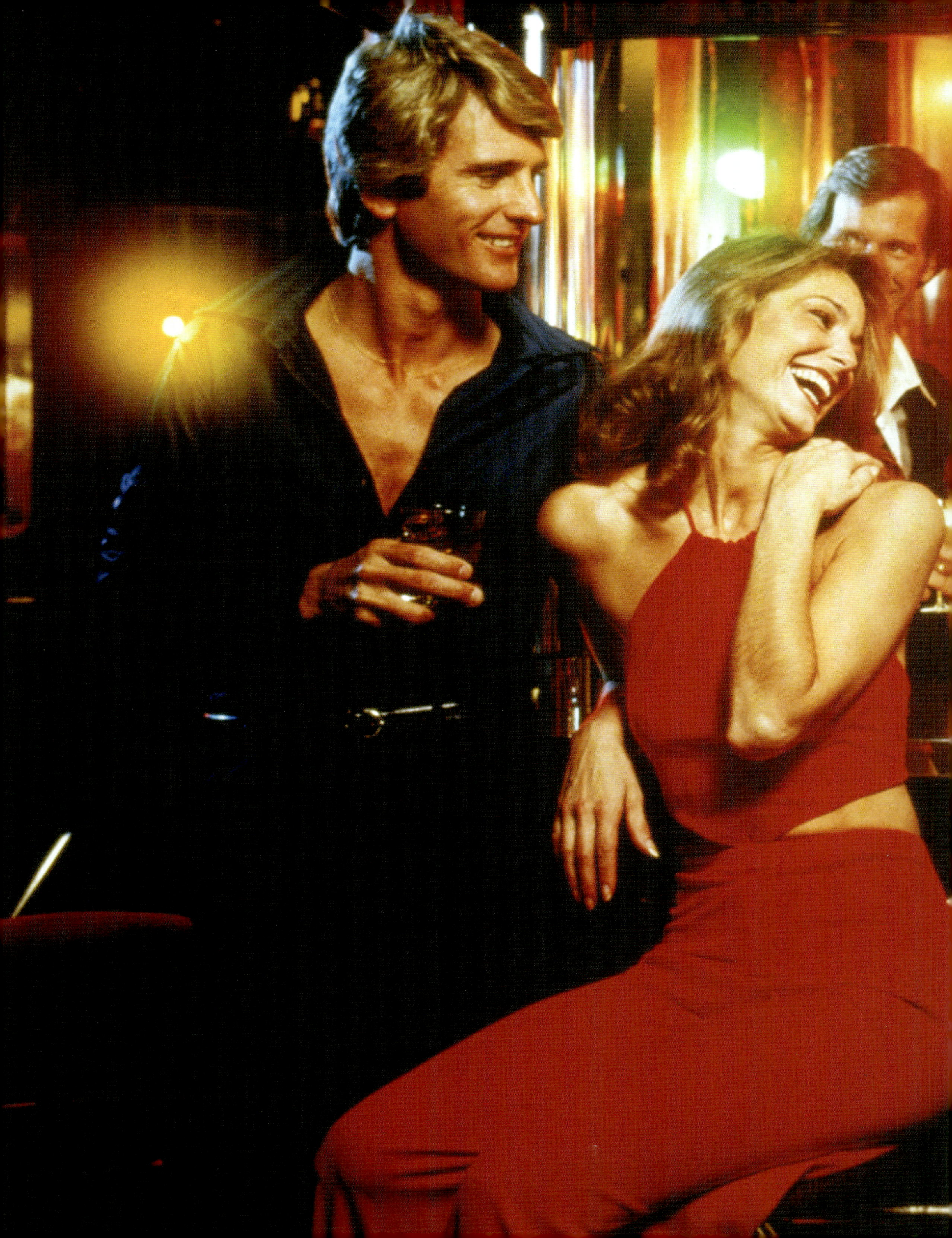

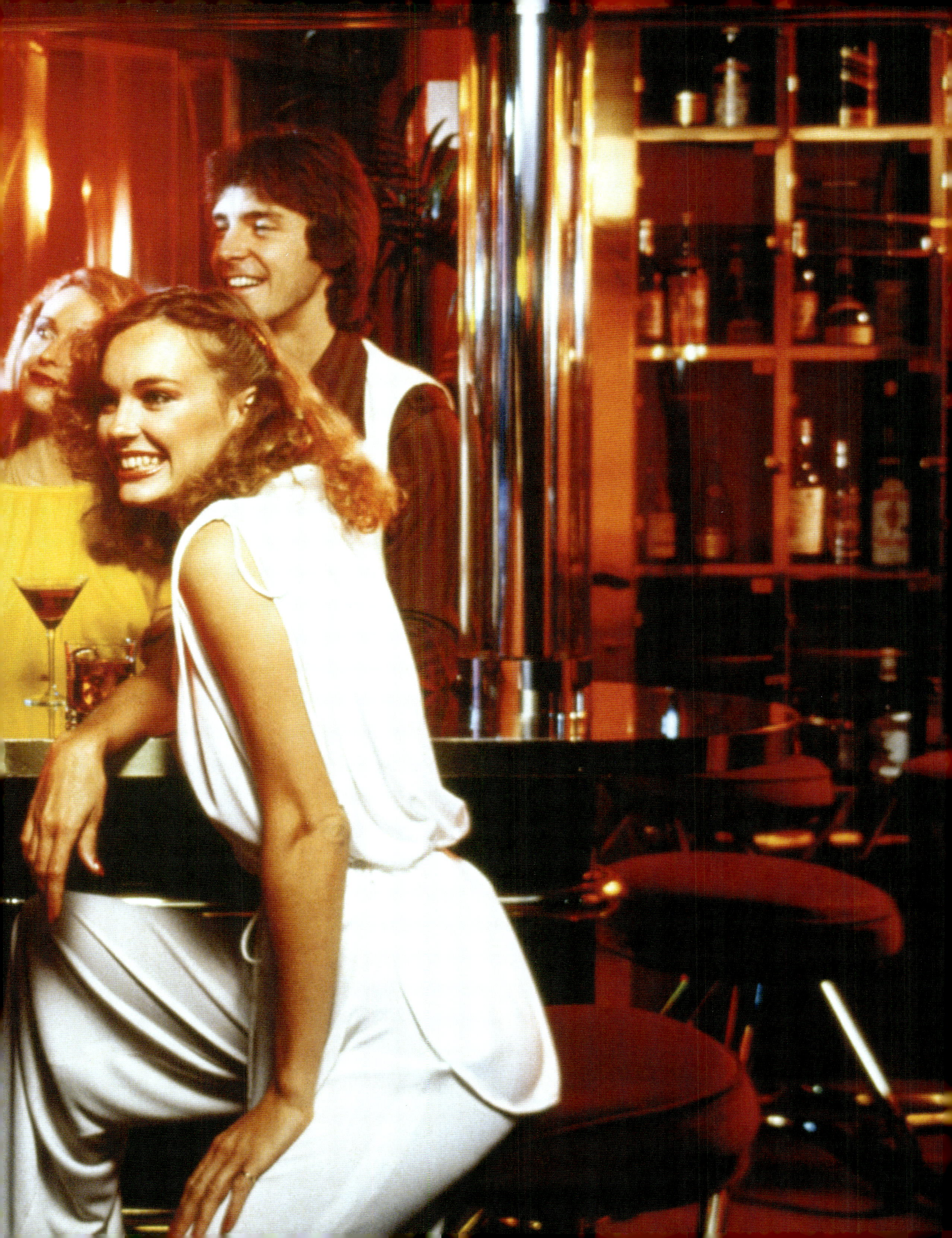

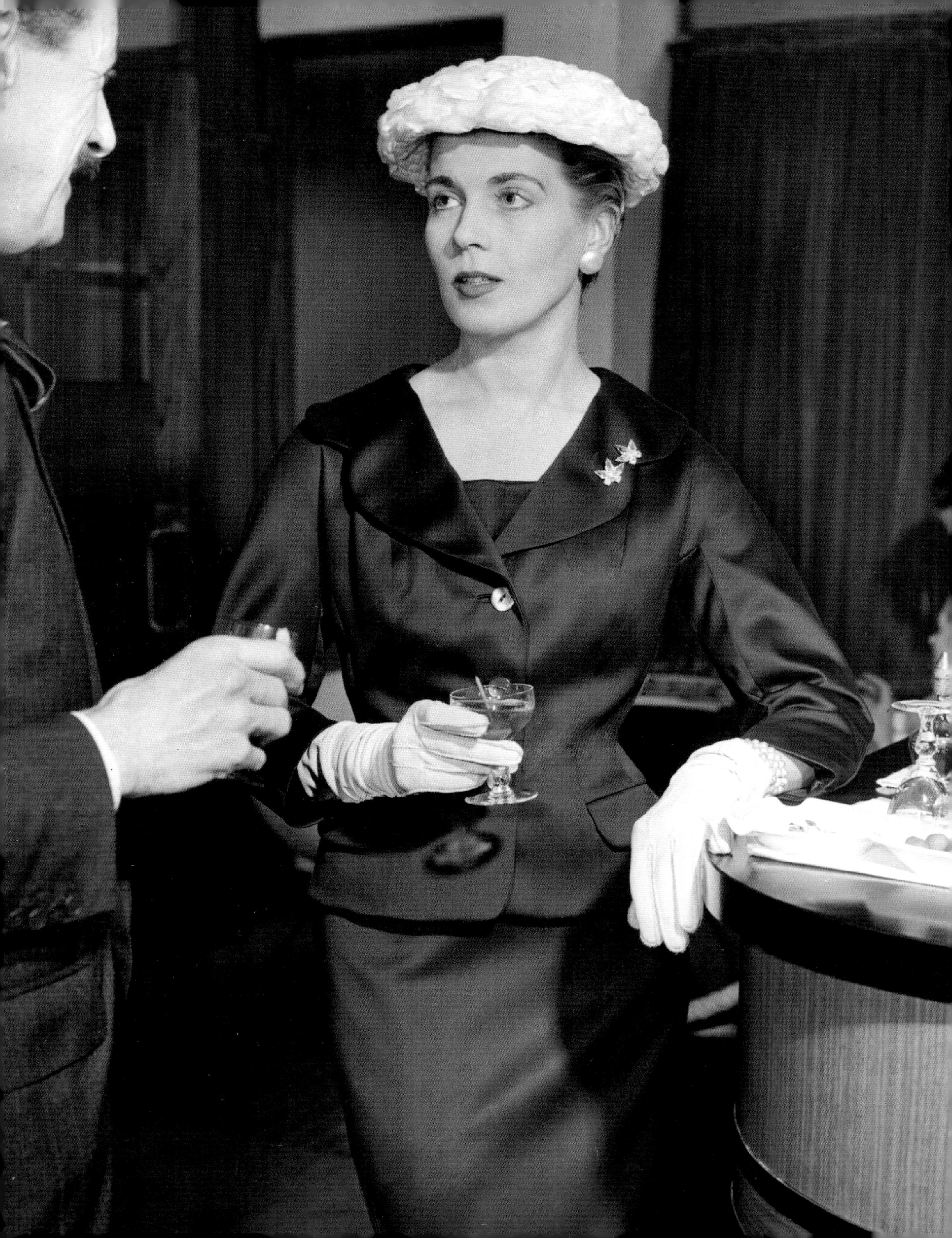

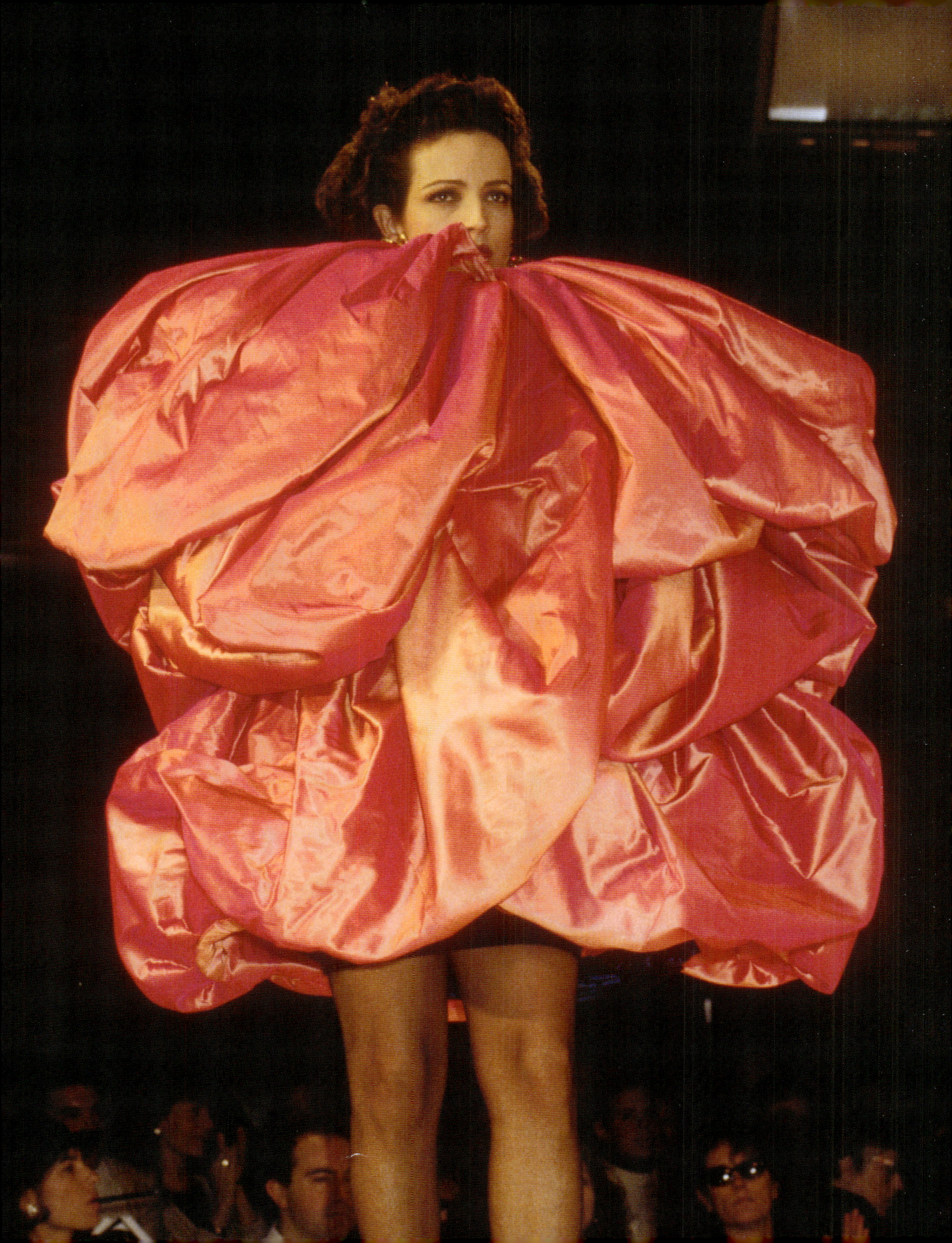

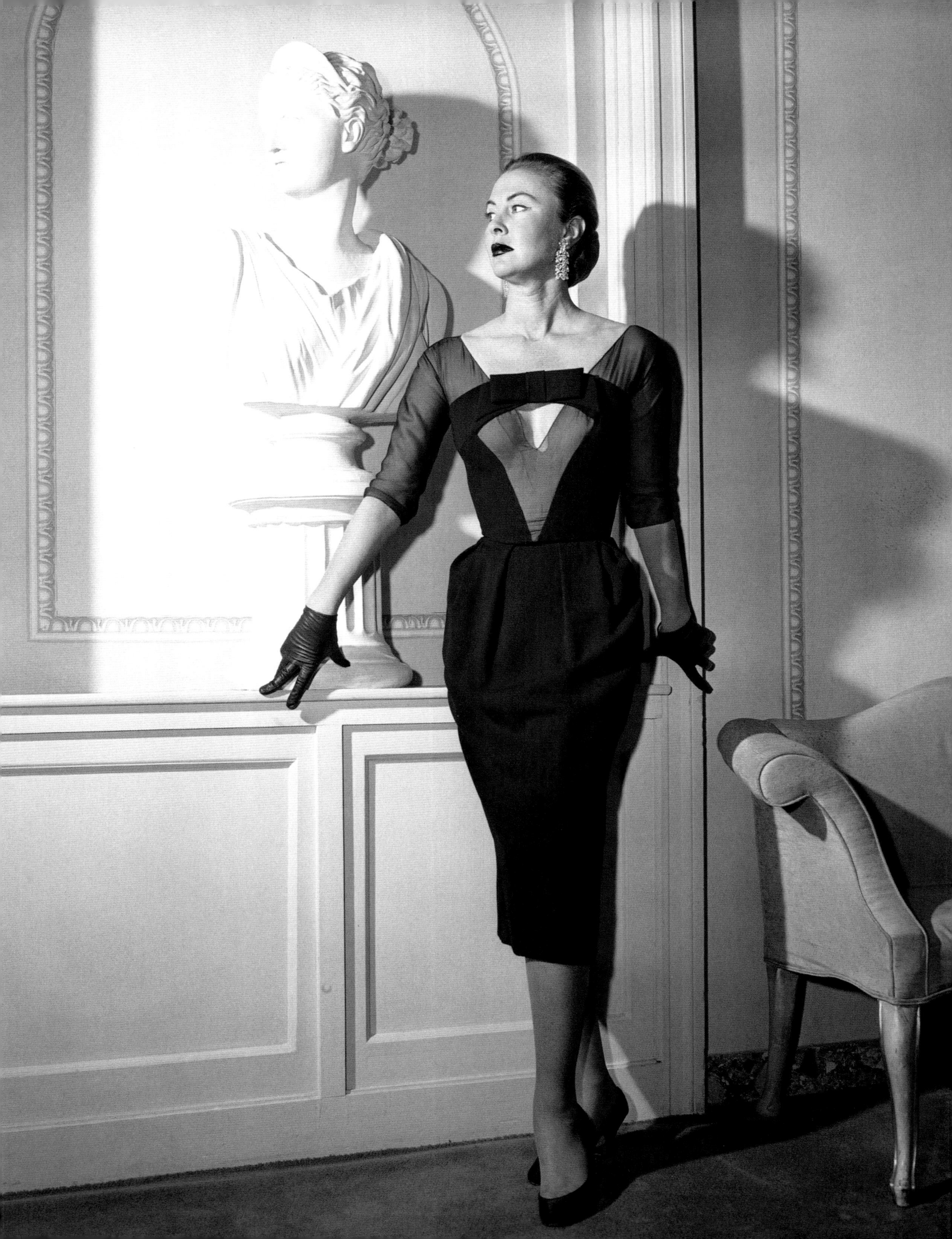

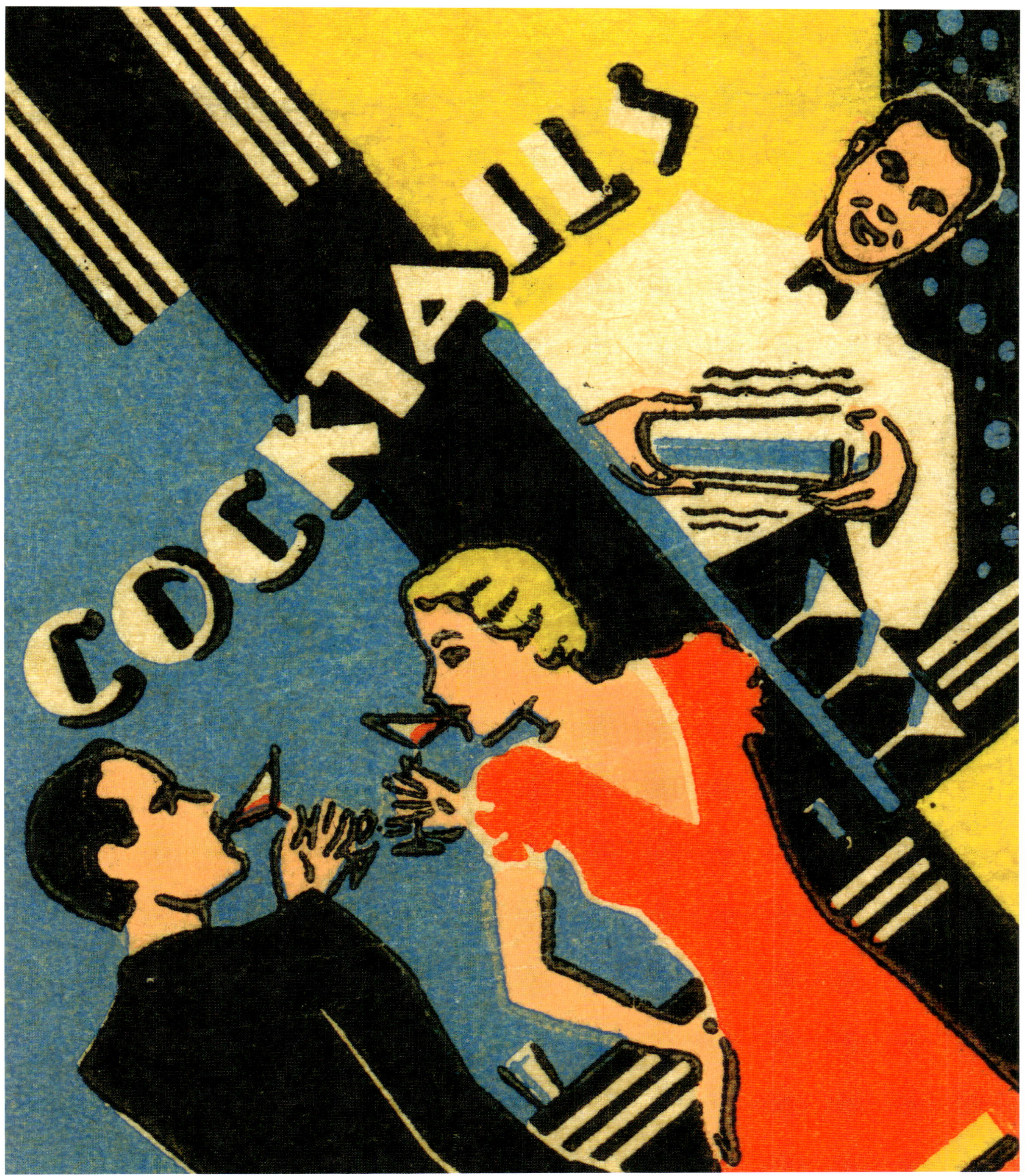

Previous pages, left: *A genteel white cap and gloves complement a satin fitted jacket and dress, 1957*; right: *Emanuel Ungaro's exuberant cocktail dress channels a more-is-more aesthetic, 1989.* Opposite: *Oleg Cassini serves up classic cocktail-hour style in a crepe sheath and chiffon with plunging neckline, 1958.* This page: *A circa-1930 matchbook portrays a fashionable night out, courtesy of a dapper bartender and his shaker.*

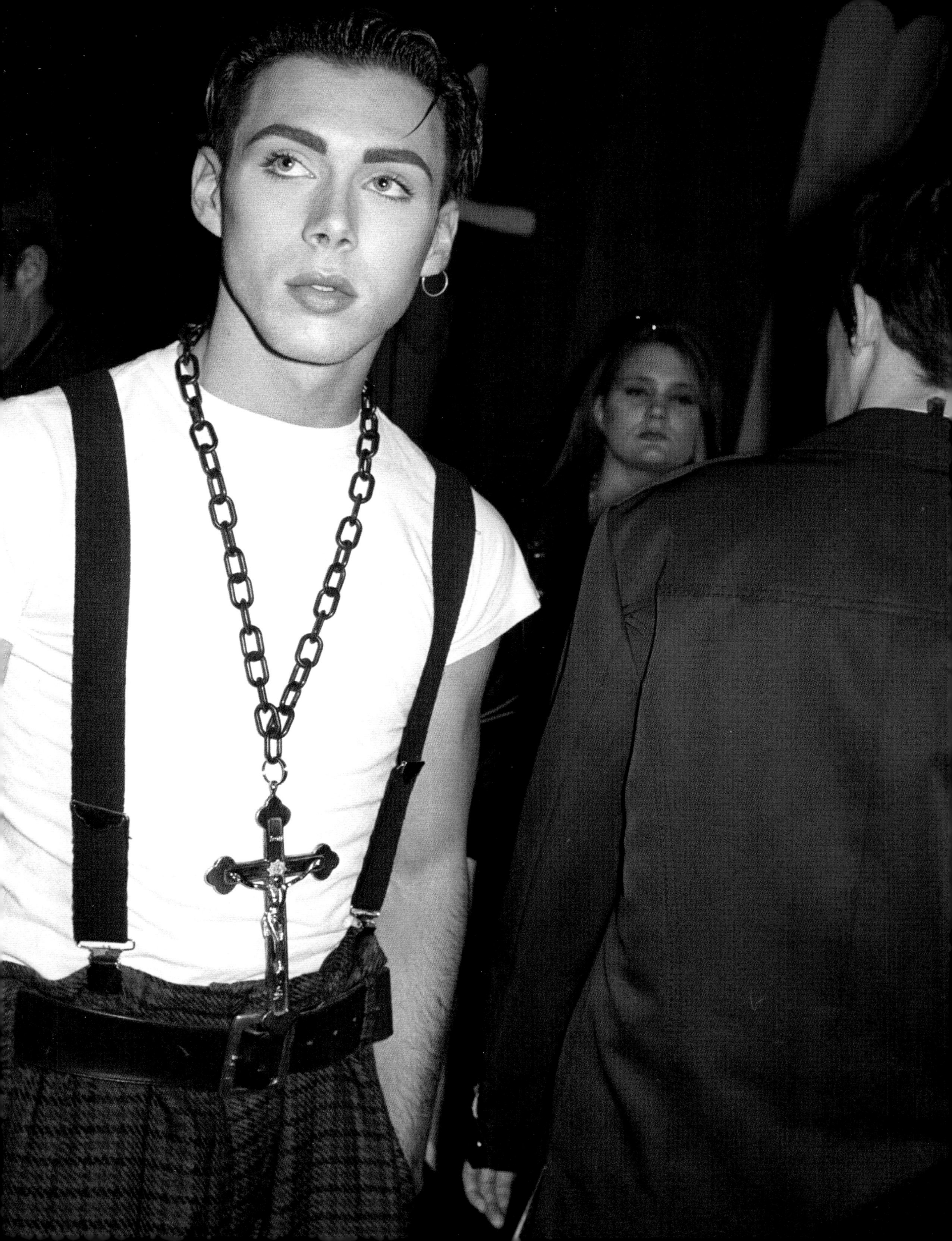

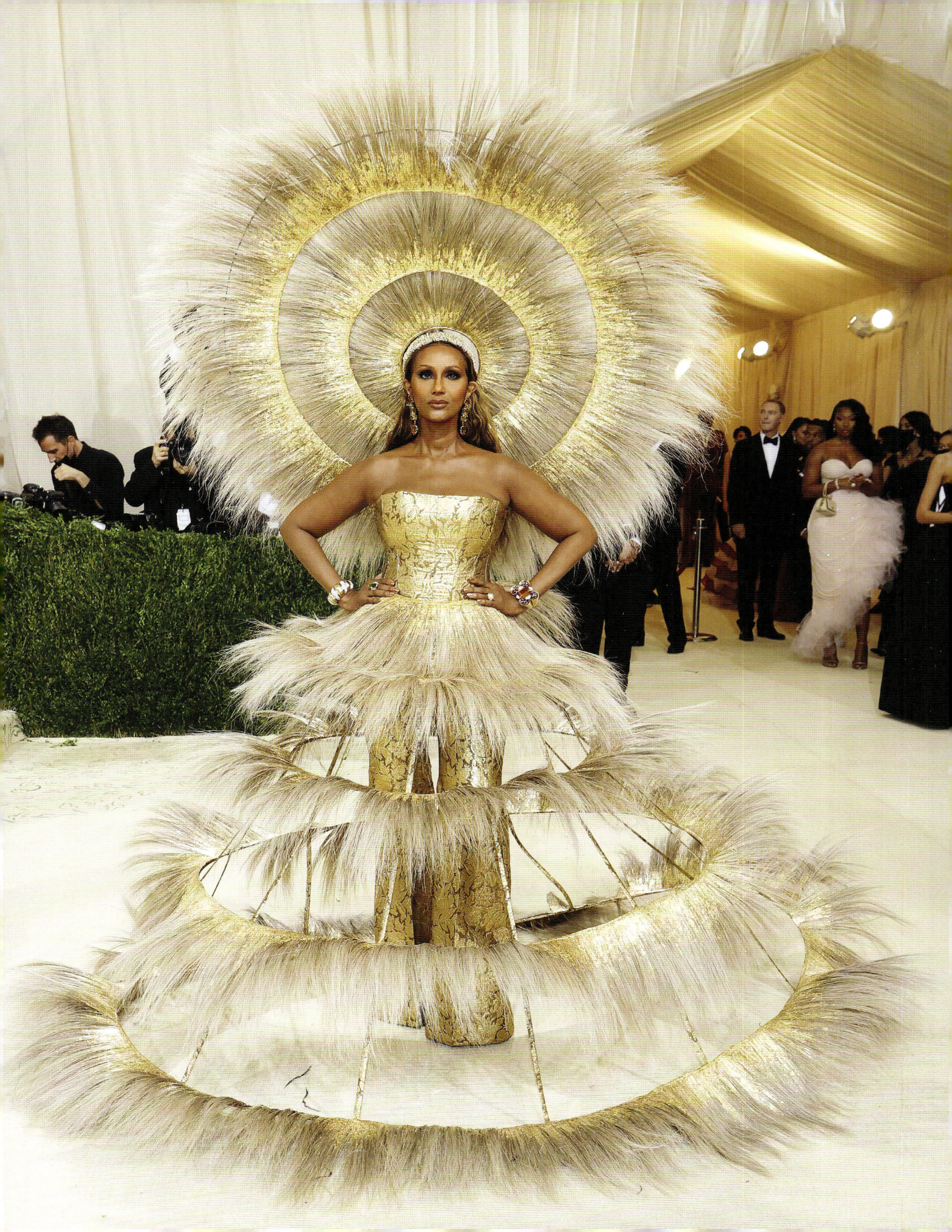

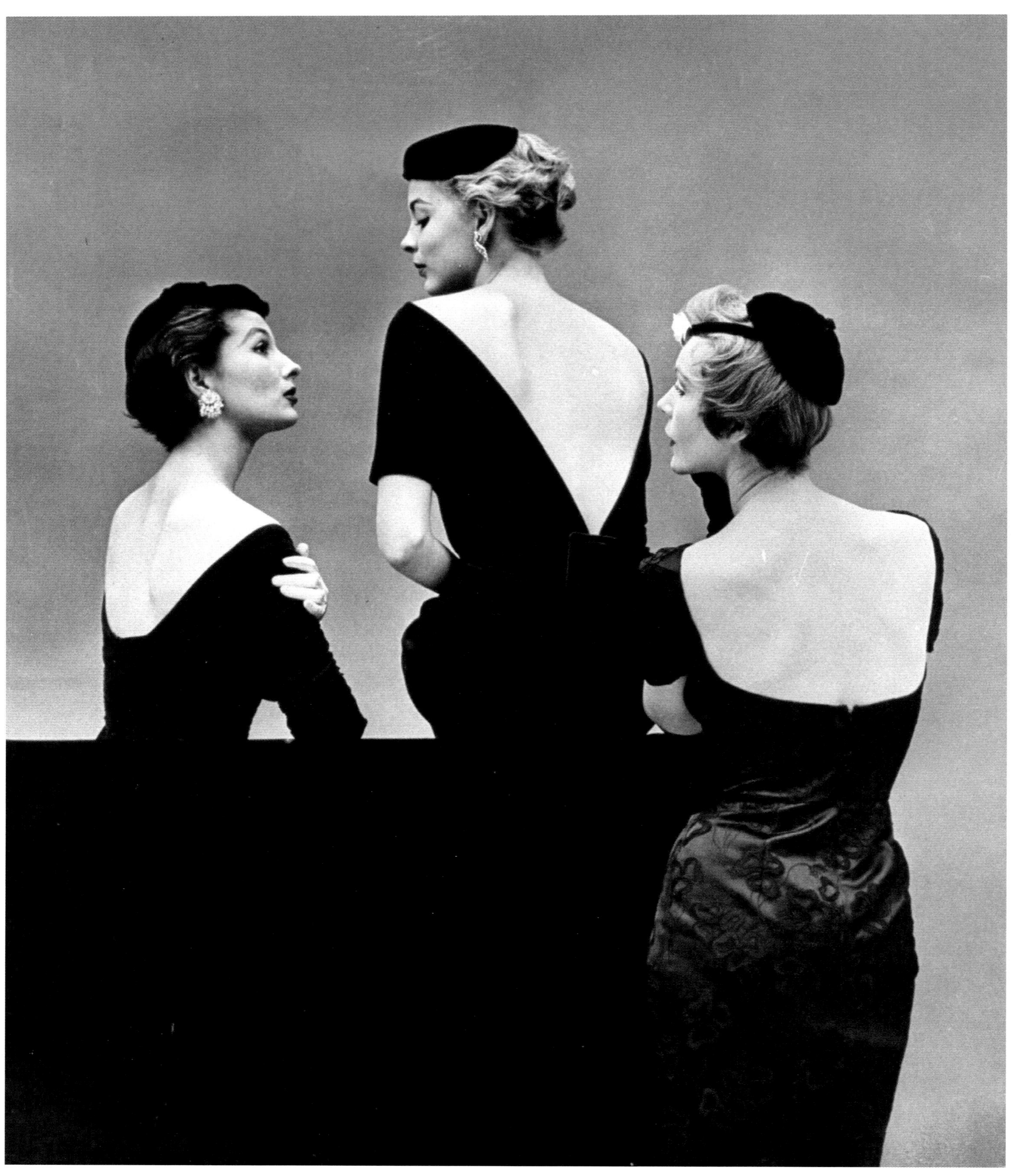

Previous pages, left: *A 1992 New York partygoer rocks the status quo with androgynous flair*; right: *In a tiered, gilded feather cage overskirt and matching headpiece, supermodel Iman takes cocktail couture to otherworldly heights at the Costume Institute's Met Gala, 2021.* This page: *Three backless gowns from 1953 embody the allure of the "little black dress."* Opposite: *A silk cocktail dress by courtier Jacques Griffe has a detachable cape for a dramatic entrance, 1956.*

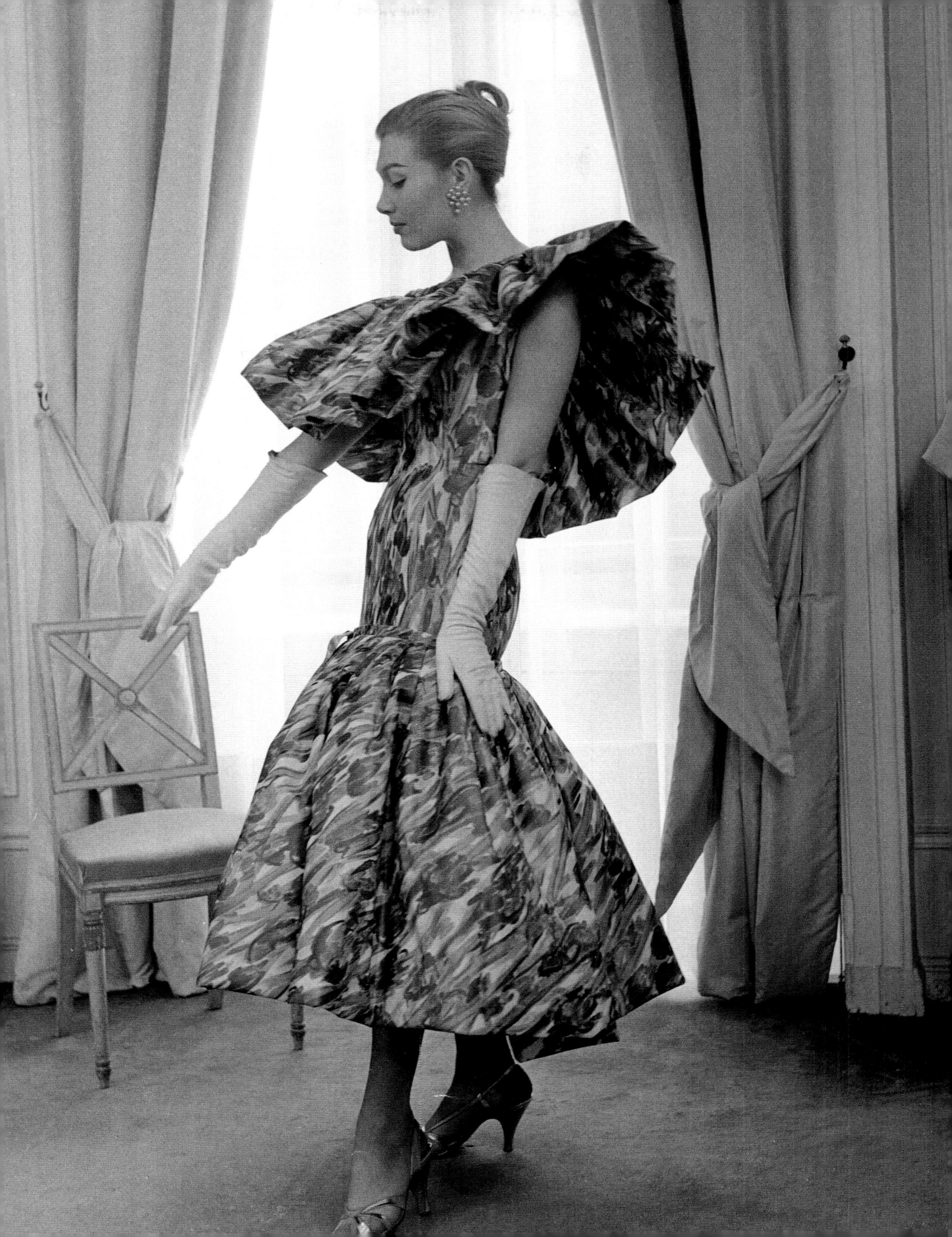

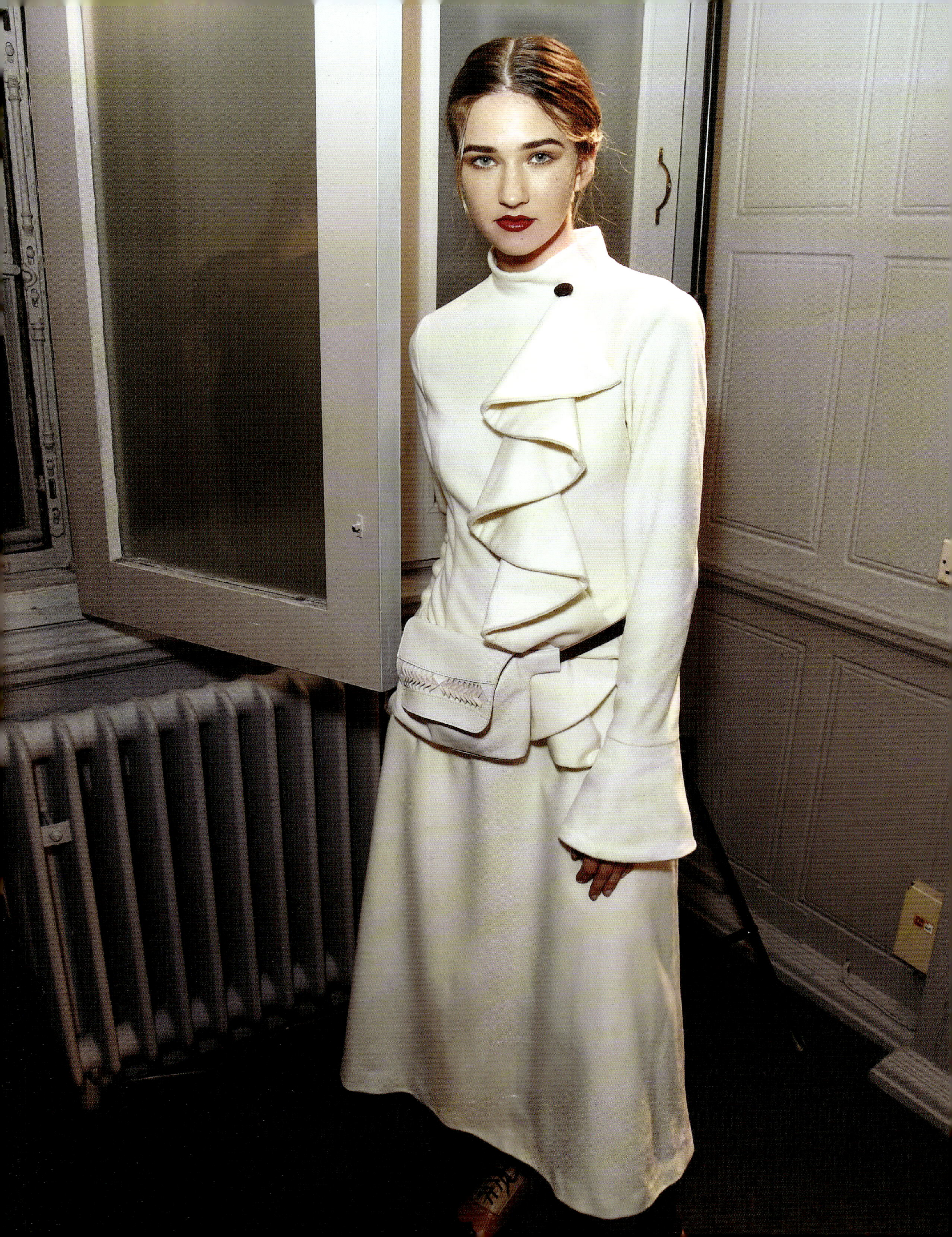

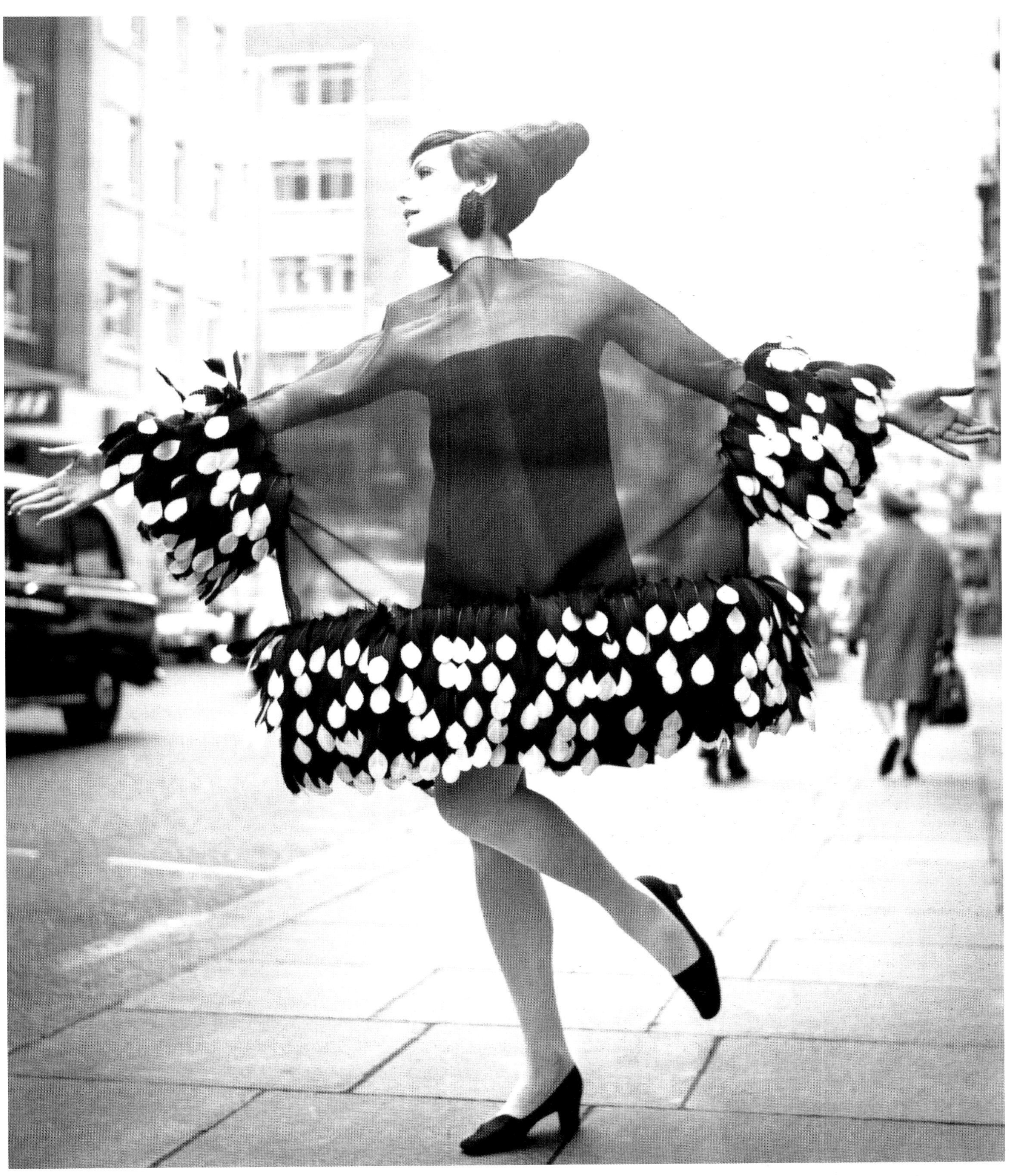

Opposite: *Designer Doris Kath's contemporary twist on a romantic era elevates the modern cocktail scene, London Fashion Week, 2019.*
This page: *With a cocktail dress and feather-trimmed sheer organza cape, Marc Bohan for Christian Dior wittily blends elegance with carefree charm, 1967.*

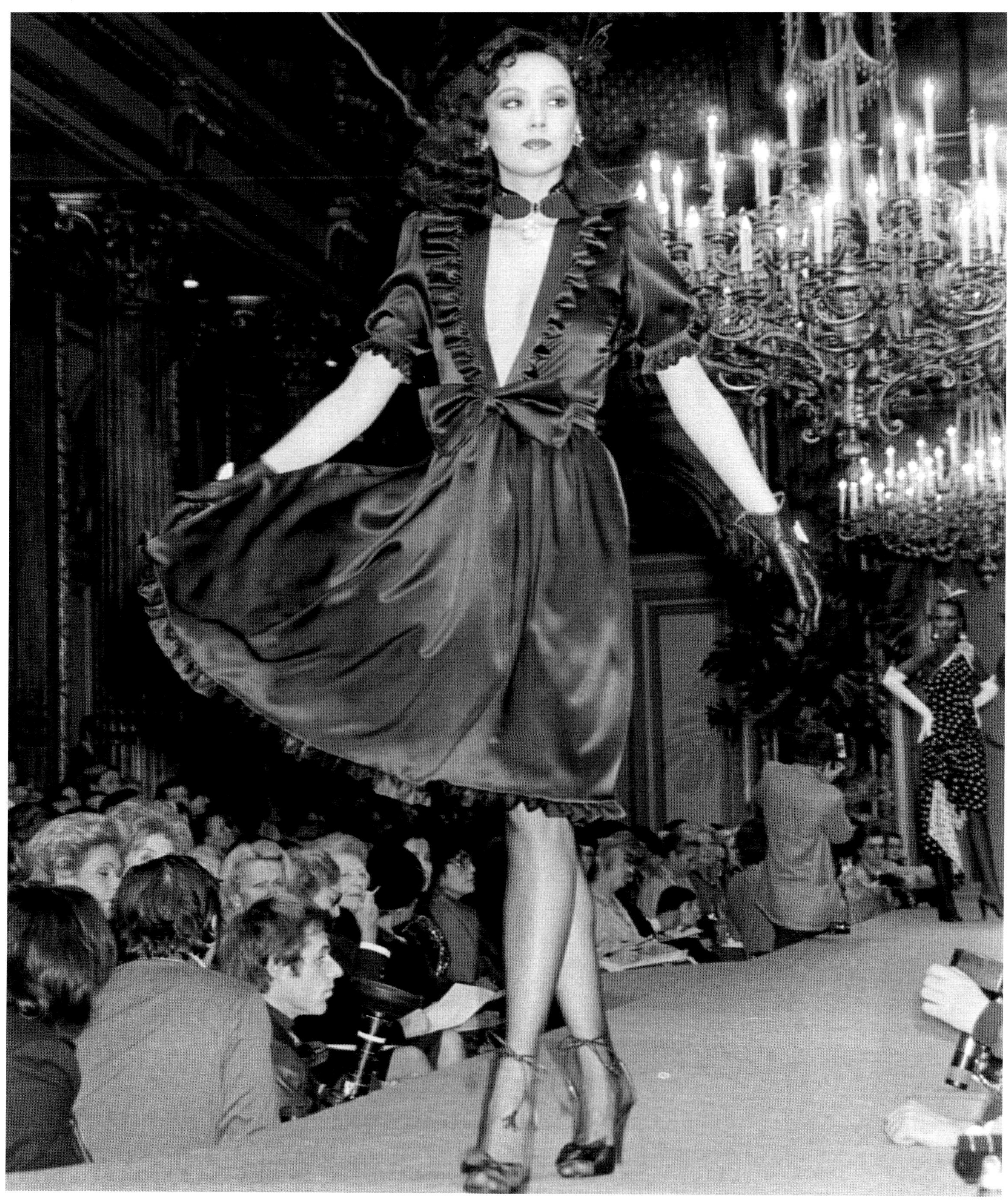

This page: *A model twirls on the runway in a Yves Saint Laurent cocktail dress, its bows and ruffles channeling the sophistication of a bygone age, 1980.* Opposite: *Designers like Yeung Chin continue to shake and stir traditional cocktail couture.*

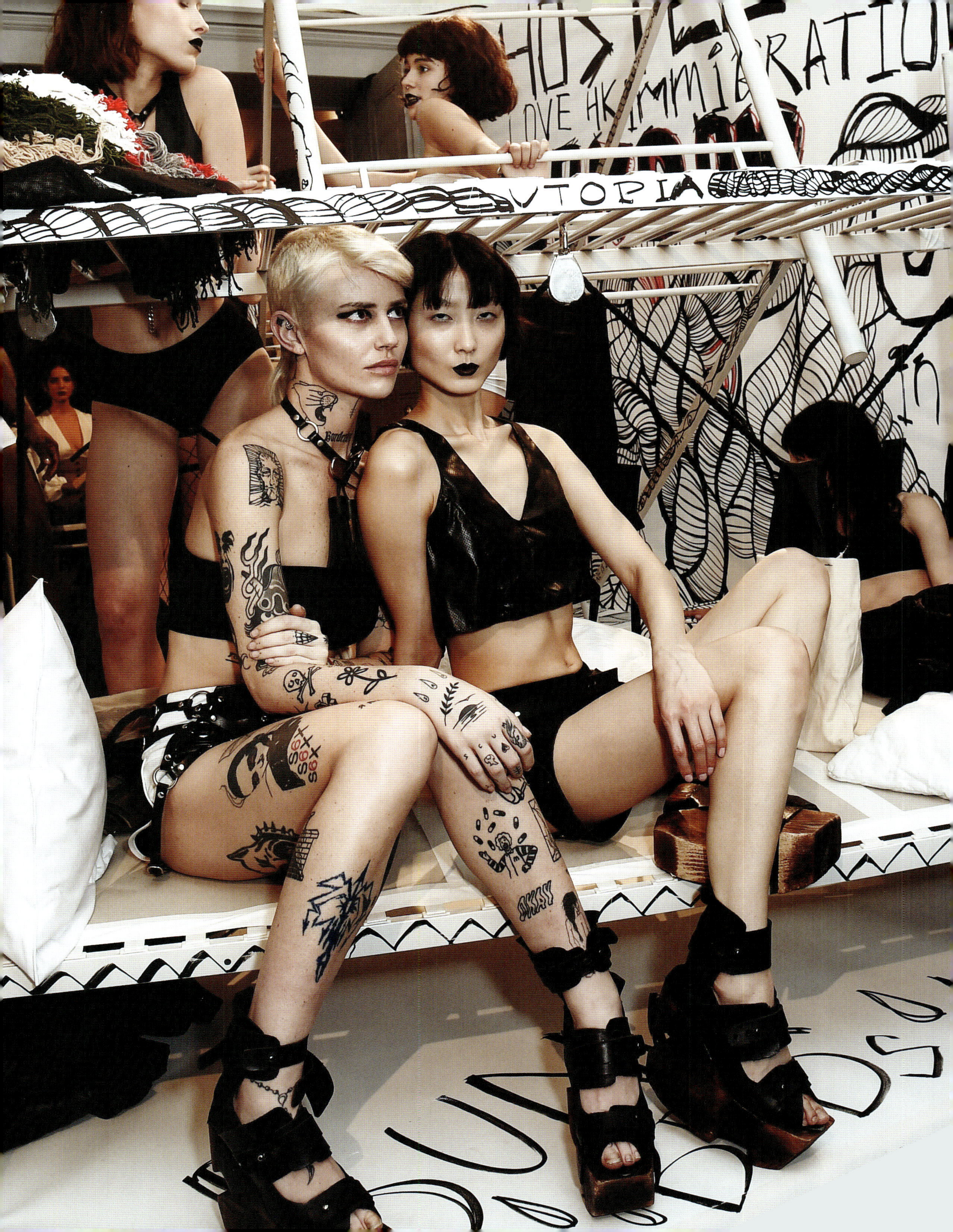
LOVE HK
UTOPIA

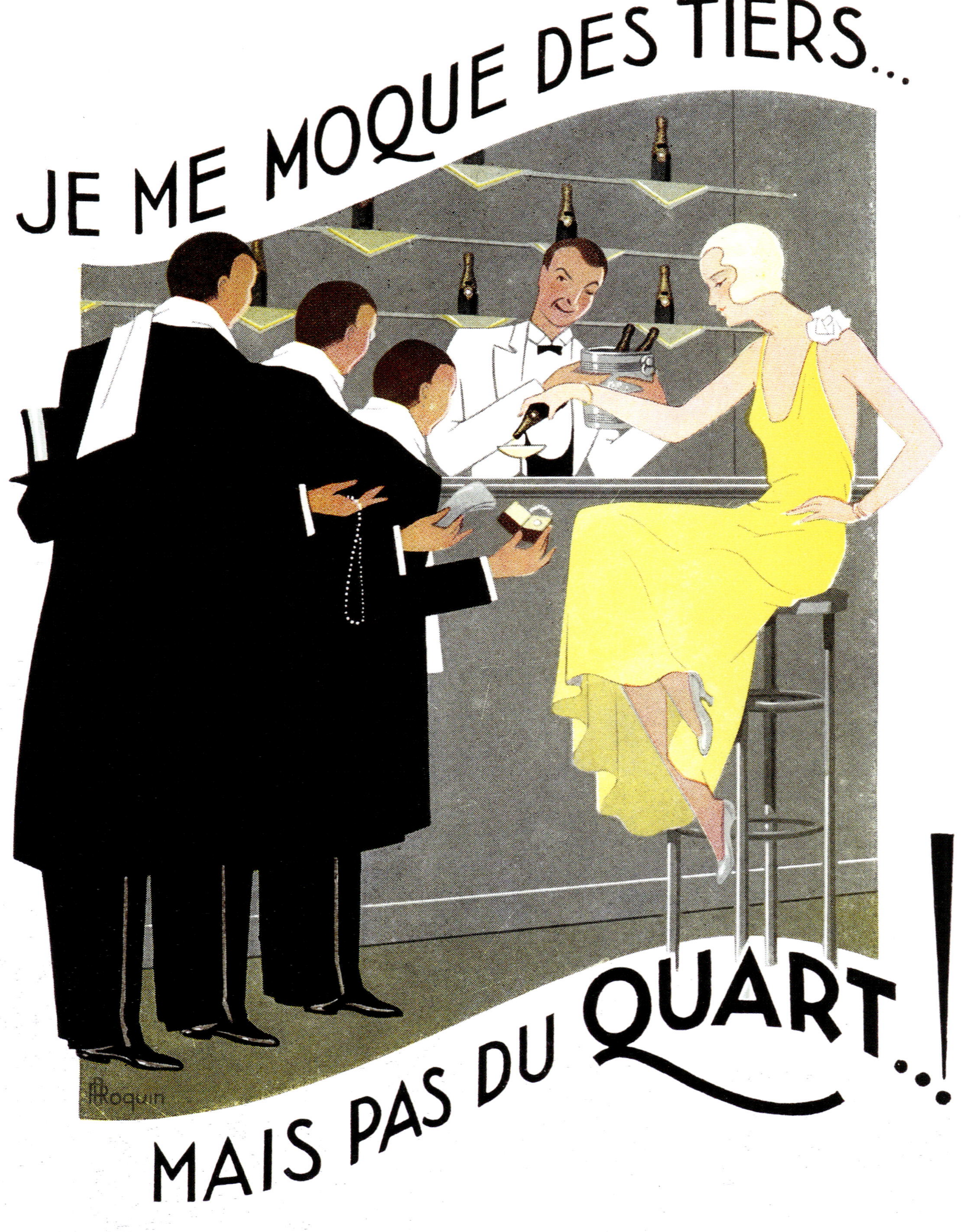
JE ME MOQUE DES TIERS...
MAIS PAS DU QUART...!
Roquin
POMMERY & GRENO

ART, DESIGN & CULTURE

THE ART OF COCKTAIL PARTIES

It's fitting that the first drinkable distilled spirit was called "aqua vitae." Through the ages, spirits—and the gatherings and conversations centered on their imbibing—have sparked revolutions and inspired artistic masterpieces. Rituals involving spirits have taken us closer to the divine. Spirits have linked us to our identities, from Scotch whisky and Cuban rum to Kentucky bourbon.

Creativity leads to magic, especially when spirits are involved. From art and design to film and music—and even a cocktail party for the ages—humans create extraordinary things from simple ingredients (plus a dash of finesse and a twist of daring).

Savoring Life's Palette

If you love bonding over a finely crafted cocktail, you're part of a rich tradition. From ancient Roman feasts to Jazz Age gatherings, the art of sharing drinks has inspired artists. Take Édouard Manet's *Un bar aux Folies Bergère* (1882) (*A Bar at the Folies-Bergère*)—the painting transports the viewer into a Parisian music hall, where the barmaid has seen it all and pours with a knowing smile. Or Archibald Motley's 1926 painting *Cocktails*, a vibrant snapshot of laughter and camaraderie, where friends come together to toast life's joys and forget the world's troubles.

The synergy of Greek *sympínein* (to drink together) bridges art and design, eras, and individuals. Illustrator Leonetto Capiello captured the scintillating brilliance of the Paris 1920s art scene in a vermouth poster that evokes the rushing excitement

Opposite: *In an early twentieth-century Champagne ad, a stylish woman much prefers a quarter bottle of Pommery et Greno over the expensive gifts of a trio of suitors.*

of the modern age. Classic burlesque inspires modern vedette Dita Von Teese, whose cabaret performances featuring a huge martini glass in turn inspired pop superstar Taylor Swift's music video for her song "Bejeweled." And like Athena springing from the head of Zeus, iconic libations have emerged from art, such as the Bellini, a sunset-hued masterpiece dreamed up by Giuseppi Cipriani at Harry's Bar in Venice, inspired by Giovanni Bellini's paintings. As the saying goes, "We drink first with our eyes." With cocktails as captivating as works of art, let's all signal the bartender for another round.

Lights, Camera, Bottoms Up!

No film captures the bittersweet essence of love and loss like 1942's *Casablanca*, set amid the turmoil of World War II. At Rick's gin joint in French Morocco, intrigue swirls like notes from Sam's piano as Humphrey Bogart's Rick and Ingrid Bergman's Ilsa exchange longing glances. The movie features the French 75 (named after a French World War I field gun), whose combination of gin, lemon juice, sugar, and Champagne matches the film's blend of sweetness and bite. On the drier side, a Vodka Martini—shaken, not stirred—epitomizes James Bond's cool sophistication. Since 1962's *Dr. No*, Bond has saved the world with vodka and dry vermouth garnished with lemon twist in hand. (For a taste of the literary 007, try a Vesper Martini—gin, vodka, and Lillet—from Ian Fleming's first Bond novel, *Casino Royale*.)

Philip Marlowe, the tough private detective in Raymond Chandler's 1953 novel *The Long Goodbye*, will take a gimlet: "A real gimlet is half gin and half Rose's Lime Juice and nothing else. It beats martinis hollow." Meanwhile, The Dude (Jeff Bridges) in *The Big Lebowski* (1998) quaffs a White Russian (vodka, coffee liqueur, and milk) in his bathrobe. Also in the 1990s, a certain pink vodka-based cocktail was the talk of the town with Carrie, Charlotte, Miranda, and Samantha in *Sex and the City*. Beneath its pretty and stylish surface, the Cosmopolitan packs a punch, much as this fashion-centric TV show also tackled serious themes of friendship, dating, and careers. In the new millennium, TV's *Mad Men*'s Don Draper (Jon Hamm) had a timeless go-to: an Old Fashioned—rye, sugar cubes, bitters, a cherry, and an orange wedge. "Make it simple, but significant," Draper advised—good advice that evokes the *savoir faire* of self-made *élégante* Holly Golightly (Audrey Hepburn) in 1961's *Breakfast at Tiffany's*.

All About the Rhythm

Music can guide the cocktail hour from appetizers to the final Zombie. Chill lounge tunes ease conversation into the night, while Glenn Miller can keep the golden feel-good vibe alive. Hits from Nancy Sinatra to Taylor Swift fuel pop singalongs while jams like Montell Jordan's "This Is How We Do It" get everyone moving. And when the last guests linger too long, hosts drop a hint, like Madonna's "The Power of Good-bye," and give a final toast.

The Thin Man (1934) kicks off with Nick Charles, played by William Powell, schooling bartenders on their craft: "The important thing is the rhythm. Always have rhythm in your shaking. Now, a Manhattan you shake to foxtrot time; a Bronx, to two-step time; a dry Martini you always shake to waltz time." Like mixing the perfect cocktail, orchestrating a cocktail party is all about the rhythm. Conversation and music flow like a jazz riff, but without the right tempo, they can stall.

Create to Shake and Stir

From the sleek forms of Art Deco to the sassy styles of the 1950s and today's anything-goes vibes, design has been a megaphone for cocktail culture's allure. Advertisers have dished out promises of adventure and excitement, tempting patrons with illustrated visions of international watering holes and far-flung escapes. Nights out are steeped in cocktail chic, promising tipplers a multitude of festive, fantastic, and exotic ways to set quotidian cares aside for the evening. Tiki culture, pioneered by Donn Beach, whisked patrons away on a kitschy trip to the tropics with tiki torches and thatched roofs. Hors d'oeuvres ("outside the work") became extraordinary moments of tartlets, crudités, skewers, or canapés. Today, a chic speakeasy might lurk behind a humble pizzeria, and city hotel terraces awe with sky-high views. Every sip and every experience can be a toast to the unpredictable and the sublime.

However, for any cocktail party, there is one elusive yet perfect ingredient: style. True style is one's own. Will your next party be a tropical oasis, a lush garden, or a winter wonderland? Will it be a festive holiday bash, a mysterious costumed ball, or a charity gala to spread the love? Will you deck out your home bar with vintage whimsy, or serve with Baccarat crystal (or both, why not)? Brush up your mixology skills: Add a Boston shaker to shimmy and twist-handled bar spoons to stir. Toss in julep strainers, muddlers, and festive glassware to clink from coups to rocks glasses to flutes and highballs. But above all, invite guests who keep everyone's spirits high. After all, a cocktail party isn't sixty minutes of schmooze and drinks. It has the power to stop time, tantalize the senses, and create moments that linger long after the last sip.

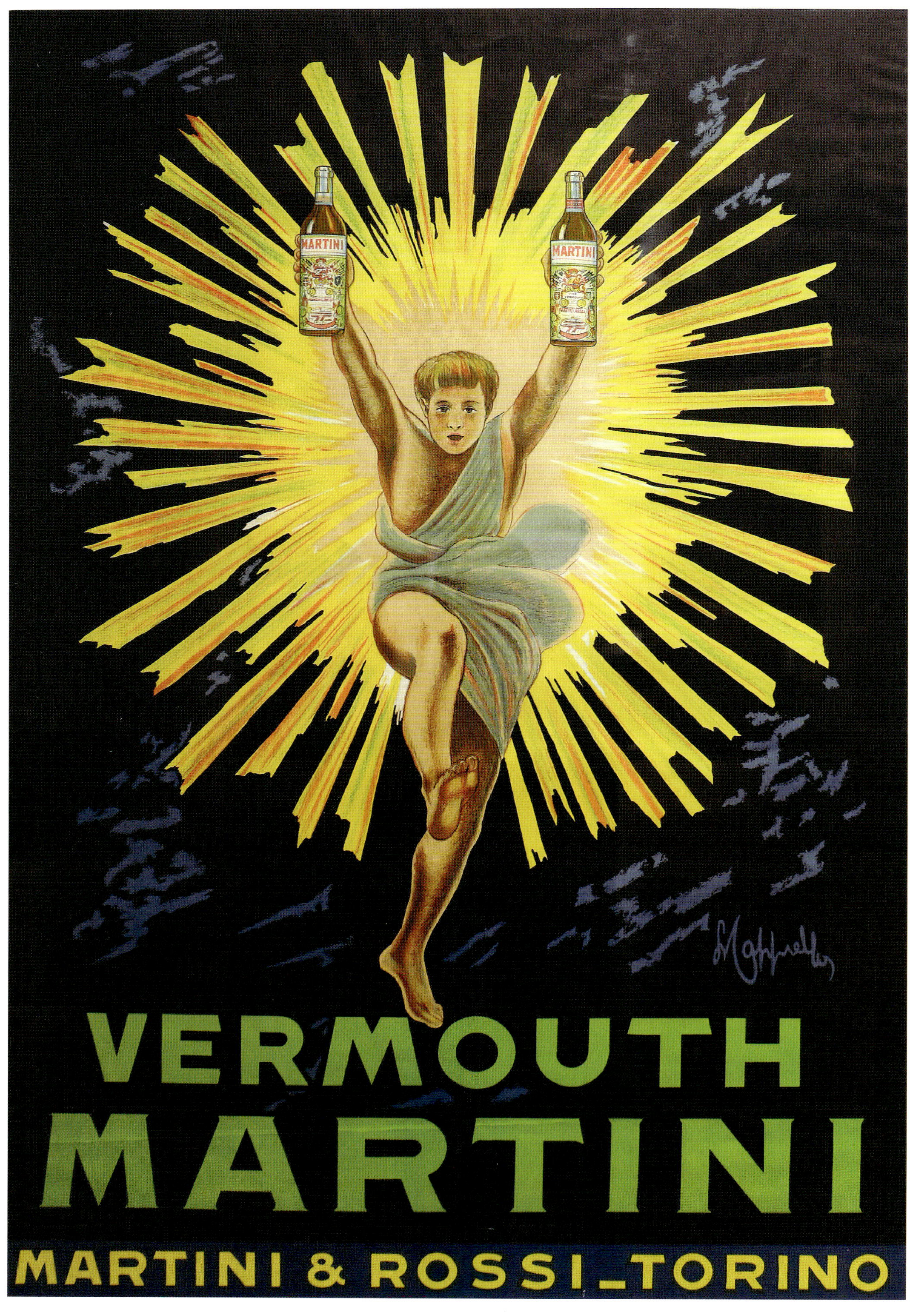
MARTINI
MARTINI
VERMOUTH
MARTINI
MARTINI & ROSSI_TORINO

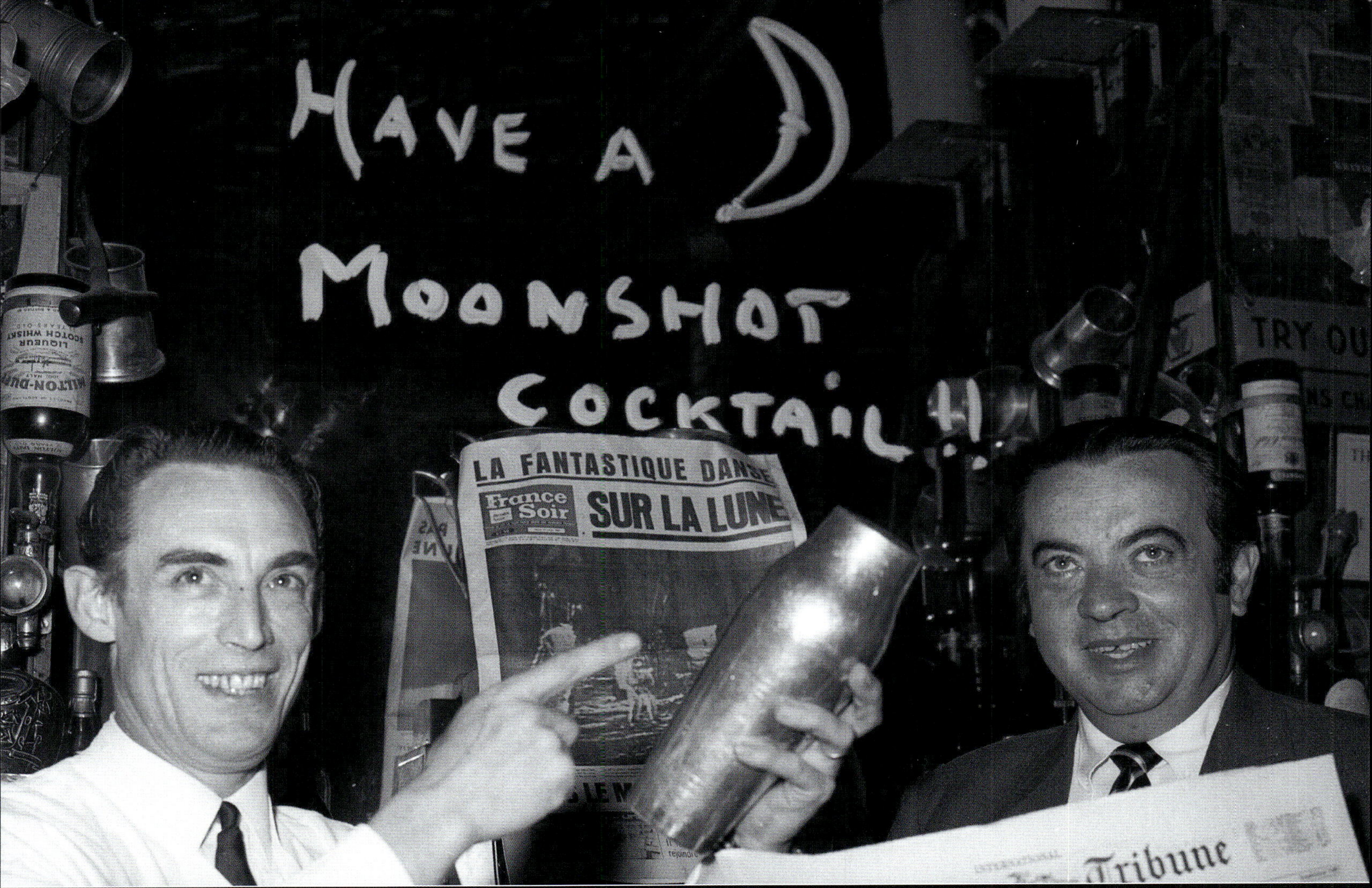

HAVE A
MOONSHOT
COCKTAIL !!
LA FANTASTIQUE DANSE
France Soir
SUR LA LUNE
Tribune

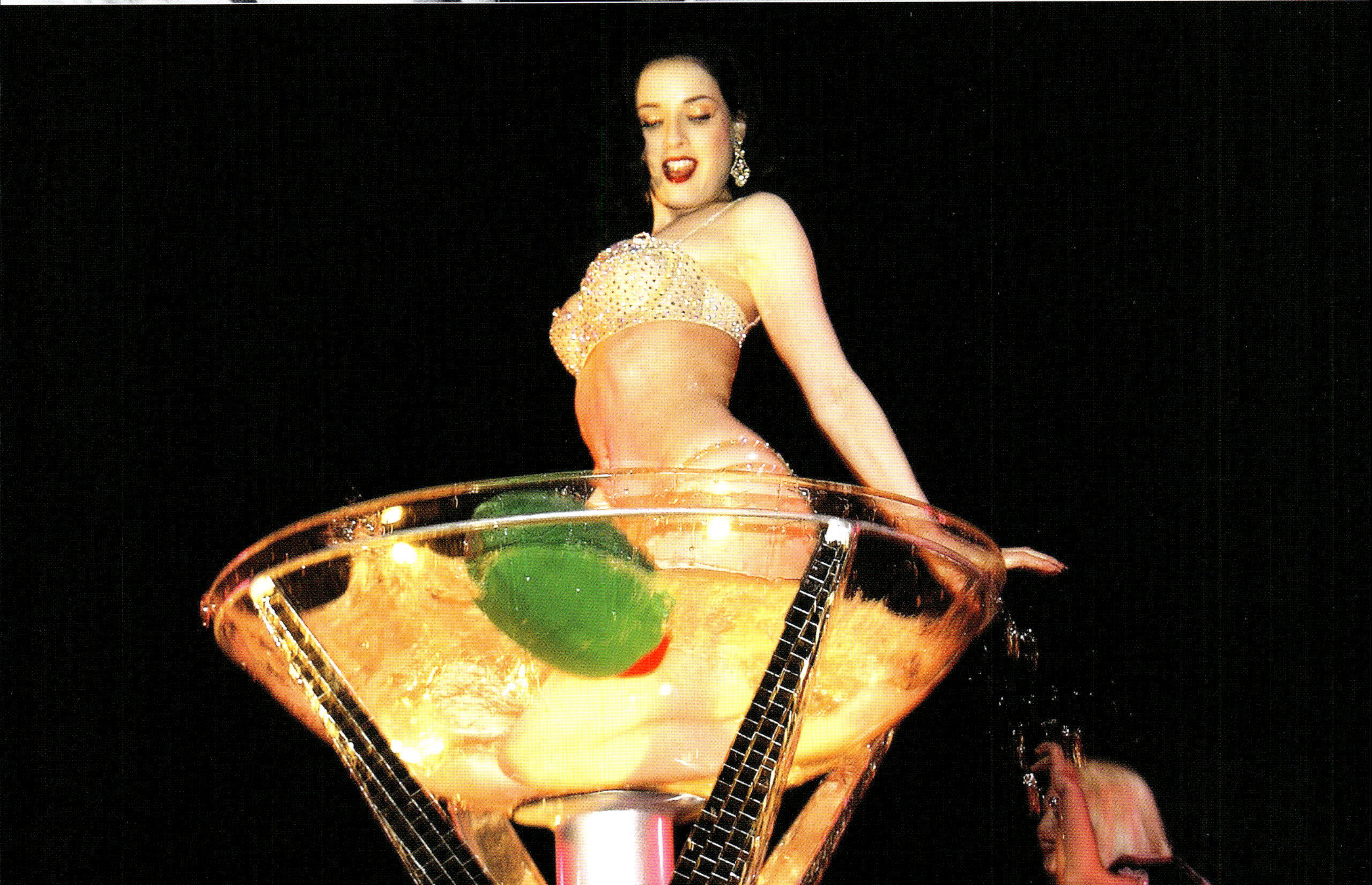

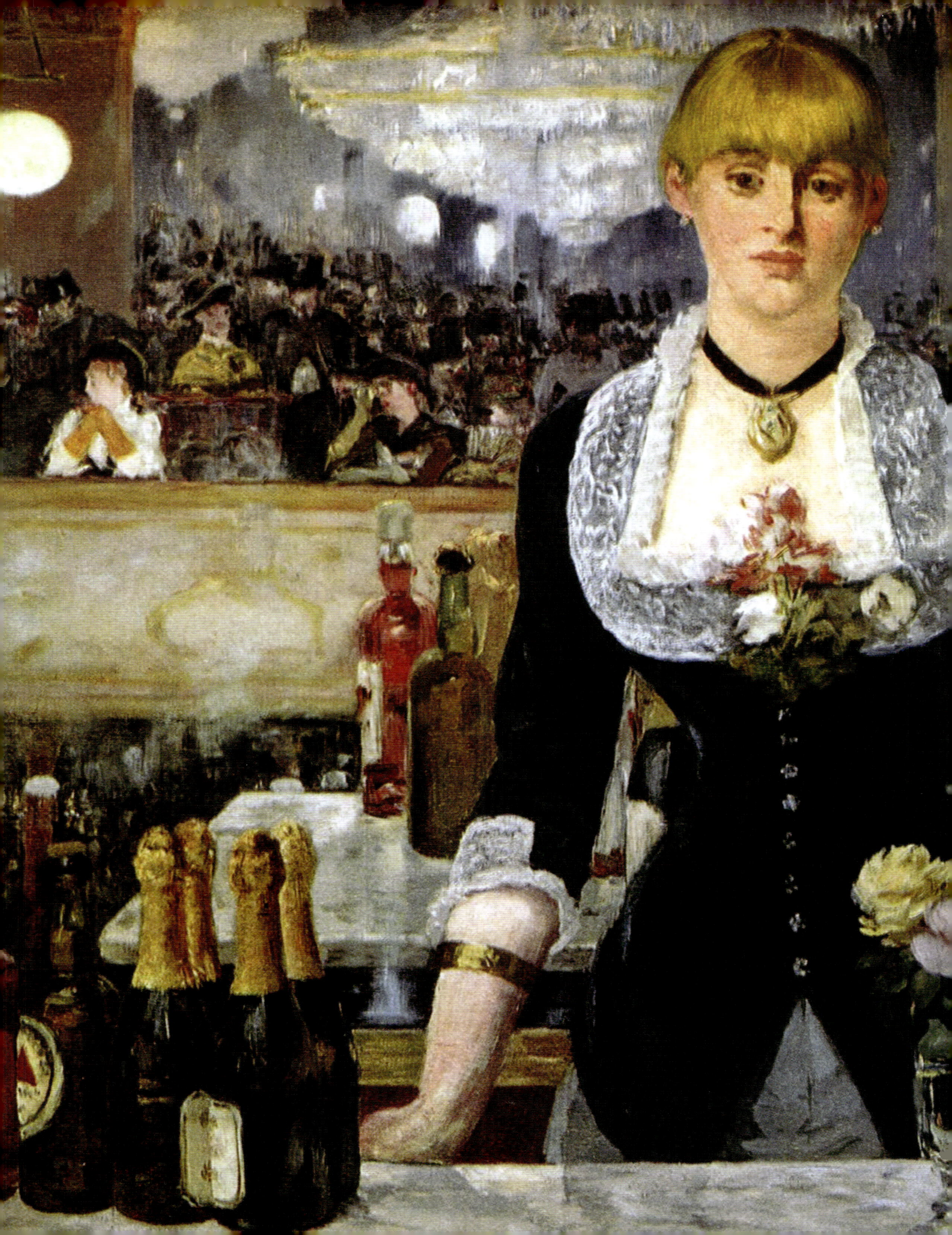

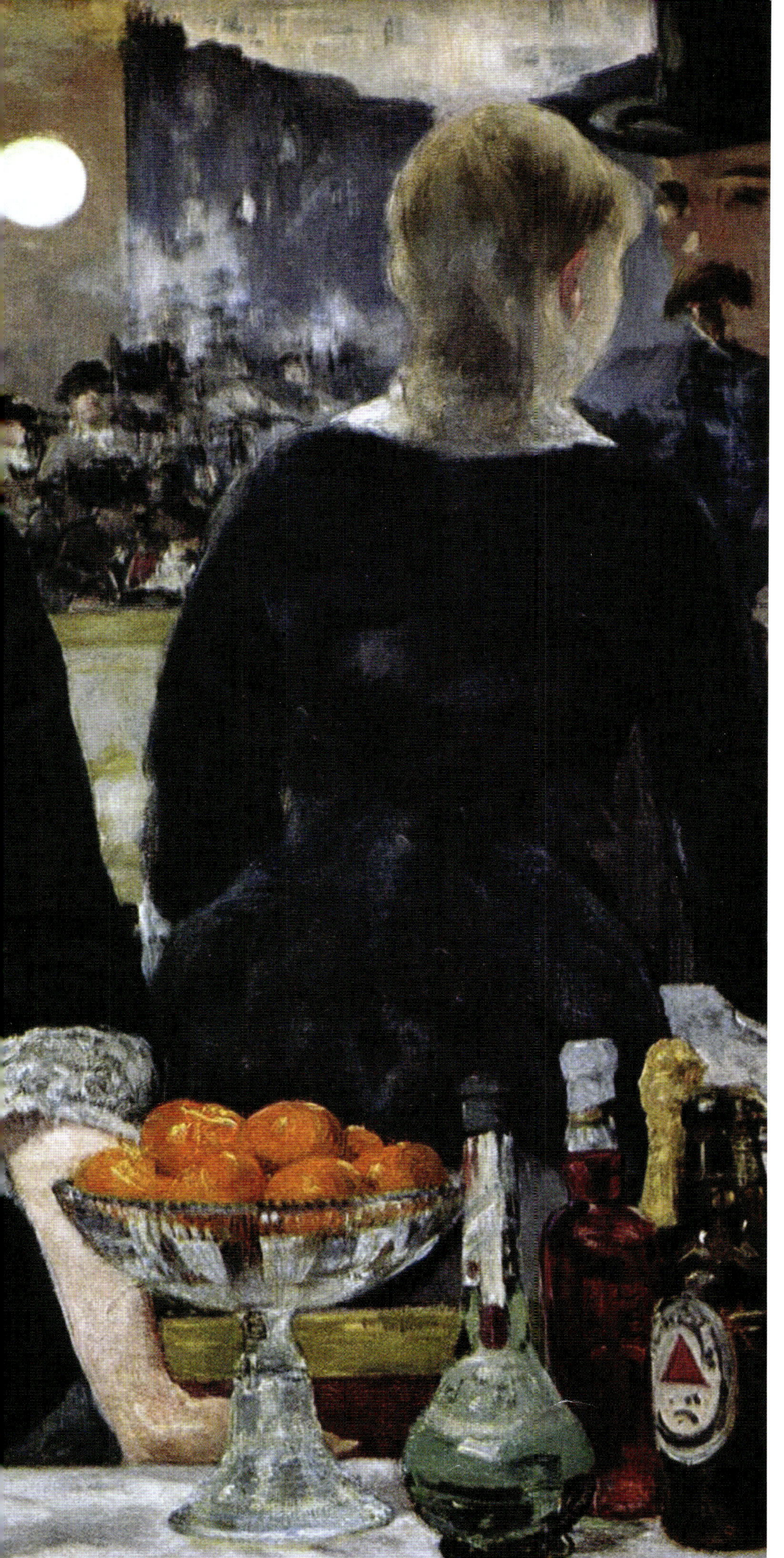

Previous pages, left: *A dynamic advertisement for vermouth expresses the electric excitement of the Parisian art scene in the Roaring 20s*; right: (top) *Apollo 11's Neil Armstrong and Buzz Aldrin's 1969 moonwalk inspired the potent "Moon Shot," at Harry's Bar in Paris*; (bottom*) "Queen of Burlesque" Dita Von Teese splashes in a larger-than-life martini glass for her spectacular strip-tease act*. Opposite: *Édouard Manet's eye for detail portrays the pleasures of Paris's famed nightclub—complete with world-weary barmaid—in* Un bar aux Folies Bergère *(1882).*

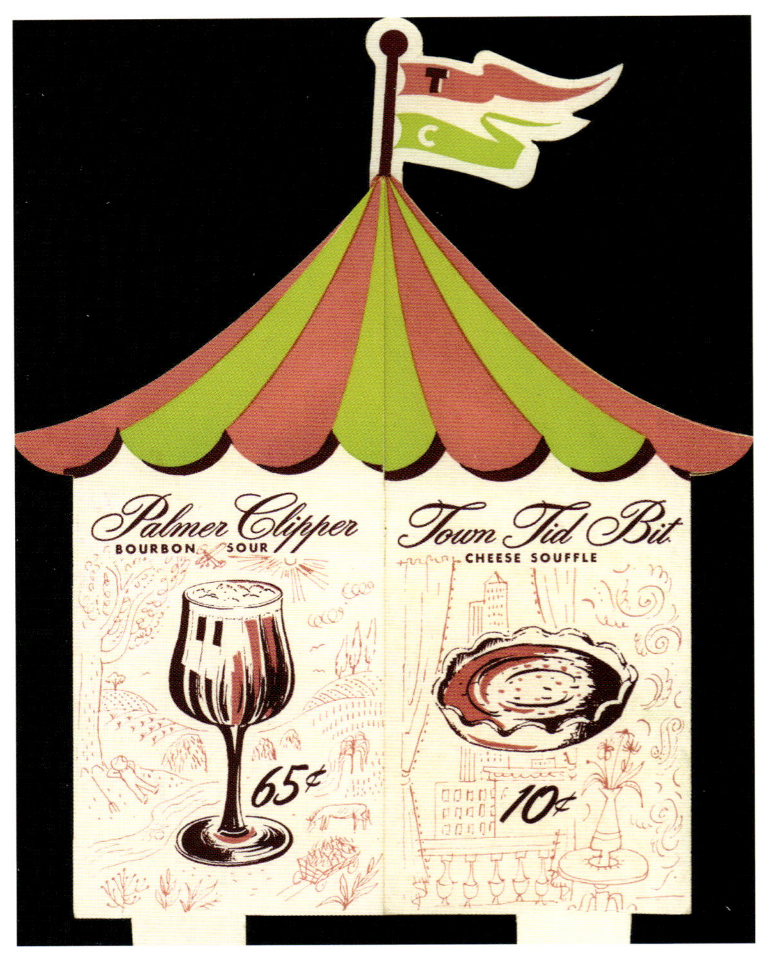
Palmer Clipper
BOURBON SOUR
65¢
Town Tid Bit
CHEESE SOUFFLE
10¢

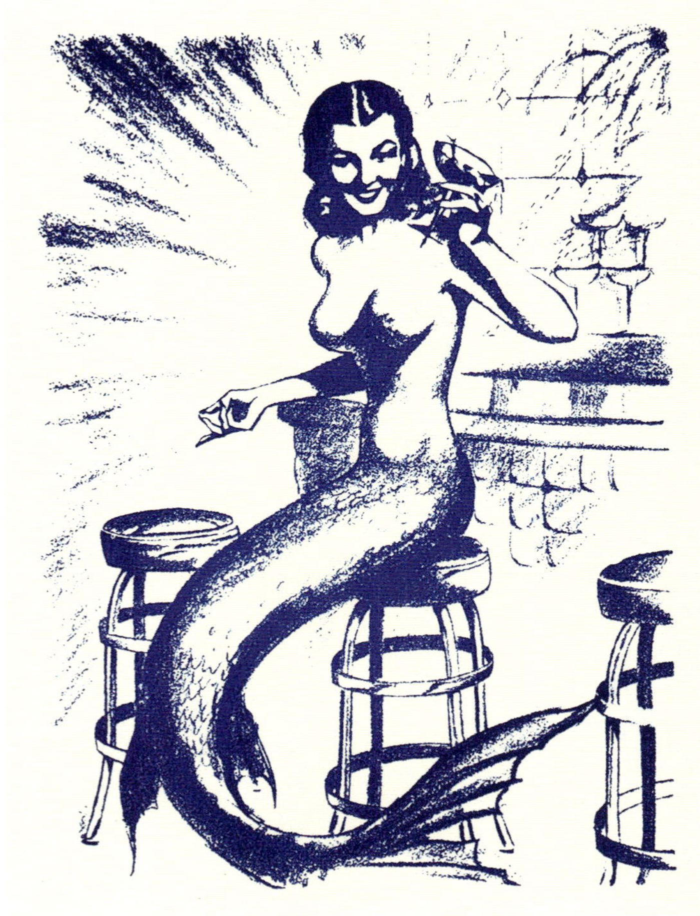

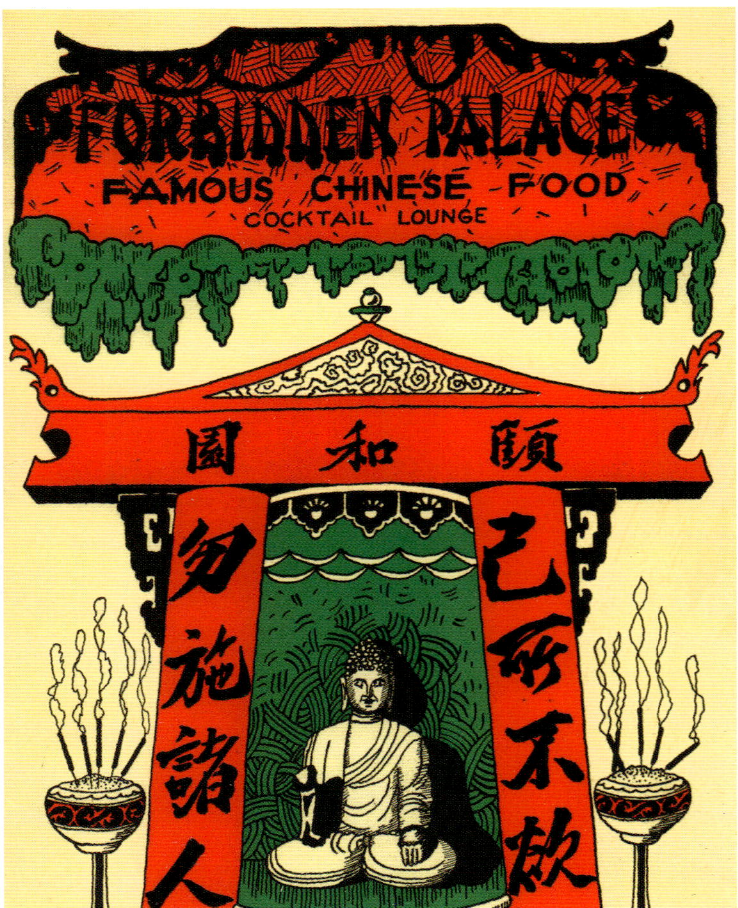
FORBIDDEN PALACE
FAMOUS CHINESE FOOD
COCKTAIL LOUNGE
頤和園
己所不欲
勿施諸人

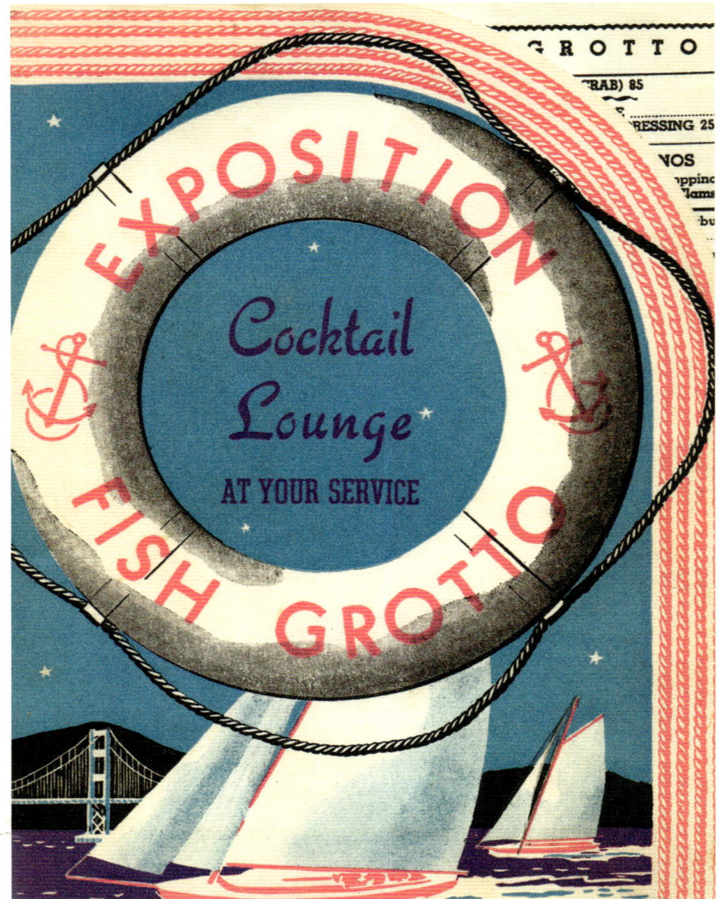
GROTTO
EXPOSITION
Cocktail Lounge
AT YOUR SERVICE
FISH GROTTO

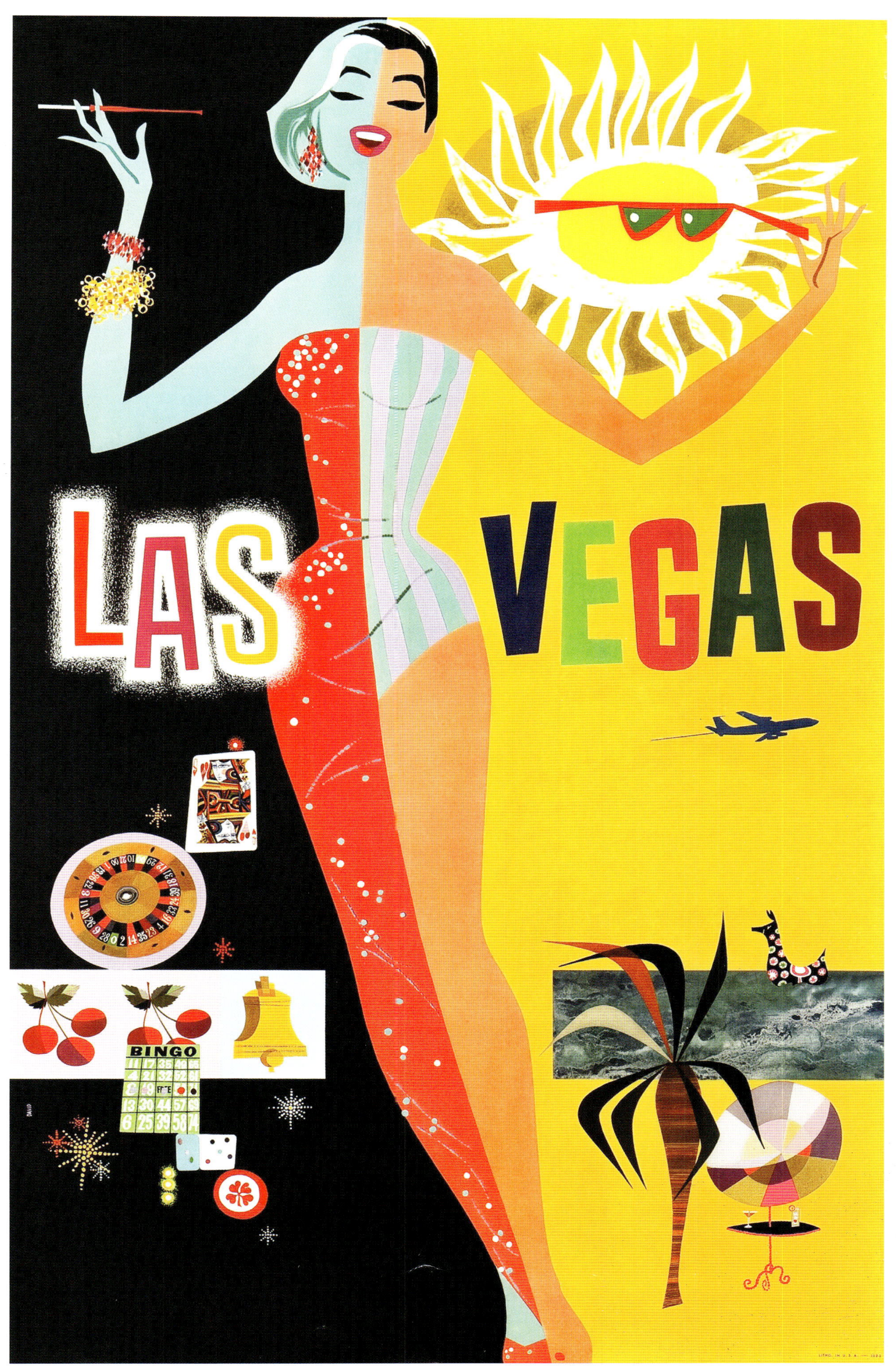
LAS VEGAS
BINGO

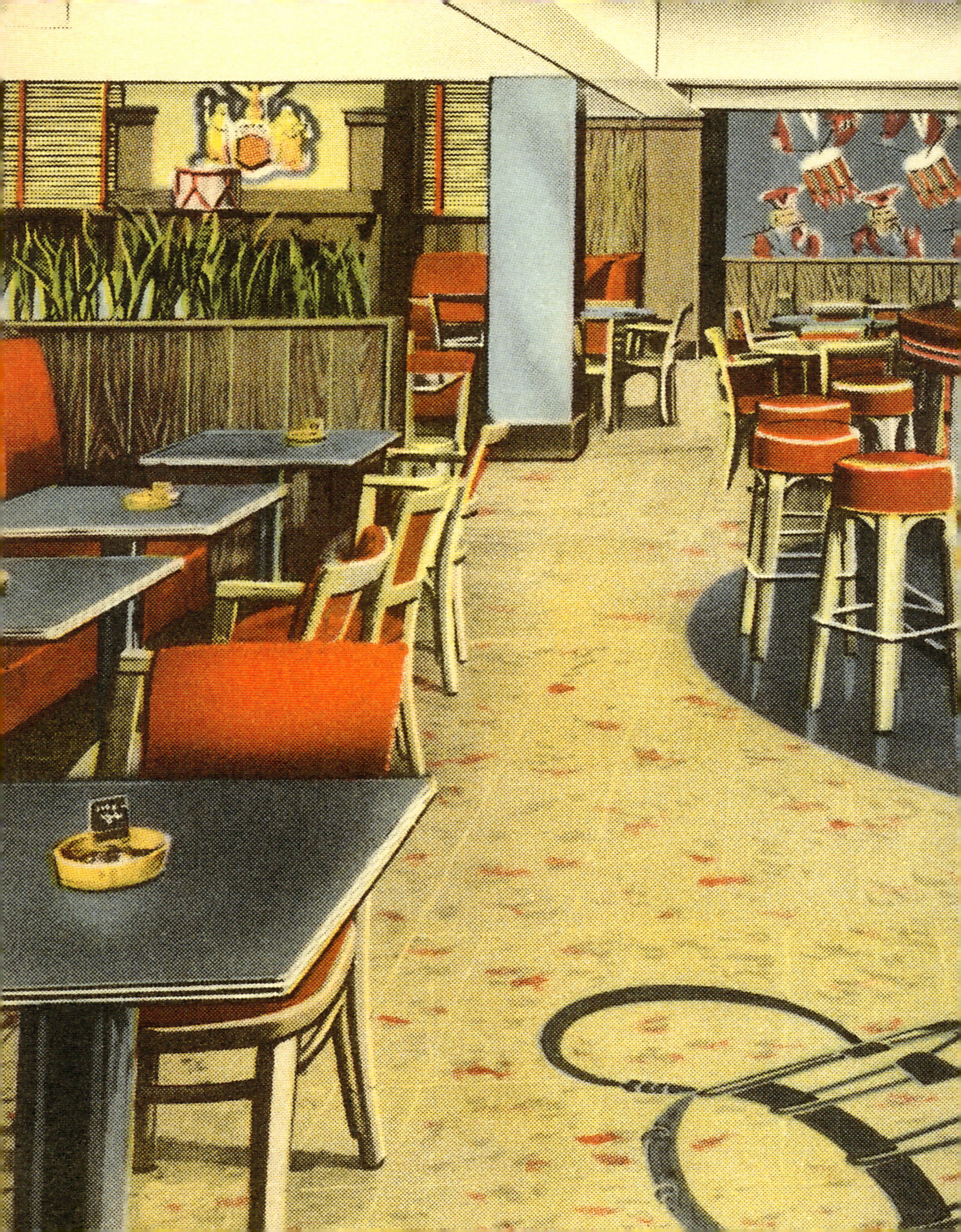

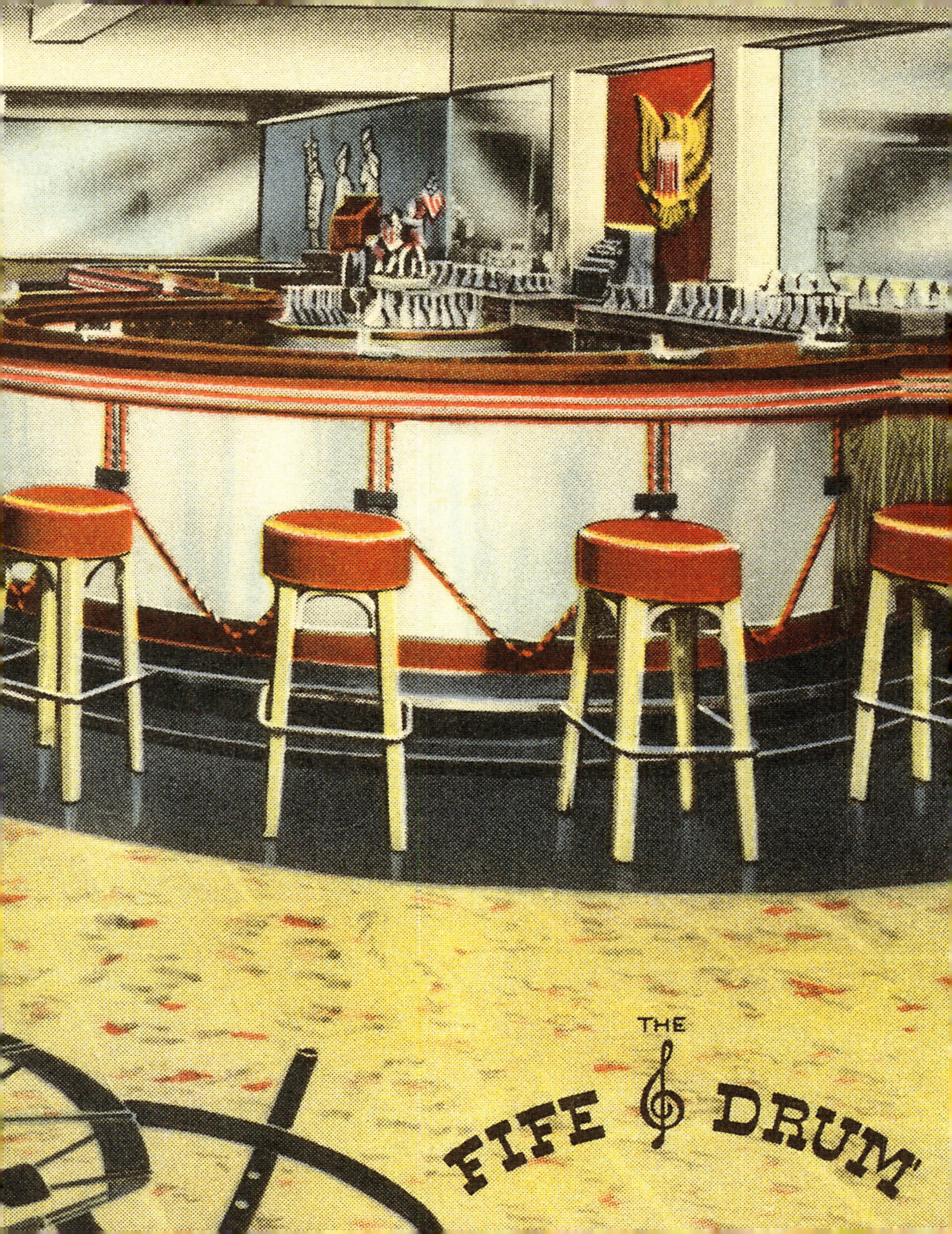
THE
FIFE DRUM

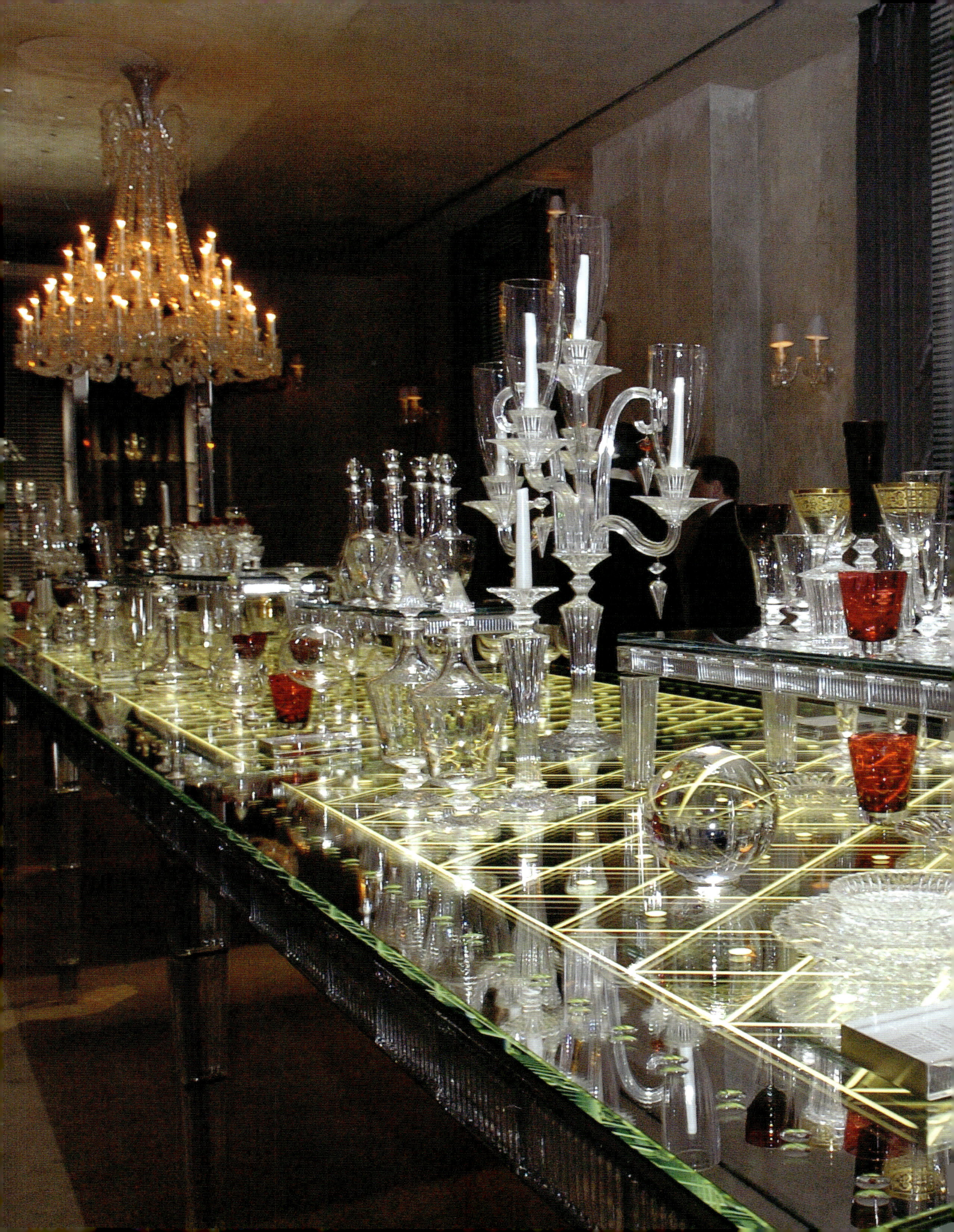

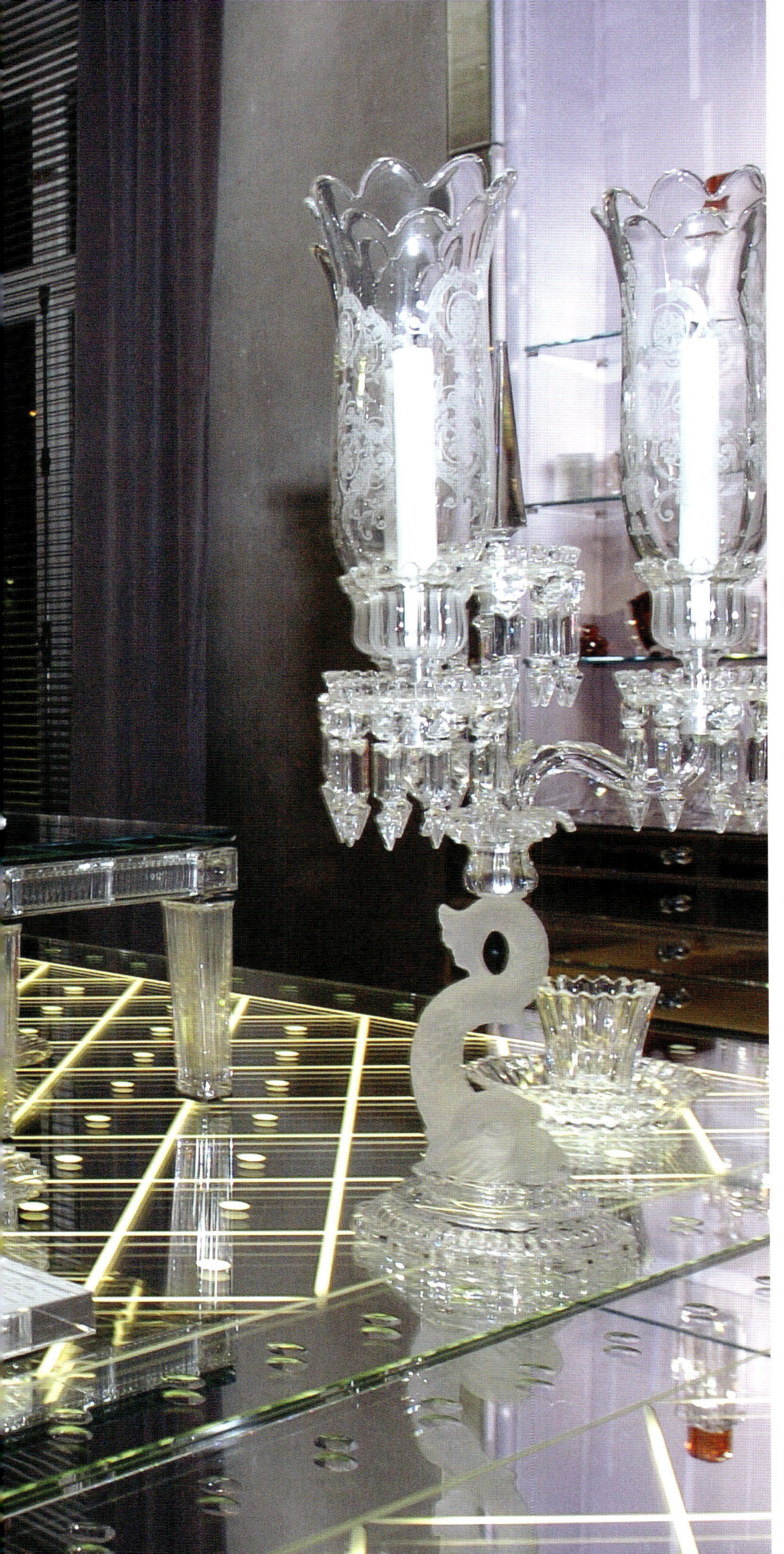

Pages 142–43, left: (clockwise from top left) *A 1960 menu features a Bourbon Sour for sixty-five cents; A beguiling mermaid gives a toast on a vintage Mermaid Lounge coaster; A 1940 menu from San Francisco's Exposition Fish Grotto showcases a nautically themed cocktail lounge; The Forbidden Palace cocktail lounge serves escape to faraway lands, 1942*; right: *In Sin City, the fun never stops, as depicted in renowned illustrator David Klein's poster for Las Vegas, 1960*. Pages 144–45: *A 1940s upstate New York restaurant offers a smart place to rendezvous at the Fife & Drum cocktail lounge*. Opposite: *Baccarat glassware, a symbol of refined taste, captures the light at a cocktail party.*

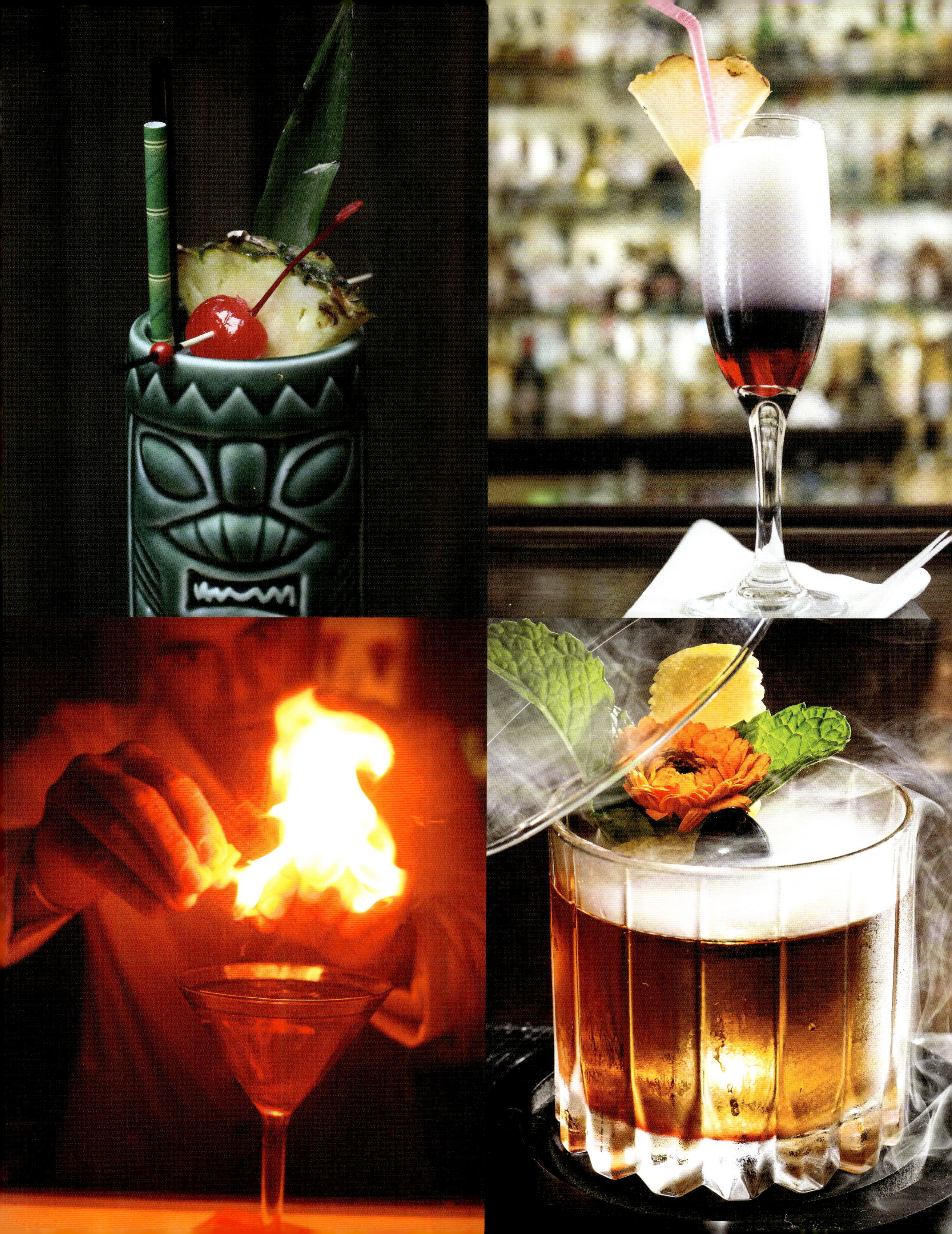

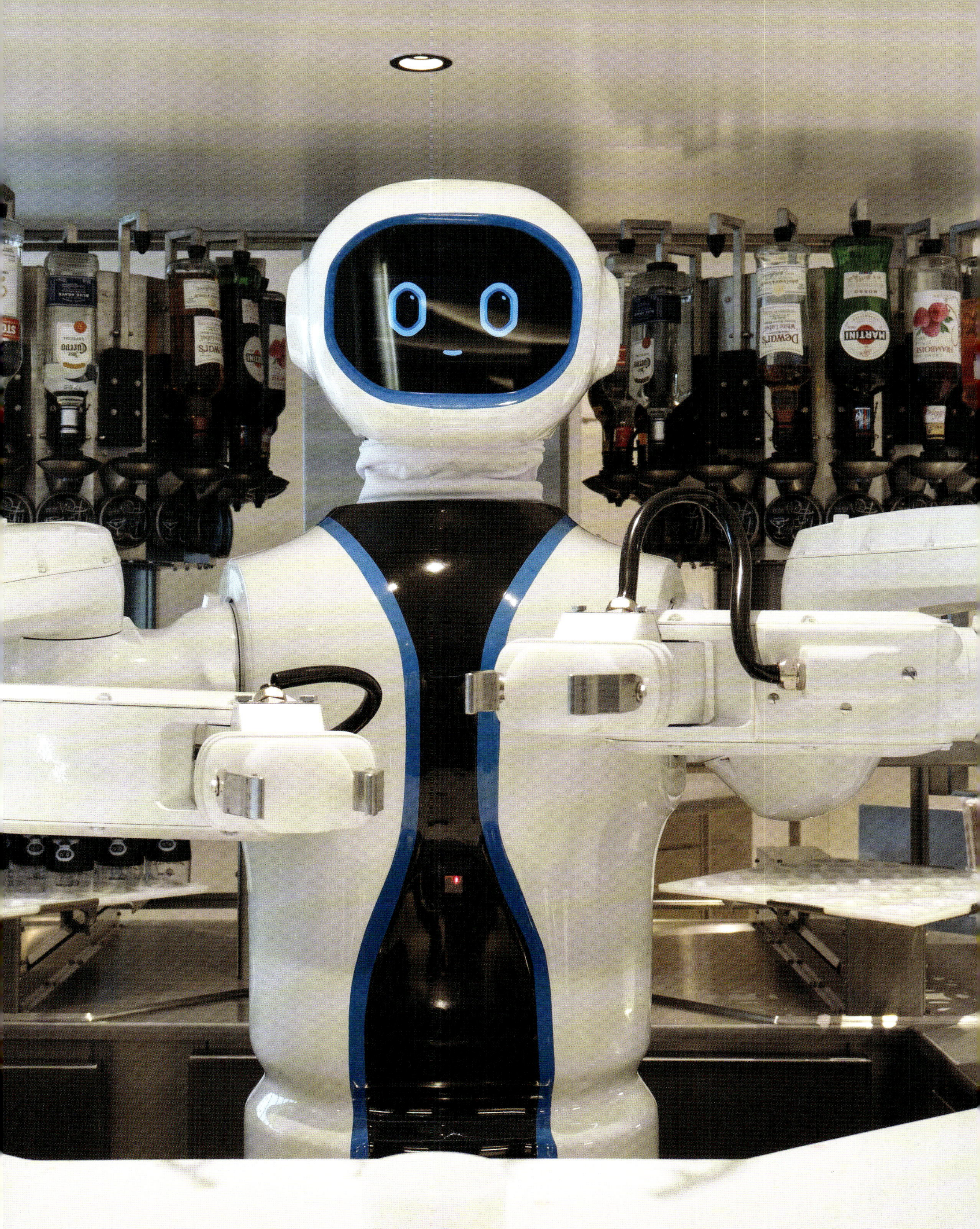

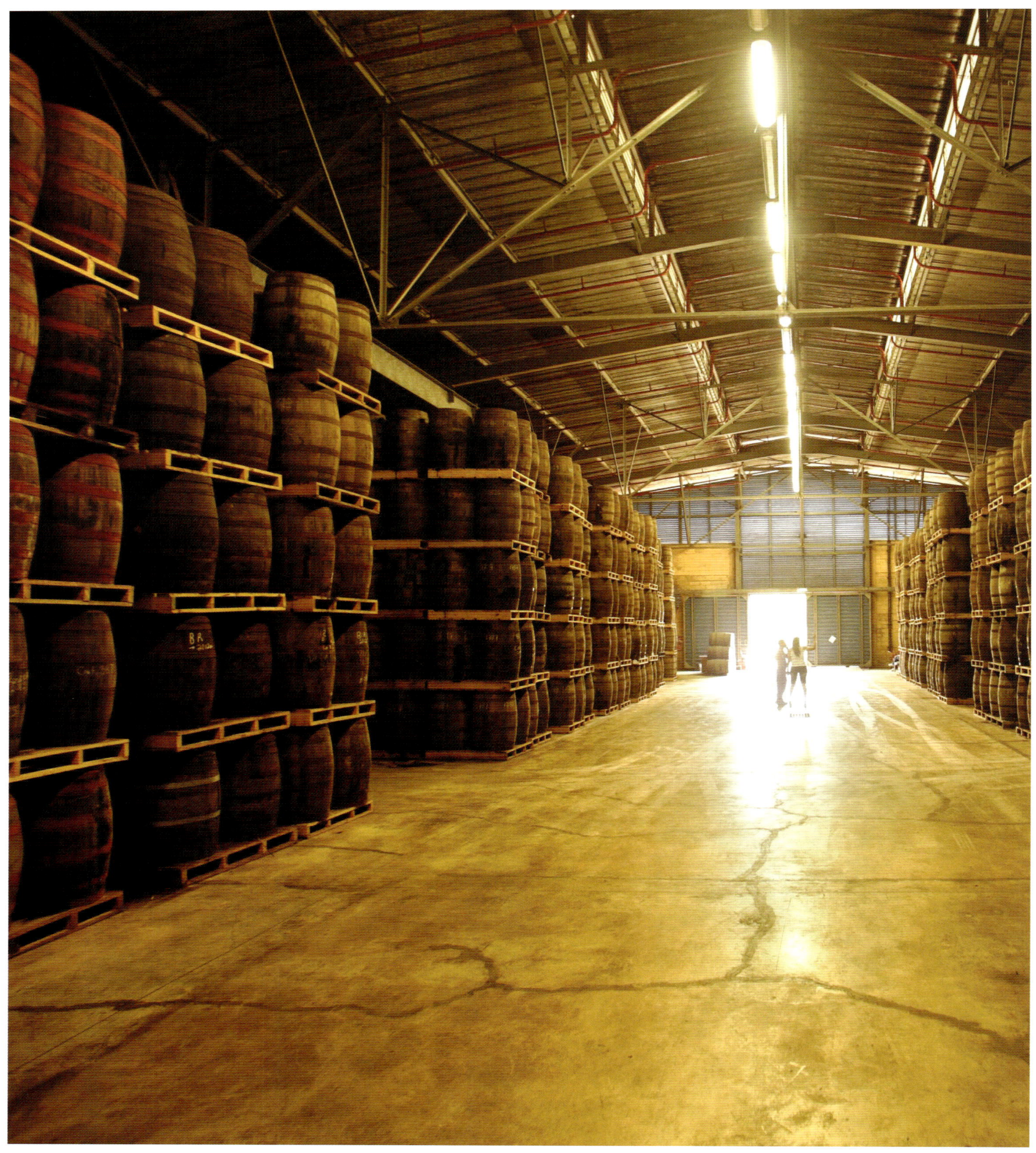

Pages 148–49, left: (clockwise from top left) *A potent Zombie beckons from the Honi Honi Tiki Cocktail Bar, Hong Kong; A cocktail in a champagne glass with straw and pineapple slice refreshes in Sancti Spiritus, Cuba; A Peach Manhattan bridges the political divide at the Watergate Hotel, Washington, DC; A bartender burns an orange peel above a Negroni to extract citrus oils;* right: *A robot bartender takes an order on an ocean liner cruising the North Sea.* This page: *White oak barrels filled with aging rum await their time at the Havana Club rum factory in Cuba.* Opposite: *Barrels of sake donated to the temple at the Tokyo's Meiji Shinto Shrine are used during purification rites.*

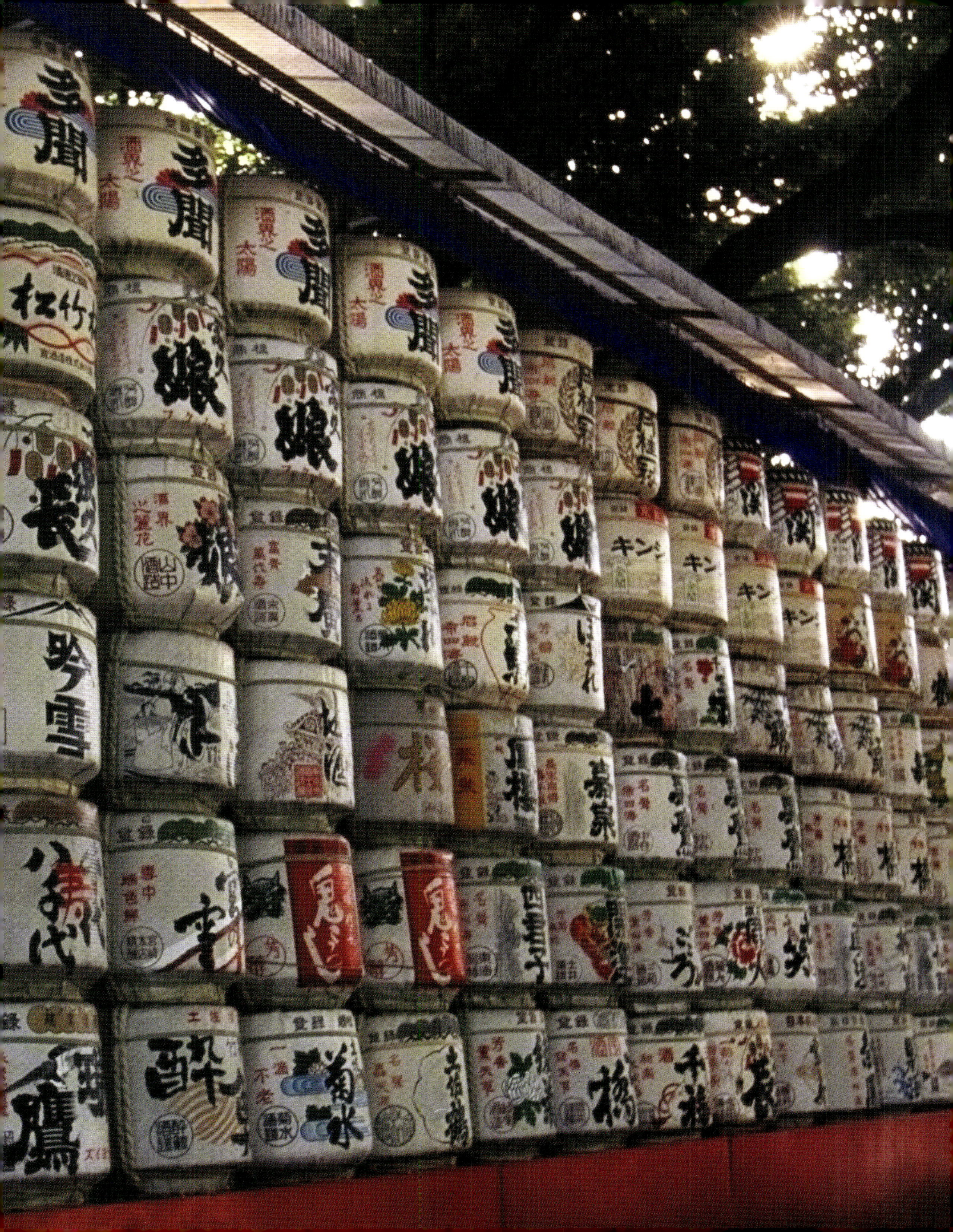
酒界之太陽
松竹梅
吟雪
キンシ
菊水
土佐鶴

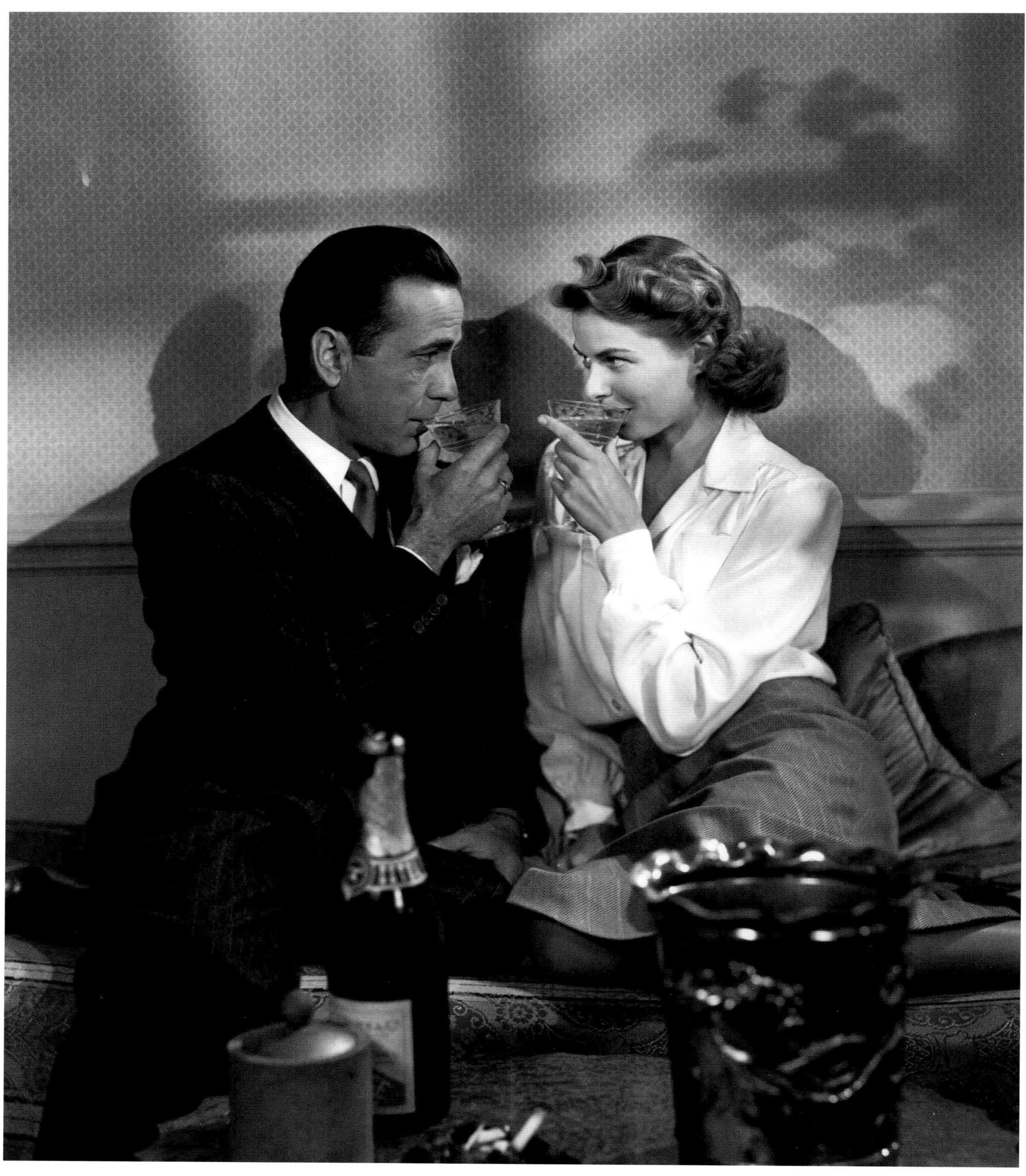

This page: *Rick (Humphrey Bogart) and Ilsa (Ingrid Bergman) share a drink in a scene from* Casablanca *(1942)*. Opposite: *The Martini (shaken or stirred) was made famous by secret agent James Bond—played by debonair actors like Sean Connery and Roger Moore*. Following pages: *A chic LBD, an impeccable updo, a dash of panache—Holly Golightly (Audrey Hepburn) is unforgettable in* Breakfast at Tiffany's *(1961), directed by Blake Edwards.*

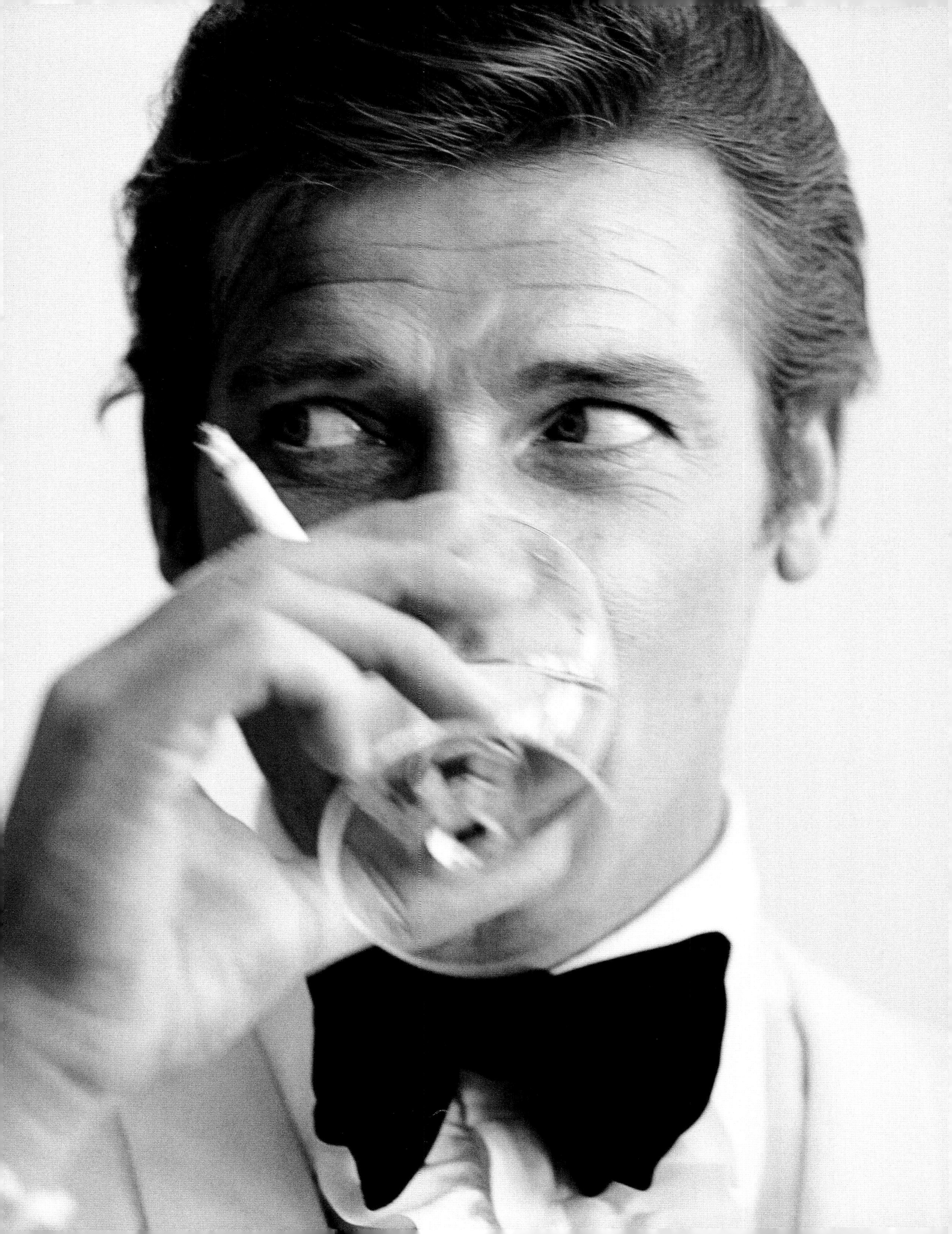

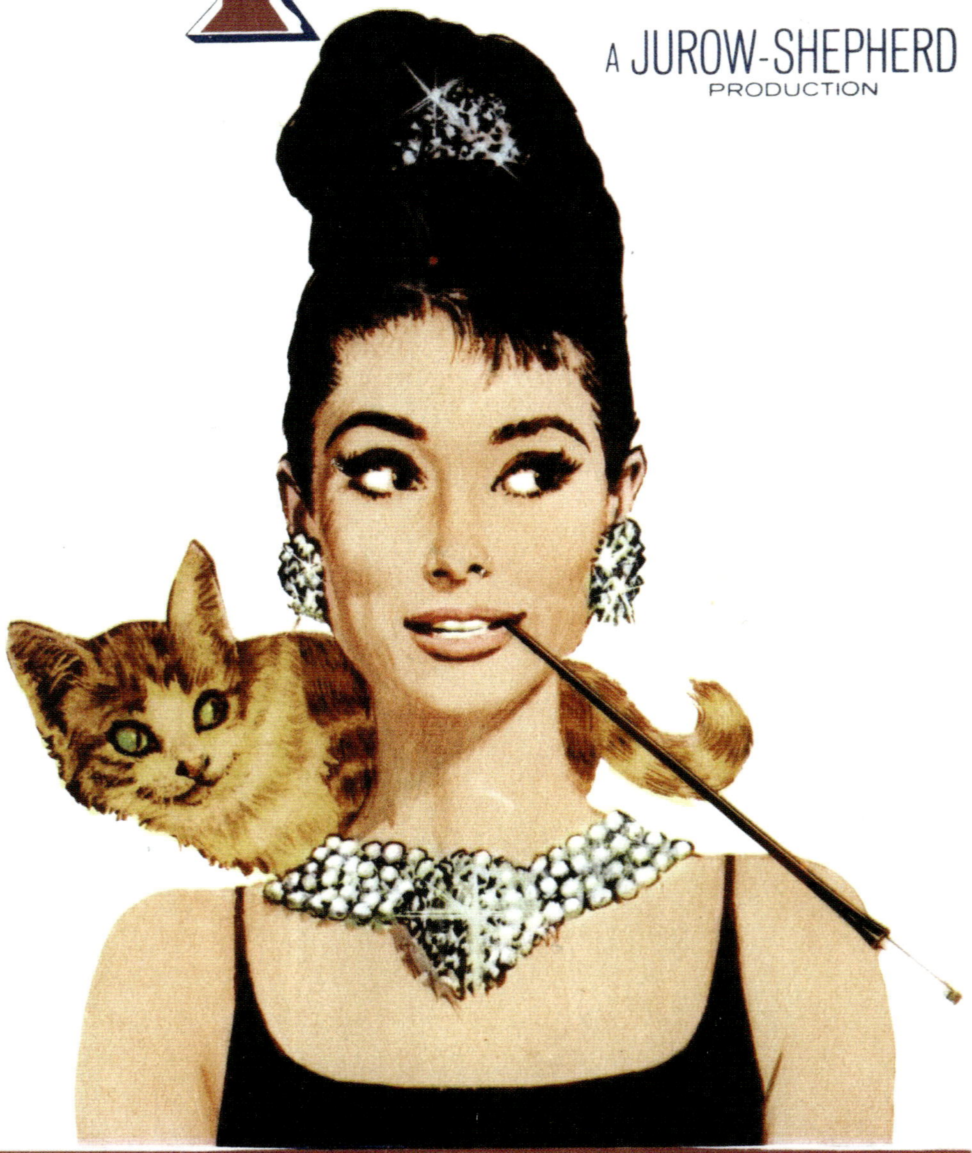
AUDREY HEPBURN
AS THAT DELIGHTFUL DARLING, HOLLY GOLIGHTLY, IN
BREAKFAST AT TIFFANY'S
A JUROW-SHEPHERD PRODUCTION
ALSO STARRING
GEORGE PEPPARD
CO-STARRING
PATRICIA NEAL · BUDDY EBSEN · MARTIN BALSAM AND MICKEY ROONEY
DIRECTED BY
BLAKE EDWARDS ·

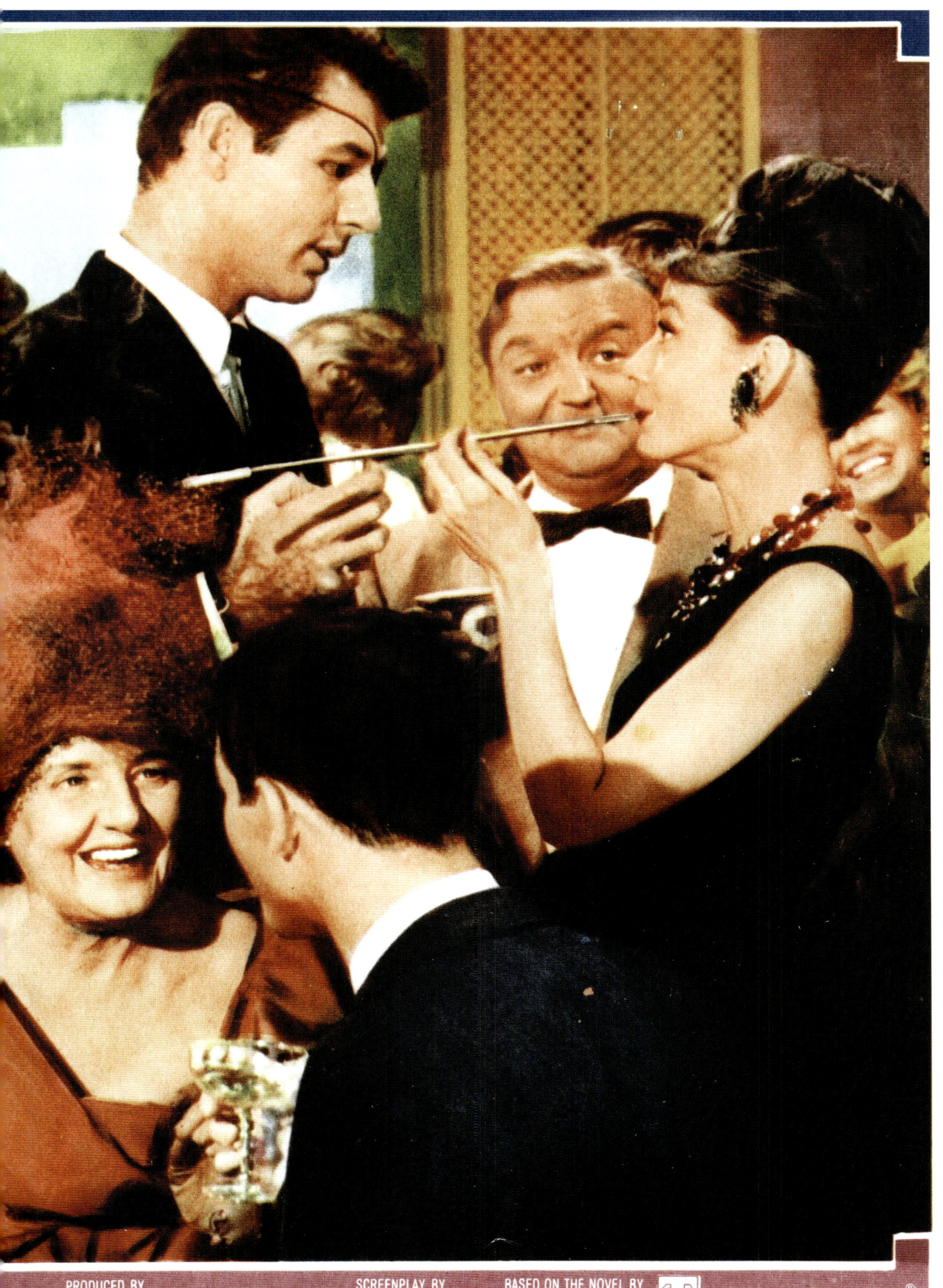
PRODUCED BY
JUROW AND RICHARD SHEPHERD
A PARAMOUNT RELEASE
SCREENPLAY BY
GEORGE AXELROD
BASED ON THE NOVEL BY
TRUMAN CAPOTE
MUSIC — HENRY MANCINI
TECHNICOLOR

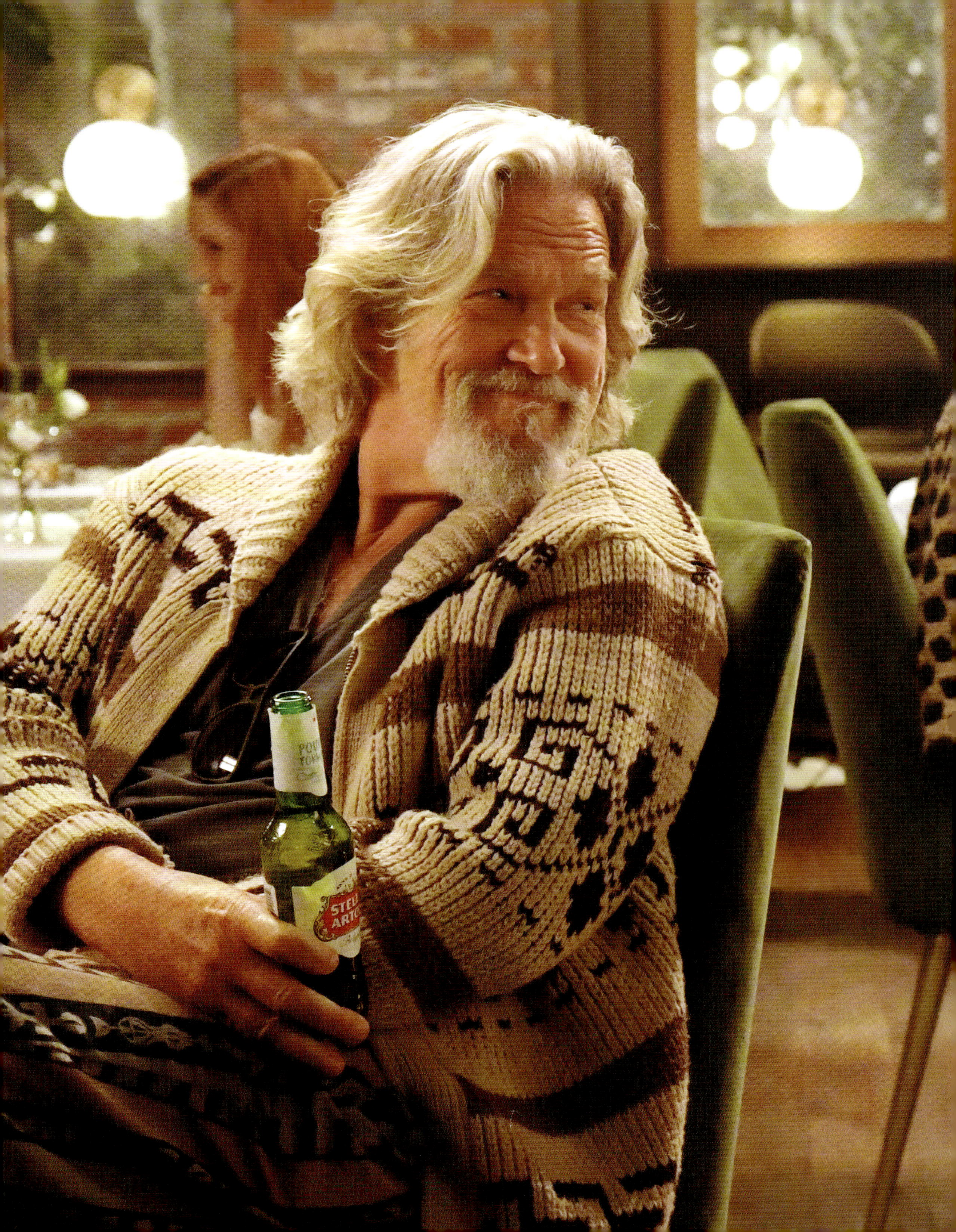

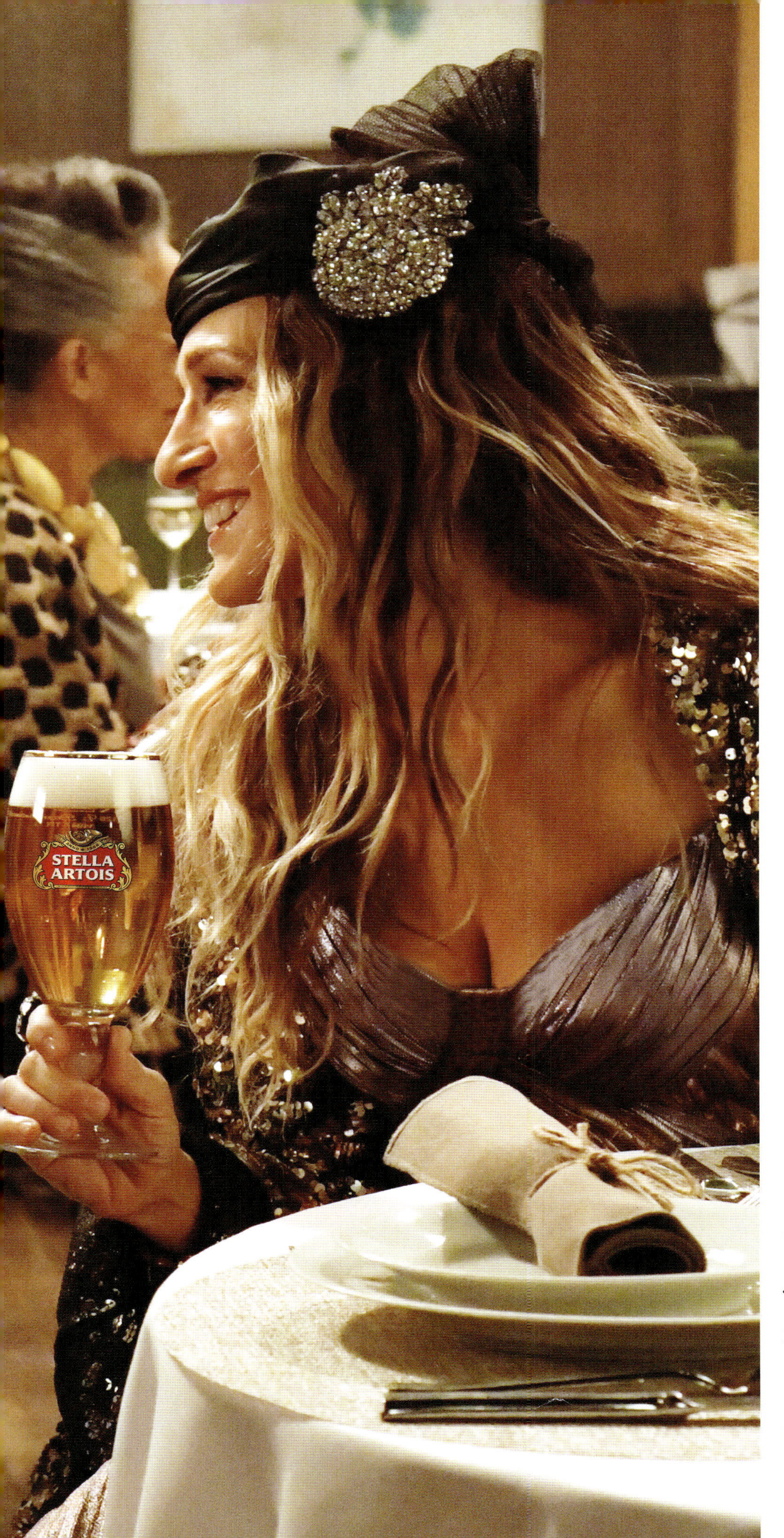

Opposite: *The Dude (Jeff Bridges) and Carrie Bradshaw (Sarah Jessica Parker) clink glasses in a 2004 Super Bowl ad—sans their usual White Russian and Cosmo.* Following pages, left: *Tom Cruise shows off epic tricks as a flair bartender in a scene from* Cocktail *(1988);* right: *Ursula Andress raises a glass to 007 in Jamaica for the 1962 James Bond film,* Dr. No.

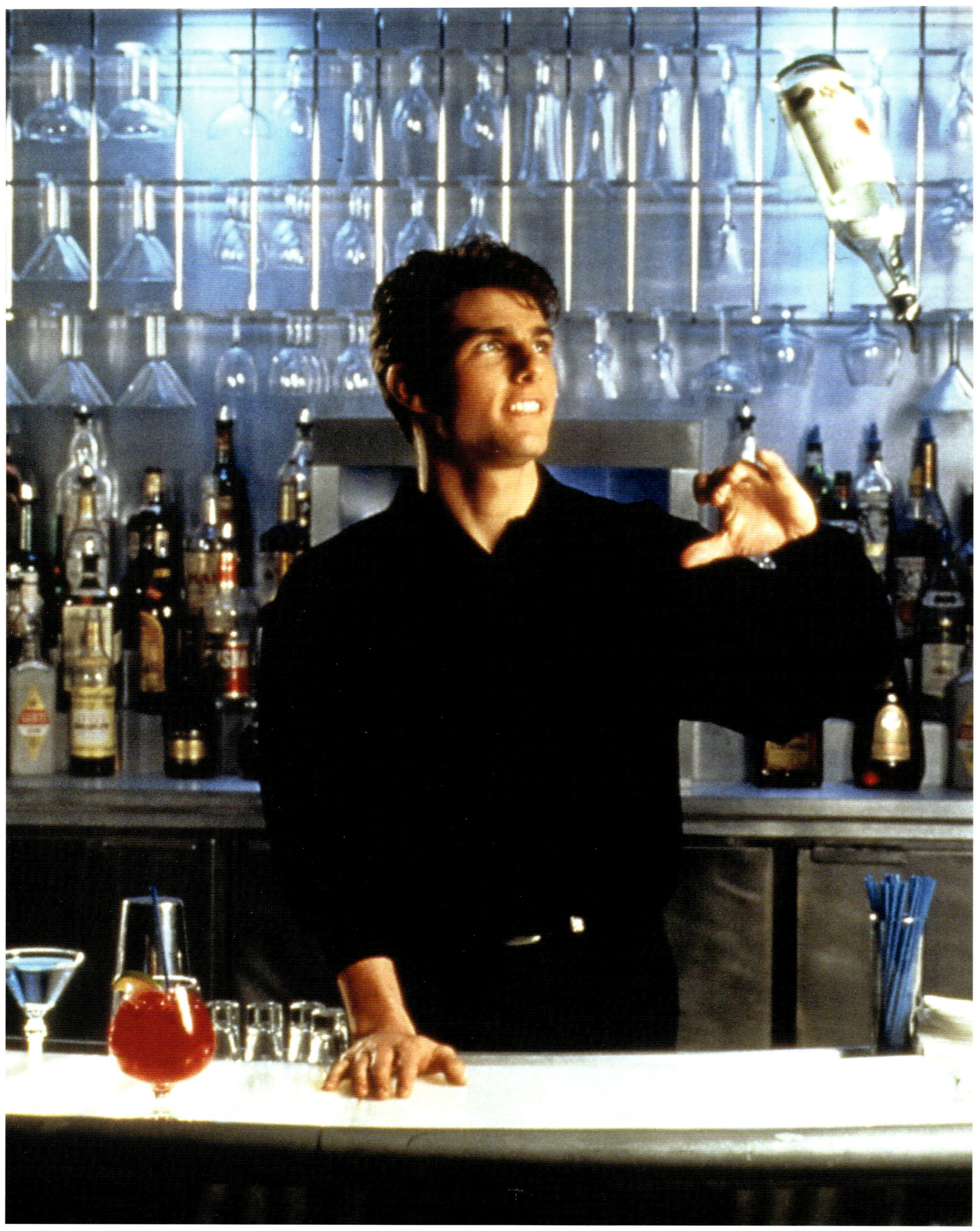

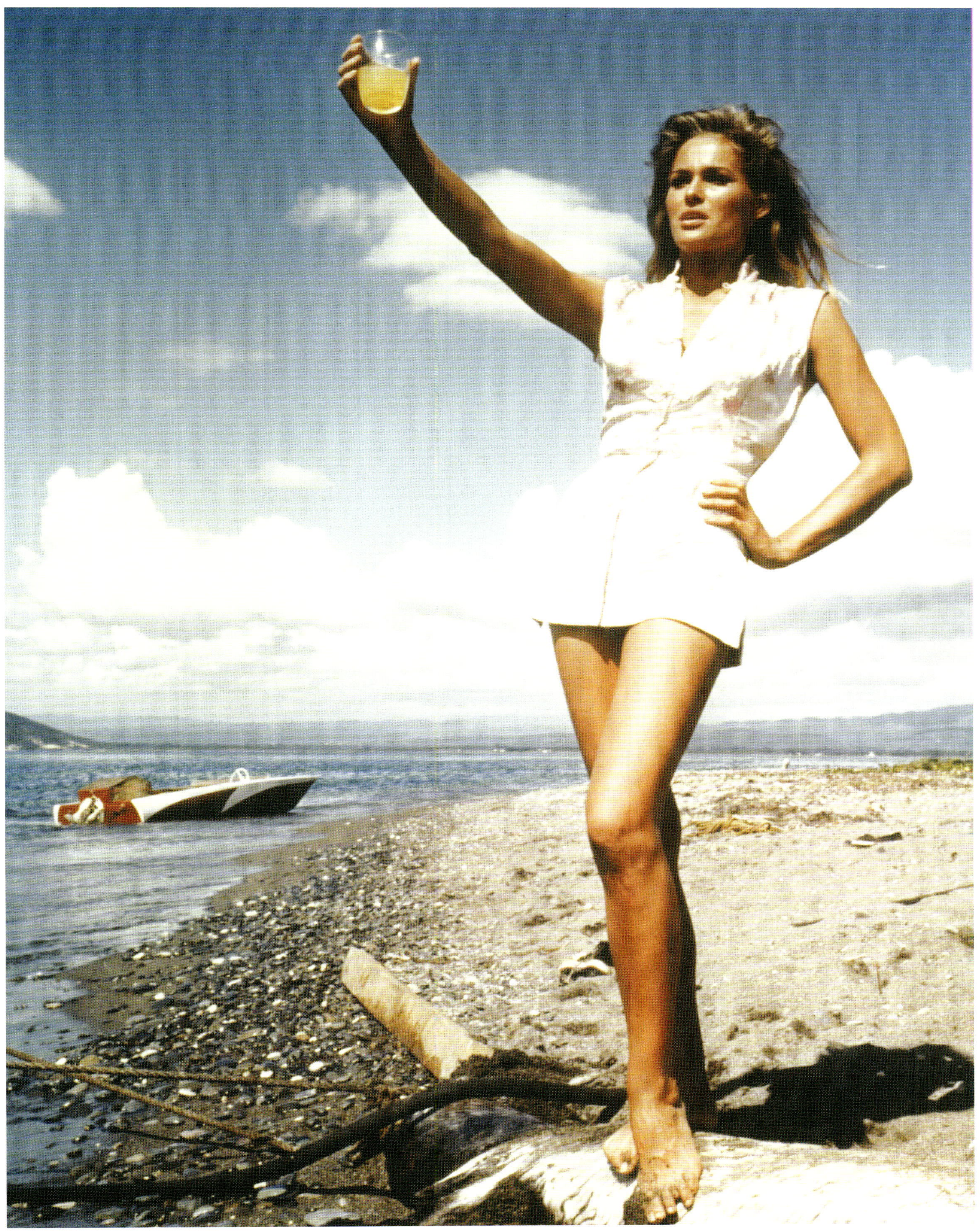

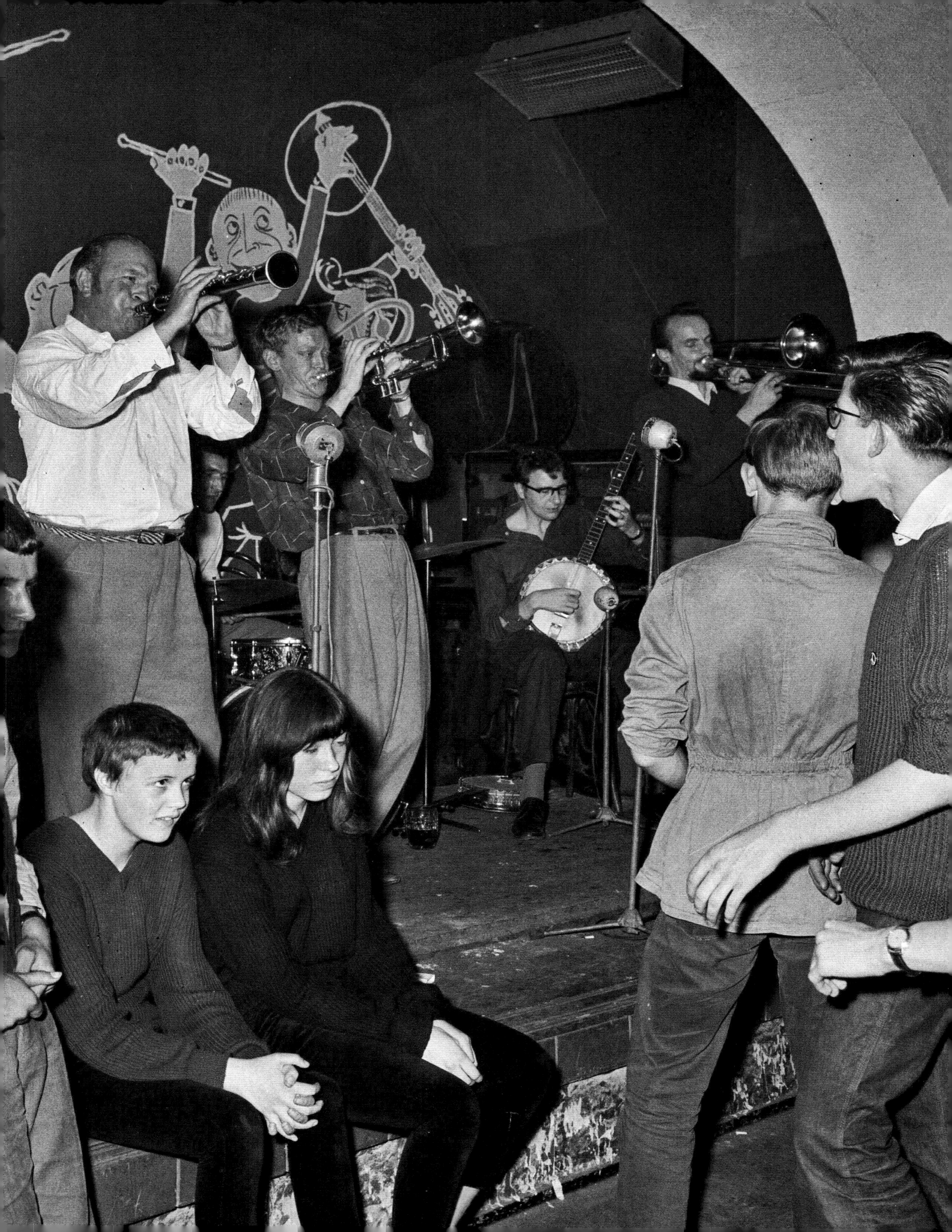

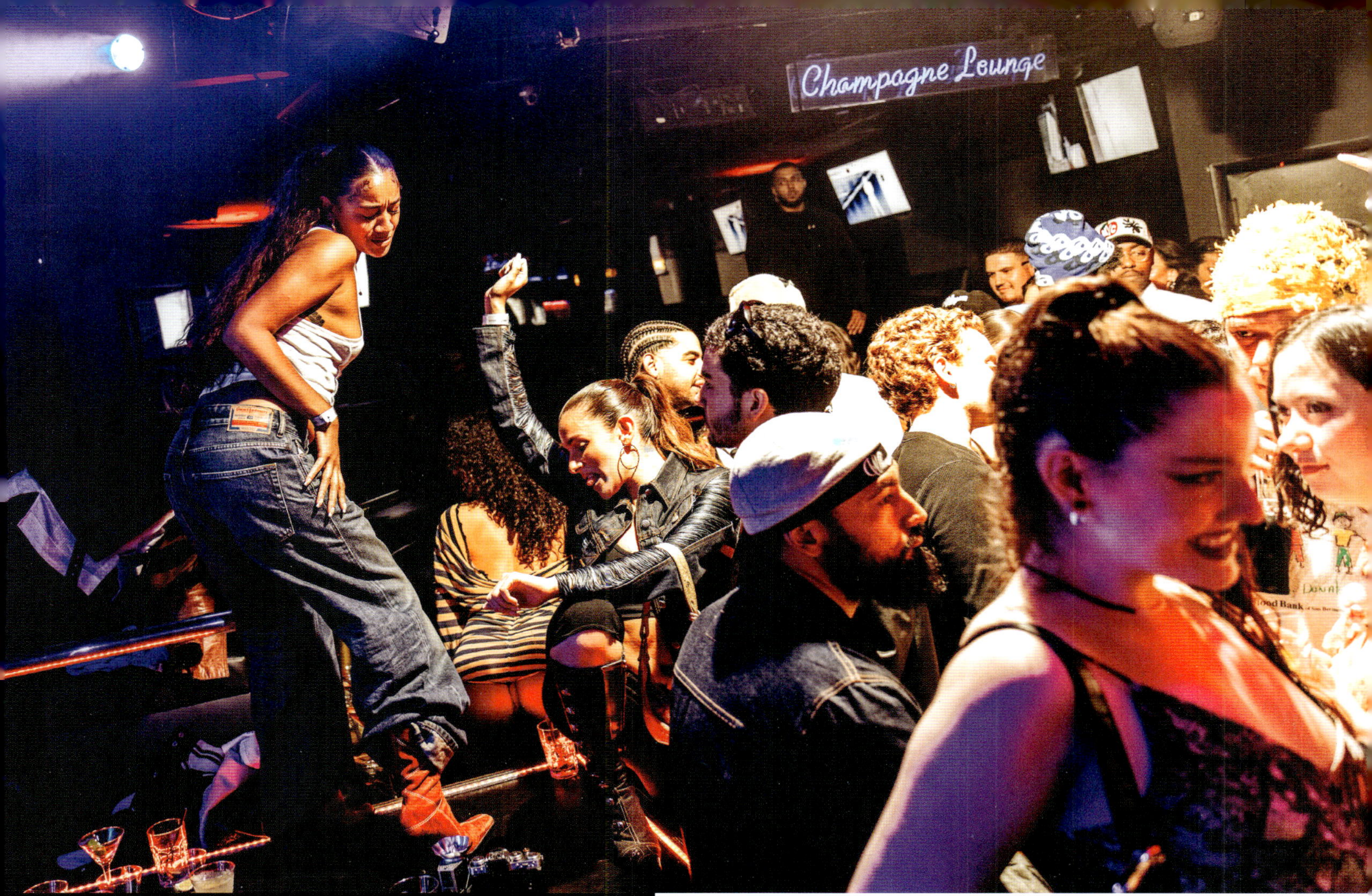

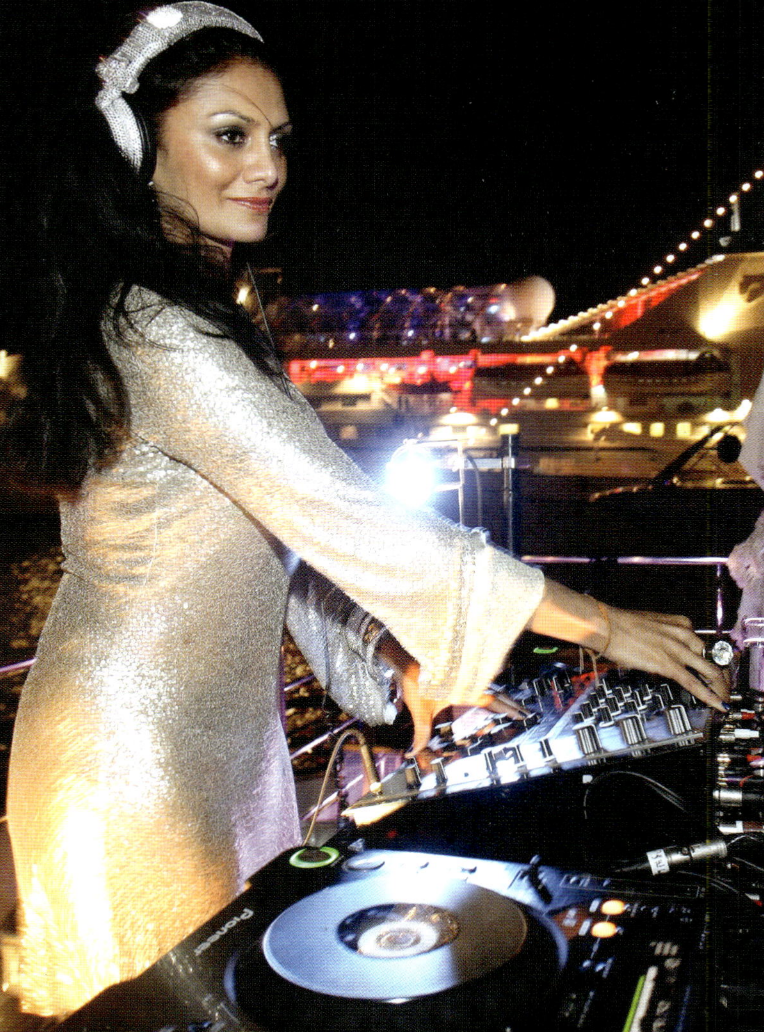

Clockwise from left: *Cool jazz heats up a hotel bar on Eel Pie Island on the Thames, 1961; Dance vibes take over a Met Gala party at New York's Sapphire, 2024; A DJ amps up a super-yacht cocktail party in Monaco, Monte Carlo, 2008.*

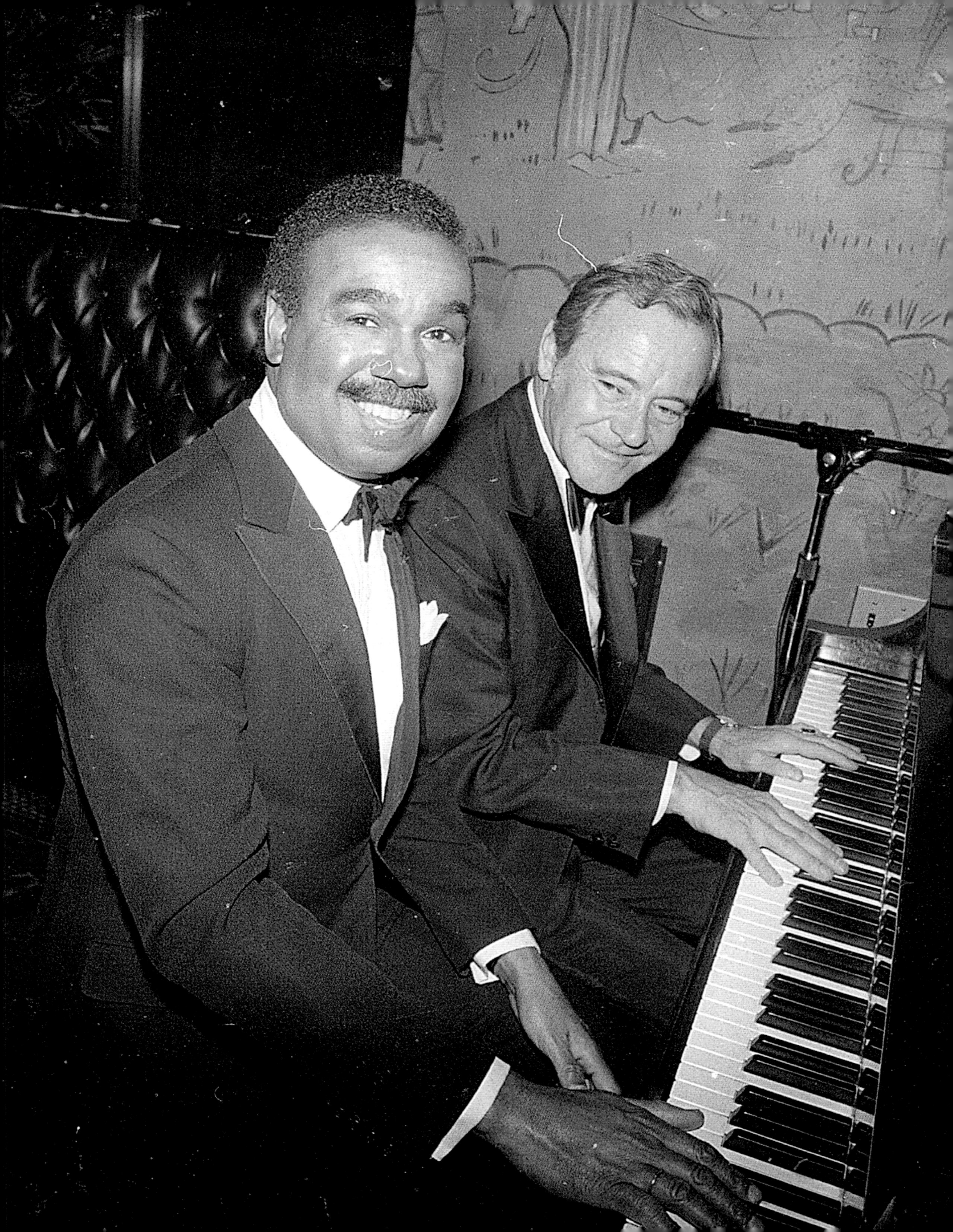

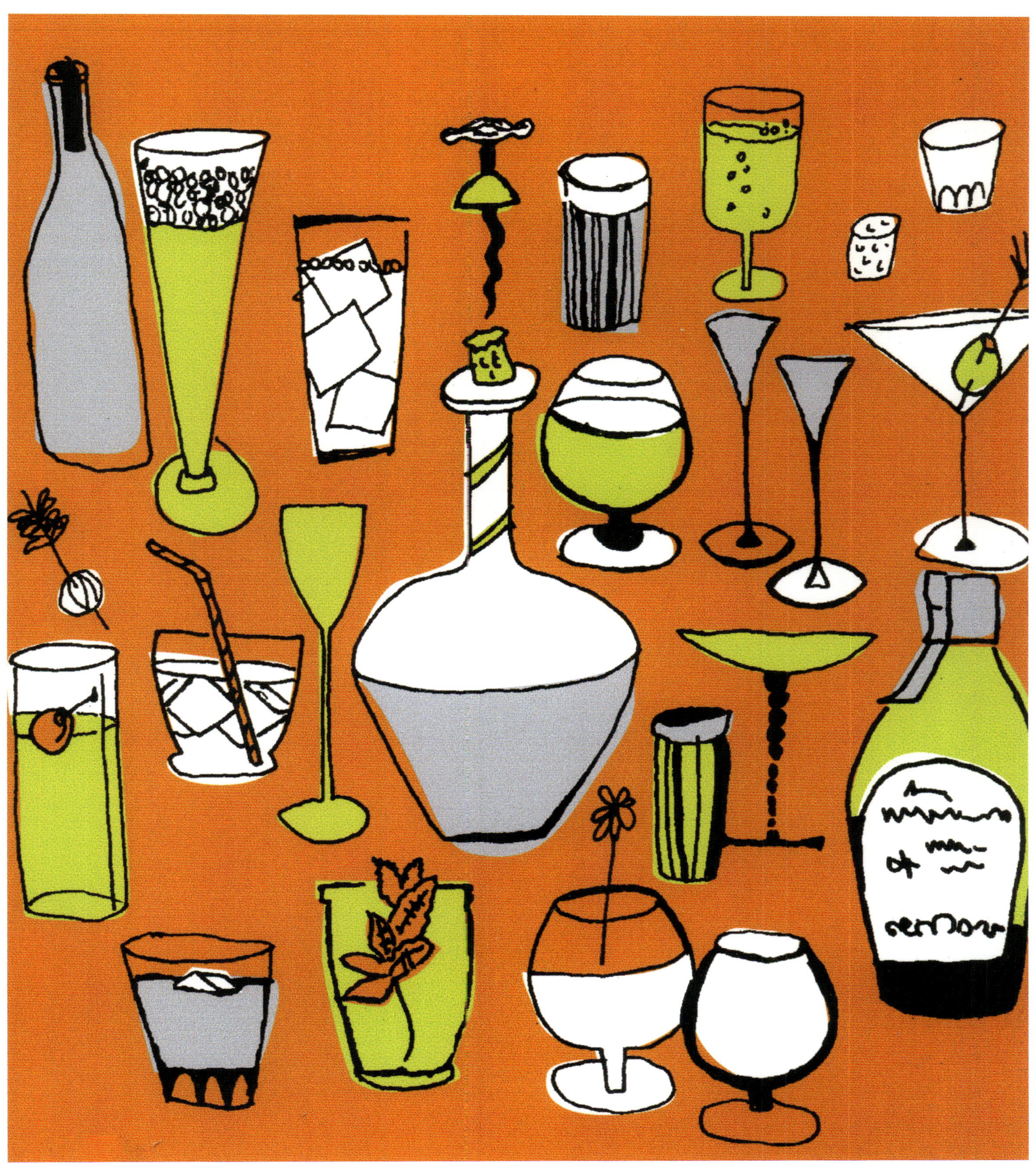

Opposite: *Music orchestrates a feel-good mood—like Bobby Short (and his pal, Jack Lemmon) tickling the ivories at Bemelmans Bar at the Hotel Carlyle, 1982.* This page: *Glassware enhances a drink's qualities, from ice-cold Gin and Tonics in highballs to sophisticated Manhattans in martini glasses.* Following pages, clockwise from top left: *Like martini glasses from the legendary Hemingway Bar at Paris's Ritz Hotel, glassware can make every sip sing; A smorgasbord of retro hors d'oeuvres showcases penguins composed of olives and hard-boiled eggs; Delicious hors d'oeuvres elevate the mood, especially when offered to guests with élan.*

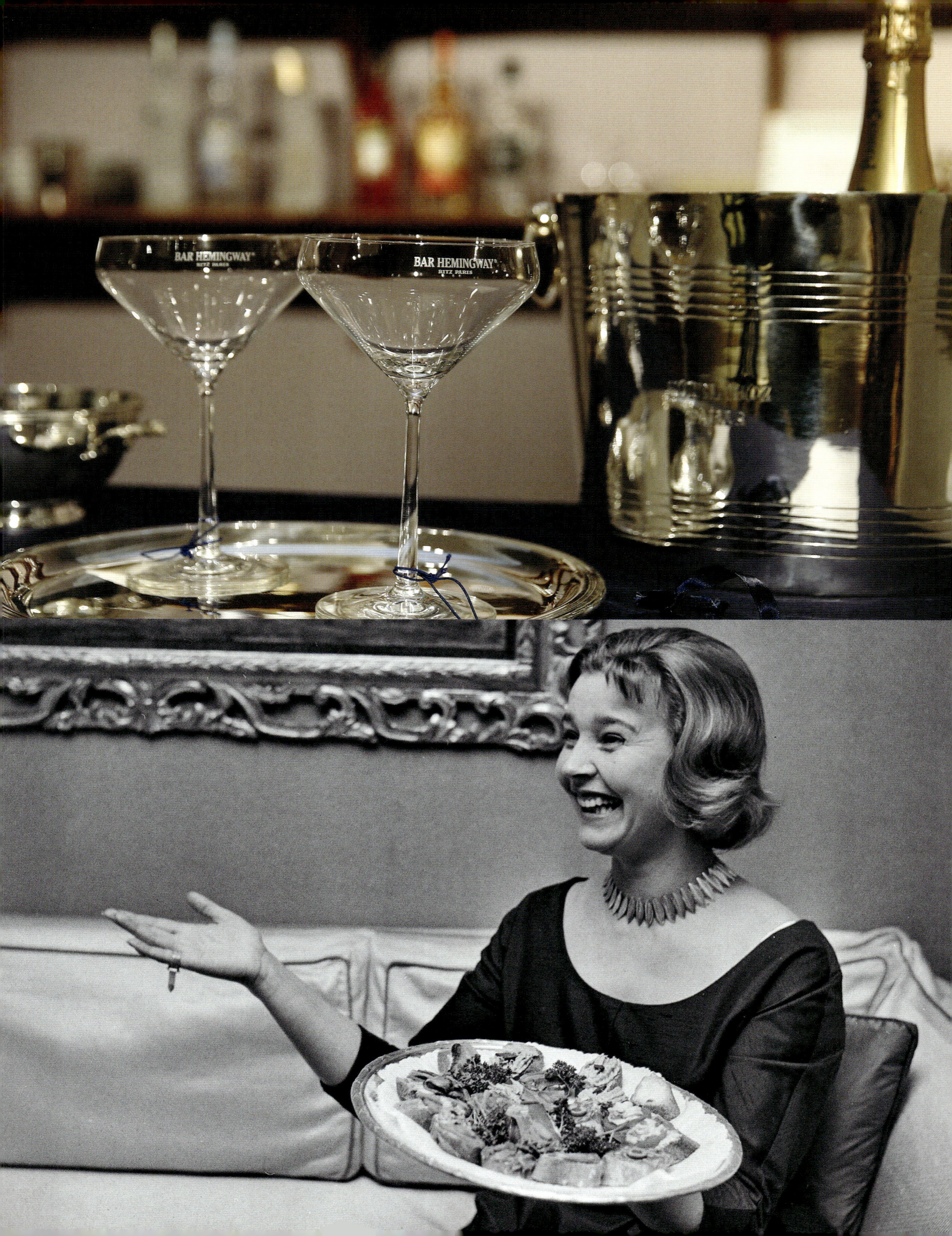
BAR HEMINGWAY
RITZ PARIS
BAR HEMINGWAY
RITZ PARIS

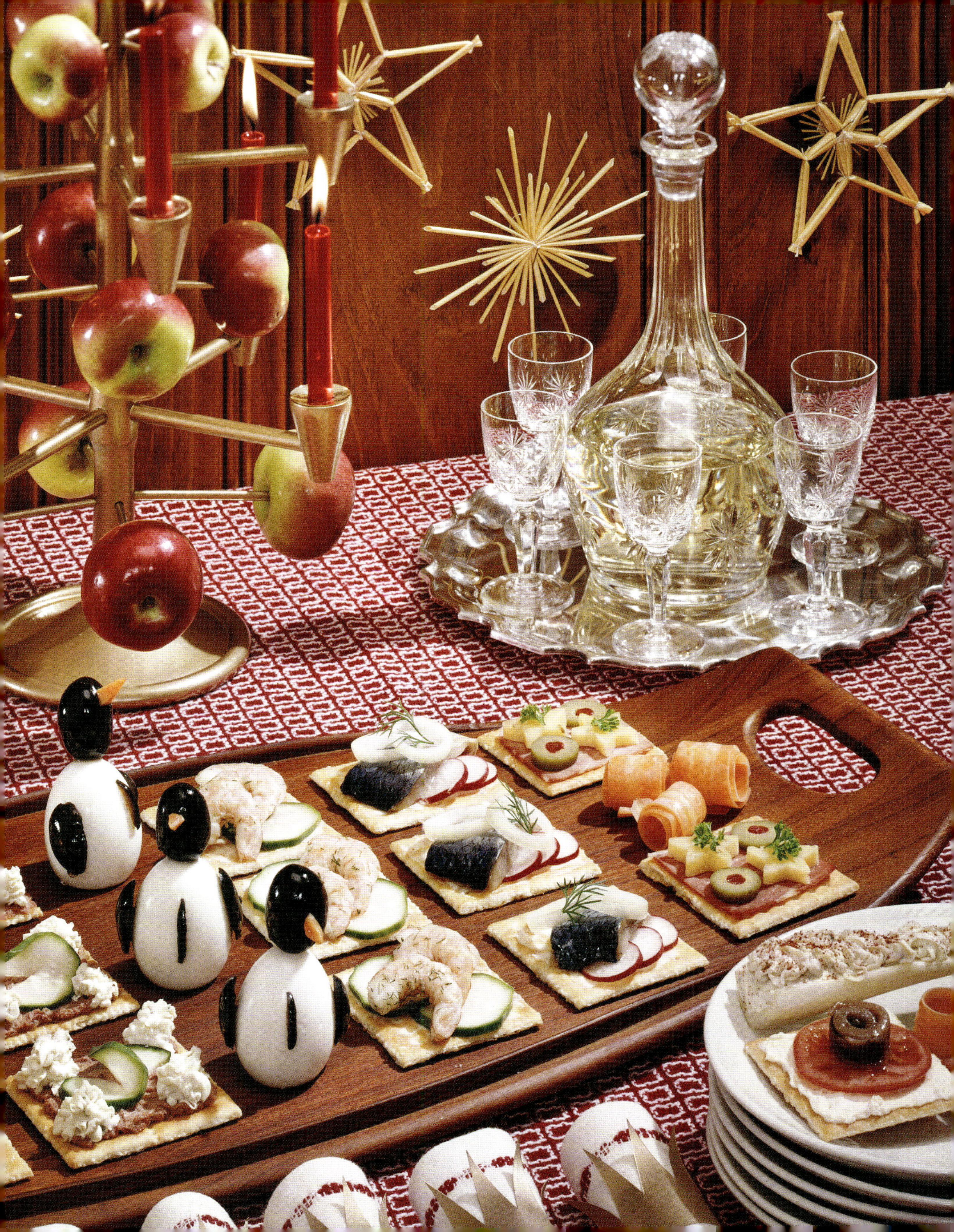

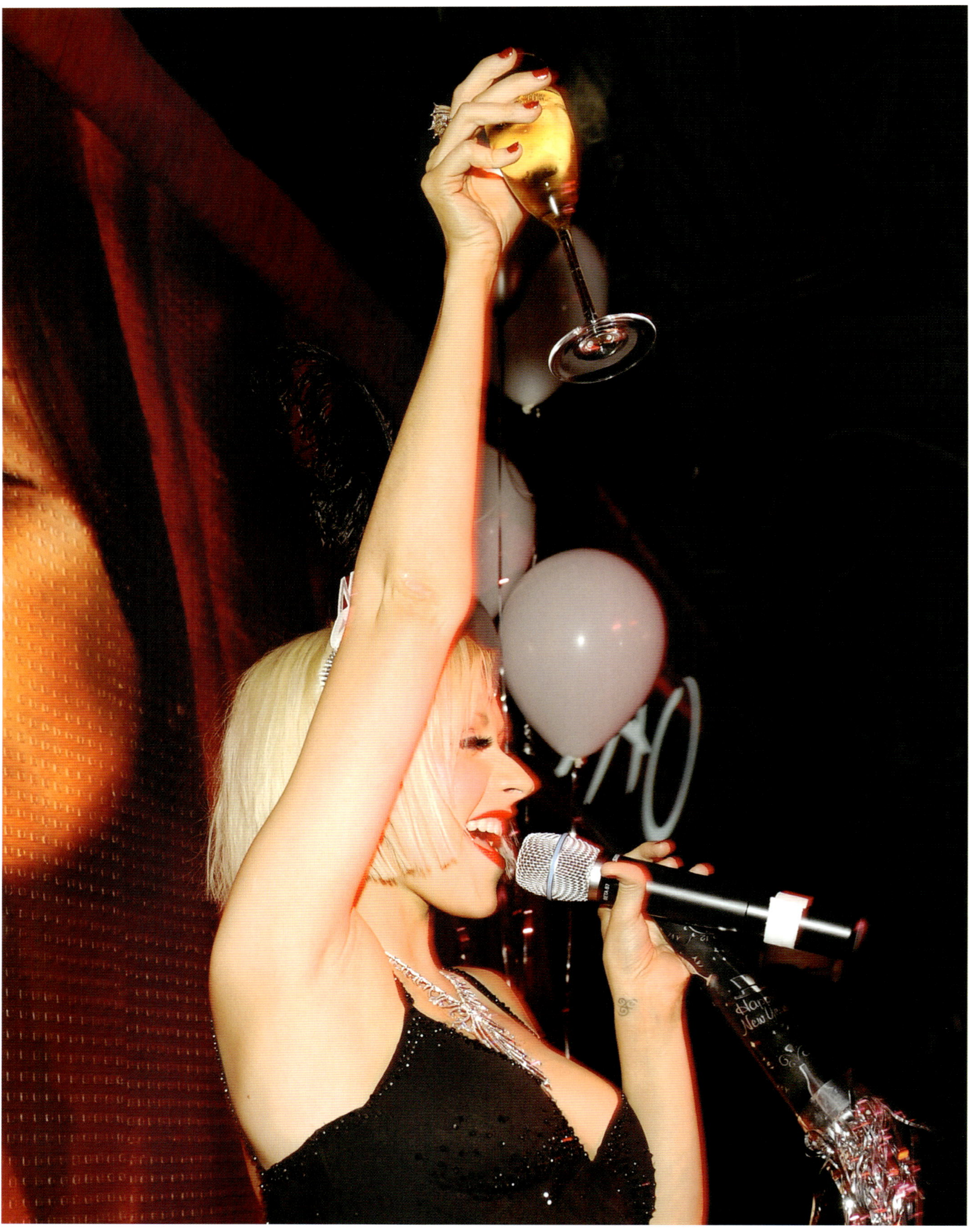

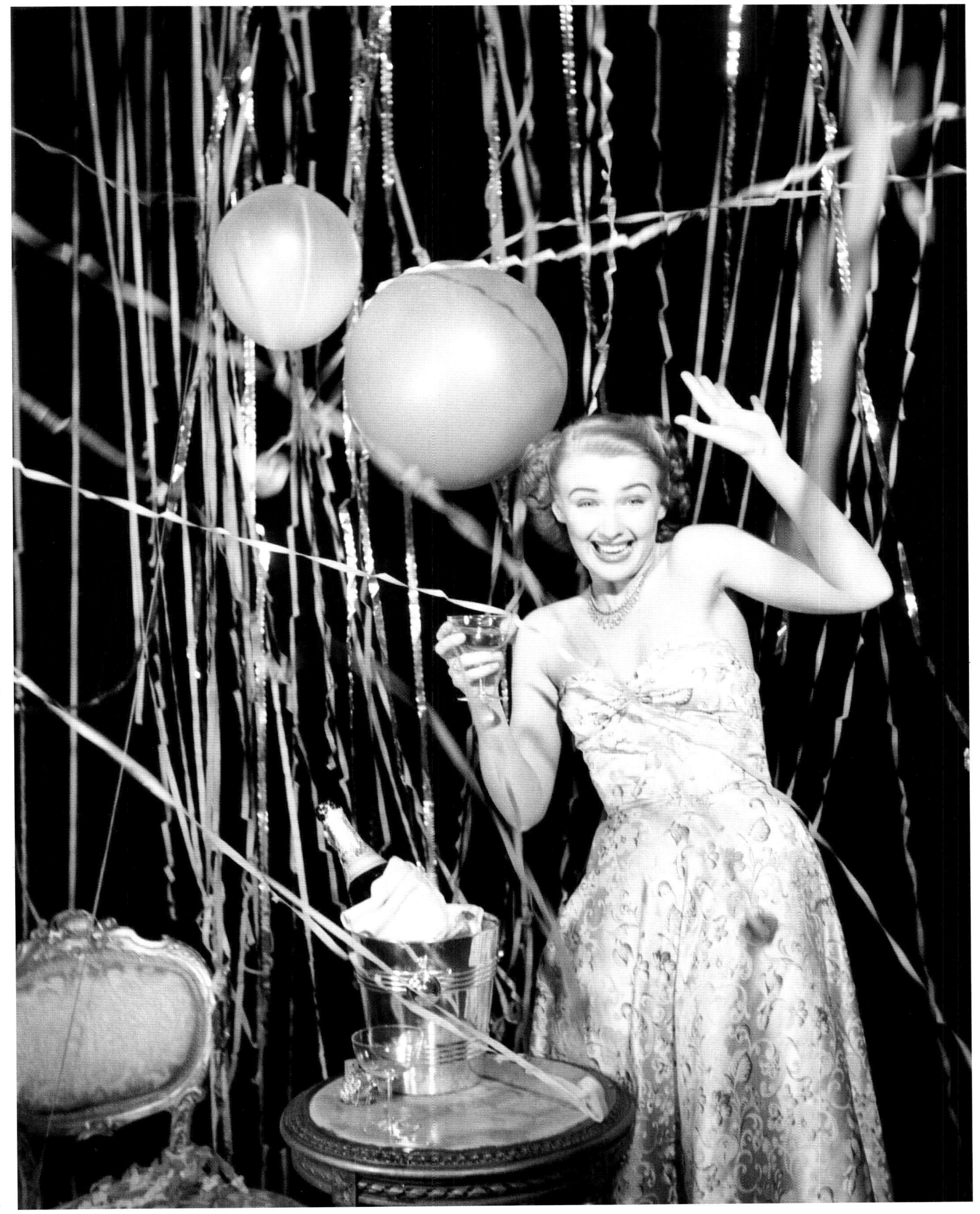

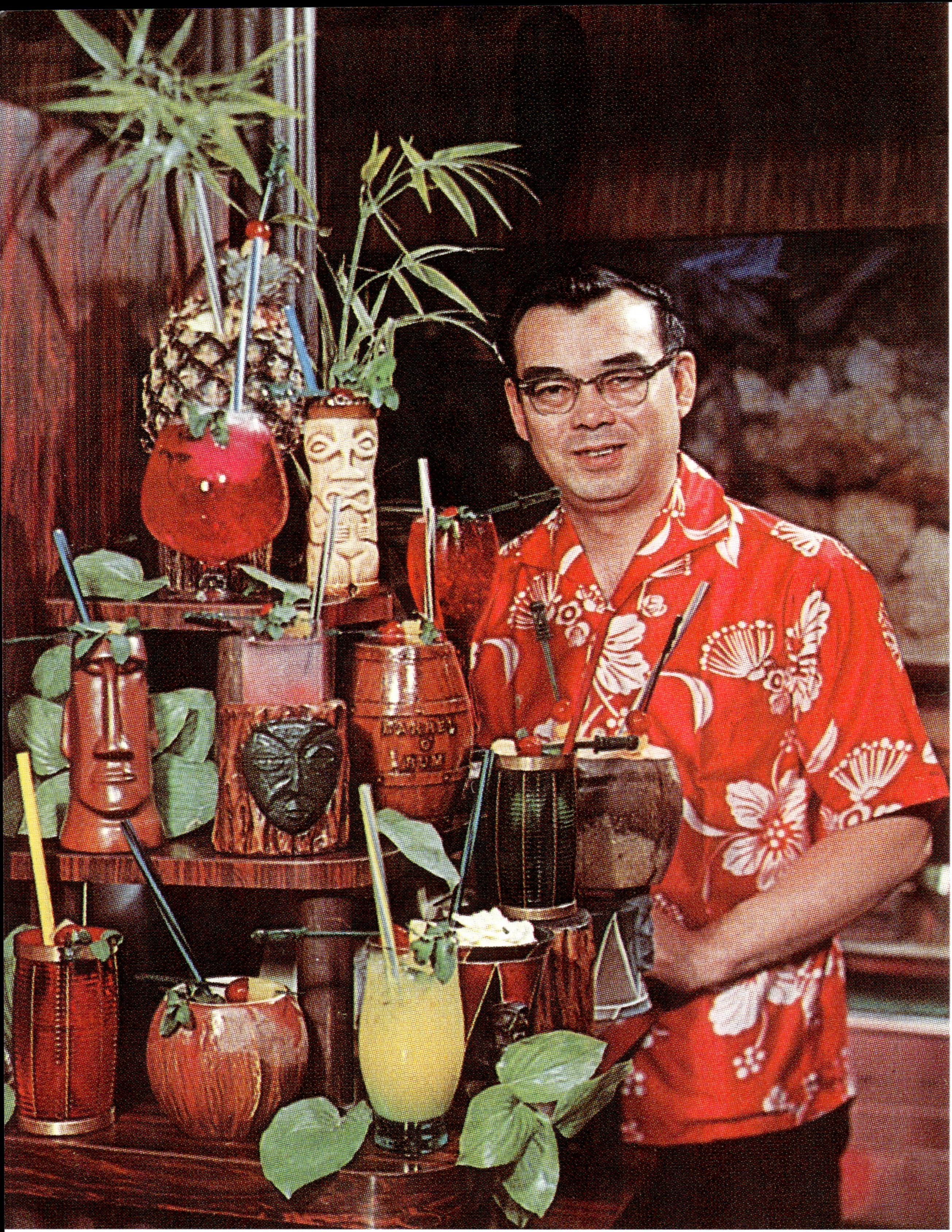

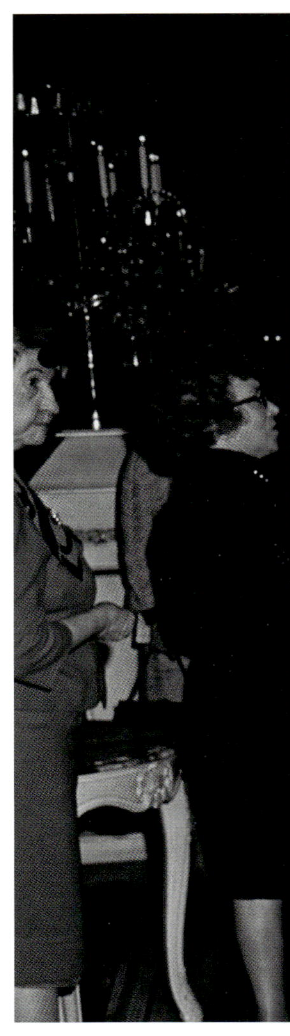

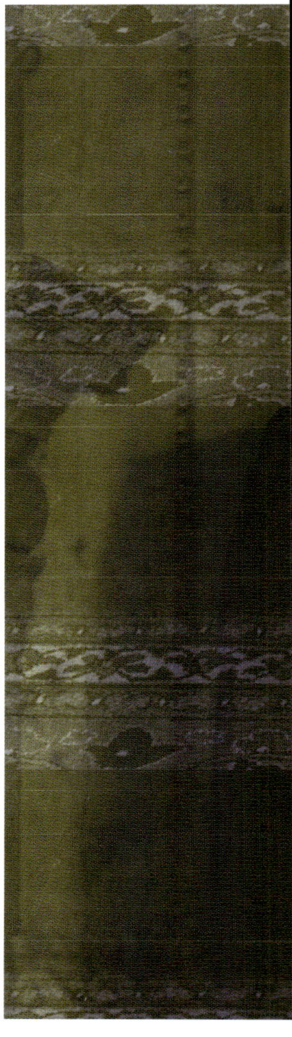

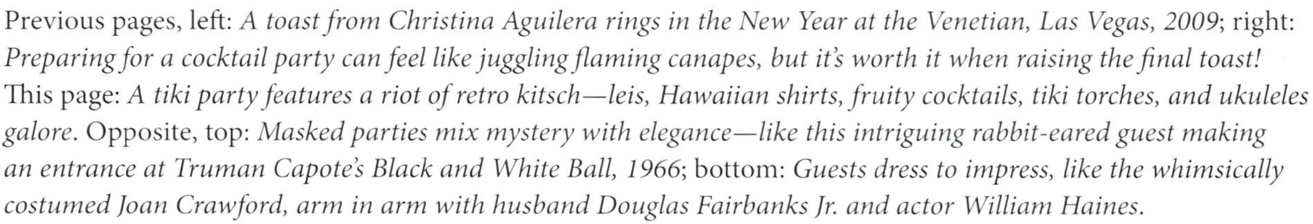

Previous pages, left: *A toast from Christina Aguilera rings in the New Year at the Venetian, Las Vegas, 2009*; right: *Preparing for a cocktail party can feel like juggling flaming canapes, but it's worth it when raising the final toast!* This page: *A tiki party features a riot of retro kitsch—leis, Hawaiian shirts, fruity cocktails, tiki torches, and ukuleles galore*. Opposite, top: *Masked parties mix mystery with elegance—like this intriguing rabbit-eared guest making an entrance at Truman Capote's Black and White Ball, 1966*; bottom: *Guests dress to impress, like the whimsically costumed Joan Crawford, arm in arm with husband Douglas Fairbanks Jr. and actor William Haines.*

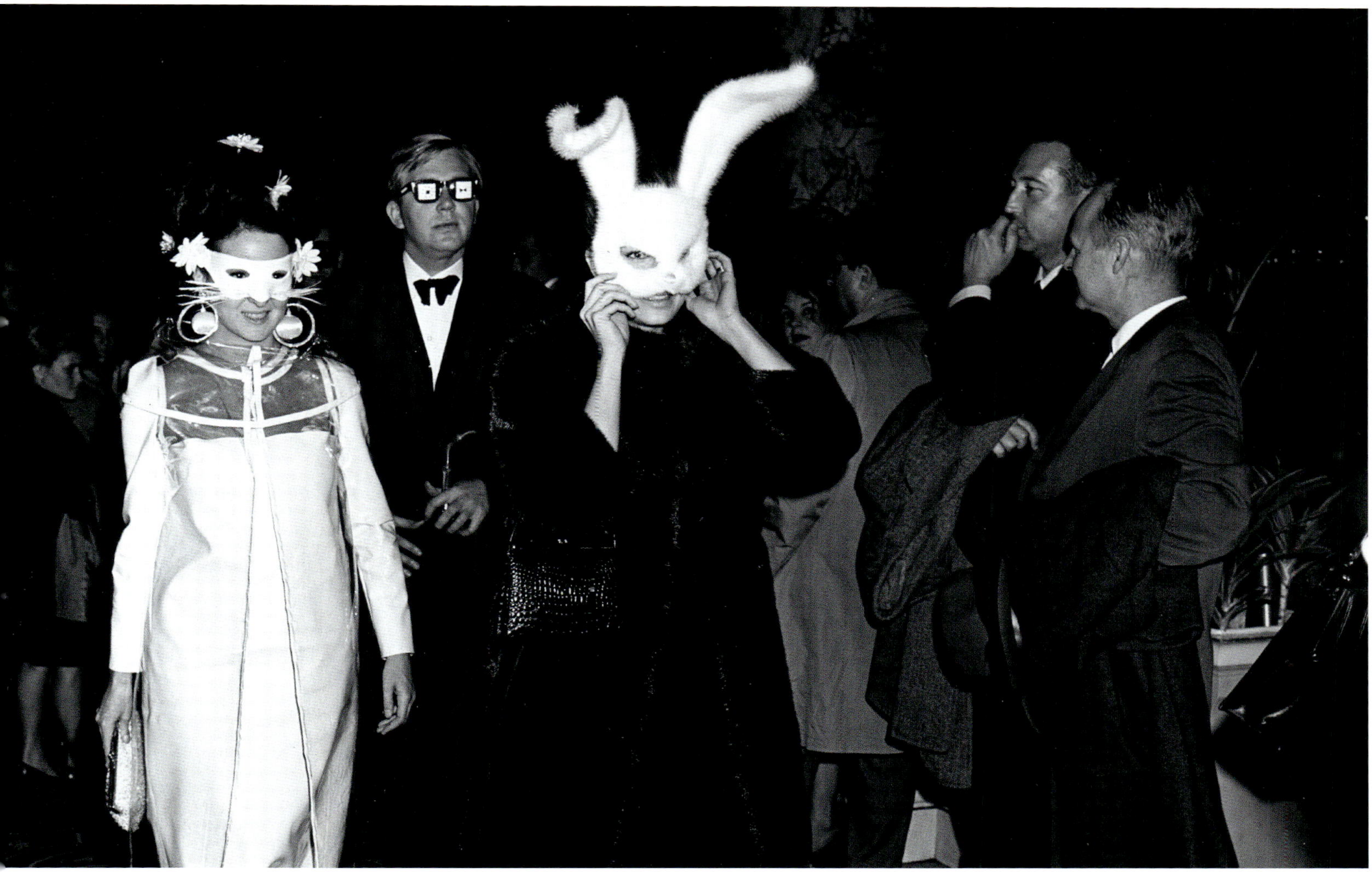

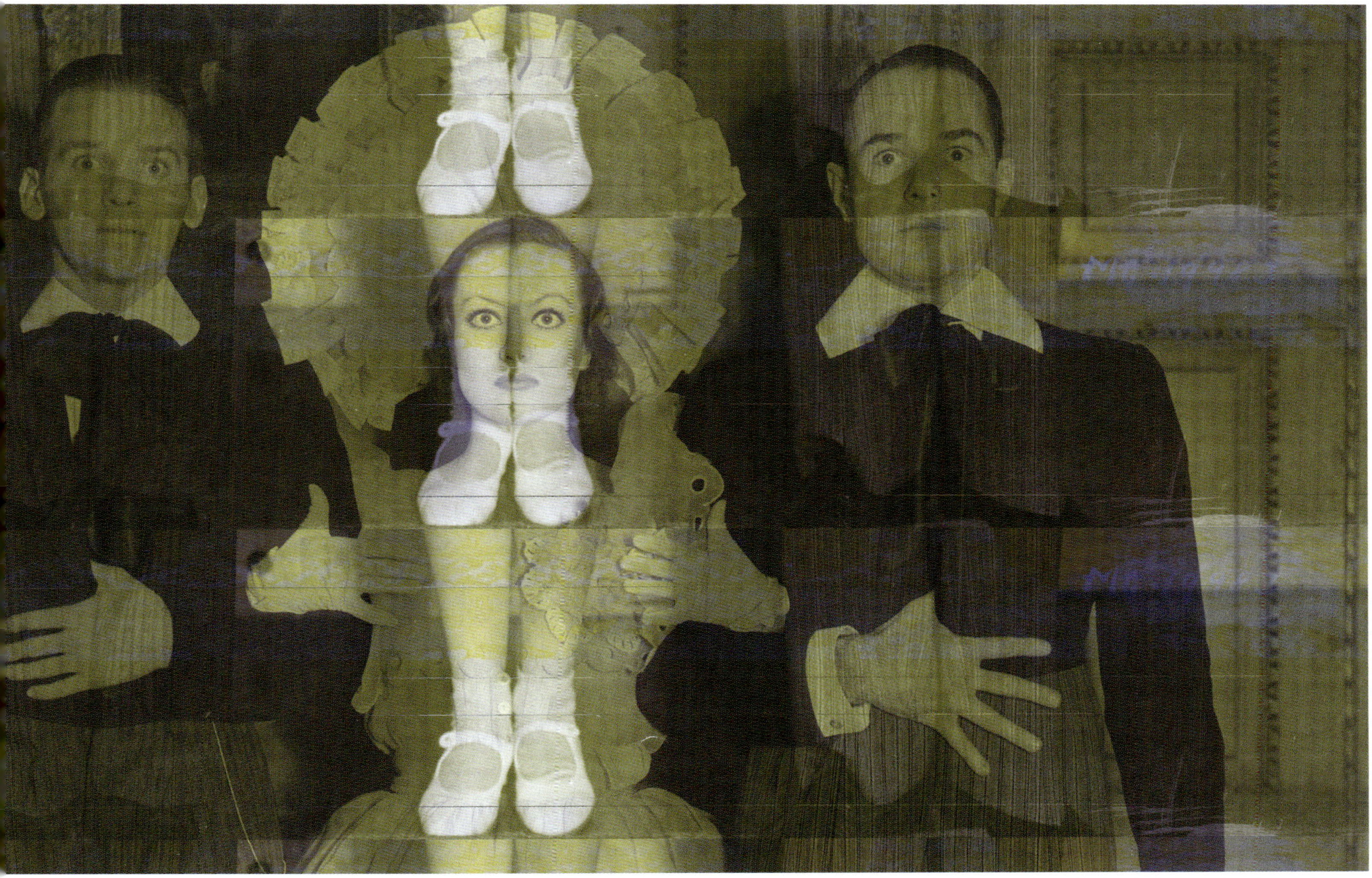

COCKTAIL RECIPES

OLD FASHIONED

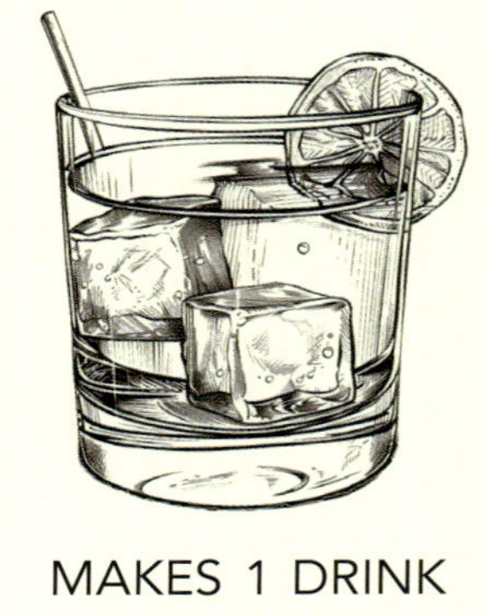

MAKES 1 DRINK

¼ OUNCE SIMPLE SYRUP, OR TO TASTE
2 TO 3 DASHES ANGOSTURA BITTERS
SPLASH OF WATER
2 OUNCES RYE WHISKEY OR BOURBON
1 ORANGE TWIST AND/OR 1 MARASCHINO CHERRY, FOR GARNISH

In a mixing glass, stir together the simple syrup, bitters, and water to combine. Add the whiskey (or bourbon) and stir. Strain into a rocks glass with ice. Gently squeeze the orange twist over the glass, and garnish with the orange twist and/or a maraschino cherry, as preferred. Cheers!

NEGRONI

1 OUNCE GIN
1 OUNCE SWEET VERMOUTH
1 OUNCE CAMPARI
ORANGE TWIST OR SLICE, FOR GARNISH

In a mixing glass filled with ice, stir together the gin, sweet vermouth, and Campari until well chilled. Strain into a rocks glass over ice. Garnish with the orange twist or slice. *Cin cin!*

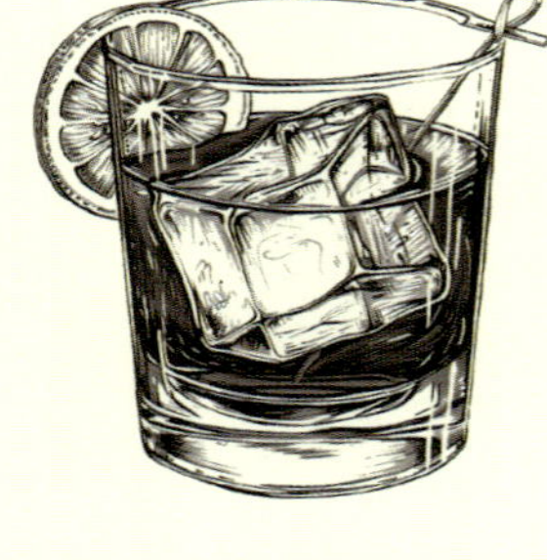

MAKES 1 DRINK

MOSCOW MULE

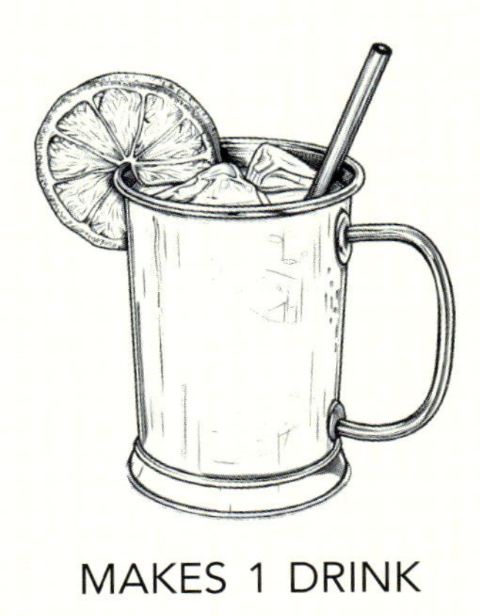

MAKES 1 DRINK

2 OUNCES VODKA
½ OUNCE LIME JUICE, FRESHLY SQUEEZED
½ CUP GINGER BEER
1 LIME WEDGE, FOR GARNISH

In a Moscow Mule mug filled with ice, stir together the vodka, lime juice, and ginger beer until well chilled. Garnish with a lime wedge. *Za zdorovye!*

MOJITO

3–5 MINT LEAVES, TO TASTE
1½ OUNCES WHITE RUM
½ OUNCE LIME JUICE, FRESHLY SQUEEZED
¼ OUNCE SIMPLE SYRUP, OR TO TASTE (OPTIONAL)
SODA WATER, TO TOP

In a cocktail shaker, lightly muddle the mint leaves. Add the rum, lime juice, and simple syrup (if using). Top with a splash of soda water and shake until well chilled. Strain over a tall Collins glass filled with ice. *¡Arriba, abajo, al centro y pa' dentro!*

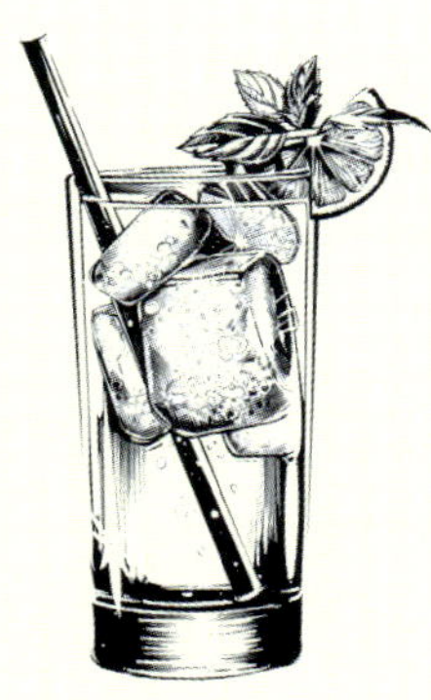

MAKES 1 DRINK

COCKTAIL RECIPES

DRY MARTINI

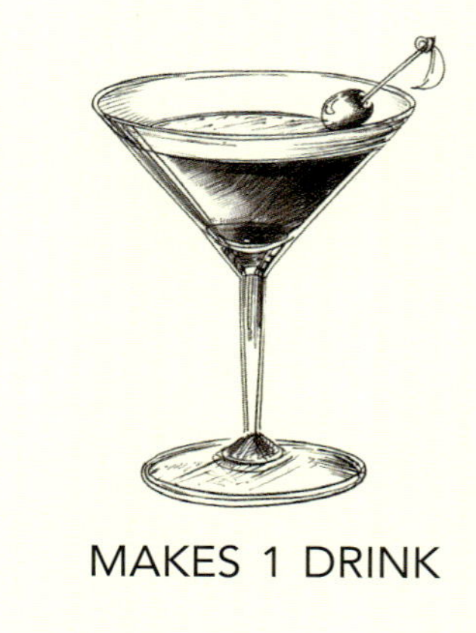

MAKES 1 DRINK

2 ½ OUNCES GIN
½ OUNCE DRY VERMOUTH, OR TO TASTE
1–3 GREEN OLIVES OR LEMON TWIST, FOR GARNISH

Chill a martini glass. Into a mixing glass (or cocktail shaker) filled with ice, add the gin and dry vermouth. Stir (or shake) until well chilled. Strain into the chilled martini glass. Garnish with the green olives or a lemon twist, as preferred. Here's mud in your eye!

MARGARITA

¼ TEASPOON SEA SALT (FOR RIM)
LIME WEDGE (FOR RIM)
1½ OUNCES TEQUILA
1 OUNCE TRIPLE SEC
¾ OUNCE LIME JUICE, FRESHLY SQUEEZED
¼ OUNCE AGAVE NECTAR OR SIMPLE SYRUP, OR TO TASTE (OPTIONAL)
LIME WHEEL OR WEDGE, FOR GARNISH

Sprinkle the salt onto a plate. Wet the rim of a margarita glass with a lime wedge and dip the moistened rim in the salt. In a cocktail shaker filled with ice, add the tequila, triple sec, lime juice, and agave nectar (if using). Shake until well chilled. Strain into the salt-rimmed margarita glass. *¡Salud!*

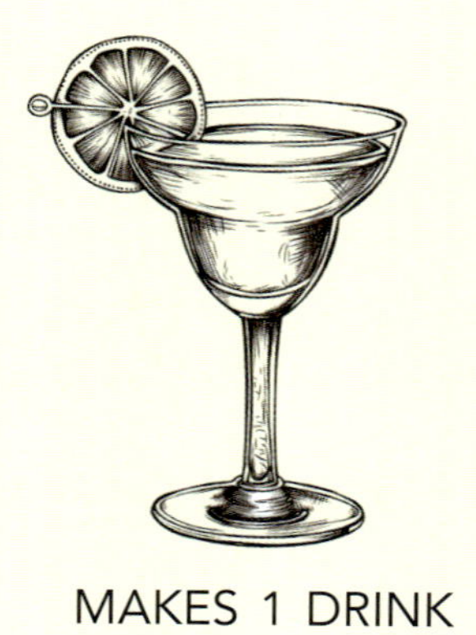

MAKES 1 DRINK

ESPRESSO MARTINI

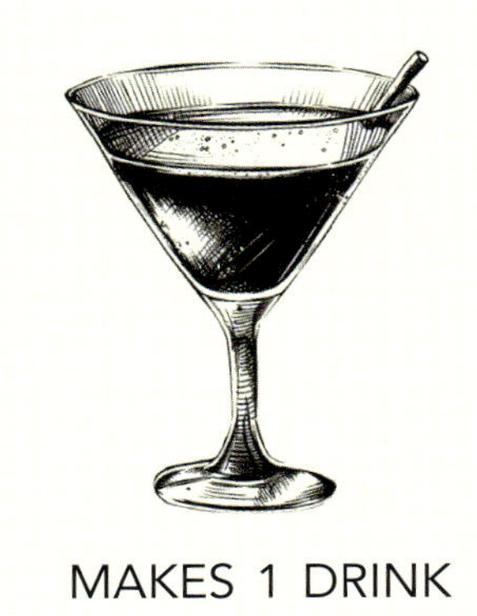

MAKES 1 DRINK

1½ OUNCES VODKA
1 OUNCE COFFEE LIQUEUR
1 OUNCE ROOM-TEMPERATURE ESPRESSO OR COLD BREW CONCENTRATE
¼ OUNCE SIMPLE SYRUP, OR TO TASTE (OPTIONAL)
3 COFFEE BEANS, FOR GARNISH

Chill a coupe glass. Into a cocktail shaker filled with ice, add the vodka, coffee liqueur, espresso, and simple syrup (if using). Shake until well chilled and strain into the chilled coupe glass. Garnish with the coffee beans. Bottoms up!

LONG ISLAND ICED TEA

½ OUNCE GIN
½ OUNCE RUM
½ OUNCE TEQUILA
½ OUNCE TRIPLE SEC
½ OUNCE VODKA
1 OUNCE LEMON JUICE, FRESHLY SQUEEZED
COLA, TO TOP
LEMON SLICE OR WEDGE, AS GARNISH

To a tall highball glass filled with ice, add the gin, rum, tequila, triple sec, vodka, and lemon juice. Top off with a splash of cola and stir to combine. Garnish with a lemon slice or wedge. Enjoy!

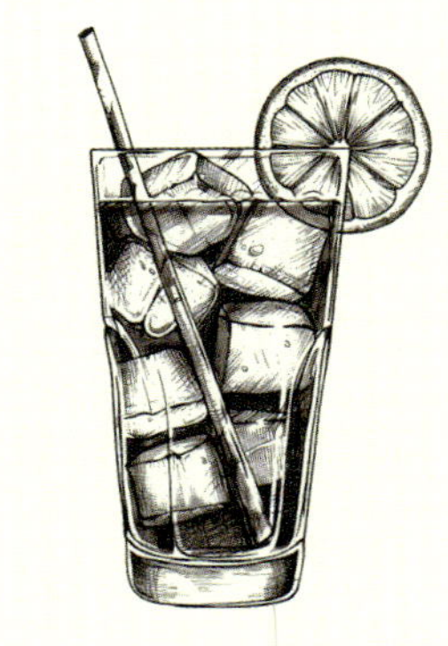

MAKES 1 DRINK

PHOTO CREDITS

Cover (front and back): © Slim Aarons/Hulton Archive/Getty Images; p. 2: © Fred Lindinger/United Archives/Getty Images; p. 4: © Bettmann/Getty Images; p. 6: © John Springer Collection/CORBIS/Corbis via Getty Images; p. 9: © Rose Hartman/Getty Images; p. 10: © Enrico Spanu/REDA&CO/Universal Images Group via Getty Images; pp. 14–15: © Slim Aarons/Getty Images; p. 16: © Laslo Irmes/RDB/ullstein bild via Getty Images; p. 17: © Hulton Archive/Getty Images; p. 18: © Jay L. Clendenin/Los Angeles Times via Getty Images; p. 19 (top): © Eric Bard/Corbis via Getty Images; p. 19 (bottom): © Keystone-France/Gamma-Rapho via Getty Images; p. 20: © Slim Aarons/Hulton Archive/Getty Images; p. 21: © Nicky Digital/http://NickyDigital.com/Corbis via Getty Images; pp. 22–23: © Michael Putland/Getty Images; p. 24 (top): © Peter Bischoff/Getty Images; p. 24 (bottom): © Junko Kimura/Getty Images; p. 25: © David Keeler/Getty Images; pp. 26–27: © Paul Chinn/The San Francisco Chronicle via Getty Images; p. 28 (top): © Hulton Archive/Getty Images; p. 28 (bottom): © Ron Galella, Ltd./Ron Galella Collection via Getty Images; p. 29: © Circa Images/GHI/Universal History Archive/Universal Images Group via Getty Images; pp. 30–31: © Edward A. Hausner/New York Times Co./Getty Images; pp. 32–33: © Slim Aarons/Hulton Archive/Getty Images; p. 34: © Hulton Archive/Getty Images; p. 35: © Sergi Reboredo/VW PICS/Universal Images Group via Getty Images; pp. 36–37: © Slim Aarons/Hulton Archive/Getty Images; p. 38: © Bettmann/Getty Images; p. 39: © Charley Gallay/Getty Images for Betsey Johnson; pp. 40–41: © Stefanie Keenan/Getty Images for NET-A-PORTER; p. 42: © Underwood Archives/Getty Images; p. 43: © Roger Viollet via Getty Images/Roger Viollet via Getty Images; p. 44: © Slim Aarons/Hulton Archive/Getty Images; p. 45: © Daily Mirror/Mirrorpix/Mirrorpix via Getty Images; p. 46 (top): © Thomas Janisch/Getty Images; p. 47 (bottom): © Jean Marc CHARLES/Gamma-Rapho via Getty Images; p. 48: Bettmann/Getty Images; pp. 48–49: © Austrian Archives/Imagno/Getty Images; pp. 50–51: © Jeffrey Greenberg/Education Images/Universal Images Group via Getty Images; p. 52: © Bettmann/Getty Images; p. 56: © Fin Costello/Redferns; p. 57 (top): © Dima Korotayev/Epsilon/Getty Images; p. 57 (bottom): © Robin Platzer/Getty Images; pp. 58–59: © Ron Galella/Ron Galella Collection via Getty Images; p. 60: © M. Garrett/Murray Garrett/Getty Images; p. 61: © Fairchild Archive/Penske Media via Getty Images; pp. 62–63: © FPG/Archive Photos/Getty Images; p. 64: © Sonia Moskowitz/Getty Images; p. 65 (top): © Rita Barros/Getty Images; p. 65 (bottom): © Bettmann/Getty Images; p. 66: © Bettmann/Getty Images; p. 67: © Lee Celano/WireImage for William Morris Agency(WMA); pp. 68–69: © Jacques M. Chenet/CORBIS/Corbis via Getty Images; pp. 70–71: © Evening Standard/Getty Images; p. 72: © Ron Galella/Ron Galella Collection via Getty Images; p. 73: © ullstein bild/ullstein bild via Getty Images; p. 74: © Slim Aarons/Hulton Archive/Getty Images; p. 75: © Bettmann/Getty Images; p. 76: © Steve Eichner/Penske Media via Getty Images; p. 77: © Fairchild Archive/Penske Media via Getty Images; p. 78: © The Denver Post/Denver Post via Getty Images; p. 79: © Graphic House/Archive Photos/Getty Images; p. 80: © Steve Eichner/WWD/Penske Media via Getty Images; p. 81 (top): © Fox Photos/Getty Images; p. 81 (bottom): © Walter Rudolph/United Archives/Universal Images Group via Getty Images; p. 82: © Underwood Archives/Getty Images; p. 83: © Hulton Archive/Getty Images; p. 84: © Bettmann/Getty Images; p. 85: © Arthur Grimm/United Archives via Getty Images; p. 86: © Vinnie Zuffante/Getty Images; p. 87: © Los Angeles Examiner/USC Libraries/Corbis via Getty Images; p. 88: © Bettmann/Getty Images; p. 89: © Rebecca Smeyne/Getty Images; p. 90: © Pierre Vauthey/Sygma/Sygma via Getty Images; p. 94: © Slim Aarons/Getty Images; p. 95: © Guy Marineau/WWD/Penske Media via Getty Images; p. 96: © Susan Wood/Getty Images; p. 97: © Anwar Hussein/Hulton Archive/Getty Images; p. 98: © Ron Galella/Ron Galella Collection via Getty Images; p. 99: © Harry Benson/Daily Express/Hulton Archive/Getty Images; p. 100: © Hulton Archive/Getty Images; p. 101: © DeAgostini/Getty Images; p. 102: © Heinz Kluetmeier /Sports Illustrated via Getty Images; p. 103 (top): © JB Lacroix/WireImage; p. 103 (bottom): © Agnese Galleani/WWD/Penske Media via Getty Images; pp. 104–105: © Fairchild Archive/WWD/Penske Media via Getty Images; p. 106: © Taylor Hill/Getty Images; p. 107: © Rose Hartman/Archive Photos/Getty Images; p. 108: © Ron Galella/Ron Galella Collection via Getty Images; p. 109: © Hulton Archive/Getty Images; pp. 110–111: © General Photographic Agency/Getty Images; p. 112: © Bettmann/Getty Images; p. 113: © Eamonn McCormack/BFC/Getty Images; pp. 114–115: © TV Times via Getty Images; pp. 116: © Edward Berthelot/Getty Images; p. 117 (top): © Peter Bischoff/Getty Images; p. 117 (bottom): © Gamma-Keystone via Getty Images; p. 118: © Fairchild Archive/Penske Media via Getty Images; p. 119 (top): © Hulton Archive/Getty Images; p. 119 (bottom): © Slim Aarons/Getty Images; pp. 120–121: © Tom Kelley/Getty Images; p. 122: © Brian Kirley/Hulton Archive/Getty Images; p. 123: © Pierre Vauthey/Sygma/Sygma via Getty Images; p. 124: © Bettmann/Getty Images; p. 125: © Jim Heimann Collection/Getty Images; p. 126: © Fairchild Archive/Penske Media via Getty Images; p. 127: © Mike Coppola/Getty Images; p. 128: © Sharland/Getty Images; p. 129: © Savitry/Picture Post/Hulton Archive/Getty Images; p. 130: © Eamonn McCormack/BFC/Getty Images; p. 131: © Hulton-Deutsch/Hulton-Deutsch Collection/Corbis via Getty Images; p. 132: © Fairchild Archive/WWD/Penske Media via Getty Images; p. 133: © Eamonn McCormack/BFC/Getty Images; p. 134: © Stefano Bianchetti/CORBIS/Corbis via Getty Images; p. 138: © Fine Art Images/Heritage Images via Getty Images; p. 139 (top): © Bettmann/Getty Images; p. 139 (bottom): © Robert Mora/Getty Images; pp. 140–141: © Universal History Archive/Universal Images Group via Getty Images; p. 142 (top left): © Jim Heimann Collection/Getty Images; p. 142 (top right): © Pierce Archive LLC/Buyenlarge via Getty Images; p. 142 (bottom left): © Jim Heimann Collection/Getty Images; p. 142 (bottom right): © Jim Heimann Collection/Getty Images; p. 143: © Buyenlarge/Getty Images; pp. 144–145: © Found Image Holdings/Corbis via Getty Images; pp. 146–147: © Eddy LEMAISTRE/Corbis via Getty Images; p. 148 (top left): © Jonathan Wong/South China Morning Post via Getty Images; p. 148: (top right): ©Roberto Machado Noa/LightRocket via Getty Images; p. 148 (bottom left): © Andrew Lichtenstein/Corbis via Getty Images; p. 148 (bottom right): © Scott Suchman for The Washington Post via Getty Images; p. 149: © Planet One Images/UCG/Universal Images Group via Getty Images; p. 150: © Sven Creutzmann/Mambo Photo/Getty Images; p. 151: © DEA/G. SOSIO/Getty Images; p. 152: © Warner Brothers/Getty Images; p. 152: © Peter Ruck/BIPs/Getty Images; pp. 154–155: © LMPC via Getty Images; pp. 156–157: © Lester Cohen/Getty Images for Stella Artois; p. 158: © Touchstone Pictures/Getty Images; p. 159: © Screen Archives/Getty Images; p. 160: © Evening Standard/Hulton Archive/Getty Images; p. 161 (top): © Jeenah Moon for The Washington Post via Getty Images; p. 161 (bottom): © Francois Durand/Getty Images; p. 162: © Bettmann/Getty Images; p. 163: © Jim Heimann Collection/Getty Images; p. 164 (top): © Chesnot/Getty Images; p. 164 (bottom): Evening Standard/Hulton Archive/Getty Images; p. 165: © L. Fritz/ClassicStock/Getty Images; p. 166: © Denise Truscello/WireImage; p. 167: © WATFORD/Mirrorpix/Mirrorpix via Getty Images; p. 168: © Found Image Holdings/Corbis via Getty Images; p. 169 (top): © Ray “Scotty” Morrison/WWD/Penske Media via Getty Images; p. 169 (bottom): John Kobal Foundation/Getty Images); p. 175: © Silver Screen Collection/Getty Images;

Opposite: *Jayne Mansfield settles in for cocktail hour, circa 1955.* Following pages: *Singer Josephine Baker unwinds after a show in Venice, Italy, circa 1940. Cheers!*

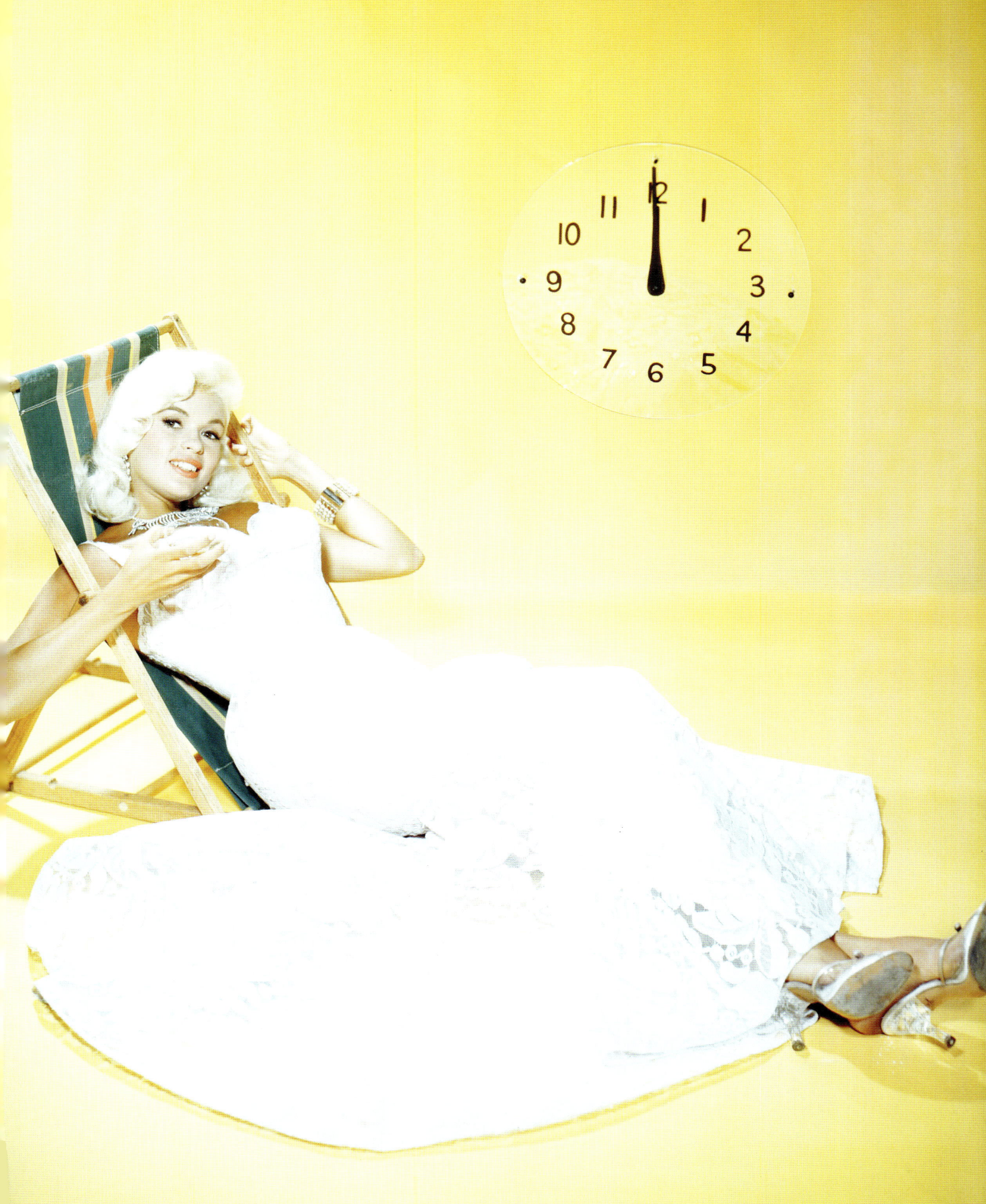

The Stylish Life: Cocktail Parties

Writer: Elizabeth Smith
Editorial Coordinator: Maureen Gallagher
Copy Editor: Brita Vallens
Photo Research: Maureen Gallagher
Design by Liz Eno
Production by Liz Eno
Color separation by Asia Pacific, China

Published by gestalten, Berlin 2025

ISBN 978-3-96171-666-1
Library of Congress Number: 2014958647

Printed in the Czech Republic by PBtisk a.s.

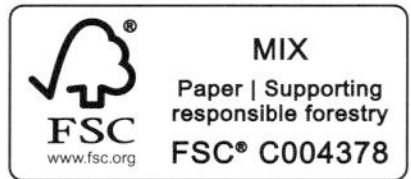

For more information and to order books, please visit www.teneues.com and www.gestalten.com

Die Gestalten Verlag GmbH & Co. KG
Mariannenstrasse 9–10
10999 Berlin, Germany
hello@gestalten.com

Düsseldorf Office
Waldenburger Straße 13
41564 Kaarst, Germany
verlag@teneues.com

teNeues Press Department
press@gestalten.com

Bibliographic information published by the Deutsche Nationalbibliothek. The Deutsche Nationalbibliothek lists this publication in the Deutsche Nationalbibliografie; detailed bibliographic data is available online at www.dnb.de

https://instagram.com/teneuespublishing

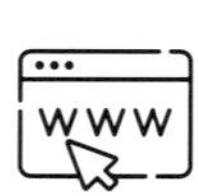

www.teneues.com